"This book is a tremendous contribution impact of war largely unseen through ign
us individually and as nations to tackle mythologies contrived to glorify wars at the cost of the moral wellbeing of those sent to fight them—and to stop ignoring the costs to any nation's collective soul."

—JODY WILLIAMS

Nobel Peace Prize, Founding Coordinator, International Campaign to Ban Landmines

"*War and Moral Injury* is not only a work from the conscience, but from the heart. This earnest and moving collection of essays, poems, memoirs and meditations gives us a much-needed view of what it is to be human in the face of war, of how we are not made to kill, and of how doing so injures the human soul. A stunning and essential book."

—HELEN BENEDICT

Columbia University, author of *Wolf Season, Sand Queen,* and *The Lonely Soldier.*

"If you are a non-combatant interested in a life with depth, with real humanity, then allow yourself to be guided into the inner darkness of war, and beyond, by the courageous, no bull-shit, truth-bearing veterans in this volume. While the focus is on the consequences for conscience and soul when the blood of war is visible on your hands, in the process a precious window is opened for all of us to grapple more honestly, more humbly and more hopefully with accepting our share of responsibility for violent conflicts, with transforming the profoundly dehumanizing legacy of war, whether justified or not."

—WILHELM VERWOERD

Philosopher and International Peace and Reconciliation Worker, Director of the International 'Beyond Dehumanization Project', author of *My Winds of Change*

"*War and Moral Injury* is a profound and courageous reader that gathers the voices of warriors, chaplains, reporters, poets, and scholars to open an honest place for our generation to deepen the timeless conversation about what constitutes Moral Injury and how we might restore our humanity by repairing and atoning for what violence has done to all of us. In a world increasingly numb to what we do to each other, it is clear that unless the wounds of war are forthrightly addressed, the violence will keep permeating the societies we live in. This book and the integral voices it carries helps to stop the cycle of violence and to begin to heal the trespass."

—**MARK NEPO**

author of *More Together Than Alone* and *Seven Thousand Ways to Listen*

"This brilliant, timely, and compelling collection of essays, poems and reflections on the experience of war from those who fought the fight and are still fighting war's demons, sheds urgently needed light on the moral "wounds" of our combat veterans and how we, our society, and especially faith organizations can reach out to assist them in their time of need."

—**JOHN SCOTT**

Retired United States Major General, Deacon, Roman Catholic Church, Diocese of Phoenix, Arizona

"Moral Injury, an ancient idea with a new name, is not PTSD. But, like PTSD, it deserves in-depth exploration. Meagher and Pryer compiled such an exploration with disparate viewpoints from poets to professors, and from warriors to chaplains. Moral Injury's guilt and shame festers in darkness. *War and Moral Injury: A Reader* brilliantly sheds a much-needed, antiseptic light on this terrible wound."

—**COLONEL CLARK C. BARRETT**

Iraq War veteran, infantry officer, and military ethicist

"As a field battalion surgeon in Vietnam, I am a witness to the moral and physical injury inflicted by war. Thanks to the contributors for the healing made possible by the compassion and wisdom that is woven into every page of this magnificent volume."

—**LARRY DOSSEY**
author of *Recovering the Soul* and *Healing Word*

"This compilation of essays and poetry is a large and important step in our understanding of the tremendous psychic wounds that typically result from participation in war. No one is immune. In my military career I witnessed many—including career special operations soldiers—who found their lives undone by this wounding. This book offers varied insights into the phenomenon of moral injury and sends a clear message to those afflicted—you are not alone and there is a way out of the hell you have found yourself in. For therapists, counselors, and healers, it provides understanding and effective methods for bringing our warriors home and, in the process, healing the society. An important work."

—**PAUL L. HENDERSON**
Retired Lieutenant Colonel, United States Amy Special Forces

"An invaluable guide on the path to a fuller understanding of moral injury."

—**DAVID WOOD**
Pulitzer Prize journalist, author of *What Have We Done: The Moral Injury of Our Longest Wars*

"Honoring our military veterans is right and necessary. However, it too often leads to glorifying war itself. The stories in this collection are a powerful antidote to that false logic. They tell us that while respecting veterans' bravery and sacrifice we must not forget the true nature of war: when unnecessary, a crime, and even when necessary, something to grieve, not celebrate."

—**ARNOLD R. ISAACS**
former Vietnam war correspondent, author of *Without Honor: Defeat in Vietnam and Cambodia* and *Vietnam Shadows: The War, Its Ghosts, and Its Legacy*

"As William Tecumseh Sherman remarked, "War is hell." This book explores that truism and offers a way to find the journey out of hell. In the opening pages, you will find a reason for the descent into hell: "no matter what crackling pain and anger you carry in your fists, my friend, it should break your heart to kill."

—ROBERT G. CERTAIN
Chaplain, Retired United States Air Force, Military Chaplains Association past president

"The finest resource yet on Moral Injury, this collection—historical, literary, contemporary, scholarly, and experiential—offers us all deep knowledge to understand and address the suffering revealed in these pages."

—RITA NAKASHIMA BROCK
co-author of *Soul Repair: Recovering from Moral Injury After War*

"This wide-ranging collection of different intellectual disciplines, professions, and voices provides many doorways into one common room—a deeper appreciation of war's costs on both individual humans and our common humanity. This excellent volume adds to our growing understanding of Moral Injury—one of the signature wounds of the post-9/11 era—and what is required to heal it."

—ELIZABETH A. STANLEY
former United States Army intelligence officer, associate professor of security studies, Georgetown University, author of *Paths to Peace*

"By bringing together multiple voices—warriors and poets, scholars, journalists, and chaplains—this book is a rich, nuanced approach to the complex issue of Moral Injury, which can and does arise in all manner of conflict situations, not just war. It will work on readers like a haunting portrait, lingering in heart and mind long after the last page is read."

—ELIZABETH EOWYN NELSON
Pacifica Graduate Institute

"This wonderful collection of writings goes to the moral and spiritual heart of the psychological wounds of war, so poorly understood through the general and somewhat misguided term, posttraumatic stress disorder. It should be essential reading for all those working with veterans and their loved ones, and I hope that many isolated veterans will find in these pages words that can help them find their way home."

—ROGER BROOKE

Professor of Psychology and Director, Military Psychological Services, Duquesne University

"Recent decades have brought increased attention to PTSD as a cost of war. The post-911 conflicts have added traumatic brain injury. But soldiers have always known that the dangers are deeper, threatening their very moral foundations. This brilliant book gathers an amazing collection of material, from poetry through social science to philosophy, that illuminates the dark forces that war can unleash."

—STEPHEN SOLDZ

Director, Social Justice and Human Rights Program, Boston Graduate School of Psychoanalysis

"Dutifully edited by two of the top scholars and military experts in the field, *War and Moral Injury* is invaluable not only for our returning veterans, but also for non-military readers. It should be read by anyone concerned about sustaining and strengthening the health of our nation's military and its veterans into and beyond the 21st century."

—LIONEL BEEHNER

West Point Modern War Institute Director of Research

"*War and Moral Injury* presents compelling perspectives on the emerging science of Moral Injury, the existential trauma that can accompany even such legally justifiable combat actions as the taking of human life. This volume's diverse views will help those who suffer the unseen wounds of moral trauma and serve a heuristic value in generating future scientific study."

—MICHAEL D. MATTHEWS

West Point Professor of Engineering Psychology, author of *Head Strong: How Psychology is Revolutionizing War*

War and Moral Injury

War and Moral Injury

A Reader

Edited by

ROBERT EMMET MEAGHER
and DOUGLAS A. PRYER

Foreword by

William P. Nash and Christa Davis Acampora

CASCADE *Books* · Eugene, Oregon

WAR AND MORAL INJURY
A Reader

Cascade Books
An Imprint of Wipf and Stock Publishers
199 W. 8th Ave., Suite 3
Eugene, OR 97401

www.wipfandstock.com

PAPERBACK ISBN: 978-1-4982-9678-6
HARDCOVER ISBN: 978-1-4982-9680-9
EBOOK ISBN: 978-1-4982-9679-3

Cataloguing-in-Publication data:

Names: Meagher, Robert E., editor. | Pryer, Douglas A., editor. | Nash, William, P., 1952–, foreword. | Acampora, Christa Davis, 1967–, foreword.

Title: Book title : War and moral injury : a reader / edited by Robert Emmet Meagher and Douglas A. Pryer ; foreword by William P. Nash and Christa Davis Acampora.

Description: Eugene, OR : Cascade Books, 2018 | Includes bibliographical references and index(es).

Identifiers: ISBN 978-1-4982-9678-6 (paperback) | ISBN 978-1-4982-9680-9 (hardcover) | ISBN 978-1-4982-9679-3 (ebook)

Subjects: LCSH: War—Moral and ethical aspects. | War neuroses. | Veterans—Mental health—United States. | Post-traumatic stress disorder. | War—Psychological aspects.

Classification: U22 .W38 2018 (paperback) | U22 .W38 (ebook)

Manufactured in the U.S.A.   04/04/18

This book is dedicated
to the beloved memory of Desiree Joy Pryer,
to all those wounded by war,
and to the healers.

Contents

Reporters

Chaplains

Scholars

Permissions

Portions of Michael Putzel's "Survivor's Guilt and Recompense" appeared in *The Price They Paid: Enduring Wounds of War*, Washington, DC: Trysail Publishing, 2015. Used by permission of Michael Putzel.

Peter Marin's "Living in Moral Pain" first appeared in *Psychology Today* (November 1981) 68–80. Used by permission of Peter Marin.

Tom Frame's "Moral Injury and the Influence of Religious Conviction" first appeared in Tom Frame, ed., *Moral Injury: Unseen Wounds in an Age of Barbarism*, Sydney: University of New South Wales Press, 2015. Used by permission of Tom Frame.

A version of Shannon French's and Anthony Jack's "Connecting Neuroethics and Military Ethics to Help Prevent Moral Injury" originally appeared as "Dehumanizing the Enemy: The Intersection of Neuroethics and Military Ethics" in David Whetham, ed., *Responsibilities to Protect in Theory and Practice*, The Netherlands and Boston: Brill/Martinus Nijhoff Publishers, 2015. Used by permission of Shannon French and Anthony Jack.

A version of Erik Masick's "A Moral Injury Primer for Military Commanders and Lawyers" first appeared as "Moral Injury and Preventive Law: A Framework for the Future," *Military Law Review* (2016): 223–89. Used by permission of Erik Masick.

Jonathan Shay's "Moral Leadership Prevents Moral Injury" are his prepared remarks for the 2010 Command and General Staff College Ethics Symposium (Nov. 16, 2010), http://www.cgscfoundation.org/wp-content/uploads/2014/03/FtLvnEthicsSymposiumReport-2010.pdf. Used by permission of Jonathan Shay.

A short version of Edward Tick's "Military Service, Moral Injury, and Spiritual Wounding," first appeared in *The Military Chaplain*, 89:1, Spring 2016, 4–8. Used by permission from *The Military Chaplain*.

Contributors

D. William Alexander is a Visiting Fellow at the Centre for Trauma, Asylum and Refugees at the University of Essex in the United Kingdom, where he specializes in working with those who have been exposed to (or have participated in) acute political violence throughout the world. Educated at Fordham University, the Johns Hopkins Hospital, the University of Essex (PhD), and Pittsburgh Theological Seminary (DMin), David is a former paratrooper with combat experience in Afghanistan, and has been working with moral themes in analytically informed therapeutic interventions for veteran clients and their families for the past ten years.

Brad Allenby is President's Professor of Civil, Environmental, and Sustainable Engineering, and of Law; Lincoln Professor of Engineering and Ethics; and co-chair of the Weaponized Narrative Initiative of the Center for the Future of War, at Arizona State University. He moved to ASU from his previous position as the Environment, Health, and Safety Vice President for AT&T in 2004. He received his BA from Yale University, his JD and MA (economics) from the University of Virginia, and his MS and PhD in Environmental Sciences from Rutgers University. He served as an officer in the US Army Corps of Engineers from 1972 to 1975.

Doug Anderson served as a Marine corpsman in Vietnam. He has published three books of poems: *The Moon Reflected Fire* (winner of the Kate Tufts Discovery Award), *Blues for Unemployed Secret Police,* and *Horse Medicine*, and a memoir, *Keep Your Head Down: Vietnam, the Sixties, and a Journey of Self-Discovery.* He has taught in the MFA programs at the Pacific University of Oregon and Bennington College, Smith College, and the University of Massachusetts. He has won numerous prestigious awards and fellowships, and twice held a residency at Fort Juniper, the former home of the poet Robert Francis. He is present working on a novel about the Vietnam War.

Tyler Boudreau served twelve years in the Marine Corps. In 2004, he deployed to Iraq as an infantry officer, after which he resigned his commission and returned home to Massachusetts. Boudreau is author of the book *Packing Inferno: The Unmaking of a Marine* (Feral House) and other related articles.

Tony Camerino is a retired Air Force Reserve officer. A combat veteran of Bosnia, Kosovo, and Iraq, he conducted or supervised over 1,300 interrogations during Operation Iraqi Freedom. He started his career as a Special Operations helicopter pilot before joining the Office of Special Investigations, where he conducted major felony investigations and counterintelligence operations in fifteen countries. He is the author of the memoirs, *How to Break a Terrorist* and *Kill or Capture*. Tony worked as a technical advisor and writer on the hit show, *Person of Interest*. He is a fellow at UCLA's Burkle Center for International Relations.

Bob Darlington was born December 26, 1923 in Wilmington, Delaware. He graduated from George School in Newtown, Pennsylvania, and attended Swarthmore College. Because of his Quaker background, Bob claimed conscientious objector status as World War II began. He quickly gave up this status as he watched others take on the responsibility of going to war. Bob left Swarthmore to serve with the 10th Mountain Division in Italy, where he was awarded a Bronze Star. Bob received his Bachelor's and Master's degrees in architecture, becoming a teacher and architect. After 1969, he lived in Massachusetts, where he passed away on January 19, 2014. His poem "These Old Scars" is being published here for the first time.

Bill Edmonds is a lieutenant colonel in the US Army and the author of *God Is Not Here: Torture, Trauma, and the Moral Injuries of War*. With over twenty years in the military, he has served in various positions throughout the Department of Defense and with other US government agencies. Bill received a BA in International Relations from California Polytechnical University and an MS in Defense Analysis, with an emphasis on terrorist networks and terrorist financing, from the Naval Postgraduate School in Monterey, California. He is currently stationed in Europe with his wife, Cheryl, and two daughters, Natalie and Ava.

Euripides created over ninety dramas in his roughly seventy-five-year lifetime, which overlapped those of his mentors and rivals, Aeschylus and Sophocles. For nearly all of his adulthood, Athens was at war with Sparta and its allies in a ferocious and protracted internecine contest known as the

Peloponnesian War. Owing to the fact that every adult Athenian citizen, unless disabled, was required to serve in the military until age sixty, Euripides surely knew combat firsthand and often. His works reveal his love of Athens, his disdain for self-serving politicians, his hatred of war, and his compassion for all of its victims, especially women.

Tom Frame joined the Royal Australian Navy as a sixteen-year old cadet midshipman in January 1979. He served at sea and ashore before resigning to train for the Anglican ministry in 1993. After parish work, he was Bishop to the Australian Defence Force (2001–2007) and then Director of Saint Mark's National Theological Centre (2007–2014). He was appointed Director of the Australian Centre for the Study of Armed Conflict and Society (ACSACS) and Professor of History at University of New South Wales (UNSW) Canberra in July 2014. Tom Frame is the author or editor of thirty-five books, including *Where Fate Calls: The HMAS Voyager Tragedy* and *Living by the Sword: The Ethics of Armed Intervention*.

Shannon E. French is the Inamori Professor in Ethics, Director of the Inamori International Center for Ethics and Excellence, a philosophy professor with a secondary appointment in the School of Law at Case Western Reserve University, the General Hugh Shelton Distinguished Visiting Chair in Ethics for the US Army Command and Staff College, and associate editor for the *Journal of Military Ethics*. She taught philosophy for eleven years at the US Naval Academy and served as Associate Chair of the Department of Leadership, Ethics, and Law. Her many works on military ethics include *The Code of the Warrior: Exploring Warrior Values, Past and Present*.

Peter Fromm, a retired US Army lieutenant colonel, is currently the Deputy G1 for US Army Japan at Camp Zama, Japan. He holds a BA in social science from San Jose State University and an MA in philosophy from Indiana University, Bloomington. During his career, LTC Fromm served with the 1st Battalion (Ranger) 75th Infantry; the 82d Airborne Division; the 1st Cavalry Division; the 2d Armored Division; and as a principal staff officer with US Army Japan. He also taught English, philosophy, and ethics for several years at the US Military Academy, West Point.

Hamilton Gregory is the author of *McNamara's Folly: The Use of Low-IQ Men in the Vietnam War*, and he appears in a YouTube video entitled "McNamara's Folly." He served in Vietnam as a US Army intelligence agent from 1968 to 1969, where, using a false name and posing as a civilian journalist, he worked on a team that recruited and trained Frenchmen and Southeast

Asians for espionage missions in Cambodia. He is a life member of two veterans' organizations—Vietnam Veterans of America and Disabled American Veterans. He lives in Asheville, North Carolina.

Anthony I. Jack uses brain imaging to investigate the tension between Analytic and Empathetic thinking in the brain. His work examines implications of this tension for ethical leadership, coaching, self-management, and philosophy. He is educated in Philosophy (BA), Psychology (PhD), and Cognitive Neuroscience (postdoc), and publishes in all three areas. His research includes collaboration with both the Department of Organizational Behavior and the School of Nursing at Case Western Reserve University. He leads the Brain, Mind and Consciousness Laboratory and is Research Director of the Inamori International Center for Ethics and Excellence.

Stephen Karakashian is an American psychotherapist who has worked with Fr. Michael Lapsley and the Institute for Healing of Memories in South Africa and the United States. He lives in Portland, Oregon.

Pete Kilner, PhD, retired in 2017 from the US Army as an infantry lieutenant colonel after twenty-eight years of service. As Professor of Leader Development and Organizational Learning at the US Military Academy, he taught courses on Ethical Reasoning, Just War, and Officership. He deployed five times to Iraq and Afghanistan to research small-unit combat leadership, interviewing nearly four hundred soldiers. He regularly leads discussions on the moral justifications of war and of killing in war for both military and civilian audiences. He co-authored two books and has penned more than eighty articles on ethics, leadership, and instructional design.

Timothy Kudo deployed as a captain to Iraq and Afghanistan between 2009 and 2011 with Alpha Company, 1st Battalion, 8th Marines. He's currently an associate with the consulting firm McKinsey & Co. in New York. Before joining the military he taught middle school math in the Bronx with Teach For America. He is a native of Santa Monica, California.

Michael Lapsley, SSM, is a South African Anglican priest and social justice activist. During the height of apartheid repression, he became chaplain to students at both black and white universities in Durban, and spoke out on behalf of schoolchildren who were being shot, detained, and tortured. After he was exiled by the South African Government in 1976, he joined the African National Congress (ANC) and became one of their chaplains. In April 1990 he received a letter bomb in the post. He now runs the Institute for Healing of Memories in Cape Town and works with veterans in the US. He is the author of *Redeeming the Past: My Journey from Freedom Fighter to Healer*.

Kristen J. Leslie, MDiv, PhD, is a feminist pastoral theologian and United Methodist pastor who addresses issues of survivor resilience in the aftermath of sexualized violence on college campuses, in the US military, and in Rwanda. She is the Professor of Pastoral Theology and Care at Eden Theological Seminary in Saint Louis, Missouri, and author of *When Violence Is No Stranger: Pastoral Counseling with Survivors of Acquaintance Rape*. She has served as a subject matter expert for the US Navy and the US Air Force, equipping chaplains to provide pastoral care in situations involving military sexual trauma. She is a regular lecturer for Warfighter Advance, Inc., a therapeutic retreat setting serving veterans and service members who have experienced post-traumatic stress, Moral Injury, and military sexual trauma.

Sean Levine holds Masters Degrees in Theology, Biblical Studies (Asbury Seminary, 2003, 2008), and Divinity (Saint Vladimir's Orthodox Theological Seminary, 2010). He serves as an Orthodox Christian Priest on active duty in the Army's Chaplain Corps, and has deployed twice to Iraq and twice to Afghanistan. As the Vice President of the Board of Directors for Trauma and Resiliency, Inc., Father Sean specializes in the spiritual aspects of PTSD and Moral Injury, and he has spoken about these issues at Saint Vladimir's Seminary, the EMDRIA Annual Conference, the Open Center in New York City, and at Fort Bliss in El Paso, Texas.

William P. Mahedy, Jr. devoted his life to veterans. After serving as an Army chaplain in Vietnam, he worked with veterans from every war from the Spanish American War through to the present conflicts. He co-founded in 1979 the National Veterans Outreach Program, which enabled the establishment of over three hundred Vet Centers in all fifty States, Washington, DC, and US protectorates. He later co-founded the Veterans Village of San Diego, which has served as a model for many programs across the country. His book *Out of the Night* has helped countless veterans suffering from the unseen wounds of war. Bill passed away in 2011.

Stefan J. Malecek, PhD, was a Social Work/Clinical Psychology Specialist in Vietnam 1968–1969. He worked for seventeen years on psychiatric units in the San Francisco Bay Area before returning to garner his PhD in 2006. He had a private practice from 2008 to 2013, with 100 percent PTSD vets.

His books include the first and second Paul Marzeky mysteries, *Crazy Tales of Combat Psychiatry*, and *Unwitting Witnesses*. In press is also *Crucible of Shame: Trauma and Transformation*. He is currently working on a book entitled *The Real Work Begins When You Retire*.

Peter Marin lives in Santa Barbara, California and has spent much of his life writing about, and defending, the "insulted and injured" in our midst—those whose marginality gives them access to truths the rest of us may both lack and need. He presently works defending the rights of the homeless and indigent in California and elsewhere.

Erik D. Masick is an active duty officer in the Army's Judge Advocate General's (JAG) Corps. A former enlisted Soldier and infantry officer, he holds an A.A. from the Valley Forge Military College (Valedictorian), a B.A. from Binghamton University, a J.D. from the University of Maryland School of Law, an LL.M. from the Judge Advocate General's School, and recently graduated with honors from the Command and General Staff Officer Course. He has done three combat deployments, and he recently published "Moral Injury and Preventive Law: A Framework for the Future" in the *Military Law Review*.

Steve Mason, a former Army captain and decorated Vietnam combat veteran, was named the National Poet Laureate by the Vietnam Veterans of America. Mason's poem "The Wall Within" was read at the 1984 dedication of the Vietnam Veterans Memorial in Washington, DC and has the distinction of being the only American work of poetry on display at the war memorial in Hanoi. His books include *Johnny's Song: Poetry of a Vietnam Veteran*, *Warrior for Peace*, and *The Human Being: A Warrior's Journey toward Peace and Mutual Healing*. Diagnosed with lung cancer as a result of wartime exposure to Agent Orange, he died in 2005.

Robert Emmet Meagher is Professor of Humanities, Hampshire College, Amherst, Massachusetts. After studies at the University of Notre Dame and the University of Chicago, he taught at Indiana University and Notre Dame, and has held visiting professorships at numerous colleges and universities, including Trinity College Dublin and Yale. His publications include a list of books, translations, and original plays, most recently *Herakles Gone Mad: Rethinking Heroism in an Age of Endless War* and *Killing from the Inside Out: Moral Injury and Just War*. He has led and served in a range of programs to understand and heal war's inner wounds.

William Allen Miller received the Purple Heart and Bronze Star with V Device from action in Vietnam. He appears in the film "Straight Talk: Veterans in the Classroom," produced by Robbie Lepzer, narrated by Kris Kristofferson. Al co-authored and performed in the 2010 play *Ambush on "T" Street*. He is the 2015 winner of the Amherst Writers and Artists prize for poetry with his poem, "David," which is being published here for the first time. Al has spoken in classrooms about his war experiences for more than thirty years.

Eric Newhouse, a retired newspaper editor who won the Pulitzer Prize in 2000 for a year-long series of stories about alcohol abuse in Montana, is the author of the books *Alcohol: Cradle to Grave* and *Faces of Combat: PTSD and TBI*. His book *Faces of Recovery*, a sequel to *Faces of Combat*, was published in 2017. For more information, visit his website at http://www.ericnewhouse.com/.

Chester Nez at age eight was sent to a school run by the Bureau of Indian Affairs and given his English name, Chester, after Chester A. Arthur. While at a government-run boarding school in Tuba City, Arizona, Nez was recruited into the Marine Corps and served as a Navajo code talker in the Pacific Theater in WWII. After the war he worked as a painter for twenty-five years at a VA hospital in Albuquerque. On July 26, 2001, Nez was one of the five living code talkers who received the Congressional Gold Medal from President George W. Bush, and in 2011 he wrote his memoir *Code Talker*.

Wilfred Owen enlisted in the Artists' Rifles in 1915, Commissioned as a 2nd lieutenant with the Manchester Regiment, he was sent to the front in 1916 where he and his men held a flooded dugout for fifty hours under heavy shelling. After being hospitalized for a concussion he returned to battle and barely survived an artillery shell that dismembered his friend. It was when being treated in Scotland for shell shock that he met Siegfried Sassoon who became his mentor and friend. After returning to combat he was killed on the 4th of November 1918, one of the last casualties of the war.

Charles Pacello, who hails from a family of veterans, is a former Air Force officer now serving as a Life Coach and Healing Expert for PTSD, Depression, and Trauma. An author, inspirational speaker, humanitarian, actor, and core facilitator with the Mindful Warrior Project, he serves on the Board of Directors of Soldier's Heart, an organization that tends the emotional, moral, and spiritual wounds resulting from military service. Recently, he graduated from Goddard College with a Master of Arts Degree in Psychology and Theater. He can be reached via his website, www.char-liepacello.com.

HC Palmer, an assistant poetry editor at *Narrative*, was born in Kansas and served with the US Army's First Infantry Division in Vietnam in 1965–1966 as a battalion surgeon. Specializing in internal and sports medicine, Palmer practiced in San Diego, New Orleans, and Kansas. He is retired and lives in Lenexa, Kansas, with his wife, Valerie.

David W. Peters served as an enlisted Marine and an Army Chaplain, deploying to Baghdad, Iraq, in 2005. His writing about war and Moral Injury has been published by Oxford University Press, and he is the author of two books, *Death Letter: God, Sex, and War* and *Post-Traumatic God: How the Church Cares for People Who Have Been to Hell and Back*. David currently is a Writer/Instructor at the US Army Chaplain Center and School at Fort Jackson, South Carolina, and the Associate Rector at Saint Mark's Episcopal Church, Austin, Texas. Follow him on Twitter @dvdpeters or Instagram @ trail.padre, or read more about his work at www.davidwpeters.com.

Joshua E. S. Phillips has reported from Southeast Asia, the Middle East, South Asia, and Central America. His work has appeared in the *Washington Post, Newsweek, The Atlantic, The Nation, Salon*, the *San Francisco Chronicle*, and the *Atlanta Journal-Constitution*, among other publications. He has produced broadcast features for NPR, PRI, the BBC, Reveal, PRX, and Al Jazeera. Phillips won a Heywood Broun Award and Alfred I. DuPont–Columbia University Award for excellence in broadcast journalism for his American Radio Works documentary, *What Killed Sergeant Gray*.

Douglas A. Pryer retired as a lieutenant colonel from the US Army military intelligence corps in 2017, last serving as a political-military advisor in the Joint Staff J-5, Strategic Plans and Policy, Deputy Directorate-Middle East. His military experience includes five years supporting combat operations in Iraq, Afghanistan, and Kosovo. His book, *The Fight for the High Ground*, and essays on warfare's moral and psychological dimensions have earned numerous military writing awards. He is currently pursuing a PhD in International Politics at the University of Aberystwyth, Wales, UK, where he lives with his wife, Sonie, and two children, Leo and Brooke.

Michael Putzel is a journalist and author who covered Vietnam, Cambodia, and Laos for two-and-a-half years as a war correspondent for The Associated Press. He went on to report many of the biggest running news stories of his generation, including the Watergate scandal and (from Moscow) the collapse of Soviet Communism. He is the author of *The Price They Paid: Enduring Wounds of War*, which won the 2015 Indiefab Gold Awards' "War and Military Nonfiction Book of the Year" for its story of the most intense helicopter battle in history and this battle's lifelong impact on the American warriors who survived it.

Monisha Rios is a disabled Army veteran, autoethnographer, clinical social worker, human rights advocate, and activist. As a witness to and survivor of military sexual violence in a variety of contexts, Monisha focuses most of her work on exposing and eradicating the problem in society, among the ranks, in armed conflict, and within communities directly impacted by the US military. Having incurred moral wounds from her military experiences, she strives to propel the conversation on Moral Injury beyond stereotypical, heterosexual, male combat narratives. Monisha will soon complete a PhD in Humanistic Psychology, specializing in Transformative Social Change at Saybrook University.

Siegfried Sassoon joined the Sussex Yeomantry on the 4th of August, 1914, the day that England declared war on Germany, and was a year later commissioned a 2nd lieutenant with the Royal Welsh Fusiliers. For his exceptional valor and calm under fire he received the Military Cross and the nickname Mad Jack. In 1917 he delivered his "declaration against the war" to Parliament, calling for a negotiated peace, to no avail. A gunshot wound to the head, a case of friendly fire, ended his combat career but not his life. He remains one of the most celebrated poets of the twentieth century.

William Shakespeare, the national bard of England and arguably the greatest wordsmith of the English language, lived from 1564 to 1616. While works have been translated into virtually every major world language and his plays performed more widely and adapted more variously than those of any other playwright, relatively little is known of his personal life and appearance. Records suggest that he died a relatively sudden death in 1616 at the age of fifty-two.

Jonathan Shay received a BA (1963) from Harvard University and an MD (1971) and PhD (1972) from the University of Pennsylvania. From 1987 until his recent retirement, he served as a staff psychiatrist at the Department of Veteran Affairs Outpatient Clinic in Boston, Massachusetts. In 2001, Shay served as Visiting Scholar-at-Large at the US Naval War College; from 2004 to 2005, he was Chair of Ethics, Leadership, and Personnel Policy in the

Office of the US Army Deputy Chief of Staff for Personnel, and he held the 2009 Omar Bradley Chair of Strategic Leadership, US Army War College. In 2007 he was awarded a prestigious MacArthur Foundation Fellowship.

Edward Tick, PhD, transformational psychotherapist, educator, and author, works internationally on the psycho-spiritual and cross-cultural healing of military, war, and violent trauma. He is Director of Soldier's Heart (www. soldiersheart.net) and has been pioneering innovative healing with veterans and other trauma survivors for over forty years. He has served as the US military's subject matter expert trainer on healing post-traumatic stress disorder and Moral Injury and has taught at numerous universities. He is the author of six books, including the groundbreaking *War and the Soul*. His newest publications are *Warrior's Return* and the audio set *Restoring the Warrior's Soul*.

Brian Turner served seven years in the US Army. He was an infantry team leader for a year in Iraq with the 3rd Stryker Brigade Combat Team, 2nd Infantry Division. Prior to that, he deployed to Bosnia-Herzegovina with the 10th Mountain Division (1999–2000). Turner is the author of a memoir, *My Life as a Foreign Country*, and two collections of poetry, *Here, Bullet* and *Phantom Noise*. He is the recipient of the Poet's Prize, and fellowships from the Guggenheim Foundation, the Lannan Foundation, the NEA, USA Artists, and the Amy Lowell Traveling Fellowship. He curates *The Kiss* series for *Guernica* and he is the founding director of the MFA program at Sierra Nevada College in Lake Tahoe.

Foreword

WILLIAM P. NASH
and CHRISTA DAVIS ACAMPORA

Most of the themes that have coalesced in recent years around the concept of Moral Injury have been around a long time. The term may be relatively new to this context, but the central ideas are ancient: that there can be dire consequences for wrongdoing, both for the wrongdoer and for the wronged, and that those consequences can endure for lifetimes and even ripple across generations. Some consequences are internal, like the painful and sometimes overpowering emotions of shame, guilt, and anger, or losses of the competency, value, and trustworthiness of our core selves. Other consequences are external, such as losses of resources or social standing, or being expelled from the group, figuratively or literally.

Another enduring theme is that we don't all agree on what's right and what's wrong, even in peacetime. In situations of conflict, it can be daunting to find the least bad option in each situation, and to find it before it's too late. Some moral standards are culturally defined; others are very personal. We are not equally invested in moral rules and their consequences, from person to person and over the course of each of our own lives. Yet we are all experts at denying our own wrongdoing, exactly for fear of its consequences. We can also too easily convince ourselves that consequences don't exist or that they simply don't matter. Thus, Moral Injury is in no way unique to the battlefield, as the contributions to this volume attest.

There are also ancient themes of hope feeding the Moral Injury conversation—hope springing from how tenaciously we can fight to right perceived moral wrongs, to atone for our sins and to seek atonement from those who have wronged us; how we can remain compassionate with ourselves and others in the face of deep shame and anger; how we can find xxiv Foreword

meaning in chaos; how we can forgive ourselves and others, even when it makes no sense at all to do so; and how we can become better people, day by day, given the chance.

These themes appear in the most ancient of writings, including the world's sacred texts. It would be hard to find a great novel, movie, poem, or song that didn't touch on one or more of these themes, comedically or tragically. The imperatives and challenges of living a life of meaning and purpose, and the consequences of perceived failure to live up to moral expectations, are just that central to who we are.

Though we may be familiar with these seemingly universal themes, we haven't yet woven them into a sturdy fabric of actionable understanding when it comes to Moral Injury. The concept has not one definition but many. We can list any number of potentially morally injurious events in various life situations, but we don't yet have a robust theory to reliably predict what else we haven't thought of that belongs on this list. We can describe some of the biological, psychological, social, and spiritual characteristics of Moral Injury as a state of being, but we don't know which of those characteristics might be necessary and sufficient for recognizing Moral Injury in ourselves or others. And though many approaches have been proposed for moral repair as a process of rebuilding after Moral Injury, we don't yet know what works and what doesn't, or for whom.

We are still the proverbial blind men and women unwittingly describing the parts of an elephant that are close enough to touch, yet we have no idea how trunk, ears, tusks, and tail might possibly fit together on one beast, or even whether what we perceive are truly aspects of just one entity.

If conversations about Moral Injury are to advance understanding and lead to rational action, they must transcend boundaries of perspective, language, and ideology. We need books like *War and Moral Injury: A Reader*, to provide a platform for many voices, many perspectives, many experiences, regardless of whether they appear to converge on any common themes. We are way too early in the game to limit ourselves to only one or a few perspectives. Nothing should be excluded until we are much further along in our understanding

That's one reason we decided to write this foreword together, as the result of our own Moral Injury dialogue, so that our gateway into this important book would also be multidisciplinary.

Here's a cautionary tale about the potential dangers of prematurely narrowing the conversation about Moral Injury. It comes from the early decades in the life of the concept of post-traumatic stress disorder (PTSD), a psychiatric diagnosis that overlaps with Moral Injury in definite but unclear ways. The diagnostic criteria for PTSD that first appeared in the third edition of the American Psychiatric Association's *Diagnostic and Statistical Manual of Mental Disorders* (DSM-III) in 1980 were drawn from two precursor constructs: post-Vietnam syndrome and rape trauma syndrome. Importantly, the DSM-III criteria for PTSD were formed from the features that appeared to be common to *both* syndromes, such as nightmares, flashbacks, avoidance of reminders, and overdrive of the sympathetic nervous system. But what happened to the features thought to be characteristic of one or the other syndrome but not both? They were ignored. Among the orphaned features of post-Vietnam syndrome were the following, copied from a 1981 paper by Matt Friedman, the psychiatrist who became the first executive director of the VA's National Center for PTSD.[1]

> Guilt figures strongly in post-Vietnam syndrome and includes not only survivor guilt because close friends were killed in combat, but also guilt about Vietnamese (especially women and children) who were killed in the line of duty. A feeling of betrayal may accompany the guilt as the combat veteran becomes convinced that society and the government have failed to acknowledge or reward his personal military sacrifice. The result is an abiding distrust of the Veterans Administration, the Armed Forces, and other organizations.

And of course, Vietnam was not the first war in which guilt and anger over perceived violations of moral expectations were recognized. WWII aircrew pilots who heaped devastation on civilian cities reported similar experiences lasting for years after they returned. And there were many other instances.

Omitting the gnawing moral aspects of post-Vietnam syndrome from the criteria for PTSD cleared the way for scientific conceptions of psychological trauma to narrow even further and become mostly, if not solely, about fear conditioning. Subsequent editions of DSM required exposure to an event that threatened one's own life or limbs for the diagnosis of PTSD to apply. And psychological treatments for PTSD were based on learning theory (since conditioning is a form of learning), supported by decades of basic research using rat models of fear conditioning as a proxy for PTSD. Concern is growing that the disappointing performance of talking treatments for PTSD may be traced to the narrow conception of PTSD as a disorder of fear and brain fear circuitry.

It doesn't seem surprising that guilt never figured as strongly in rape survivors as it did in in combat veterans, but what about anger over perceived betrayals of trust? Tragically, there is evidence that rape survivors

1. Friedman, "Post-Vietnam Syndrome," 933.

who expressed significant anger were criticized by their care providers for what was conceived to be a maladaptive coping response on their part. Anxiety was to be expected; anger was not—despite evidence over many decades that anger, rage, and hatred are common among survivors of serious assault, especially at the hands of someone known and trusted.

There is a palpable note of urgency in much of this book. Urgency for what? Urgency for the authors to act through their writing, perhaps, because moral injuries task the injured to *do* something about it: to neutralize a recognized moral danger or at least to warn others about it, to comfort others who are morally injured while encouraging their rebuilding work, and to atone, of course, and to seek atonement. There may be urgency to share what has been experienced and learned to expand our store of information about Moral Injury, and urgency to motivate others to act.

We are honored to add our voices to this important work, and to respond to the authors' call. We are determined. And hopeful.

William P. Nash
Director of Psychological Health, US Marine Corps, former Navy psychiatrist embedded in the 1st Marine Division during the Second Battle of Fallujah, and researcher in combat-related PTSD, loss, and Moral Injury

Christa Davis Acampora
Professor of Philosophy with expertise in moral psychology and modern European philosophy, most recently organizer of *The Experience of War: Moral Transformation, Injury, and Repair,* a series of programs and public events sponsored by the National Endowment for the Humanities

Introduction

ROBERT EMMET MEAGHER
and DOUGLAS A. PRYER

I open my eyes, and Saedi is bent over the still-crying prisoner. He whispers in his ear, and cigarette smoke escapes his nose to float up in the air and twirl around the one hanging light bulb. I hear more sobs, which become suckling whimpers.

I feel a deep loss.

I despair.

I need to escape.

I must escape, or I will become lost.

I quickly leave the cell and climb the stairs to the room. Outside, the sun is just beginning to rise.

—LIEUTENANT COLONEL BILL EDMONDS

So Lieutenant Colonel Bill Edmonds describes the gestation of his own inner torment in a torture chamber in Iraq and his ascent to the light—an ascent that prefigures his own spiritual rebirth, years later, when he leaves this darkness behind him to find self-forgiveness, strength, and new life. He calls this wounding torment "Moral Injury."

What is this Moral Injury that Edmonds and others in this collection describe? Many believe it to be the signature wound of today's wars, a wound that all too often goes unrecognized and improperly treated. Some in this volume go further and see it as the inevitable wound of all war. The psychiatrist Jonathan Shay, who popularized the term and who is a contributor to this volume, uses it to mean a profound sense of betrayal of "what's right," either by a "legitimate authority" or by oneself (selection 39). A majority of leading mental health researchers and clinicians define the sources of Moral Injury more broadly, stating it can result from "perpetrating, failing to prevent, bearing witness to, or learning about acts that transgress deeply held moral beliefs and expectations."[1] Symptoms widely associated with Moral Injury include guilt, shame, a loss of trust (in yourself, others, or God), feelings of powerlessness or hopelessness, depression, anxiety, anger, re-experiencing of the moral conflict, and self-destructive behaviors (suicidal ideation, substance abuse, high-risk behavior, the sabotaging of close relationships). Not all our authors, however, regard medicalized descriptions of Moral Injury, and the recommended therapies emergent from them, as adequate to explain or address the pain they have suffered or witnessed. If there were consensus regarding the etiology and treatment of Moral Injury, there would be no need for this volume, which offers many diverse views and voices.

Despite this lack of consensus, it is clear that Moral Injury is as old as the human record. We see it in the "mark of Cain" borne by the first fratricide, when he was banished in shame. We hear it in the lament of Sophocles' boy-warrior Neoptolemos, who learns the hard way, the only way, that "All is disgust when one leaves his own nature and does things that misfit it."[2] We recognize it too in the elaborate system of penances imposed on Christian warriors in the Middle Ages, recompense for every life taken in battle, no matter how valiant the warrior or how just (even holy) the Church declared his cause to be. We witness it too in the refusal of so many RAF bomber crews to take Communion before their life-taking missions over Germany and occupied Europe, despite the odds against their safe return. We read it today in heartrending notes left behind by honored veterans who have found the burden of life after war too heavy to bear for even one more day. However unable we are to agree on a single understanding of Moral Injury, or any one account of its causes, symptoms, or cure, we somehow know it when we see it.

The late great anthropologist Claude Lévi-Strauss, abandoning the search for the one true version of any myth, argued that the truth of a myth is to be found in the sum of all of its versions. While Moral Injury is anything but a myth, the same principle holds true for all of its widely variant understandings. Together they shed more light and advance the common cause further than any one of them can reasonably aspire to do on its own.

1. Litz et al., "Moral Injury and Moral Repair in War Veterans," 695.
2. *Philoctetes* (lines 902–3).

Clinicians of every stripe and school, Native American healers, Yoga instructors, practitioners of Asian medicine, theologians, chaplains, pastors, rabbis, imams, parents, friends, fellow veterans, companion dogs, therapy horses—these and many others in no clear order—all may play a critical role in understanding and healing the pain of those who go off to war and return visibly intact and invisibly anguished. Whatever sheds light, whatever helps, is worth knowing and sharing—this at the very least is a sound point of departure.

This volume began several years ago with a conversation and meeting of minds that was initiated and fostered, as so often happens today, on the Internet. It was, on the face of it, an unlikely alliance and friendship that ensued between a career military officer and a life-long peace activist, a combat veteran and a college professor. Their—our—point of contact and convergence was Moral Injury or, more precisely, what each of us independently was wrestling with and writing about it. This book began with our reading of each other's work, our listening to each other's voice, and our recognizing in that voice a partner—not a "partner in crime" as the saying goes, but rather a "partner in care" for those wounded in war, wounded so deeply and invisibly that their rending pain is still mostly unrecognized, misunderstood, and unaddressed.

No matter how relatively neat and discreet might be the entry wound of a Moral Injury, the exit wound is inevitably messy and devastating, wide in its reach and incalculable in its damage. Moral injuries are not easily contained. The would-be firewall between our military and civilian worlds, between the war zone and the home front, is in the end illusory. There can be no effective, much less ethical, quarantine installed between the morally injured and the seemingly unscathed. All apparent signs and vocal disclaimers to the contrary, it is the nation that goes to war when it sends its sons and daughters, fathers and mothers, brothers and sisters to kill and be killed. Those same warriors, at the end of the day, bring their war, our war, home with them to the nation, to their neighborhoods, to their families, to us, home to roost, as it were.

Consequently, the divide between seasoned warrior and would-be peacemaker, between Pentagon planner and classroom instructor—a divide that one might imagine insurmountable—came to nothing in the face of what we each knew to be a national and human crisis. Listening to others, to one another, can do that—tear down walls, cut holes in fences, dissolve differences, reveal common ground. It has been our hope that in widening that conversation, and opening it out to enlist the rich diversity of voices represented between the covers of this book, that a national conversation and community of concern might be fostered. That conversation, we know, is already going on, and that community already taking shape. It is also our hope that this volume will contribute significantly to both.

From the start, the aim of this book project has been to provide for veterans and active-duty military, as well as their families, clinicians, clergy and caregivers, scholars and students, politicians and the concerned general public, an invaluable resource. As we envisioned it, the common cause of every voice in this volume would be to inform the national conversation on war and its deepest wounds and to advocate for the wounded, not only to reveal trauma but more importantly to point out possible paths of healing, and, finally, to instill hope in all those whose grasp on it is loosening. Hope, after all, begins with knowing that one is being heard, understood, and reached out to.

In building this volume "from the ground up," we reached out first to veterans and asked for their voices, their stories, their poems, their wisdom. The tales of Moral Injury that they tell are both varied and similar: there are stories of killing, witnessing or committing torture, suffering military sexual assault, being cruelly hazed, participating in nuclear preparedness exercises, feeling the failure to protect comrades, loved ones, or civilians, ministering to the broken, and despairing. These tales, though, also include stories of healing. It is these stories that we thought especially important to include.

Next, we assembled an international "university" of other professions and disciplines: psychiatry, psychology, philosophy, classical studies, law, comparative religion, theology, journalism, and poetry. In doing so, it was our avid hope that this volume might encourage further cross-disciplinary and international study among scholars on this vital, universal topic. It would indeed be a terrible shame were scholarship pertaining to Moral Injury to remain stove-piped within different disciplines and more or less confined to a handful of nations.

When choosing what work to include, we looked for writings that were accessible and authoritative. By "accessible," we mean work that service members, veterans, and their loved ones would want and be able to read without having to cut their way through thickets of jargon or unnecessarily dense prose. So, we did not include some undeniably valuable clinical or empirical studies, though these are cited liberally throughout the book. We encourage readers to dive into that growing scientific literature themselves. One would do well to read, for example, the foundational article by Brett Litz and his colleagues, "Moral Injury and Moral Repair in War Veterans: A Preliminary Model and Intervention Strategy," as well as Shira Maguen and Litz's "Moral Injury in Veterans of War," an excellent survey of clinical studies of Moral Injury up to 2012. By "authoritative," we had in mind work by scholars and authors, many already known and noted, who have brought to their writing a depth of research, learning, and personal experience, together with insight and integrity. Most of the contributions collected here are either original or thoughtful reconsiderations of previously printed work. Some seminal work, such as Peter Marin's classic post-Vietnam reflections on "Living in Moral Pain" (selection 27), WWII Navajo code talker Chester Nez's account of his ritual path to healing (selection 23), and Tyler Boudreau's penetrating Iraq War commentary "The Morally Injured" (selection 13), are here reprinted in their original forms.

In sum, under one cover, the varied materials in this volume comprise studies, essays, memoirs, and poetry—in our view, representative of the finest out there—whether already written, previously published, or created specifically for this collection. To assist readers in selecting readings from this veritable cornucopia of material, we grouped authors into five sections: Poets, Warriors, Reporters, Chaplains, and Scholars. There is admittedly some artificiality in this distinction. Many of our authors wear more than one of these caps. Erik Masick, for example, is not only a military lawyer; he is also an active-duty Army officer and former infantry soldier. He is thus both a scholar and warrior. However, placing his essay in the Scholar section was an easy choice, for what his essay most fully teaches us is firmly grounded in Erik's expertise as a lawyer, rather than his combat-zone experience (selection 37).

It is important to note that, while we focused on veterans' views and voices, Moral Injury is not something with which only veterans are afflicted. Civilians on the battlefield may also find cause to lose trust in themselves, in others, or in God, and after this loss of faith, feel helpless to remedy their situation. Our focus on the stories of veterans is due to the literature being so rich here, and because veterans are, we believe, the population that is most at risk for Moral Injury. We also have very personal reasons for this narrow scoping. We ourselves both know and care deeply about many veterans suffering with Moral Injury, and one of us believes he himself has been afflicted with it.

While the stories in this volume are military ones, non-veterans with Moral Injury themselves, or who care for someone with this condition, should well be able to relate to, and learn from, these stories of injury and healing. We advise and ask, though, that those who consider themselves to be morally injured proceed slowly and cautiously while reading this book. Some stories could re-open poorly healed wounds. If you feel that happening, please put this book down, seek the assistance or companionship that will help you, and resume reading only once you are sure that you are ready to do so.

All readers, take note: this book presents a strong, vivid, to some painful or challenging argument against war. It does not, however, argue that war is never necessary. Several of this book's authors, while recognizing the vital role of the military, offer options to leaders for reducing the chance that their troops will be afflicted with Moral Injury in the exercise of their duties. At the same time, all the voices in this book are at one in reminding us what war can and often does do to the psyches of warriors who survive it. One of the most alluring and enduring of modern myths is that well-trained, physically protected warriors can as a rule kill without being killed, without suffering a kind of death themselves. War, the authors in this volume make clear, kills not only those it buries in the ground. It can just as surely kill the souls of warriors who, having marched off to war and Moral Injury, return home, where, standing tall while the music plays and their hometowns cheer, feel inside that they are forever lost.

War, therefore, is far harder to comprehend and to recover from than we wish to believe it is. This is especially true of modern war, when, generally, it is not our own loved ones who fly off to wage it. Most of us today don't have an immediate family member or friend who is a combat veteran, and, even when we do, our loved ones don't come home to us at sunset, direct from a battle fought that morning, blood-splattered, slimed with gore, with fresh wounds needing treatment. Rather, they are gone from us for months, perhaps a year or more, and when they return, their physical wounds have been cleaned and treated and, in most cases, have completely healed. By the time we see and hug them, our loved ones may not display any visible injury at all. They may even look "good as new."

The distancing and sanitizing of modern war make it more bearable for those at home and thus, tragically, far more likely to happen and be accepted. Separated from war by time and oceans, those at home may hear stories and see images that horrify them, but this horror possesses none of the haunting immediacy of actual personal memory. Secondhand thoughts and images of war are more like dreams we can choose to wake up from and forget—or, in today's world, like channels we can instantly escape with a push of a button on our remote, or as easily as exiting a website or closing an app. This physical and temporal remoteness—true, for example, of every American conflict since the Civil War—has meant that even when something like an entire generation feels the horrors of war, their bitter memories typically morph into the next generation's nostalgic dreams of victory and heroism.

Here we must acknowledge a great gap in this text as in nearly every other on the subject of America's wars and veterans: the deaths and wounds, physical and spiritual, inflicted on the "others," our enemies, especially our "civilian enemies." When we walk the blood-soaked soil of the Gettysburg battlegrounds, we acknowledge and feel the pain of all who suffered and died there, and understandably so; but when we approach the awesome sacred gravity of the Vietnam Wall, we are less likely to bear in mind and mourn the loss of the estimated two million Vietnamese lives taken in that same war. As it happens, one of the editors was recently reminded of that fact by a Vietnam veteran who was central to the creation of the Vietnam Memorial. It is chastening to remind ourselves too that the war Americans know as the Vietnam War is known in Vietnam as the American War. How can we forget that every war has at least two sides? "Easily" is perhaps the answer that first comes to mind.

Amidst this awful cycle of war and forgetting, this book stands defiantly hopeful. Its authors equip veterans with ways to better understand the moral injuries with which they may be afflicted, reassure veterans that they are not alone, and help them to realize that, just as physical amputees can learn to live well in the aftermath of their injuries, spiritual amputees can restore their lives and rediscover joy. For readers who are caregivers, the authors offer different frameworks for understanding, dealing with, and treating the morally injured. And for readers who have neither gone to war nor interacted closely with those who did, the authors serve collective notice of war's enduring cost, lest these readers—via nostalgic dream, irrational fear, the incomplete calculation of self-interest, or fleeting passion—endorse yet another unnecessary war and send others off to fight it.

Robert Emmet Meagher
Douglas A. Pryer

In support of this shared effort, the Editors and Contributors are donating their royalties to Soldier's Heart, an organization whose work is presented at the end of this book.

Poets

Now what god can unfold for me so many terrors?
Who can make a song of slaughter in all its forms—
The deaths of captains down the entire field,
Dealt now by Turnus, now by Aeneas, kill for kill?
Did it please you so, great Jove, to see the world at war,
The peoples clash that would later live in everlasting peace?

—Virgil, *The Aeneid* (tr. Robert Fagles)

It used to be said that in the old wars fought by the Irish clans that they had an agreement. I don't know if this is true, but I love the idea, that no matter how much they slaughter themselves with broadswords and knives and whatever else those maniacs used, that they should always spare the poets. Don't kill the poets, because the poets had to be left to tell the story.

—David Blight

The poet is the priest of the invisible.

—Wallace Stevens

1

BRIAN TURNER

Sadiq

It is a condition of wisdom in the archer to be patient
because when the arrow leaves the bow, it returns no more.
   —SA'DI

It should make you shake and sweat,
nightmare you, strand you in a desert
of irrevocable desolation, the consequences
seared into the vein, no matter what adrenaline
feeds the muscle its courage, no matter
what god shines down on you, no matter
what crackling pain and anger
you carry in your fists, my friend,
it should break your heart to kill.

Eulogy

It happens on a Monday, at 11:20 a.m.,
as tower guards eat their sandwiches
and seagulls drift on the Tigris River.
Prisoners tilt their heads to the west
though burlap sacks and duct tape blind them.

The sound reverberates down concertina coils
the way piano wire thrums when given slack.
And it happens like this, on a blue day of sun,
when Private Miller pulls the trigger
to take brass and fire into his mouth:
the sound lifts the birds up off the water,
a mongoose pauses under the orange trees,
and nothing can stop it now, no matter what
blur of motion surrounds him, no matter what voices
crackle over the radio in static confusion,
because if only for this moment the earth is stilled,
and Private Miller has found what low hush there is
down in the eucalyptus shade, there by the river.

PFC B. Miller
(1980–March 22, 2003)

2

HC PALMER

After War

A Six-Word Story

I'M HOME ALIVE. Well, not really.

If I Die in a Combat Zone

IF I MUST BE KILLED,
I wish to be killed by a sniper.

His efficient nail
does not require a tree

or an IED. I want him to remember
me, magnified, lit up,

hanging on his crosshairs.
I want him to believe

in a different war we might have
been comrades,

in a different war he might have
loved me.

3

WILLIAM ALLEN MILLER

David

I don't remember clouds or the color of the sky,
      the sound of birds.
Who his father might have been, the significant trees in his
      life as a child,
the way he ran to go home at the end of a day.
      The things
he passed that told him who and where he was, or if he had known
      the loyalties of a dog.
When I think of him I say "David," though I never
      heard his name.
When we found him you couldn't tell if he was Asian, Anglo, or African
      not as if anything was equal.
I don't know if he had ever known the unity of a ball game. I think he might
have been
      Chinese American from California.
I wonder if his grandfather had ever taken him fishing. We wrapped him in
a poncho
      that would protect him from the rain,
tied the poncho to a bamboo pole, carried him as if we were all
      going home that night in a pilgrimage of the bewildered.
I regret the way we dropped him to the ground near morning,
brushing one palm against the other as though we were finished.

All the Voices Are in the Water

All the voices are in the water.
Maybe now will be the last time
I have to write about this.
Maybe prayer will change something.

He tried to talk to me after three rounds
in his chest. I can't tell from here if he reached for me.
Someone is dying near you, someone is leaving,
and the old expectations for mourning are gone.

I shot him in the delicate pink bubbles of his lungs.
He would drown in his blood, in the water. We drown in water.
Would a brave man, a principled man, take his own life in response?
In the realization of what I have done
I ask the question.
In a direct line of cause and effect,
taking from another the gift of life
I have asked, should mine be offered, taken? Should life be chosen?

After the weight settled, after I left the place of his killing.
After the stories of Christ, after the story of Cain comes home.
After murder, you understand it doesn't matter what you call it,
whether you train or are trained for it, or plan on your own,
          it's the same.

I wondered where I could stand
coming out of the hooch.
A large rock said it could take my weight.
I listened to his voice fade, listened
to him say bullets in my chest, rounds in the lungs.
All the oceans breathing why he should live,
as his voice came down the scale of living,
after no more effort could come from him.

After his voice stopped, he left his body.
I met him and he told me who he was,
that he would have lived in *community, in respect.*
He was a higher form of me, and I shot him.

I couldn't hear, the light turned pale green,
those who were moving moved in a dream light without shadows.
Sound like the light gravel roar under water,
a sound from the other side of the forest.
I shot him the second time to stop it.
The rifle bucking, what was in me then is in me now—
can love be here?

There is no other way out, no down the alley,
no holidays, no citations, no shiny ribbons.
No doorway through the underworld, no other path,
no way to leave, no way to walk away from him lying there.
Then I heard the sound water makes.
Water coming through green fog asked my soul to return.

From a seep in the side of a mountain
water was collecting on a shelf of limestone,
pouring into other water waiting.
Do you bless the water? Do you acknowledge spirit?
God and goddess pass through when we drink from a glass of water,
when the heart beats, when our jism explodes, when we piss,
when you touch me, when I touch you.
Water came to me after I killed that boy.
Blood came to me, the sound it makes
falling into water came to me.

Siddhartha with the ferryman: the ferryman says
all the voices are in the water.
I went back, the hooch was burned.
They gave me pictures of his family,
taken from his breast pocket.

I went back there to fill myself with it,
the smell, where the flies land,
where his hands stopped.
What I had done.
There was only ash, white papery ash of bamboo and grasses.
All the voices are in the water.
My eyes focused and from the ash a seated Buddha rose.

4

DOUG ANDERSON

Bamboo Bridge

We cross the bridge, quietly.
The bathing girl does not see us
till we've stopped and gaped like fools.
There are no catcalls, whoops,
none of the things that soldiers do;
the most stupid of us is silent, rapt.
She might be fourteen or twenty,
sunk thigh deep in green water,
her woman's pelt a glistening corkscrew,
a wonder she is; I forgot.
For a moment we all hold the same thought,
that there is life in life and war is shit.
For a song we'd all go to the mountains,
eat pineapples, drink goat's milk,
find a girl like this, who cares
her teeth are stained with betel nut,
her hands as hard as feet.
If I can live another month it's over,
And so we think a single thought,
A bell's resonance.
And then she turns and sees us there,
sinks in the water, eyes full of hate;
the trance broken.
We move into the village on the other side.

5

STEVE MASON

From A History Lesson

Since Vietnam,
three things
hold my universe together:
gravity, centrifugal force
and guilt.

It is so strange, therefore,
that the war is over for me
just like it's over for you.
Over.
And
over
again . . .

From In Victory or Defeat

From any nation
each man
returning from war
stands alone in the rubble
of his personal Homecoming.

In victory or defeat,
his former life has collapsed
under the undeniable weight
of debunked values.
His cultural upbringing is in ruins.

He enters a world of his own creation.

The institutions
of education and government,
marriage, marketplace and church
have been kicked out—
one "flying buttress" at a time,
until the whole of it collapsed
under his rude questioning.

Each new man
sifts the smoldering ruin
of his former life
for some uncharred thing of value—
some remnant truth
he can salvage—
that he can hold up
(still warm to the touch)
and say, "With this, I begin again."

From One with It All

Truly,
you and I have much in common.
It is in our blood, it is in our souls;
we cannot be vaccinated or indoctrinated
against our humanity.
Not for any cause. Not for any reason.

6

EDWARD TICK

The Wounded Warrior

I met him over a quarter century ago. His face and head were young, handsome, intent, with a sweep of curly hair. His thighs, torso and arms were honed and sleek. His left arm thrust forward and body crouched.

But both his legs were missing below the knees, both arms above the elbows. Above his rippled stomach a great gash cut across his chest, separating his heart and left shoulder from the rest of him, now connected by a rod.

His head too had been knocked off, then restored. Though his eyes, nostrils and mouth flared, his lips were cracked, nose broken, skin torn.

Ravaged and exhausted body. Mind stunned and confused, repositioned but not restored. Heart and body separated. Heart broken.

Yet enduring. Striving to protect to the last breath. Resolute against suffering. A will that propels the body beyond its pain. Strength and devotion that stand their ground until he can stand no more.

This was the spirit I met in a statue called "The Wounded Warrior" in Athens, Greece. It was carved around 300 BCE and originally from Delos, a sacred island reserved for pilgrimage and worship. This statue shows us PTSD set in marble. Any combat survivor looking upon the Wounded Warrior looks upon his own spirit.

> For my city and my fathers
> I stood my ground
> until Ares' stinging sword
> claimed my swift, strong legs.
> Still I cry out to you

with a man's fierce cry,
my marble battle cry.
Still I rise to face you
grasping my marble battle shield,
my shield of duty and honor.

7

BOB DARLINGTON

These Old Scars

They fought well, killed many that day
Then lay down their arms and came to us . . .
      boldly
      calmly
      confidently . . .
And the youngest had a smile and a sneer on his face.

They were six, these enemy . . .
At last close, touchable close.
Not close as a squint-eyed man
On the other end of a gun is close
      hands doing rapid things to end you . . .
Nor as the presence
Who lobs in a mortar shell
      from over the hill somewhere
      is close . . .
But gun-prod close . . .
      shapeless in ersatz
      hands high
      faces strangely scrubbed-looking.

Now they stood and waited . . .
      amused

half-insolent
casual
Almost in control . . .
their captors indecisive
puzzled . . .
this was new, this prisoner business.

Only a squad but more ground over the hill
more Italian earth to be bled over
more Italian sun to be sweated under.
And no man to spare for prisoners.

No man to spare.

There are questions one faces . . .
and there are other questions . . .
and a warm Apennine afternoon blows cold
a bright sun turns gray.

The six stood on . . . waited looked.
Stark on the crest a broken tree . . .
The farmhouse, white-stuccoed and red-tiled
shell-pitted
gutted
dead
sat eternally on raw spring earth . . .
Across the valley the broken bell tower.

This ancient land knew death.

No word passed . . .
and we lowered
on the lieutenant . . .
the mantle of decision.

To the men shivering in damp holes
looking blank future in the face
in the dark . . .
Had come that morning a command . . .
"Take no prisoners . . ."

Afterward it started, and the day was hard
Friends died that day . . .
>> turned gray on the still earth
>> sent comrades on into solitude.

Then suddenly a lull
And there were prisoners . . .
>> sand in the offensive
>> a dead weight
>> baiting the conscience.

No word was yet spoken
>> no man designated . . .
Then with the lieutenant's voice
>> the great emptiness of the sky
>> came into our hearts.

>> "We were told . . ."
an empty voice, too . . .
>> "No prisoners.   Sergeant."

One needs blind hearts
To pass the fires of hell,
>> *unscathed.*

Today we carry deep scars.

Thin voices only
Ill at ease
With, the half-words of rebellion . . .
>> "It hardly seems . . ."
>> "A dirty trick . . ."
>> "What the hell . . ."
Strange protest in that articulate land
>> yet the balance wavered and reversed,
>> seemed to settle safely.

Tension fled
Sweet breath was drawn again
>> and turned rotten . . .
>> "Hell, finish it!"

The years of memory fade
The scars heal over . . .
>*but the wounds remain*
A deep parting of the mind
>*aching with the adverse weathers*
>*of the soul . . .*

The six are gone.
We left them there . . .
>grotesque on the mountainside
>the raw earth of spring . . .
And went on . . .
>to take no more as ordered
They were collected
>duly catalogued, classified
>and buried . . .

But they lie there still
>*condemned to the changeless season . . .*

And a dozen scars smolder.

8

WILFRED OWEN

The Parable of the Old Man and the Young

So Abram rose, and clave the wood, and went,
And took the fire with him, and a knife.
And as they sojourned both of them together,
Isaac the first-born spake and said, My Father,
Behold the preparations, fire and iron,
But where the lamb for this burnt-offering?
Then Abram bound the youth with belts and straps,
And builded parapets and trenches there,
And stretchèd forth the knife to slay his son.
When lo! an angel called him out of heaven,
Saying, Lay not thy hand upon the lad,
Neither do anything to him. Behold,
A ram, caught in a thicket by its horns;
Offer the Ram of Pride instead of him.
But the old man would not so, but slew his son,
And half the seed of Europe, one by one.

Strange Meeting

It seemed that out of battle I escaped
Down some profound dull tunnel, long since scooped
Through granites which titanic wars had groined.

Yet also there encumbered sleepers groaned,
Too fast in thought or death to be bestirred.
Then, as I probed them, one sprang up, and stared
With piteous recognition in fixed eyes,
Lifting distressful hands, as if to bless.
And by his smile, I knew that sullen hall,—
By his dead smile I knew we stood in Hell.

With a thousand fears that vision's face was grained;
Yet no blood reached there from the upper ground,
And no guns thumped, or down the flues made moan.
"Strange friend," I said, "here is no cause to mourn."
"None," said that other, "save the undone years,
The hopelessness. Whatever hope is yours,
Was my life also; I went hunting wild
After the wildest beauty in the world,
Which lies not calm in eyes, or braided hair,
But mocks the steady running of the hour,
And if it grieves, grieves richlier than here.
For by my glee might many men have laughed,
And of my weeping something had been left,
Which must die now. I mean the truth untold,
The pity of war, the pity war distilled.
Now men will go content with what we spoiled.
Or, discontent, boil bloody, and be spilled.
They will be swift with swiftness of the tigress.
None will break ranks, though nations trek from progress.
Courage was mine, and I had mystery;
Wisdom was mine, and I had mastery:
To miss the march of this retreating world
Into vain citadels that are not walled.
Then, when much blood had clogged their chariot-wheels,
I would go up and wash them from sweet wells,
Even with truths that lie too deep for taint.
I would have poured my spirit without stint
But not through wounds; not on the cess of war.
Foreheads of men have bled where no wounds were.

"I am the enemy you killed, my friend.
I knew you in this dark: for so you frowned
Yesterday through me as you jabbed and killed.

I parried; but my hands were loath and cold.
Let us sleep now. . . ."

Soldier's Dream

I dreamed kind Jesus fouled the big-gun gears;
And caused a permanent stoppage in all bolts;
And buckled with a smile Mausers and Colts;
And rusted every bayonet with His tears.

And there were no more bombs, of ours or Theirs,
Not even an old flint-lock, nor even a pike.
But God was vexed, and gave all power to Michael;
And when I woke he'd seen to our repairs.

9

SIEGFRIED SASSOON

Survivors

No doubt they'll soon get well; the shock and strain
Have caused their stammering, disconnected talk.
Of course they're "longing to go out again,"—
These boys with old, scared faces, learning to walk,
They'll soon forget their haunted nights; their cowed
Subjection to the ghosts of friends who died,—
Their dreams that drip with murder; and they'll be proud
Of glorious war that shatter'd all their pride . . .
Men who went out to battle, grim and glad;
Children, with eyes that hate you, broken and mad.

Suicide in the Trenches

I knew a simple soldier boy
Who grinned at life in empty joy,
Slept soundly through the lonesome dark,
And whistled early with the lark.

In winter trenches, cowed and glum
With crumps and lice and lack of rum,
He put a bullet through his brain.
No one spoke of him again.

You smug-faced crowds with kindling eye
Who cheer when soldier lads march by,
Sneak home and pray you'll never know
The hell where youth and laughter go.

10

WILLIAM SHAKESPEARE

From The Tragedy of Richard III

Richard

Give me another horse! Bind up my wounds!
Have mercy, Jesu!—Soft, I did but dream.
O coward conscience, how dost thou afflict me!
The lights burn blue; it is now dead midnight.
Cold fearful drops stand on my trembling flesh.
What do I fear? Myself? There's none else by.
Richard loves Richard, that is, I [am] I.
Is there a murderer here? No. Yes, I am.
Then fly! What, from myself? Great reason why:
Lest I revenge. What, myself upon myself?
Alack, I love myself. Wherefore? For any good
That I myself have done unto myself?
O, no. Alas, I rather hate myself
For hateful deeds committed by myself.
I am a villain. Yet I lie; I am not.
Fool, of thyself speak well. Fool, do not flatter.
My conscience hath a thousand several tongues,
And every tongue brings in a several tale,
And every tale condemns me for a villain.
Perjury, perjury, in the highest degree;
Murder, stern murder, in the direst degree;

All several sins, all used in each degree,
Throng to the bar, crying all "Guilty, guilty!"
I shall despair. There is no creature loves me,
And if I die no soul will pity me.
And wherefore should they, since that I myself
Find in myself no pity to myself?
Methought the souls of all that I had murdered
Came to my tent, and every one did threat
Tomorrow's vengeance on the head of Richard.[1]

From The Life of King Henry V

King Henry

O God of battles, steel my soldiers' hearts.
Possess them not with fear. Take from them now
The sense of reck'ning [or] th' opposèd numbers
Pluck their hearts from them. Not today, O Lord,
O, not today, think not upon the fault
My father made in compassing the crown.
I Richard's body have interrèd new
And on it have bestowed more contrite tears
Than from it issued forcèd drops of blood.
Five hundred poor I have in yearly pay
Who twice a day their withered hands hold up
Toward heaven to pardon blood. And I have built
Two chantries where the sad and solemn priests
Sing still for Richard's soul. More will I do—
Though all that I can do is nothing worth,
Since that my penitence comes after all,
Imploring pardon.[2]

1. Shakespeare, *The Tragedy of Richard III*, V.iii.189–219.
2. Shakespeare, *The Life of Kind Henry V*, IV.i.300–316.

11

EURIPIDES

From Herakles Gone Mad

Chorus of Veterans

Leaning on our staves,
A procession of propped-up old men,
We make our way slowly to a great house,
To the shelter of its roof
And the comfort of an old man's couch.

Like aged birds, their plumage drained of all color,
We sing a pitiful song.
Our laments are all we have left.
We are no more than ghosts, only half here,
Things of the night or of dreams,
Trembling, wanting to help, useless.
. . .
Keep going. Don't give in to weariness.
Drag yourself along, the way a horse pulls a heavy load
Up a steep, rocky slope, one exhausting step at a time.
When you lose your footing, reach out.
Grab hold of a hand or robe.
We are all old now. We stand or fall together.
The same as in our spear-bearing youth,
When we stood as one in the toil of battle

And brought home only glory
To our fatherland.[1]

(Translated by R. E. Meagher)

---

1. Euripides, "Parados," *Herakles Gone Mad*, 75.

Warriors

O child what is happening to you? Where have you left us and gone to? You're raving and possessed. Why? It must be the killing you've just done.

—Euripides, *Herakles Gone Mad* (tr. R. E. Meagher)

I became a fucking animal . . . Y'know, I wanted—. They wanted a fucking hero, so I gave it to them. They wanted a fucking body count, so I gave them a body count. I hope they're fucking happy. But they don't have to live with it. I do.

—Anonymous Vietnam Veteran

12

BILL EDMONDS

God Is Not Here

Memories from war never just fade away. If left alone, they come alive to seep and reach through time with searching and grasping claws. Ignored, they consume, just as they once consumed me. However, with the help of a small community of empathetic friends and family, I was able to find my healing voice: writing. Writing gave me the means to "live with" every painful experience: rethinking every thought, every word, and every choice until I was able to create the meaning of my experiences that I required, so I could put my memories where they belonged: in my past.

In other words, I learned what the psychologist and Zen master Joseph Bobrow has been telling the world: "What we cannot acknowledge, we cannot process. What we cannot process, we cannot transform. What we cannot transform, haunts us."[1]

Healing from Moral Injury is thus possible, but it can be a long and lonely journey, especially if the injured remain quiet. The very first step then, before any healing can happen, is to break the silence . . .

---

1. Bobrow, "Waking Up from War, Part 2." Bobrow is the founder of the *Coming Home Project*, a nonprofit organization devoted to providing expert consultation for community-based organizations that address collective and individual trauma.

Iraq: 2005

After almost two years of fighting, my country finally acknowledged it was fighting an insurgency. If we wanted to win—or at least if we wanted an honorable exit plan—training the Iraqi Security Forces had to become a strategic priority. So, the US military hastily formed a new organization called the Iraqi Assistance Group, and I eagerly volunteered. I was young and idealistic, but I would soon learn that ideals are sometimes unachievable in the real world.

And few places are as real as Mosul.

I lived on a small Iraqi base called "The Guest House," located in the center of town, a jumble of religions, ethnicities, and tribes seeking revenge for some past but not forgotten wrong. I arrived in the wake of the Abu Ghraib scandal, at the height of the insurgency and our own counterproductive policies and actions. Mosul was chaos, a city where evil people could reach their full potential.

My job was to advise an Iraqi intelligence officer and interrogator, whom I'll call "Saedi," Arabic for "sir." Saedi had been doing this work for over thirty years, first as a Peshmerga, a Kurdish guerilla fighting against the Saddam Hussein regime; then as a member of the Asayish, the notorious Kurdish Intelligence service; and then, when I met him, as a new colonel in the recently formed Iraqi security forces. It should come as no surprise, then, that Saedi was freakishly skilled at interrogation and torture.

My job was to teach, coach, and mentor him, but I was unable to give orders. Instead, I used rapport to nudge him in the right direction—to help him defeat the insurgency in one corner of the city and, if possible, to deter him from resorting to the worst forms of abuse. I immersed myself in the experience.

In that life, it didn't take long for Iraqi rules to become apparent, and Saedi's first rule was this: do what's necessary. "I don't have the luxury of civility," he would remind me daily. "These men are killers, lives hang in the balance, and Iraqi rules allow me only three days to interrogate. If I don't get enough evidence or a confession, then I have to release them back onto the streets. And you know—you *know!*—they'll kill again, more of my countrymen, or, perhaps, another American."

Iraq: Month 2

I am giving a class to the Iraqi intelligence officers and soldiers on the treatment of detainees. As I stand in front of the small class, I look up at the twirling fan, and I swear the fan is in an uncontrollable wobble. I take a step to the side, then I look down and read my flashcards. Sweat rolls down my face and, sometimes, splatters my notes. I move my hands to the side so the drops won't smudge the pencil.

The class is animated. My Iraqi students ask lots of questions, and as has happened in other classes, I find some way to talk about the importance of treating prisoners humanely. We discuss Abu Ghraib and how to not allow that to happen here. "It is vital for the Iraqi citizen and the world community to respect and trust the Iraqi military." I speak about how it is the Iraqi officer's responsibility to monitor the prison guards and to avoid abusing prisoners. But it's frustrating, for both the Iraqis and me, since this last point of my lecture doesn't seem to resonate with them. I have to remember that I am dealing with a completely different culture. The Iraqi legal system is based on confessions, and since confessions are required to find a person guilty and keep them in prison, confessions are what interrogators try to get.

It seems so easy to say, "No beating the prisoners," until I'm actually standing here teaching men who themselves have been beaten many times before. No matter how many times I wag my finger, I can see their minds turning and them thinking: "But this prisoner is a terrorist. He has killed women, children, or a soldier friend of mine. If he confesses, he will go to jail. Why should the world care if this requires that I hurt him? How typical of you hypocritical Americans."

It is a long road to change such deeply ingrained beliefs. Sometimes, I feel like Sisyphus, and I'm conflicted about this feeling as well. As an adviser, I am not in charge. I have no control and can only show the way. There are times, though, when something clicks. When I point out that "not every person captured is guilty," it seems that the Kurds and Shia, who've suffered so much under Saddam, and that even some of my Sunni students, understand. When I explain that if you beat prisoners, you will be just as likely to create a terrorist as to stop one, I get some nods of agreement.

But the daily cycle quickly becomes an eternity. There are countless patrols, playing chicken with fate, and then returning to the prison on my base, where some of those I interrogate wanted my death on the streets, the same insurgents who kidnapped, shot, assassinated, and planted IEDs. They stumble dirty and blindfolded through Saedi's prison door, often to be abused. My arguments against torture aren't working, and I have to admit, at least to myself, that I'm torn about torture as well.

I know prisoners were—and still are—abused throughout the Middle East. Nowhere was this truer than in Iraq under Saddam Hussein. It is one of the reasons why torture is still used to extract confessions. In Iraq, an interrogator cannot turn away from this simple, hard-to-swallow fact: to gain a confession—to get the words you most want to hear—torture almost always works. But often such tactics are unnecessary.

Most insurgents whom we interrogate are motivated more by personal benefit than by religious conviction. When we confront them with facts, they become weak and timid, most cry, and almost all soon confess. They are afraid. They should be.

Although torture is used, I've learned that success comes more from prisoners' fear of torture than from actual torture. The prisoner's imagination is often an interrogator's most powerful ally. But then there is the occasional anomaly where this maxim does not hold true—the devout Muslim terrorist, the man who believes that the more suffering he endures, the greater his pleasure in paradise will be.

But what is torture, anyway? It seems everyone has a different definition. Is it abacination, boiling, crushing, drilling, flaying, garroting, hamstringing . . . waterboarding? Is it putting a gun to a prisoner's head—*click*? Is it making the prisoner stand up and then sit down, over and over again? Is it giving him water but not letting him pee? What about sleep deprivation? Or detaining a relative? Is it releasing him and then letting the whole town know that he talked with me, the American? Is it telling him his nephew is sick and that he won't get to see him before the nephew dies? Is it having a fake doctor strip search him to "check" him, then you're telling the town, his friends, family, and fellow terrorists that he is gay? Is it no sunlight? No bed? No female companionship? No window? No daily walk outside?

I think, too, on my own definition of what constitutes torture. Does my definition change depending on who I have in my prison cell? I know it does. I feel my bar adjust every single day. But I have a responsibility to try to deter behavior that meets my definition of torture.

I am told: "Teach, coach, mentor. Enable your counterpart." Why? "To capture and kill terrorists. Oh, and try to deter abuse in the process." How? "You're Special Forces. Use your experience and judgment." Well, that is what we get trained and paid for, so instead of crying that the sky is falling, I'm working on changing my students' and Saedi's proclivities. I need to find a way to convince them.

So, my arguments turn pragmatic. I appeal to strategic consequences. "Look," I begin, "there are serious consequences if you torture prisoners. Just look at what happened in Abu Ghraib. The use of torture encourages international and—more importantly—local support for the terrorist's cause."

When this line of reasoning doesn't seem to hold any water, I try to appeal to tactical consequences. "Look, torture produces unreliable information. And if you torture devout prisoners, this will just increase their resistance and will only prove to them that their cause is just. It's possible that you are torturing an innocent civilian who will eventually be released. These tales of abuse will spread in the community and only strengthen the citizens' support for the terrorist."

But this mostly gets me glazed and unbelieving looks. After the class, I wonder: Is morality somehow different in war? Is right-and-wrong only black-and-white where choices are easy? When you move from the professor's abstract lecture to a dirty and dark basement prison filled with terrorists and surrounded by a city full of killers, does the immediate benefit of torture become easier to see?

So, I've become desperate. When talking to Saedi, I make use of the things that he values most—relationships, honor, his family, and his tribe. I use his friendship with me. I attack the spots where he is psychologically vulnerable while expressing sympathy for his perspective. It seems I'm learning from Saedi. I'm manipulating him even as he manipulates me.

I say: "I know that these terrorists are cowards who do not have human rights. I know they have information that may save some innocent lives. I, like you, have no sympathy for them. However, just listen to me. We are good friends and you know I will always be honest with you. If you torture them, you will get me into trouble. If you torture them, you risk the reputation of your unit. If you torture them, you're alienating the very community we need on our side. The risks are just not worth the possibility that this asshole has information which he may tell us."

This particular approach works, at least for a while, but it is tenuously tied to our "friendship." I also fear that I have become the same type of person that I'm desperate to stop. By protecting these terrorists, have I raped a boy, or kidnapped a girl, by proxy? Has my black-and-white coffee-shop reasoning killed an American, or a helpless and innocent Iraqi woman or child? I see so no clear right or wrong choices, only shades between bad and worse.

As the days become weeks, as the dozen of prisoners become hundreds, my world focuses down to the struggle to answer one existential question, the answers to which place my very soul in jeopardy, no matter the choices I make: What is "right action" when fighting wrong? Is there a path to "most good" when trying to stop terrorists from killing little boys and girls?

Iraq: Month 6

Shoeib kneels and then curls up on the cold cement floor. "I think he's ready to confess," Saedi softly tells me.

Shoeib slowly rises to sit cross-legged. His head is bent over, and he cries. His entire body shakes, and he doesn't look up. There is a sandbag placed over his head so that he can't see, and I wear an itchy black wool ski mask.

During interrogations, I never wear my US military uniform, but I always wear this mask. This disguise lets me conceal my identity as an American. Americans have been in Iraq for too long, and these killers have learned that we will protect them. They know that an American will hold back Iraqis' heavy hands. Therefore, when I enter a cell, I hide in the dark shadows of deep corners. I become just another Iraqi soldier taking notes. Saedi, on the other hand, never wears a mask. He despises the prisoners, and he wants each one to see the power of his crinkled eyes and glowing smile.

It is early morning, and the sun has yet to rise. The cell is damp and cold, and I'm tired. I pass to Saedi a silent twirl of a finger. Let's start this show.

"How many operations have you done?" he asks Shoeib, slowly rising from his seat to move close. Saedi yanks the sandbag off the prisoner's head. Then the question is quickly repeated and followed by a swift and well-deserved fist and foot. Shoeib falls forward, his head on the floor.

I smile because this time, we know—*know*—what this man has done. There are no more guesses; we just need him to document his confession with a smudgy thumbprint.

Shoeib is broken and will confess at any moment. I just know it. All of Saedi's hitting and kicking serves to quicken the inevitable, to turn Shoeib's thoughts away from the inner sanctum of self-pity where selfish killers retreat under interrogation. Today, Saedi's abuse is not only a tactic to get a confession. He is also taking personal satisfaction from it.

I smile and nod to my partner.

"Speak!" Saedi screams. "If you talk, I may not spend all my time focusing on you."

"I have done ten operations," Shoeib says with lowered eyes and pitiful sobs.

"What type of operations?" demands Saedi.

"Cutting off the heads, or killing them by a bullet to the head."

Saedi and I just sit there and glare—for almost a minute we let the silence become a deafening roar—and then the questions start again. "Describe to me your operations."

"In four operations, my job was to hold the legs of the person. I was to keep them still and to stop them from kicking. Six times I was told to do the killing myself. I would either cut off his head or shoot him in the back of the head."

"Who were these people you killed?" Saedi asks with quiet loathing.

"I don't know. I would get a call from Mohammed. He would tell me to be at a certain house. Mohammed and some other people I don't know would kidnap someone and bring them to the house. I would either hold the legs or do the killing myself as they made a videotape."

Shoeib starts to cry. Then he raises his hands above his head and wails, "Wa-Allah, Saedi, Wa-Allah!" From only a few feet away, I feel the shimmers of evil come off this man who dares to sit here and plead for God's help. Well, God is not here.

Night after night, these men confound me with their acts of inhumanity. I try to stop my slide into their darkness, and so far I've succeeded, barely, but tonight is different. When Shoeib wails for some higher power's assistance, I feel a fracture slide down the center of my chest. For the first time in my life, I fervently want to kill another human being. I want to reach across this small prison cell and let my shadow fly.

As I feel my darkness intensely and taste this killer's pleas, I can hear everything, even the now-silent prayers of his victims. I can see everything, every drop of moisture that slides down the cinderblock walls. I hear perfectly every breath, every heartbeat, and every shuffle of booted feet. I'm conscious of every scent, and the odors speak of the excitement, the anticipation, the fear, and the hatred that we all feel. Then suddenly it vanishes.

I open my eyes, and Saedi is bent over the still crying prisoner. He whispers in his ear, and cigarette smoke escapes his nose to float up in the air and twirl around the one hanging light bulb. I hear more sobs, which become suckling whimpers.

I feel a deep loss.

I despair.

I need to escape.

I must escape, or I will become lost.

I quickly leave the cell and climb the stairs to the roof. Outside, the sun is just beginning to rise. Mosul is beautiful in the early morning, and I need only a few minutes in the crisp early light. I desperately need the rebirth of a sunrise because beneath my rage is guilt: This isn't the first time that I've seen Shoeib. Two months ago, he was captured by the Iraqi Army and brought to Saedi's prison, the same prison where he wails in the room below me. But two months ago I chose a different path, I made the decision to protect him. I told Saedi, "No, on no account." So, two months ago, Shoeib didn't confess, and after a few days, Saedi released him back onto Mosul's streets.

So, today, when Shoeib confessed to those ten executions? Instantly, those deaths became my fault, and those weren't the first, nor the last deaths, that I'll have to account for.

Iraq: Month 10

As the days became months, something unexpected happened inside of this prison. I've opened my eyes—I changed my mind: Torture isn't *really* about doing what's necessary or choosing the lesser of two evils. Torture isn't about the rational weighing of costs and benefits. It's not about being tougher or less "squeamish" than weaker people. The seldom-acknowledged truth is that there is a natural and often unconscious human impulse to inflict and condone brutality against bad people, and then our minds contort to rationalize, to defend the indefensible.

This understanding isn't hypothetical: it is experiential. I daily witness these mental gymnastics, and I constantly force myself to stand in the way of my own—and of others'—descent into a moral abyss. And some days I lose these arguments. I'm afraid of where I'll go, and that I've lost myself.

For me, the final metric for any discussion of "right" and "wrong" is this: Am I willing to hurt another person in order to prove the preconceptions of fallible people? And the level of "torture" or "pressure" or "enhanced interrogation techniques" only increases until my preconceptions are proven true. If I were to remove the conditional clauses in my reasoning, would I still be right? Do I definitely commit a "wrong" in the hope it will possibly result in a "right" at some point in the distant future? Am I willing to risk every negative consequence because the absence of evidence proves I am right, and the longer my faith remains hidden, the more pressure I feel necessary to apply?

Am I absolutely certain of my own infallibility? No, I am not God. I'm human, and my absolute certainty is certain proof of my absolute ignorance.

And torture? Torture is the last refuge of the sadist or the incompetent.

What I've learned is that a more effective way to protect Americans and advance our nation's interests is to be a competent interrogator: dominating the battle of wits, learning personal details about prisoners, preparing rigorously for interrogations, controlling every atmospheric nuance, and building relationships, relationships that entice prisoners to talk.

The rational part of me understands these truths, but on this base, reality seems condensed and comes at me in a thick and steady pour. Every day, I talk with such horrible people, but each devil has a face and a heart that I come to know as intimately as my own. When I enter the cell and I hear their stories, I feel the relentless pull to slide down their rabbit hole. . . .

And I'm scared. I'm terrified of losing myself.

So I've decided to stop interrogating. But my self-imposed isolation hasn't helped with the cognitive dissonance, because every day I know that horrible things are happening inside of that prison, and by not being next to Saedi, I'm choosing to let this happen. And for that, I can't forgive myself.

Iraq: Month 11

It's cold, fucking colder than I would have ever imagined it could be. There's ice on the ground and frost on the bushes. Even the feral dogs are no longer barking, they just whimper from the shadows, and I still don't feel like talking—to anyone. I like to just stand behind the door that opens onto my rooftop. I stare out at Mosul through the rusted iron bars that once held glass. These bars feel like my prison, and I miss the human connection of the interrogation.

Iraq: Month 12

Tomorrow, I leave Iraq. Tomorrow begins the journey to a dream.

I came to Iraq loathing radical Muslims. I leave with more complex and nuanced feelings. I tell myself I've been successful, that I stopped terrorists from killing innocent people. But at what cost? Did it require becoming evil?

I'll return home with no visible wounds, but I'm different. Something has changed, inside.

Six Years after Leaving Iraq: Behavioral Health Clinic

"Why are you here? The intake sheet doesn't mention specifics."

The voice comes out of nowhere. It's out of place and surprises me but hints that I need to find another human in the growing remoteness. Where is a hand? . . . and then I see a man. He enters the exit to step on a carpeted floor, and I look up to see posters on the wall, the same posters on Determination, Inspiration, Teamwork, and Confidence that hang in so many military offices. As my mind adjusts from the prison dark, the fog begins to clear.

"Why are you here?" the man repeats.

I'm confused but then remember.

I came home from Iraq many years ago, and now I'm in a counselor's office.

I slip out of the present so easily and so often that I hardly notice and am often shocked by a sound or touch. Like now—from seeing a killer whom I desperately wanted to kill, to finding myself floating in this doctor's office chair. The echoes are so real that I hear the screams and want to slide into the room's dark corners. I look down to the center of my chest, to search for the crack that must be there.

And what is he asking?

"Major Edmonds, why are you here?"

"I need help. I'm fucking desperate." But these words are trapped and I can't say them. Instead, I whisper: "There is Iraq, which was six years ago. Then there is the present. Where do I start?"

"Tell me what you want. Whatever you think is important. The order doesn't matter."

"There are too many things happening to me, too many things going wrong, and I'm scared.

"I no longer have an appetite. I've lost over fifteen pounds, and I'm not trying to lose weight. I barely eat anything at all. I get only a few hours of sleep a night. I wake up early, really early, every morning, and can't fall back to sleep. And when I do wake up, I don't feel tired. Sometime later in the day, I slump down exhausted, to fall asleep in a chair or on a nice patch of soft green grass. And my stomach really, really hurts. Then there are the headaches, intense headaches that come on so suddenly and from nowhere. The pain sits right here, right behind my right eye, and it thumps and thumps, fuck, fuck, fuck . . . and makes it difficult to think."

But these words only echo inside. What I have the courage to say is, "I can't sleep. I wake up early and feel exhausted all day. And I feel awful. My stomach hurts, and I have intense headaches." Then I go quiet.

I rest my head in my hands, thinking that if I had really told the truth, about everything, about all of my symptoms, he would connect the dots to some rare and fascinating ailment that is the cause of my fucked-up thinking—a brain tumor, perhaps? But, no, life is never that easy because there is so much else that is going on, so much that is happening, so much that I am thinking, so much that I am feeling, and so much that I can't talk about but . . . God, I have to. I have to tell someone. I have to, if not for me, then for my family.

"Is that all?" he asks.

No.

"It has been going on for a long time now. I've tried to focus on creating a new life—a new job, a new wife, and starting a family. But I can't leave Iraq behind," I say, and then go silent. But if you press an ear to my chest, you'd hear the details. There are the flashbacks, the constant thoughts and memories ricocheting inside. Fuck! I'm constantly thinking. I'm sitting in a doctor's office chair but it's not real. Behind the veneer that is the present world, I'm living inside of a basement prison, reliving every session of torture, and thinking about all of the suffering and death that I've allowed to happen.

Whatever is going on, of all the things that are happening, what terrifies me the most is how telling the truth will affect my job and the respect of those at work. If I lose my security clearance, how can I take care of my family? I wouldn't know what to do.

But these words are trapped, and my surface stays silent.

He nods. "Okay. You're constantly thinking about Iraq. And you're not feeling well." His legs are crossed, and a notebook rests on the arm of his chair.

"Anything more?" he asks me.

Yes. It's obvious he doesn't hear me shouting. Because lately, I've started to imagine doing something really, really stupid, like jumping off a cliff or driving my car off the side of the road . . . there I am, hands on the wheel, and I see a tight corner approaching. My speed stays constant and my hands stay locked on the 10 and the 2. I close my eyes, and I imagine myself floating. I am smiling. There is no fear, and I feel a . . . a weight lifting. It's a blissful release, and well, I just feel, which feels good, and it reminds me of how I felt in Iraq, how it felt to stand up in the turret with my head exposed and death all around me. Does he realize that being so close to death is addictive?

But, no, of course he can't understand me, so I don't tell him about these ideations. I barely even whisper them to myself.

"What?" I ask as I raise my head, as I'm pulled back from the car that is crashing through a roadside barrier, and floating . . .

"I asked," says the doc, "if there was anything more you want to talk about."

What an ass. No, I don't "want" to talk, you fuck.

"Major Edmonds? Is there anything more?"

Yes, there is so much more, but I don't know how to put Iraq into words. How, every day, during both sleep and wakefulness, I'm living inside of a basement prison. But I don't have the words to describe that inner fight, how every day I was forced to make a choice—and how every day, over and over again, no matter the decision, I made a soul-crushing wrong choice, and how the other stresses of war, the daily expectation of death, the failing war strategy, the isolation, the austere environment, and the stressful girlfriend back home, how these other things only compromised my mental resiliency. Over time, my mind slowed, and then I just . . . turned off. I shut down.

"When something hurts so badly, it eventually stops hurting," I want to tell this mental-health professional, and then I want to continue: "And I'm losing. I have a family I desperately love. Can you help?"

After seventy minutes of talking, the mental health professional tells me that my symptoms don't fit the PTSD profile, that nothing is wrong. "You're okay," he tells me. "You just need to learn how to handle your stress. You can take some stress management classes, but I don't think we need to talk anymore."

Later, I decide to tell my commander, about Iraq, about everything, seeing mental health and about what's bothering me, and to him I'm a malingering drama queen, a security risk, and weak. But both offer some truly helpful parting advice. "Continue your writing. Writing might do some good," offers the therapist. And "find a new job, elsewhere. And be quiet about it," says my boss.

So I do. I find a new job, move my family across the country, and begin to write.

Every morning for four years I wake up early to relive and relive again every thought, every word, and every choice. Every morning I wake up early to confront my Enemy—each and every painful memory.

For years, the Enemy and I sit in the same room together and just glare at each other from a distance. But then one day, something changes and I realize I can look him in the eye. Then, sometime later, I discover I can move my chair closer, millimeters at a time. Soon, I am close enough to feel his breath on my cheek. That's when the screaming begins. Then the hate becomes loathing, and then revulsion turns to disgust. Suddenly, we're conversing, never friends, just enemies who are talking, suffering a different perspective. And when I think I understand, I change my viewpoint. I stand up, move myself to another angle, and start the process all over again. Over time, the cognitive dissonance harmonizes.

Then I start the process over again, but with a new memory.

For years I do this, daily jotting down what's trapped, inside. Writing takes the place of the conversations I needed to have with someone else. It's traumatic, but also therapeutic, giving me the space to breathe, to finally process and transform each painful memory. Writing—the art of turning thoughts into words—allows me to make the sense of my experiences that I required to learn self-forgiveness.

Today

It has been such a twisted and savage journey, but I don't regret my experiences since they've come with an understanding: There is a weight to all moral choices, but, in war, this weight can become a burden that literally injures, even kills. This is the natural consequence when a basically good person's choices result in the suffering and death of both the guilty and the innocent. Unfortunately, this difficult truth is often wished away, as we can see by such commonplace euphemisms as "hard decision-making." However, seventeen years of wars and counting are making this self-deception next to impossible, to the point that today, there's even a new term for what we've long glossed over. This term is "Moral Injury," and it describes a controversial and misunderstood form of trauma that many believe is the signature wound of our wars in Iraq and Afghanistan.

Bill Nash, an eminent psychiatrist and an expert on Moral Injury, believes that there are limits to human endurance, that war, by its very nature, often pushes people to and sometimes beyond their limits, and that one way war does this is by relentlessly attacking, and sometimes utterly defeating, our very necessary moral beliefs.[2] If this is true, can warfighters who are unable to reconcile what they've seen or done with the person they once were, ever fully come home? That is, can wounds to moral identity ever truly heal?

I learned it's possible, but the obstacles are daunting, especially when admitting the very existence of the injury raises uncomfortable questions that most nations would prefer to ignore. Instead of taking actions to better safeguard service members from Moral Injury before, during, and after going to war, we've unconsciously allowed a destructive national narrative to form, one that ensures that the most harmful of conditions becomes the norm: silence. "Manage out of sight and alone," those who suffer from moral injuries are effectively told.

But it doesn't have to be this way. It's possible to change course, and the most important first step is for warfighters to accept their hidden injuries and to take charge of their own healing. This is where communities can help, and their role is so very simple and requires such minimal effort: listen. Attend to the stories of those who's injuries are less *visibly* apparent, in whatever forms those experiences are communicated. Provide for them, in any way you can, a safe, nonjudgmental, and compassionate space in which

2. Wood, *What Have We Done*, 20–21.

to share their experiences, an environment where they can, possibly, learn self-forgiveness.

When warfighters come home and re-enter communities who truly empathize—who try to understand the true cost of the wars we all have chosen and are willing to share the moral burdens of those wars with their veterans—the weight of what we are asked to do in our country's name suddenly becomes . . . lighter.

And the consequences can be life-saving.

13

TYLER BOUDREAU

The Morally Injured

On a summer evening in 2004, I participated in the search of an isolated farmhouse in Yousifiyah, a small town along the Euphrates River in the northern Babil province of Iraq. I was an infantry captain in the Marine Corps. We staged our trucks out of sight from the house until darkness fell. Then we moved in with terrible speed, our engines roaring, our hearts racing, and our hands tight on loaded weapons. We felt some fear during these missions, I suppose, but that emotion always seemed peripheral or almost disingenuous. Our heavy breaths rose from something else. I don't think "thrill" would be too strong a word. There was something about these raids that served neither cause nor country, just our own lust for excitement.

Missions, however, are not initiated for the thrill (not explicitly, anyway), but in response to what is known as "actionable intelligence"; information gathered on the ground through various sources and agents, processed through intelligence staffs, handed up and down the chain of command, until it becomes the basis of an operation. In this case, the specific farmhouse was not suspected but was located in the general vicinity of another house that was, and so was targeted for good measure. The search itself was conducted flawlessly: I watched from my vehicle as the Marines knocked on the front door. A man answered and, through an interpreter, they politely explained that we needed to search the premises for weapons and bomb-making materials. They asked him if he'd mind stepping outside with his wife and children while we looked around. The man was cooperative and amiable. There was no shouting or pushing. The Marines wore friendly smiles. They stepped gently through the house and were careful to replace anything they moved. Outside, other Marines chatted playfully with the kids and gave them pieces of candy. When the search was complete and nothing was found, we thanked the man and apologized for the inconvenience. It was over. Not a shot was fired, not a drop of blood or a tear was shed, and yet, as we withdrew from that farmhouse and roared off into the night, I felt something inside me begin to hurt.

What can I call that hurt?

Since the invasions of Iraq and Afghanistan, there's been a lot of talk about the "invisible wounds" of war. I've talked a lot about them myself. Thousands of veterans have come home in a state of near mental collapse, harried by their memories of the battlefield. Some of those veterans have ended up addicted to drugs or alcohol, or in jail, or homeless. Others have lost their jobs, their families, or their savings. Many of them, unable to face their nightmares any longer, have resorted desperately to suicide. And when the veterans, and the families and friends, and the communities all cried out, "What do we call this? What do we call this thing that has torn our young soldiers apart?" the resounding answer was *post-traumatic stress*. That was the lesson we learned from the Vietnam War.

To nearly anyone who'd care enough to listen—counselors, doctors, ministers, peace activists, folks in the community—I would bellow again and again, "I'm hurting!" And they were all sympathetic, they really were, and they'd assure me, nearly every one of them, that I was experiencing this thing called post-traumatic stress. (It seems to be an affliction freshly discovered after every war.) Of course, I'd heard of it before. When I was a rifle company commander, at least a dozen of my Marines were medically discharged after we came home from Iraq for PTSD. A dozen more were punitively discharged for having suddenly picked up a drug habit in the wake of war. There was talk that they were trying to get out of our upcoming deployment, scheduled nine months after we got home. But I felt this drug epidemic wasn't so much about escaping the future deployment as much as it was about escaping the past one. Drugs probably seemed like the most effective means to get their heads out of Iraq. So yes, by the time I left the military, I'd already heard plenty about the debilitating effects of post-traumatic stress. But was that what was going on for me? Could I really call my farmhouse episode *traumatic*? I think that would be a difficult argument to make.

And what about all those times when the searches were not so benign? What about the orders I gave, from time to time, to use a heavy hand? What about the patrols I dispatched that returned to base with young Marines in body bags? What about the approval I issued to snipers over the radio one night to shoot a man armed only with a shovel? (He was suspected of digging a hole for a roadside bomb.) Could any of these scenarios be called traumatic for me? In each case, there was violence felt and inflicted by somebody, absolutely, but my role was indirect; I was too far off to even hear the shot that felled that man with a shovel. Would any clinician in good conscience diagnose me with PTSD for those experiences alone? I was in Camp Fallujah in 2004 when the news of Abu Ghraib broke, just a few miles down the road from the infamous facility. Several of us gathered around to examine the glossy pictorial of the tortured Iraqi prisoners. The images were distressing, certainly, but I doubt I'd pick up any disability benefits for having seen them. And yet, for all these things, including the pictures, I felt that hurt again.

After resigning my commission in 2005, I came home to Massachusetts and was diagnosed with PTSD by the Department of Veterans Affairs (VA). I'd been shot at and shelled enough to explain away my very turbulent emotions. I accepted the diagnosis from the VA and from everyone else, and I'm sure that my condition was in part that, but inwardly I knew that the greatest pain I felt was not linked to those moments when violence was being directed at me but when I was involved in inflicting it on others. Post-traumatic stress just didn't seem to fit. So what could I call this pain? It felt a lot like guilt, so that's what I started calling it, but in the *Diagnostic and Statistical Manual of Mental Disorders* (DSM) under PTSD there is no mention of guilt, except for "survivor's guilt," which is about being alive while one's comrades are dead, not about harming others. There has been no official name for this type of guilt, and that has struck me since getting out of the military as a significant gap in the discourse on war casualties.

The term "Moral Injury" has recently come afloat, and it applies to exactly the kind of guilt I'm talking about. Though not everyone agrees exactly on the definition, it's a term being used more frequently now across the medical community and among political activists, various faith groups, and others. "Moral injury" is capturing attention in the media and veterans' organizations. Even the military has begun to recognize Moral Injury as a category of wound that service members are facing. Researchers from the VA describe "Moral Injury" as "involving an act of transgression that creates dissonance and conflict because it violates assumptions and beliefs about right and wrong and personal goodness."

Generally speaking, "Moral Injury" is meant to displace the more severe sense of guilt, and to give space for the kinds of wounds we inflict on ourselves that come inherently with the wounds we inflict upon others. It resonates with the notion that killing hurts the killer, too, even in self-defense or in the line of duty, and that no *justification*, legal, political, religious, or otherwise, can heal those wounds. The problem with the word "guilt" is that it seems to load a disproportionate burden on the shoulders of individual veterans. A man might wring his hands and say in anguish, "I killed!" But it's not as though he thought it up and did it on his own. There were other factors and other agents involved. There were greater circumstances to consider. Even war crimes can't be owned exclusively by the perpetrators. Moral injury is about the damage done to our moral fiber when transgressions occur by our hands, through our orders, or with our connivance. When we accept these transgressions, however pragmatically (for survival, for instance), we sacrifice a piece of our moral integrity. That's what Moral Injury is all about.

Moral injury does not replace post-traumatic stress. It works alongside it. An event could be both traumatic and morally injurious, or it could be only one without the other. VA researchers have found that the two manifest themselves in similar ways. For example, both have been connected to symptoms of "re-experiencing" and "avoidance," while generally "hyperarousal" is associated only with PTSD and not Moral Injury. What we'll probably discover in the future is that most symptomatic veterans are suffering from both PTSD *and* Moral Injury. So far, roughly two million Americans have served in Iraq and Afghanistan. A now well-known RAND study conducted in 2008 suggested that about 20 percent of them will have symptoms of PTSD. It's very likely those figures reflect a lot of moral injuries as well; however, at the time of the study, scarcely anyone had heard the term.

The problem for now is that while "Moral Injury" is gaining traction in the public discourse, it is still viewed by the VA and the military as a medical issue, and those who suffer from it as "patients." Moreover, the concept of Moral Injury is in its nascent stages, remains widely unfamiliar, and is, therefore, not yet available as a formal diagnosis or a commonly understood condition for people to rally around. So when veterans or soldiers feel something hurt inside themselves, there is still only one brand to choose—PTSD. That's not good. It's not always accurate. And it renders soldiers automatically into mental patients instead of wounded souls.

Since post-traumatic stress has been, so to speak, the only game in town, it has served as something of a one-size-fits-all response to any mention of grief by a veteran. This default medicalization of a veteran's moral angst has created an ongoing dilemma for the mental health community. They are confronted all the time with veterans who are struggling, searching, digging, aching to know whether their personal actions and their wars were just or unjust.

"What do I say to that?" one provider will ask.

"I just try to honor their experience without judgment," another will respond.

These are typical comments I've heard time and again at the many conferences, events, and gatherings I've attended over the past five years related to combat stress.

While these veterans' questions undoubtedly relate to their mental health, the answers do not fall squarely within the providers' field of expertise or within any treatment for PTSD. Furthermore, a clinician's suppression of subjectivity while attempting to navigate such morally treacherous terrain is neither possible nor desirable. As a veteran, I really can't imagine a more disheartening scenario than being stuck in a room with a person listening with stony detachment as I grapple exasperatedly with the moral implications of my actions in war. I'd rather say nothing at all. And the consensus I've gathered from the clinicians I've met (and I've met quite a few) is that they'd rather stick with therapy and leave the larger moral questions to someone else. But why? If PTSD is the only diagnosis available for these invisible wounds of war, then who can we turn to for help, if not the doctors?

PTSD as a diagnosis has a tendency to depoliticize a veteran's disquietude and turn it into a mental disorder. What's most useful about the term "Moral Injury" is that it takes the problem out of the hands of the mental health profession and the military and attempts to place it where it belongs—in society, in the community, and in the family—precisely where moral questions should be posed and wrangled with. It transforms "patients" back into citizens, and "diagnoses" into dialogue. At this stage of American history, it's hard to imagine just what that might look like, but, all the same, it's an attempt that must be made. It's far too easy for people at home, particularly those not directly affected by war (and right now that's about 98 percent of the population) to shed a disingenuous tear for the veterans, donate a few bucks, and whisk them off to the closest shrink . . . out of sight and out of mind. As long as the invisible wounds of war are medical, there is no incentive in the community or in the household to engage them. After a while the veterans themselves become invisible.

So, in practical terms, what does a Moral Injury look like? The question, while succinct, has a broad and rather ambiguous answer. The word "war" itself contributes to the ambiguity, particularly today, because neither efforts in Iraq or Afghanistan are truly wars in the conventional sense. Officially, they're characterized as counterinsurgency operations, but it would be most accurate to call them occupations. Of course these days, "occupation" is not a label favored in political circles; however, it does give a more precise picture of just what today's combat tour is all about. That's important if we want to understand the nature of the mental and emotional crises that follow in its wake. It's easy to imagine the famous battles of the past in the trenches, and the beaches, and the mountains, and the jungles, all of them covered with corpses and steeped in blood. The American consciousness has been imbued with these images through every mode of popular culture. But occupations look much different.

In Iraq, with the exceptions of the invasion itself, the assault on Fallujah, and a few other small-scale battles, the most typical engagements between Americans and Iraqi insurgents, seen day-to-day, have been minor skirmishes that would hardly register in the most detailed historical accounts. The amount of violence witnessed by the average soldier deployed to Iraq or Afghanistan is quite low relative to that experienced in past wars. But again, this is a poor comparison, because, really, Iraq isn't a war—not anymore. At any rate, the fact remains that the US presence in Iraq has been far more perilous for Iraqis than it has for Americans. Even the most conservative statistics demonstrate that clearly.

However, mentioning the several hundred thousand Iraqi people killed since the US invasion in 2003, or the two and a half million displaced, or the millions more without money or medical care, appears to be taboo in the American media, the government, and in social circles. Nobody wants to talk about the Iraqis. It's always about *the troops*. But "Moral Injury" by definition includes the memories of those who have been harmed. Without the Iraqi people, the troops can have no moral injuries to speak of. And the only way Americans can fathom the meaning of this term, "Moral Injury," is to acknowledge the humanity of the Iraqis. The two ideas are inseparable. What I've found most difficult for people to grasp (and for a while this was hard for me, too) is the full range of "moral injuries" sustained in Iraq; because it's not always about the killing. This is where the precision of the word "occupation" is so helpful, because one has to imagine just what the troops are involved in to get an accurate sense of their reactions to it.

I once watched an old video of some Vietnam veterans giving testimony of war crimes that they'd either witnessed or participated in. What was most stunning about these testimonies, besides the gruesome events that they described, was the extraordinary stoicism with which they described them. Later, I listened to veterans of Iraq and Afghanistan talk about their roles in what they called "atrocities." The strange thing was that hardly any of their stories were particularly atrocious by the typical wartime standards. And yet these men cried. They wept and wept as they testified to deeds such as striking a man, or ransacking a house, or terrorizing families, or maybe even shooting a civilian. They described the daily grind of driving in and out of towns, patrolling through the streets, searching houses, detaining suspected insurgents, questioning locals, and all the while trying to stay alive. These were sad stories, to be sure, but somehow disproportionate to the word "atrocity" and to the intense emotions displayed by the tellers, particularly in contrast to those Vietnam testimonies that were, by any standard, horrendous. I thought maybe my contemporaries were being a little melodramatic.

Then last year, I discovered some of that same melodrama lurking in myself. I was watching a documentary about Iraq with a friend of mine (not a veteran). Midway through the piece, a short video clip was shown of two soldiers searching an Iraqi home. The footage was uneventful, boring even, capturing nothing but a bit of walking around and some chitchat between the Americans and the family. Then one of the soldiers, clad in body armor, sunglasses, and an automatic rifle, feeling in an amorous mood, I suppose, leaned toward a young Iraqi man in the living room and gave him a hug. The Iraqi submitted with limp arms and an unenthusiastic smile. The soldier, maybe nineteen or twenty years old, laughed. The other soldier laughed, too. And that was it. The footage ended.

I felt my face get hot with rage. I blurted something out in anger, something profane, to match the profanity of what had just been presented in this documentary without so much as a comment from the narrator.

"What?" my friend asked me. "What's wrong? Where's the harm in a hug?"

"There is harm in a hug!" I shouted. "Can't you see?"

But he didn't see. He couldn't grasp the magnitude of what had just happened. And in explaining my reaction I felt almost obligated, morally beholden, to express myself with fury. I wasn't angry at my friend. I was angry at how this type of atrocity could be shrouded in a guise of bonhomie. And I couldn't avoid that word, by the way—*atrocity*. So I used my ire to make up for the apparent mildness of the scene.

The trouble is that no matter how that Iraqi man felt about the hug, there's nothing he could have done to stop it. He couldn't say no to the hug. And there was no one who could help him. Nobody at all could stop that American soldier from hugging that Iraqi man—and you could see in their faces, they both knew it. That's what an occupation looks like. And that's the harm in a hug.

For all my years in the military, all my time training with guns, and alongside artillery, and tanks, and aircraft, I never comprehended the full force, the *weight*, of the United States military until I witnessed its massive presence in Iraq as one body. Then I began to grasp the grave reality of American foreign policy and the extent of what it means to be a superpower on earth. It means nothing can stop us from going anywhere and doing anything we want to do, whether bombing, or building, or shooting, or hugging—anything. There may be limits, legal limits, political limits, moral limits, but I know now that those limits will never be recognized until after they've already been broken; then we'll decide retrospectively whether or not to honor them. When that Iraqi man was hugged by the soldier, he felt, in that instant, the embrace of total American power. That was the harm. That was the atrocity that I could only convey through exaggerated emotion. And that was when I understood the melodrama of my comrades who also used emotion to try to make the very same point.

Through these ostensibly mundane stories, we cried out to the world, "Our moral fibers have been torn by what we were asked to do and by what we agreed to do."

Moral injury does not necessarily imply that the injuries are inflicted by others, like when a soldier is ordered to perform a morally dubious task, although the term does leave room for that. In some cases, we injure ourselves through acts of commission or omission, through direct participation or indirect approval. Back at that farmhouse in Yousifiyah, I remember fighting an urge to go inside, just to look around. I had no tactical reason to go in, but then I didn't need much excuse; I was a captain, after all. But, at the same time, I was reluctant. Somehow I knew that crossing that threshold would increase my culpability in this occupation. If just being present on a search, if feeling the thrill of it, was a moral affliction upon my soul, then wandering into this home, uninvited, unnecessarily, and purely out of curiosity, would surely be a larger wound to bear. So I stayed outside. I think at that point in the deployment I'd already begun to sense what I was doing to myself and what I was quietly standing by, allowing my country to do to others.

"Moral injury" is a term that loosens the noose a bit around the necks of veterans who are harangued by enormous personal guilt and distributes the responsibility for their actions (justified or not) more evenly among the chain of command, the government, and maybe even the American people. Simultaneously, Moral Injury reaches out to those who may be too quick to exculpate themselves. It broadens the burden of responsibility for acts that may not be criminal by the strict letter of the law but that are clearly hurtful to other people and, therefore, morally questionable. It implicates all participants of war, whether commanding, supporting, or just standing idly by, and it gives a name for the hurt that comes from doing so. It pulls moral transgressions that are not necessarily traumatic out of the mental health profession and into society, into the living room, and makes these notorious "invisible wounds" all of our problems, not just the problems of the VA. Moral injuries are not about benefits or blame. They're not about treatment or medications. They're not about disability. They are about our society and our moral values. A Moral Injury is not inherently the same thing as a war crime, though clearly the two ideas overlap. But when we talk about war crimes, we seek justice; when we talk about moral injuries, we seek a deeper understanding of our humanity. We seek healing, in some spiritual sense.

The goal for now is to get the idea of "Moral Injury" out there, get it heard, get it recognized universally as a wound that must be healed communally, not medically. And the first step is understanding what a Moral Injury looks like in an occupation environment. No doubt, it will sound strange to those accustomed to the more traditional war stories, because occupations look so much different. There aren't going to be staggering American casualty statistics. There won't be massive armies clashing on the fields of battle. There aren't going to be blood-spackled bodies stacked up around fighting holes or littered in the trenches. There won't be any glorious combat actions and medals of honor to go with them. It's not going to be material for thrilling stories that yank you to the edge of your seat. In an occupation, Moral Injury just isn't going to look like that. It's going to be dull. It's going to be a man with a shovel or a farmhouse search.

It's going to be a hug.

14

DOUGLAS A. PRYER

What We Don't Talk about
When We Talk about War

For the past four years, I've read and written about Moral Injury, a process akin to a difficult, perilous passage at sea. The stories I've read of veterans whose identities were broken or lost in the storm-tossed waters of war have troubled and threatened to capsize the ship that is my own soul. I may not have witnessed as much violence as some of them experienced, but I've endured enough. After all, as William Styron unforgettably describes in his novel, *Sophie's Choice*, the greater horror often lies in our choices rather than in actual acts of violence.

Harder than opening myself up to the stories of broken warriors has been bringing myself, in these turbulent waters, to make landings on the nightmare-shrouded shores of sometimes suppressed memories. Better it would be, I've often felt, to keep such memories at a distance, as if they were islands with submerged, dangerous reefs safely viewed only from afar.

There has been no real choice for me in this matter, though. I must learn to live with painful memories. If not, I feel in my bones that I will someday find my ship caught up in such strong currents of moral dissonance that it could be broken upon hidden reefs that I had thought—had wished—were far away.

The Shades of Abu Ghraib

In July 2003, the Abu Ghraib prison reopened as the US military's consolidated interrogation facility in Iraq. I was an Army captain then, part of the team managing interrogation operations for all of Baghdad. Once open, I called the prison almost daily, asking interrogators there to pull my division's former prisoners from the prison's general population and take them to their "hard site" for questioning.

My division never received a single piece of actionable intelligence back from the prison. Those guys must be the worst interrogators ever, I thought. But in war, especially a counterinsurgency, you can't afford to leave any stone unturned in the search for intelligence. So, I kept up a steady stream of requests.

The lack of any useful intelligence from Abu Ghraib was an indicator that something terribly wrong was happening there. Other indicators were theater policy memos that endorsed so-called "enhanced" interrogation techniques. However, perhaps because my immediate leaders spoke so strongly against such techniques, it never occurred to me that our prisoners at Abu Ghraib were being abused. This thought didn't dawn on me until, with the rest of the world, I viewed shocking photos of naked pyramids, faux electrocution, and dogs raging at nude prisoners. When I saw those photos, not just the war, "I" felt suddenly lost.

For long afterwards, I wondered if any of the suspected insurgents whom I had asked Abu Ghraib interrogators to question were in those photos. Then I learned that nearly all the depicted prisoners were alleged criminals rather than insurgents. A group of soldiers—their characters at least partially undone by a command climate gone awry—had randomly pulled reputed criminals out of the prison's general population for some late-night fun.

But this fact made me feel only slightly better, since I also learned that there were photos of worse abuses that President Obama elected not to release, photos that reportedly involve crimes like rape and may depict suspected insurgents. I learned, too, that Abu Ghraib interrogators had routinely directed such approved techniques as "Forced Nudity, "Stress

Positions," and "Use of Military Working Dogs" on suspected insurgents—
practices I consider torture and profoundly wrong.[1]

Many American soldiers feel tainted by what happened at the prison.
I suspect I feel tainted more than most. It makes me nauseous to think that,
by making calls to that prison and asking for certain prisoners to be inter-
rogated, I was probably part of a causal chain that led to the torture of other
human beings. How could I have not understood what was happening?

I've forgotten the names of the Iraqis whom we sent to Abu Ghraib.
It's possible that I could remember some of their names under hypnosis and
then, perhaps, look for and find a few of them. Or—and this thought haunts
me—it's possible that I may someday meet them in the afterlife, as Odysseus
in Hades met the accusatory shades of warriors he once knew.

What would I say to them? It wasn't my fault? I'm sorry?

Beyond PTSD

After my tour in Iraq, I was awarded a Combat Action Badge for having
received enemy fire. Years later, explosions still cause me minor discomfort.
The sound of fireworks, gunfire, and engines backfiring are unsettling. But
was I traumatized by enemy fire? No, at least not deeply. My most affect-
ing combat experiences are sewn together with a thread other than life-
threatening violence. This thread is moral dissonance. It's clear to me today
that my leaders and I sometimes failed to make wise choices. To our shame,
we should've done better.

"Post-traumatic stress disorder" (PTSD), a psychological injury born
out of adrenalin and fear for one's own life or the lives of others, isn't the
best description of my injury. Yes, I feel fear, but it is a fear akin to learned
helplessness: I fear that I will fail to prevent terrible harm from happening
to those I need to protect. Hypervigilance, flashbacks, and anxiety are rarely
a problem for me, but other symptoms associated with PTSD are, like "re-
current, involuntary, and intrusive memories," "sleep disturbance," "distress

---

1. As I've discussed elsewhere, in a September 14, 2003 memo, Lieutenant General
Ricardo Sanchez, the commander of US military forces in Iraq at the time, approved
"Stress Positions," "Use of Military Working Dogs," and other so-called "enhanced"
techniques. "Forced nudity" was one of the techniques that Donald Rumsfeld, the US
Secretary of Defense, had approved for use at Guantanamo Bay, Cuba (Gitmo) and had
been approved for use by subordinate military leaders at other facilities. LTG Sanchez
did not approve its use at Iraq. Later investigators determined two main sources for this
technique's regular usage at Abu Ghraib: (1) interrogators who had worked elsewhere
such as Gitmo informally brought the technique with them, and (2) Abu Ghraib interrogators misinterpreted a statement in doctrine calling for them to control "the food,
clothing, and shelter" given prisoners (Pryer, *The Fight for the High Ground*, 47).

after exposure to traumatic reminders," "avoidance," "negative beliefs and expectations about oneself or the world," "anger," "guilt," and "shame."[2]

A growing number of mental health experts argue for the existence of a condition that better accounts for both my symptoms and these symptom's sources. This condition is called "Moral Injury." Moral Injury, one seminal article argues, can occur after "perpetrating, failing to prevent, bearing witness to, or learning about acts that transgress deeply held moral beliefs and expectations."[3] PTSD, these experts contend, is physical in origin, while Moral Injury is a "dimensional" problem.[4] Physically stressful experiences can cause PTSD, but nonthreatening events may still serve as a source of moral trauma.[5] Some physically traumatic events serve as a source of both PTSD and Moral Injury, and some symptoms associated with PTSD are more properly aligned with Moral Injury.[6] PTSD sufferers can be helped via physiological remedies like drugs, acupuncture, and Rapid Eye Movement treatment, but the morally injured require therapies designed to help them find forgiveness and regain faith in themselves and others.

Although these experts continue to collect data to refine the causes and effects of Moral Injury, exactly what Moral Injury *is* remains elusive. What some experts call a "dimensional" problem, psychoanalysts view as poor "ego" functioning, philosophers consider an "identity" issue, and theologians and clergy (as well as those of a literary bend) see as the damaging of the "soul." No other inner malady depends so much for its diagnosis on how its prescribers view the universe.

It is tempting to argue that these profound ontological differences only exist because of the relative newness with which science has begun examining the condition. Yes, the phrase "Moral Injury" is at least 300 years old, and its symptoms have been described by poets for thousands of years.[7] Science, however, did not begin studying Moral Injury in earnest until this century, and it is not yet listed as a syndrome in the *Diagnostic and Statistical*

2. National Center for PTSD, "PTSD and DSM-V."

3. Litz et al., "Moral Injury and Moral Repair," 700.

4. Maguen and Litz, "Moral Injury in Veterans of War," 1. In the mental health field, "dimensional" problems are those that involve quantitative rather than qualitative differences from a normal personality. They consist of heightened, maladaptive levels of normal reactions.

5. Ibid.

6. Ibid.

7. Bishop Joseph Butler referred to injuries that were moral in sermons in the 1720s in England. See Bishop Butler's Sermon VIII, "Upon Resentment and Forgiveness of Injuries" in *Fifteen Sermons*. Jonathan Shay and Robert Emmet Meagher are among those who have pointed to evidence of warriors' moral injuries in ancient heroic verse. See Shay's *Achilles in Vietnam* and *Odysseus in America,* and Meagher's *Herakles Gone Mad.*

Manual of Mental Disorders (DSM), the standard reference of the mental health profession. As with any new idea, it is tempting to say, any unscientific approach will lose value as relevant scientific knowledge about it grows.

We must avoid this temptation, though. Worldview uniquely impacts both the causes and cures of Moral Injury. One empirical study, for instance, showed that the "primary motivation of veterans' continuing pursuit of treatment may be their search for a meaning and purpose to their traumatic experiences" and raised the possibility that "spirituality should be more central to the treatment of PTSD [Moral Injury]."[8] There will probably always be depths of understanding to be gained about Moral Injury from a wide range of professional expertise, to include the humanities and, especially, religion.

The Warrior's Eternal, Internal Battle

The psychiatrist Jonathan Shay popularized the term "Moral Injury" in his 1994 book, *Achilles in Vietnam*. At the heart of Homer's *The Iliad*, Shay says, is a story of sullied honor.[9] Agamemnon, the Greek army's commander, "betrays 'what's right' by wrongfully seizing Achilles' prize of honor," the captured princess Briseis. Achilles is outraged, withdraws from the Greek army and the war, and "cares about no one but a small group of combat-proven comrades." When the Trojan hero Hector kills Patroclus, Achilles "is tortured by guilt and the conviction that he should have died rather than his friend," and "he goes berserk and commits atrocities against the living and the dead."

"Moral injury," Shay writes, "is an essential part of any combat trauma that leads to lifelong psychological injury. Veterans can usually recover from horror, fear, and grief once they return to civilian life, so long as 'what's right' has not also been violated."[10]

The classics are rife with examples of warriors suffering grievously from moral distress. Another Greek warrior, Ajax, is driven temporarily insane by a perceived insult and slays a herd of sacred animals. When he recovers, he "is doubly humiliated, religiously defiled, and kills himself by

---

8. Fontana and Rosenheck, "Trauma," 583. Although this study doesn't explicitly mention Moral Injury, for those familiar with the term, it's clear from the context what is meant.

9. Shay, *Achilles in Vietnam*, xx–xi. My paragraph here summarizes Shay's passage.

10. Ibid., 20.

falling on his own sword."[11] Many of Shakespeare's warriors—driven mad by guilt—kill themselves, including Othello, Cassius, and Brutus.

Literature's most famous sufferer of Moral Injury may be Kurtz in Joseph Conrad's *Heart of Darkness*. Initially an idealistic imperialist, Kurtz witnesses and perpetrates atrocities in the name of civilization. His soul becomes as afflicted as his body. Succumbing to jungle fever, he cries in a whisper at Life: "The horror! The horror!"[12]

In our era, many mental health studies have concluded that warriors' moral distress can cause enduring problems. Studies of Vietnam veterans linked guilt to PTSD, depression, violent actions, and such self-handicapping behaviors as drinking and suicide.[13] A study involving Gulf War veterans found that guilt over killing others is a significant predictor of PTSD symptoms and problem alcohol use.[14]

Such studies are supported by a staggering amount of anecdotal evidence. Some stories have gained media attention. There is, for instance, the poignant story of Noah Pierce. A young infantry soldier during the US invasion of Iraq, Pierce became distressed by several incidents, to include his accidentally crushing an Iraqi child under his Bradley. After Pierce committed suicide in 2007, his mother said that "he couldn't forgive himself for some of the things he did" and that the kind of wound he had "kills you from the inside out."[15]

There is also the sad tale of Alyssa Peterson, a young intelligence analyst who committed suicide in 2003 after being reprimanded for refusing to participate in "enhanced" interrogations.[16] Peterson's case points to an important truth about Moral Injury: unlike PTSD and Traumatic Brain In-

---

11. Ibid., 76–77. The story of Ajax as told by Shay comes from a play by Sophocles.

12. Conrad, *Heart of Darkness*, 64.

13. A 1991 study (Hendin and Haas, "Suicide and Guilt") concludes that combat guilt is the most significant predictor of both suicide attempts and preoccupation with suicide. A 1997 study (Kubany et al., "Development and Validation") finds that about three-fourths of a sample of Vietnam veterans with PTSD had multiple sources of severe war-related guilt. A 1998 study (Beckham et al., "Atrocities Exposure in Vietnam Combat Veterans") links exposure to atrocities with PTSD symptom severity. A 2009 study (Maguen et al., "The Impact of Killing in War") reports that killing is associated with post-traumatic stress disorder symptoms, dissociation, functional impairment, and violent behaviors. A 2010 study (Marx et al., "Combat-Related Guilt") associates guilt from abusive combat violence, such as harming prisoners and civilians, to PTSD and MDD (Major Depressive Disorder) among combat-deployed veterans. For a summary of other related studies, see Maguen and Litz, "Moral Injury in Veterans of War."

14. Maguen et al., "The Impact of Killing," 25.

15. Alpert and Kent, *Wartorn 1861–2010*.

16. Mitchell, "Remembering the US Soldier."

jury (TBI), it is sometimes preventable. If Peterson had not felt tormented by what she had been ordered to do, she might not have felt so distressed as to take her own life.

Moral Injury is real. It causes mental torture to the troops whose care is entrusted to America's leaders. It leads service members to drown their sorrows in alcohol or drugs, to be involuntarily separated from the service due to disciplinary action, or to voluntarily leave the service—or the world, by killing themselves. It greatly burdens the US military and civilian healthcare systems. It hurts the ability of veterans to positively contribute to society. It distresses and may lead to the physical harm of those who interact with afflicted soldiers.

Of these adverse effects, the role that Moral Injury may play in the US military's high suicide rate has attracted the most attention.

A Long Winter's Night

My deepest Moral Injury occurred when I was deployed, but it has nothing to do with combat. On Winter's Solstice 2011, while I was in Afghanistan, my oldest daughter Desiree took her own life.

Eight years earlier in Iraq, a few weeks before I saw the photos from Abu Ghraib, I had learned that someone Desi's mother and I trusted had impregnated our daughter. Desi said that this boy, who was nearly seven years her senior, had molested her for years. Since it wasn't her first suicide attempt, Desi's suicide wasn't entirely unexpected. This fact didn't make the news any less devastating.

When her mother and I had been together, Desi had been very much "Daddy's Little Girl." She had been happy-go-lucky, vivacious, and intelligent. She had been artistic, often drawing, painting, and writing poetry. For me, winter's longest night that year didn't last just one day. It lasted twenty-four hours a day, seven days a week. It followed me to America for Desi's funeral and then back to Afghanistan. It filled me, enveloped me, dulled my senses. When I wasn't numb, I felt crazed with grief.

As much as her death, it was the injustice of the way her life ended that devastated me. Desi didn't deserve what had happened to her. For a few weeks, when walking around Kabul and Bagram with a pistol and ammo, I considered ending my own life: I hadn't done enough to protect or help my little girl. And, like the titular protagonist of *Sophie's Choice*, the thought that I had too much chosen my other children (those by my new wife) over my oldest child left me guilt-stricken. But it was not just self-censure that seized me. There was a desperate need to see Desi again and comfort her. I wanted to hold her, to talk to her, to tell her how much I loved her, and to apologize for my not having done enough to keep her safe and feeling loved.

I frequently fantasized about meeting Desi in the afterlife. Sometimes, I travelled to a shadowy place in Hell to see her, and I would, like Orpheus, lead her to the bright surface above. Other times, I was trapped there with her, but found solace in seeing her, talking to her, sharing her torments with her, holding her hand, comforting her as I had failed to do adequately when she lived. Usually, I dreamed that I met Desi in a place of beauty and light, somewhere we could share smiles and laughter and hugs. Despite my Christian upbringing and this religion's severe injunction against suicide, Heaven, I knew, was where she deserved to be.

Two thoughts kept a bullet from my brain. The first thought was that, even if there were an afterlife, I couldn't be sure I would see Desi again. Perhaps we are, as the Buddhists and Hindus say, reborn when we die, or, perhaps, Desi went to a better place than I will go. A second thought proved even more important: I couldn't do that to my other loved ones, especially my new wife and two much younger children. They needed me, and they would be traumatized if I were to kill myself.

If for just a few seconds those two thoughts had abandoned me, I wouldn't have returned home. As it was, they were barely enough.

Before Desi died, she had been diagnosed with PTSD and dissociative (depersonalization/derealization) disorder. When I called her on the phone, she often sounded depressed. Near the end, she wrote two despairing emails in which she told me that she wasn't the same little girl she used to be and that she never would be this girl again. "Damaged" is how she described herself. I believe today that Moral Injury was what lay at the root of her symptoms. At bottom, she believed in neither herself nor trusted the world anymore.

Her poetry increasingly focused on death and escaping to a better place:

Just another Cloudy Day

A home of white walls and no pictures to frame,
The cries of the darkness calling my name,
A plant almost dead—dead today,
I clean up the blood, and it all falls away.
I leave in a dream to mangoes and peaches,
To sunshine and smiles and castles on beaches,
I walk on the sand, dreaming it all:
The tide pulls me in, and I drown in white walls.

The fifth and sixth lines of this poem I had inscribed on her tombstone at a cemetery in Lawrence, Kansas.

Losing Desi amplified the ill-effects of the inner conflict I've felt regarding morally-charged combat experiences. It's as if Abu Ghraib and other experiences were the taps of Poe's raven, weakening the window pane of my soul, and Desi's death was what finally shattered the glass. It's no wonder PTSD symptoms can take years to surface, for when this occurs, it may not be PTSD but Moral Injury that is the underlying problem, and it can take years for your sheltering identity to finally break under the accumulating weight of moral dissonance.

Carl Jung's idea of the self's "shadow"—a collection of seemingly random, destructive thoughts, impulses, and feelings that your cultivated ego serves to buffer you against—aptly describes what happens next. Without a strong protective identity, you can flounder in a hurricane of wild thoughts and feelings. You can be at a loss on how to cope with impulses that once you could easily manage. When confronted with such impulses, you fear your inability to do what's right—or, as in my case, enough of what's right. This fear can unnerve you, causing you to seek refuge by withdrawing from others—or to decisively protect yourself from self-censure and others from harm by killing yourself.

Endless War and Military Suicide

Since the 9/11 terrorist strikes, America has been in a state of seemingly endless war. It is impossible to accurately gauge how many cases of Moral Injury current wars have created, since the data that might tell us has not been collected. The potential for Moral Injury is certainly great. The 2006 and 2007 mental health surveys of US Marines and soldiers in Iraq and Afghanistan, for example, found that 10 percent believed they had mistreated noncombatants or damaged property "when it was not necessary."[17] How distressed today are these veterans by their own harsh self-judgment? We don't know, and this group may be only the tip of the iceberg, for mistreating noncombatants or unnecessarily damaging property are only two potential sources of Moral Injury in war.

Prior to these long wars, the active-duty suicide rate of each US military service remained steady at about 10 suicides per 100,000 service members.[18] From 2003 to 2012, this rate doubled for the Navy and Air Force, making it comparable to the rate among US civilians of like age and

17. Office of the Surgeon, "MHAT IV," 4; Office of the Surgeon, "MHAT V," 32.
18. Ritchie, "Army's Former Top Psych Doc."

gender.[19] This rate, though, more than doubled among Marines and tripled among soldiers.[20]

Some American military leaders—perhaps having overly convinced themselves of the inherent rightness of America's causes and the correctness with which US service members always fight—protest that Moral Injury cannot possibly apply to US service members in large numbers. They miss the point. It's not what they think about service members' actions that matters; it's what these service members themselves think that does. And it's clear that many American troops believe they did or witnessed something wrong downrange, sometimes even terribly wrong.

Moral injury cannot be the sole reason for the US military's growing suicide rate. Other factors include PTSD, TBI, and the increased operational tempo of all units, including recruiting, training, and test units. This high tempo can damage service members' relationships with the very people they depend upon for emotional support.

Still, it is troubling that our military rarely even acknowledges that moral distress can lead to suicide, as literature, empirical studies, and a massive amount of anecdotal evidence overwhelmingly indicate that it does. This is exactly what is happening, though. Millions of dollars are spent collecting suicide-related data, but this data largely involves misbehaviors that are rightly considered effects of psychological injury, not root causes. We know, for instance, some suicide victims drank too much before they died, but we rarely know what drove them to drink.

Until deeper causes are understood, it is impossible to meaningfully reduce or prevent such negative outcomes from psychological injury as suicide.

Preventing and Healing Moral Injury

Shay writes, "Simply, ethics and justice are preventive psychiatry."[21] Like Shay, I've become convinced that Ethics doesn't consist of purely academic, impractical restraints. Rather, Ethics is firmly rooted in human biology. Our capacity for seeing others as beings like ourselves who should be treated

---

19. Kube and Miklaszewski, "Military Suicide Rate," and US House of Representatives, "House Report 112–110." According to this news report, the Navy had 60 active-duty service member suicides in 2012, the Air Force 59. This house report gives a 2012 active forces end strength of 328,700 for the Navy and 332,200 for the Air Force.

20. Pryer, "Moral Injury and the American Service Member," 35. The sources and math for this conclusion are laid out here.

21. Shay, *Odysseus in America*, 242.

as we want to be treated is an important reason our species dominates the planet. Indeed, without innate moral forces, homo sapiens would not be able to live in groups, let alone in large, powerful nations.

Adopting a morally focused approach to war promises to reduce inner dissonance by encouraging service members to align our actions with whom we say we are. To the US military's credit as an institution, it works hard to ensure service members' actions are legal. However, just because an action (such as an "enhanced" interrogation technique) can be construed as legal doesn't mean the action is right, and during my training and combat deployments, I never once witnessed a staff debate the perceived justice of a legal act. Unless a lawyer says a tactic is clearly illegal, the average US military leader believes they have the moral "green light" to do it.

Will our nation and military learn to see morally justifiable actions as the crucible on which the psychological cost of war to America's warriors is lessened and redeemed? The answer to this question is unclear. Human beings are creatures of passion, and war displays this passion at its noblest and cruelest extremes. It stands to reason and experience that our nation will not always choose only just wars to wage, and that service members will not always perform just combat actions. However, human beings are also governed by moral forces. The great strategic and personal cost of underestimating these forces—especially within the connected world of the information age—is surely too great to go long unnoticed and inadequately addressed. Our nation will not always be able to wage just wars justly, but we must try much harder to do so.

However, even in the best of circumstances—a just war fought justly—some service members will be afflicted with Moral Injury. Consider my case. Yes, if one presidential administration had not condoned prisoner abuse, much of what has bothered me about my own combat experiences would've been diminished. My greatest source of distress, however, stems from what happened to my daughter, an unprosecuted crime that no military law or policy could've prevented.

Just as Moral Injury lay at the heart of my daughter's troubles, I believe that Moral Injury is the condition that I've been afflicted with, not Major Depressive Disorder (MDD) or PTSD. I can, for example, point to the precise time when I began to suffer from bouts of depression—a four-month period in Iraq when I learned what someone had done to my daughter, I saw the Abu Ghraib photos, my friend Captain Rob Scheetz was killed from a roadside bomb while on a futile mission for an infantry battalion commander, and a group of my soldiers were severely injured by bombs on a different futile mission for this same commander. Someday, I hope, Moral

Injury's connection with syndromes other than PTSD (such as MDD) will be better explored.

For me, healing has finally begun via religious concepts like "penance," "forgiveness" (especially self-forgiveness), and "redemption"—this, despite my lack of religious faith as an adult. After years of penance and struggling to find forgiveness, I finally feel in my heart that I can forgive others and myself for our inadequate choices—and do so in such a way that I give due honor to those whom we failed. I have finally, as Eric Newhouse writes, given myself permission to move on and "enjoy life again."[22]

My finding answers in the religious concepts of my youth rather than in modern medicine doesn't dissuade me from my belief that, at least on the shallow level of observable phenomena, Moral Injury can and must be medicalized. Until Moral Injury becomes an accepted mental health category or syndrome, therapists will continue to incorrectly mischaracterize cases of Moral Injury. Such misdiagnoses mean that patients receive prescribed, often drug-based treatments that are at best, unhelpful, and at worst, destructive. Just as disastrously, until Moral Injury is blessed off by psychiatrists as an authentic condition, political and military leaders will look for ways to ignore this condition—and societies will continue to find ways to forget about this most essential consequence of the wars they choose.

Building a New Self

Every few weeks for the past year, I've had versions of the same dream.

In this dream, I live with my wife, son, and daughter in a large, white Victorian house with a columned portico. It sits on a busy intersection in my small, Midwestern hometown. The building is not in great shape—the paint is visibly peeling everywhere—but it conveys a sense of decaying grandeur.

My family and I live in this house much as we live in our current home. Our furniture, paintings, and knickknacks are familiar, and we do the same things at the same times that we do now. Although my wife and kids are mostly happy, for me, a sense of dread underlies everything. I fear some outside danger imperils them, and I won't be strong enough, or alert enough, to protect them.

In a closet, I discover a door that opens into hallways and rooms. This secret space in our home's interior is much larger than the rooms we live in. Most of these hidden rooms are clean, well-organized, and well-appointed with somewhat antique furniture. There is a kitchen with stainless steel

22. See Eric Newhouse's essay in this volume (selection 24), "Recovering from Moral Injury."

appliances, a well-outfitted island, and everything my wife might wish or need to cook. There are bedrooms, guest rooms, toy rooms, exercise rooms, a study, libraries, and an incongruously timbered porch with a view of a green, sunlit forest. The timbered porch is an idealized version of the patio of the Wisconsin house we once lived in, while the burbling sound of a trout stream outside comes from a cabin we stayed at in Vermont. Objects of fond memory populate the rooms, such as kids' bikes, fishing rods, basketballs, and baseball gloves and bats.

Deeper inside this hidden realm, though, are dusty, cobwebbed rooms, either empty or holding scant pieces of threadbare furniture. It is in these rooms, mostly, that invisible ghosts reside. Some I recognize without seeing. There is my friend Rob Scheetz. There are my injured soldiers in Iraq. There are my unit's prisoners at Abu Ghraib. And there is, of course, my daughter Desiree. Her presence is everywhere.

At the decrepit center of this hidden dimension is a room that frightens me—a dark basement with a raging furnace. Near the furnace, I see golden treasure, enough to make my family fantastically rich. But there is also real danger. There are demons here. When I enter this room and walk toward the treasure, strong invisible hands grab me, pull me, try to rip me apart.

I escape their violent clutches and flee. Rejoined with my family, I internally debate whether to show them these secret rooms. The first few times I had this dream, I chose to keep the existence of these rooms a secret. In more recent versions, I show my wife the nicest rooms. She loves the way they look, but she is uneasy: she senses even in the well-furnished rooms the presence of ghosts. I try to convince her that we should move in anyway and that we can block off access to the cobwebbed rooms and, especially, the furnace room.

Upon waking, it has been obvious to me what this house is: it is my "self" or "soul." There are the visible places that anyone can see. Then there are the secret rooms that belong most truly to me alone. Many of these secret rooms are well-appointed with happy wishes and fond memories. Other rooms consist of derelict dreams and ghosts that I can't let go of. And the fiery furnace is where my dark, Jungian shadow burns and thrives—and the demons reside with their terrifying, incredibly strong, rending grips.

After my most recent dreaming, when I awoke, I had an epiphany: I can't expect my family or me to live in a house with hidden chambers, benign ghosts, and dangerous demons. I must build a new home, something sunlit with open spaces and fresh air, a place where we needn't be afraid.

With that realization came a sense of relief. I now knew that I must move on. I also felt ready, finally, to do so.

What will my new house look like? I no more know that than how long my physical body will live. One thing I do know is that this essay is how I'm choosing to honor and preserve the memory of Desiree and my other ghosts, living and dead. It's the marker that I'm leaving outside the old decaying house in which I've spent most of my life.

I will never forget my ghosts. (Desiree, your Daddy will always love you!) But they are now memories, more fondly remembered than not. And my demons? They will never again seize and tear me with their iron grips.

"I" won't allow that.

15

TONY CAMERINO

What Buddhism Can Teach Us about Moral Injury

Strive for your own liberation with diligence.

—THE LAST WORDS OF THE BUDDHA

After returning from Iraq in the late summer of 2006, I found myself sitting in a boutique cafe in a historic neighborhood steps away from our nation's Capitol. I settled into a comfy leather chair amongst a crowd of commuting Washingtonians and picked up a menu and a newspaper. The war was still heavy on my mind, and I was anxious to find my place again in society.

The front page of the newspaper made no mention of Iraq, and patrons nearby carried on conversations about mundane topics such as the latest mobile phone upgrades, restaurant reviews, and sports. I looked at the menu and felt like Jeremy Renner in *The Hurt Locker*, when he stands dumfounded staring at an entire aisle of cereal boxes after having returned from a tour in Iraq as a bomb disposal technician. Decisions with no life or death consequences are confounding after the intense experience of war. I felt adrift at sea, like flotsam lost to the will of the changing tides.

Suddenly I was overcome with the feeling that I had to get away. From people. From society. From everything. I needed a soul-searching trip. A walkabout. For those that have read W. Somerset Maugham's *The Razor's Edge*, the story of a World War I veteran on a mission to discover the reason behind evil in the world after having witnessed senseless death during combat, my journey would sound familiar. For the next several months I traversed backwater villages in Southeast Asia, surfing on solitary beaches and meditating in remote Buddhist temples, attempting to find answers. There's a string of beaches along Phuket's western coast where I spent most of my time alone with my thoughts sitting on my surfboard in the green waters of the Andaman Sea. I couldn't have picked a more appropriate place. Those beaches are also haunted by ghosts. It's where two years earlier a tsunami stole thousands of lives.

The villages along this stretch of Thailand's coast are tranquil communities populated by fishermen and rubber farmers, where water buffalo still roam, and where coconuts grow wild. Some of these villages have given way to the tourist trade, and a retired ex-pat crowd of Europeans and Singaporeans have built modern bungalows inside their jungles, but others are only starting to open up. It's a place where vendors in hats of woven palm fronds still carry boiled eggs and peanuts on two ends of shoulder-carried poles. Where street vendors still prepare fresh papaya salad (*som tam*) in a stone bowl with a mortar. And a place where monsoon rains push forth strong currents that create waves inside small coves carved out of the mountains for three months out of every year. It was a perfect place for deep reflection and renewal.

In Iraq I was an interrogator. I gathered intelligence from Al Qaeda terrorists and Iraqi insurgents and passed that information on to the special operations soldiers in my task force. They took the information and developed targets that they then assaulted. Those assaults yielded new detainees who I would then interrogate to get new targets. Wash, rinse, repeat. The pace was relentless, the pressure was immense, and my actions carried enormous consequences.

I once helped elicit the location of an Al Qaeda safe house from a detainee, but when our soldiers assaulted it they were ambushed and two of them were killed. I wondered if I could have done more to save them. On numerous occasions I obtained targets that were assaulted and resulted in the deaths of enemy combatants. I sometimes watched these men die in real time on a computer screen that relayed a live overhead feed of the assault. I also solicited confessions that ensured many of my detainees would face capital punishment. It was well known that for those that participated in suicide bombing operations (recruiting, training, or arming) the punishment was hanging. At the very least, we knew they'd be tortured in the new Ministry of Interior's prisons. We'd seen evidence of the new Iraqi government's methods when we received a detainee from them with iron burns covering his entire back.

But the deaths I had the hardest time reconciling myself with were those of the civilians caught in the crossfire, aka "collateral damage." And one death in particular stood out. The death of a young girl who died in a house with her father, Abu Musab Al Zarqawi, the former leader of Al Qaeda in Iraq and the man known as the father of ISIS. She was crushed when we dropped bombs on the house to kill Zarqawi, not knowing she or her mother (who also died in the bombing) were inside.

I know the arguments about collateral damage well because I've been over them a hundred times in my head. Killing Zarqawi helped bring an end to the war and saved thousands of lives. There are statistics to prove the latter if one looks hard enough. Philosophers and academics can expand on the ethics of warfare, but the argument deduces to a simple one for a soldier: Does the saving of innocent lives justify the taking of other ones? Yes or no, for most soldiers the argument ends there. But before I was an interrogator, I was a military criminal investigator, and because of my prior profession, I'd developed a deep compassion for the innocent victims of violence.

I had worked several difficult cases as an investigator involving child victims. As a result, I couldn't allow the death of Zarqawi's daughter to be brushed aside as a statistical, moral, or ethical calculation. I had seen a picture of her after the bombing, and the image of that little girl lying with her head crushed in the rubble was irrevocably burned into my memory. That memory begged many questions: Who decides which civilians are worth sacrificing? What responsibility did I bear in having participated in locating that house? What did she do to deserve to die? What kind of world do we live in that an innocent child can die in such a horrible, undeserved manner? These were questions that attacked my emotional core. After months of contemplation, meditation, and, to put it bluntly, mental agony, I found no answers. And then I decided to visit a temple in northeast Thailand, also known as Isaan, the rice-farming heartland.

Much as Iraq does, the brick and sandstone temple in Phimai just outside the city of Nakhon Ratchasima sits at the intersection of religions and cultures—between the eleventh-century Hindu Khmers of Cambodia and the Buddhists of the ancient kingdom of Siam. The temple is a leftover of the great Angkor Empire, the better known ruins in Siem Reap. Its style reflects both its original Hindu devotees and current Buddhist caretakers, a mix of orange and white stone. An open corridor lined with large square pillars leads into an inner courtyard sanctuary. On the day I visited, there were less than a handful of worshipers. I found a serene alcove inside a minor temple where I sat alone in silence before a stone Buddha garnished with orange marigolds. It was here that Buddhism finally provided a partial answer to my questions.

Although I don't proscribe to organized religion, there are elements from the philosophy of Buddhism that I find intriguing, such as the cyclical nature of the universe. I've read of some of the religion's themes being used in therapy for treating PTSD. For example, psychological therapy often involves mental exercises that put one's experiences into perspective by examining a specific event within the context of a larger picture. Perhaps my own obsession with the death of that young girl was obscuring other events, such as the time I helped elicit information that stopped two suicide bombers who were minutes away from carrying out their mission. Or the time the interrogations team I led elicited information from a detainee that resulted in the confiscation of over 500 suicide-bomb vests. Applying a Buddhist lens to my war experience allowed me to look at all the events in Iraq as part of a larger timeline. A cycle. A history that repeats itself over and over again.

Soldiers have been fighting in Mesopotamia since the beginning of civilization. I was just another soldier fighting for my country in a foreign land. I was just doing my duty like so many soldiers before me, a tiny atom in a vast universe cycling through centuries of war and peace. Why should I be so upset over one small tragedy? Buddhism teaches us that the universe balances the Ying and the Yang in all realms. Hot and cold. Wet and dry. Violence and compassion. Taking lives and saving lives. Perhaps I was merely a cog in an unstoppable wheel. And maybe the purity of my intentions could never have resulted in anything other than a less than perfect outcome, simply because I'm human and flawed.

I found some comfort in this explanation, but it's not a cure. In fact, one of the hardest lessons that I had to learn in my post-combat life is that there is no cure for what experts are now calling "Moral Injury," a condition I believe I have been afflicted with.[1] You learn to manage it like an alcoholic learns to manage his or her disease. Photographs, films, books, and the real world still trigger painful memories, sometimes causing me to spiral down

---

1. Although described for thousands of years by poets and scholars, Moral Injury has only recently become the subject of empirical study. It is thus no surprise that there is no agreement between scientists, let alone between scientists, theologians, and other scholars, as to what exactly Moral Injury is. The most popular definition at present defines Moral Injury by its causes: Moral Injury is "perpetrating, failing to prevent, or bearing witness to acts that transgress deeply held moral beliefs and expectations" (Litz et al., "Moral Injury and Moral Repair," 695).

a dark hole of self-contempt in which I question my existence, or *all* of our existences.

In the first season of the HBO drama *True Detective*, Matthew McConaughey plays a detached detective named Rust Cole who has lost a daughter. He posits: "Maybe the honorable thing for our species to do is deny our programming, stop reproducing, walk hand-in-hand into extinction, one last midnight—brothers and sisters opting out of a raw deal."

I remember agreeing with that line when I first heard it, until I remembered what I came to realize in that quiet countryside temple in Thailand. To do so would also be to erase all of mankind's positive advances. Things like modern medicine, humanitarian aid, the Geneva Conventions, space travel, and simple, everyday acts of compassion. Both good and evil exist in a constant cycle in the universe. Perhaps the best we can do, as Maugham so eloquently put it at the end of his novel, is to be like a pebble thrown into a pond causing a small ripple in the water that affects a positive change on others.

It's the closest I've come to an answer.

16

TIMOTHY KUDO

On War and Redemption

When I returned from Afghanistan this past spring, a civilian friend asked, "Is it good to be back?" It was the first time someone had asked, and I answered honestly. But I won't do that again. We weren't ready for that conversation. Instead, when people ask, I make it easy for everyone by responding, "It's fine." That's a lie, though. It's not fine.

It's not the sights, sounds, adrenaline, and carnage of war that linger. It's the morality. We did evil things, maybe necessary evil, but evil nonetheless. It's not the Taliban we killed that bother me. They knew as well as I did what can happen when you pick up a gun and try to kill your enemies. But the enemy isn't the only one who dies in war.

I joined the military when we were already long into this conflict. Aside from driving to San Francisco to protest the Iraq invasion, I quickly embraced the inevitability of these wars and relinquished their execution to the government. That was a terrible mistake. In 2006, as both wars raged and the Iraq conflict seemed doomed, I felt obligated to do something. I had no idea what I was committing to when I raised my right hand and took the oath. I realize that my decision was extreme, but it's one I felt bound to. Only now do I understand the responsibility that military members bear, not only for the lives of others, but also for the consequences of their actions.

It was on a patrol early in our deployment in September of 2010 when the Afghan farmer dropped his shovel and ran for his life. Our squad of ten dove for the ground. We looked toward the staccato crack of machine gun fire but saw nothing. A few anxious Marines fired anyway. We moved. Someone observed Taliban in a small building just ahead. We fired. It was the first time in an hour anyone had a clue where the enemy was. I saw two Afghans calmly building a wall despite the war erupting around them. Nothing made sense.

We cleared the building. As one team assaulted it, a Marine holding security spotted two armed men driving toward us on a motorcycle. Gunfire rang out from multiple directions. "Are you sure they have guns?" I asked. Nobody knew. We shot a smoke grenade as warning in case they were civilians. They paused, then resumed course. We yelled and waved for them to stop. They persisted. I thought: they might kill my Marines, but if we kill them, we might be wrong. Cracks and flashes erupted from the motorcycle. The only hard fact about the rules of engagement is that you have the right to defend yourself. You decide for yourself to pull the trigger. The Marines returned fire for ten long seconds. The motorcycle sparked where the rounds slapped the metal and drove into the bodies. The bike stopped. The men fell.

The building was empty. No bodies, no blood, no bullet casings. The fog of war lifted. I had been certain what was happening and I was wrong. The combination of confusion, chaos and adrenaline can't be explained unless you've also experienced it. We ran to the motorcycle. One Marine made a quiet plea, "Please let them have weapons. Something. Anything." They were dead. Their weapons were sticks and bindles. The muzzle flash was light glaring off the motorcycle's chrome. One man was no older than sixteen. It was late afternoon then, and, in the Muslim tradition, their family quickly arrived to bury them in the last hour of sunlight.

Even now, I don't know what led them to drive toward a group of Marines firing machine guns, despite warnings, yells, and waving. I know that our decision was right and, given the outcome, that it was also wrong. We trained to kill for years, and given the opportunity, part of us jumped at the chance to finally be Marines. Despite the school construction and shuras,[1] that's what it meant to make a difference in uniform; it meant killing our enemies. But these men weren't enemies. They were just trying to get to a home so close that their family was able to watch them die. After the shooting, the families encircled us in hysterics as they collected the bodies. It was the first and only time I saw an Afghan adult woman's face. The wailing continued in the distance as we continued on our mission.

The insanity of war means that incidents like this are accepted. By the standards of those who fight wars we actually did the right thing. The catastrophe is that these incidents occur on an industrial scale. Throughout

1. Editors' note: A shura is a council, specifically a consultative council.

Afghanistan, there are accidental civilian killings; it is war's nature. When we choose war, we are unleashing a force, much like a natural disaster, that can literally destroy everything and from which there's no going back. As ten years of conflict have shown us, nobody knows how wars end.

With six months left on our deployment I had no choice but to move on. I told myself we did what we were trained to do and that it just ended badly. I stuck with that reasoning despite feeling terrible, and soon, my emotions caught up to my logic. People say they can remember a traumatic incident like it was yesterday. I can't. Since my return, Afghanistan has melted into a feeling more than a memory. But I do remember the widows and orphans and wailing families and the faces of two men on a motorcycle. They understood they were being killed as it happened, yet they couldn't accept their fate. They died painfully. Their teeth clenched and grimacing. Their eyes open. Those eyes gave them a final pleading expression. Why did you kill us?

Back in the United States, I look at people and think: "You have no idea what right and wrong are." Much that I once held as matters of conscience is now just custom or culture. The challenging thing about ethics is you have to figure them out for yourself. What the war taught me is that first, you should always strive to do the right thing even though you can't control the outcome. Second, wrong decisions have tragic, irreversible consequences. There is no return. Nothing changes it and no lesson justifies it.

I never pulled the trigger on my rifle, but I ordered other men to kill. For an officer, there is little difference. In all militaries, individuals don't kill, groups do. We are each assigned small tasks in the orchestrated murder of our enemies, and oftentimes, this decentralization creates its own momentum. We became excellent at engineering the enemy's death. After one incident, my commanding officer told me that he was ultimately responsible. Yes, by the letter of the law, that is true. But everything we did over there we did together. We're all responsible. I feel it, and I know that the other officers and NCOs share the same moments of pride and shame. I also know that this sense of responsibility is shared all the way to the presidents I've served under, who saw the consequences of our actions at the VA hospitals at Bethesda, Walter Reed, and Dover Air Force Base.

Only the dead have seen the end of war. This is a maxim that has been used to illuminate humanity's propensity for war, but it is also an accurate reflection of many veterans' experiences. The war not only came back with us, it was here the entire time, experienced by orphans and widows. It was experienced by the widows from my unit who were unable to cook a single meal for their kids since their husband's death. During a memorial a few weeks after our return, families of the dead collapsed grief-stricken in front of their loved ones' pictures as a thousand Marines solemnly bore witness. When an officer went to the house to check on one family, the littlest one told him matter-of-factly, "My daddy is dead."

Civilians can't shoulder the responsibility for killing, but the social contract demands they care for those who do. And this is the great disconnect in our society right now, because that feeling of responsibility is still locked behind the fences of our military bases. My friends killed and died over there for America. And while many of my peers view that as sentimental, jingoistic, naïve, or (behind closed doors) stupid, those men believed so deeply in something they were willing to give everything for it. When we wage war to defend the American way of life, there's an obligation to uphold that ideal. Can we honestly say we've done that?

The Marines' Hymn states that we are "first to fight for right and freedom and to keep our honor clean." Since the shooting, I've thought about what that means and decided that it was beyond good and evil. It was an accident. War doesn't distinguish between innocence or guilt, skill or incompetence, intelligence or idiocy. But we do. We see injustice in the deaths and can't accept their inevitability. But it was fated when we decided to go to war. In that sense, we're all responsible.

After coming home, our commanders told us we earned glory for our unit, but I know it's more complicated than that. War has little to do with glory and everything to do with hard work and survival. It's about keeping your goodness amid the evil. But no matter what happens, you never work hard enough, people die, and evil touches everyone. Our lives will go on, but the war will never go away. That's why it's not simply good to be back. I thought my war was over, but it followed me. It followed all of us. We returned only to find that it was waiting here the entire time and will always be with us.

17

MONISHA RIOS

The Glue Is Still Drying

One must retreat neither from the outrage of violence nor deny it,
or, which amounts to the same thing, assume it lightly.[1]

—SIMONE DE BEAUVOIR

"Blood, Blood Makes the Grass Grow, Drill Sergeant!"[2]

I will never forget the first time I understood the pain of war from a soldier's face. It was late summer, 1997, at Fort Jackson in Columbia, South
Carolina, and I was a Private 2nd Class in the United States Army. We were
in the woods for an intense day of hand-to-hand combat and weapons training. I had to sit some of it out due to shin splints, stress fractures, and falling arches. Others with injuries sat out as well. We were a busted-looking
bunch, sitting around on logs with crutches strewn about, sleeping with our
eyes open. I was enjoying a nice shady spot under a weeping willow when
I heard the familiar voice of my favorite sergeant, Drill Sergeant Williams

---

1. Beauvoir, *The Ethics of Ambiguity*, 59.
2. This is a common phrase yelled in combat-related training.

(name changed for privacy). He had been sent to babysit while the rest of our company marched further into the woods to learn how to lob grenades.

Williams was one of the good guys. He didn't abuse his power. Rather, he intervened when other drill sergeants crossed the line, and he didn't hide his distaste for their actions. This was the drill sergeant who looked out for me and other female soldiers, making sure we didn't get harassed when he was around.

He must have felt like talking that day, because he took a seat and gathered us around to shoot the breeze. We covered a range of topics, from soldiering to our favorite foods. We asked him about his service, places he had been, things he had seen, and which Meals Ready to Eat (MREs) to avoid. He would get a far-off look sometimes as he told his stories. Every now and then he would get animated, acting out the details. It was fun until, in the naïveté of my youth, I asked the wrong question—the "did you kill anyone" question. His demeanor changed in an instant. His eyes and face darkened. His body sank into a slouch. He blinked, swallowed, looked me in the eye, and spoke: "Don't ever ask that question again, Rios."

Thick, heavy silence filled the air between us as we realized what that question and his response to it meant. It still gets to me. I blinked, swallowed, looked him in the eye, and spoke: "I'm sorry, Drill Sergeant."

He smiled as much as he could and said it was okay, I didn't know any better. Then he gave us an education. He had been in Vietnam, had fired his weapon at people who were firing their weapons at him, and hated every second of it—hated himself for doing it. He thought we were too innocent to be enlisted, that we shouldn't be where we were any more than he should have been where he was, saying things like "don't be so eager" and "hold on to yourself." He taught us what doing war taught him. He continued looking out for me through the rest of basic training. It was a sad moment when we said goodbye on graduation day.

I did not realize at the time that my own military service, though brief and far from combat, would leave me with my own deep Moral Injury. I would never be the same again.

What Sexualized Violence and Oppression Can Feel Like in the Military

Sexualized violence and oppression are not new phenomena within military cultures.[3] Throughout history, they have been synonymous with military

---

3. Although the terms "sexualized violence" and "sexual violence" are often used interchangeably, they do not always carry the same meaning or value in society.

activity, including psychological warfare. It continues in times of peace while we prepare for the possibility of war.

At Fort Jackson, I and all other women in my company received immediate "training" on how to avoid "getting raped." This erroneous training came in response to the changes Brigadier General Patricia Foote, vice chair of the Army Senior Review Panel on Sexual Harassment, called for in 1996.[4] We were instructed to "defeminize" ourselves—to not cross our legs, tilt our heads, bat our eyelashes, smile too big, make eye contact with males, laugh too much, and so on. Our number one rule was to keep our legs closed and not "whore ourselves out." And we better not dare to fail at anything, because it would make all women who serve look bad

Yet, despite my best efforts to follow these rules and "man up" so as not to "pussify" the Army, I was still chosen for sexualized public humiliation. As punishment for answering a male soldier's question about a laundry slip, I was made to lay on my back in front of my company with my legs up and open while a drill sergeant yelled sexist epithets, accused me and my mother of prostitution, told males to avoid me because I would get them in trouble, and insults related to my body parts. While I lay there, he made the male soldier do pushups. That drill sergeant psychologically oppressed me in this way throughout basic training, to the extent that he would yell disgusting things during chow about what I "really wanted" in my mouth, each time I opened it to ingest food. All of this occurred among a large number of witnesses, including other drill sergeants and NCOs (Non-Commissioned Officers).

My next duty station was Advanced Individual Training (AIT) at Keesler Air Force Base in Biloxi, Mississippi. There, a drill sergeant came into the female latrine while I was in the shower and stood on the other side of the thin curtain. He was later removed from the detachment after harassing a Muslim soldier. In a classroom full of airmen, one that I thought was my friend attacked me from behind and bit me in the back of my right arm when I told him his sexually explicit and violent conversation about rape fantasies and how women really like it rough was making me uncomfortable. He bit me so hard that each tooth mark left a dark purplish blue bruise. They were darker than the rest of the bruises. He threatened to hurt me if "I got him in trouble." Not a single person in that room did anything.

"Sexualized violence," like "racialized violence" or "feminized poverty," illustrates an intentional targeting based on a certain characteristic or vulnerability and is less connotatively charged than the latter.

4. Brigadier General Patricia Foote was one of many who paved the way for women in the US Army.

A fellow soldier who saw the injury days later made me alert the drill sergeants. I had to point out the soldier who bit me. He and a friend of his came to follow through on his threat to hurt me if I told anyone what he did, while I was surrounded by my platoon and a safe drill sergeant. Thankfully, this drill sergeant did not let him hurt me, and the soldier was removed from the base. The air force doctor who was treating my back injury and gas-chamber-induced asthma attended to the bite. He offered me a choice that would change the course of my army career. He told me things would not get any easier for me, that I would most likely be assaulted in worse ways, and that rape was in my future. On the one hand, he could recommend that I be placed on permanent profile, which would limit my MOS (Military Occupational Specialty) options but not the likelihood of being raped. Or, on the other hand, he could recommend a separation based on my injuries, and significantly reduce my chances of being raped while serving my country.

While I deliberated over the next few weeks, I thought of how terrified I felt, how depressed I'd become, how I had washed out of classes, and how unsafe and unprotected I really was in this environment. I thought of what might happen to me if I stayed in. I hadn't even been in for a year, and I did not want to return home as a failure for not handling army life as a woman. I still struggle with this sense of failure (internalized oppression) to this day. The overwhelming terror outweighed my desire for an army career. I accepted defeat and the doctor's offer to help me get out. My next stop was out-processing at Redstone Arsenal in Alabama, where I endured more sexualized psychological and physical oppression at the hands of a female captain and "her boys." It was like basic training all over again, this time with a woman leading the hatred brigade.

I stood up for myself and was retaliated against. This time the retaliation consisted of a false accusation that I was the one sexually harassing *them*. The female platoon sergeant who made the report took me aside to tell me she knew it was a lie, but that it's what I got for standing up for myself against "the boys club" and that she could not help me because it would ruin her career (another example of internalized oppression). It didn't matter that I was restricted to my room and not allowed out even to eat. Her fear was too big. Relief finally came when the captain went on leave and the first sergeant returned. I invoked the open door policy and eventually spoke with the battalion's command sergeant major. I was given jobs to do outside of the barracks until the day I was discharged.

Looking back now at what was done to me in the Army, along with all that I have learned as a clinical social worker, I have come to believe that sex and killing are inextricably linked through the concepts of power and control. As a soldier, I came to intimately understand the sense of power and control that comes with having the knowledge and ability to kill and dominate others. It is not far-fetched that sex could evoke similar, if not the same, feelings and intensity that killing presents. J. Glenn Gray described the link between sex and killing as such that

> the sexual partner is not actually destroyed in the encounter, merely overthrown. And the psychological after effects of sexual lust are different from those battle lusts. These differences, however, do not alter the fact that the passions have a common source and affect their victims in the same way while they are in their grip.[5]

In *On Killing: The Psychological Cost of Learning to Kill in War and Society*, Lieutenant Colonel Dave Grossman further connected the dots, writing: "The concept of sex as a process of domination and defeat is closely related to the lust for rape and the trauma associated with the rape victim."[6] These statements lead one to ask if the connection between sex and killing illustrates a relationship between being trained to kill and perpetrating military-related sexual violence and oppression. Does the indoctrinated lust for battle and blood become so great within that it must be discharged? Does it translate into an urge to "dominate" and "defeat" another human being sexually as the next best thing, so to speak? Further research is needed in this area, to determine the extent to which soldiers' training to kill may inadvertently increase their potential to commit acts of sexualized violence (or "Military Sexual Trauma"), and if it does, what our nation can do to limit this potential.

I have one more story to tell from my days of military service. A few months before my discharge, I once again found myself face-to-face with someone else's Moral Injury. This memory haunts me still.

Bosnia and Iraq in the Corner of a Laundry Room

I met Sergeant Sims (name changed for privacy) at Redstone Arsenal. Sims was safe, like Williams, but younger and more visibly conflicted. He was part of a small group of us that stuck together in the barracks. Any time we went into town, Sims would ask someone to make sure he didn't drink too much or go home with a random person. Being underage and uninterested in drinking, I was usually the mother hen of choice when it came to

5. Gray, *The Warriors*, 68.
6. Grossman, *On Killing*, 137.

keeping the crew out of trouble. Besides being annoying, the job was a huge responsibility. Sometimes it was risky. I had to be on guard to make sure there weren't fights, or if there were, to make sure none of us got arrested or worse. And then, of course, there were the obvious hazards faced by women surrounded by drunken men. Sims seemed to be on a mission to get his rear-end handed to him as often as possible. One night he was especially self-destructive, picking a fight with a large group of men in a Taco Bell parking lot.

We had three carloads of people with us in the drive-through line. Sergeant Sims was almost passed out in the backseat while I was in the front, tired after a long stint of babysitting drunken soldiers. To this day, I cannot stand large groups of overly drunk people. Bad things tend to happen. Such as when Sims popped his head out of the window and started yelling at a group of men standing around by their van. He was simply asking for a smoke but, being as drunk as he was, it was not communicated politely. The group postured, Sims postured, and before I knew what was happening, he was out of the car moving toward them, hell-bent on getting a cigarette and ready to scrap for one. I jumped out to wrangle him back into the car just in time to see the rest of our crew exit their vehicles with the obvious intention of defending our own. The driver of the car in front of us opened his trunk, retrieved his side arm, and moved swiftly toward the gaggle of aggression.

Just as I was about to step between Sims and one of the men from the van, someone grabbed me, and I felt his shoulder in my gut as he picked me up. It was the soldier driving our car. He tossed me into the passenger seat, jumped into the driver's seat, and sped away. I yelled at him to go back, that we couldn't leave Green and the guys. He apologized, said he was from Detroit and did not want us to die in a stupid fight like so many of his friends had back home. Thankfully, he turned around anyway. By the time we got back, the fight had broken up. Still hungry, we ordered our tacos like it was a normal day and drove back to the barracks with Sims in the back seat babbling on about not getting a cigarette after all that. I was livid.

He kept his antics going as we walked through the parking lot, up the stairs, through the common areas, and into our shared hallway. (These were integrated barracks with men and women on the same floor, whereas the barracks in Basic and Advanced Military Training were segregated to keep the male and female sleeping quarters separate.) All I could think about was the gun. The scene where the driver got it out of the trunk and walked toward the fight with it played on a loop in front of my eyes like I was watching it on a movie screen. I kept feeling the sensation of being picked up. My ribs hurt from where my friend's shoulder dug into them. That is when it all hit me. It was like I was on fire and it was spreading from the inside out. Sims approached me at that moment—the wrong moment—to complain that I had not yet given him his room key. That was it. My back was to him, and I snapped. Before I realized what I was doing, my hand was around his throat, fingernails digging into the soft parts around his esophagus. I leaned in and pinned him against the wall, glared into his eyes and said something to him through gritted teeth. I don't remember the words. I was furious with him for putting us in danger like that, over a cigarette of all things. Meanwhile, there he was, too drunk to care. I let him loose and threw his key at him. I was done.

Well, I thought I was done. A couple days later, I walked into the laundry room to find him huddled up in a corner, hugging his knees to his chest, crying and gently rocking side to side. He didn't look up when I turned on the lights, only asked if I would mind turning them off. I flipped the switch and sat next to him on the floor. I don't know how long we sat there before he started talking. When he did, it was in broken sentences between sobs and whimpers. He pieced together details of things he had seen and done, such as firing on innocent people and witnessing numerous rapes of civilians. He explained that he wasn't infantry, that he was just a helicopter mechanic who had to go where the helicopter went and follow the orders he was given, even as he questioned their legality.

I didn't believe him at first, because we were in peacetime and I thought maybe he was trying to get me to feel sorry for him after what had happened. The look in his eyes, the way he trembled as he described what too many of our fellow soldiers did to innocent people while on humanitarian missions, told me I was wrong. He explained that peacetime is a joke—we were in places we were not supposed to be, doing things we were not supposed to be doing to people we were not supposed to be doing them to—and that he wasn't supposed to be telling anyone about any of it. I held him as he described what he called his unforgiveable sins. There were times I gagged and almost threw up in the trash can. I listened as he repeated over and over again that he deserved to die a horrible death and rot in hell because he followed orders to hurt innocent people. He begged for punishment and mercy, asking me to go get him enough beer or liquor to drown him. The Taco Bell incident and all the drinking made complete sense at that point.

He was gone without a word a few days later. Someone said he went AWOL. Someone else said he went to his next duty station. I never saw or heard from him again. Sometimes I go through pictures from back then. I cannot help but wonder, when I see his, if he is still alive or if he finally drank himself to death. I may never know. Wherever he is, I hope he has peace.

Moral Injury and the Myth of Resilience

It seems that in Western society there is an overwhelming rush and push to "fix" what is perceived as broken. This is acutely felt in my field, where the price tags on clinical interventions have grown leaps and bounds while the time allotted to heal continues to shrink. The focus instead is on resilience—what is commonly understood as the ability to quickly recover or "bounce back" from adverse experiences. I have theories as to why people who have endured and/or perpetuated the unimaginable horrors of humankind at its worst are not given the gentleness and patience needed to fully move through what has happened in their lives and find what heals them. I don't think our society can handle the reality of what it does, and our suffering can be like a mirror—rather than look into it, society goes to great lengths to avoid what it might see. Hence, we are forced into unrealistic expectations for recovery.

Resilience, in the way it is promoted in this context, is a naïve, contrived myth. It is not always possible or advisable for us to "bounce back" at a prescribed rate or regain our original forms. We have encountered elements of humanity that need everyone's attention to address. That requires a willingness to look at the dark parts of ourselves that we hide and pretend don't exist. It also requires our society to listen, learn, and act on the wisdom in this pain that can lead us to become a less aggressive, more peaceful force in the world.

It has taken a lot of self-work over many years to arrive at a place where I can begin to meaningfully process all that took place while I was in the US Army. I was only seventeen years old then, just a kid with a head full of ideas and a heart full of hope for a better future. I loved my country, and I was eager to show this love through military service. I thought Americans were always the good guys. Now, nearing thirty-seven, I experience bittersweet relief every time I discover a piece of that kid hidden among the shards of my shattered life. Rebuilding is a tedious and delicate task. Each piece must be carefully and patiently considered in order to understand where it was before and where it fits now. Once placed, the pieces must be given as much time as needed to set. I have learned the hard way not to move too fast while the glue is still drying, or else the pieces slip out of place again.

Some fragments are harder to deal with than others, such as those reflecting the Moral Injury incurred along the way. On one level, this injury come from what psychologist Jonathan Shay calls "a betrayal of what's right . . . by someone who holds legitimate authority . . . in a high stakes situation," such as with institutional betrayal or interpersonal violence.[7] In another respect, it arises from an action one may take that "violates their own ideals, ethics, or attachments."[8] I still cope with feeling betrayed by my leaders, my fellow soldiers, and—yes—by my own country for permitting institutionalized sexual violence both within and outside the ranks. There is the added betrayal that comes with minimization, victim blaming, and shaming. People who survive sexual violence are often subjected to harsh, cruel judgment in society. We endure the burden of proof while we are accused of bringing it on ourselves. Even in this day and age, we are seen as responsible for the perpetrators' choices to violate our minds, bodies, and spirits. This specific oppression is often internalized, resulting in such potentially dangerous outcomes as Moral Injury.

Healing from Moral Injury is a complex, painstaking process that is unique for each person. It is not something that should be intellectualized, pathologized, and reduced by the mental health field to the point of dehumanizing the people affected by it. Shay explained how people often experience Moral Injury: "It's titanic pain that these men live with. They don't feel that they can get that across, in part because they feel they deserve it, and in part because they don't feel people will understand it."[9] In an interview with PBS, Shay gave greater importance to veterans' peers than health professionals in the healing process:

> Peers are the key to recovery—I can't emphasis that enough. Credentialed mental health professionals like me have no place in center stage. It's the veterans themselves, healing each other, that belong at center stage. . . . We are stagehands—get the lights on, sweep out the gum wrappers, count the chairs, make sure it's a safe and warm enough place.[10]

Shay essentially described the creation of a safe space within which to do this healing work.

Yet, despite the undoubtedly good intentions held by many of our colleagues, there are a vast number of veterans who do not fall within the dominant experiential category that gets the most attention. That is, since we are not Caucasian, heterosexual, male, and OIF/OEF combat veterans, it is that

7. Shay, "Moral Injury," 183.

8. Ibid.

9. Shay was interviewed and quoted by Gilbertson, "The Life and Lonely Death of Noah Pierce," then quoted in Guntzel, "Beyond PTSD."

10. Shay, "Jonathan Shay Extended Interview," WGBH's *Religion & Ethics Newsweekly*, May 28, 2010; transcribed and quoted in Guntzel, "Beyond PTSD."

much harder to find the right support to meet our needs.[11] We have to find this space for ourselves. Hence, we have online peer support groups through social media. We outliers are co-creating our own healing experiences with nature, art, and spirituality, and we are doing our best to build a community. I have found much relief in storytelling, listening, writing poetry and blogs, my emotional support dogs, walks in the woods, dance, photography, and connecting with my ancestors through shamanic journeying. I engage in advocacy and activism around these and related issues, peace especially, which helps with the despair and need for redemption that Shay aptly refers to: "Despair, this word that's so hard to get our arms around . . . It's despair that rips people apart [who] feel they've become irredeemable."[12]

The core of my redemption is rooted in an applied commitment to a non-oppressive way of living, working, and relating to other living beings. It goes beyond simply "treating" those who have been psychologically injured with standardized protocols and involves actionably shifting the paradigms that lead to military-related Moral Injury in the first place. I will soon have a PhD in psychology, with an emphasis on Transformative Social Change and Creativity, and have joined various allies in pursuit of mental health care reform in the field of psychology—a field that has historically profited from its involvement in the war-manufacturing machine. As an active member of groups like Psychologists for Social Responsibility and Veterans for Peace, a co-leader in three separate and intersecting social movements, and a macro/clinical social worker, I have found a sense of fulfillment and purpose similar to that which I felt on active duty. Although my trajectory is rooted in stubbornness, defiance, and a fight for survival, this fight is ultimately for the countless others who suffer needlessly because of our nation's character flaws.

I focus on multilevel systems change as a means of preventing military-related trauma and suicide—not only for US troops and their families, but for all the widows and orphans we have helped make, and for the cultures and environments we have helped destroy through our state-sanctioned mass violence and weapons manufacturing. Like my fellow advocates and activists, I spend a lot of time working at individual, organizational, community, state, and federal levels to address an array of issues in addition to sexualized violence in the military, such as the US Army's flawed Comprehensive Soldier Fitness Program; eliminating inequities and addressing the recurrence of sexual violence in the Veterans Administration; alleviating

11. OIF/OEF stands for Operation Iraqi Freedom/Operation Enduring Freedom.

12. Shay, interviewed and quoted by Gilbertson, "The Life and Lonely Death of Noah Pierce," then quoted in Guntzel, "Beyond PTSD."

mental health stigma and ensuring safe access to relevant care; our nation's role in torture and adherence to international human rights law; and more. It has become my life's work.

Now, as I close in preparation to mourn the loss of yet another local veteran to suicide (he chose to do it outside of his home on Memorial Day), I am reminded of a time, not that long ago, when I almost gave in. I was experiencing homelessness for the third time in my life, due to disability and domestic violence. I was working, in school, in hiding, reaching out for help from colleagues, and with very little social support. The majority of the feedback I got from colleagues and society (in the form of—once again—minimization, victim blaming, and shaming) only served to reinforce the worthlessness, hopelessness, and helplessness I already felt. "Ask for help," they would say. But when I did, I was condemned, judged, and stigmatized by my colleagues—the very people whose ethical codes mandated the opposite behaviors. There is only so much cruelty a person can take. I needed mercy, not more pain. This was just more betrayal. One night, when things were more unbearable than they had been in a long time, I thought I was going to end my life. I wrote this poem instead. It saved me.

I dedicate this poem today to my loved ones, and to every life torn to shreds by needless war:

Unbroken

I could do it, you know.
Break.
I could. I've come close
To broken.
But then I think of you.
How my breaking would break you, too.
And I pause.
I think.
I feel
You.
Broken.
Breaking me isn't worth breaking you.
I think of them.
The ones who broke me down.
The ones who still try.
Because they are broken.
I could do it, you know.

Break.
I could. I've come close
To breaking.
But then I think of them.
How my breaking would break them, too.
And I pause.
I think.
I feel
Them.
Broken.
Breaking them isn't worth being like them.
So I stay whole.
When I'd rather disappear.

18

PETE KILNER

Leadership, War, and Moral Injury

War is a breeding ground for Moral Injury. Even in a justified[1] war that is fought justly, combat soldiers are likely to intentionally kill enemy soldiers, unintentionally harm civilians, and witness levels of violence and senseless suffering that challenge their assumptions about their own moral goodness and the goodness of the world. When soldiers commit, fail to prevent, or witness acts in war that violate their own moral codes, they become susceptible to suffering long-term shame, anger, alienation, loss of religious belief, and other effects known as Moral Injury.[2]

Moral Injury among combat veterans is widespread, but it doesn't have to be. Soldiers are more vulnerable to Moral Injury when they haven't been adequately prepared to make sense of the moral tragedy of war. In this essay, I argue that there are actions that military leaders can take before, during, and after their units' combat tours that would reduce the incidence and magnitude of Moral Injury among their soldiers.[3] Ethical, proactive leaders

---

1. Biggar, *In Defence of War*, 3: "No war waged by human beings will ever be simply just; but that is not to say that no war can be justified."

2. Maguen and Litz, "Moral Injury in the Context of War"; McCarthy, *An Exploration of Moral Injury*, 92–113; Wood, *What Have We Done*, 8.

3. My argument has developed over years of research and relationships. As an active-duty US Army officer, I had the privilege to interview almost 400 US Army leaders in Iraq and Afghanistan from 2003 to 2011 over the course of five research deployments. Almost all were junior officers—lieutenants and captains—serving in battalions that were conducting combat operations. Almost all interviews were private, in-depth

can train, inspire, and lead in ways that protect their soldiers' consciences as much as is possible in war.

The military profession's battle against Moral Injury should begin prior to war, when leaders have the opportunity to teach their soldiers how to think morally about war. Military leaders' foremost responsibility is to train their soldiers to perform, succeed, and survive in combat. The ways they train them, though, are focused entirely on developing soldiers' tactical war-fighting skills. The After-Action Reviews (AARs) that are integrated into training are designed to assess and develop *tactical* decision-making (e.g., why a machine gun was emplaced at a certain location) but overlook *moral* decision-making (e.g., why it was morally right to kill an enemy combatant but not a nearby civilian).

This prevailing approach to training is amoral, ignoring the moral challenges of war. To their credit, US military leaders train their soldiers to adhere to the laws of armed conflict, which explains the commendable moral record of US soldiers in recent wars. Yet those same leaders typically explain soldiers' lethal permissions and limitations in terms of legal and professional norms, not as moral principles.[4] Those explanations are sufficient for soldiers during training, when they are firing their weapons at inanimate training aids. When soldiers deploy to war, however, they engage and kill real human beings. The amoral explanations (e.g., "it's legal"; "it's what soldiers do") that suffice in training are inadequate for such morally significant actions, leaving soldiers susceptible to Moral Injury.[5]

To protect against Moral Injury, then, leaders should integrate moral reasoning into their tactical training. In AARs, soldiers should be required to articulate their moral decision-making—using moral language—as they already do for their tactical decision-making using doctrinal and legal

---

conversations lasting one to two hours. Although the interviews focused on the leaders' experiences of combat leadership and lessons learned, issues related to Moral Injury often emerged. Typically, I embedded with a company or battalion for days or weeks at a time, so I had the opportunity to observe and talk informally with many more soldiers of all ranks. Additionally, from 2000 to 2016 I served as a facilitator in two popular online forums of Army junior officers as well as taught on the faculty at West Point. My participation in these military communities led to countless conversations with combat veterans about the intersections of leadership, lethality, and morality. I make this argument more extensively in "Military Leaders' Role in Mitigating Moral Injury," available at http://soldier-ethicist.blogspot.com/2016/11/the-military-leaders-role-in-mitigating.html.

4. This point is also made well in Toner's *Morals Under the Gun* and Imiola and Cazier's, "On the Road to Articulating Our Professional Ethic."

5. Meagher, *Killing from the Inside Out*, 142.

language.[6] For example, after a training exercise in which a soldier engaged a civilian on the battlefield who had picked up a weapon and pointed it toward friendly forces, the leader should ask the soldier not only, "Why did you engage him?" ("Because he threatened the assault element"), and "Why was that legally permissible?" ("Because the rules of engagement state that any non-uniformed person who is armed and making a threatening action is positively identified as enemy"), but also, "Why was it morally right to kill him?" ("He is fighting for an armed organization that threatens the lives and fundamental rights of the people we are protecting").

A major difference between *training for* combat and *engaging in* combat is the moral component of actual combat. Soldiers perform the same actions on the training range and on the battlefield, but their actions on the battlefield have immeasurably greater moral consequences. Soldiers who are unprepared to deal with those consequences are more liable to suffer Moral Injury. Leaders, therefore, should incorporate moral reasoning into tactical training, preparing their soldiers to succeed tactically, morally, and psychologically.

Military leaders' opportunities to prevent or mitigate Moral Injury among their troops continue while they are deployed to war. After all, the wounds that later manifest as combat-related Moral Injury typically result from acts of violence that the soldiers themselves judge to be morally wrong. Leaders on a combat deployment, then, can prevent some Moral Injury among their soldiers by setting and enforcing standards that make unjust acts less likely to occur and by continuously helping their soldiers make sense of their wartime experiences.

A simple way that leaders can reduce the likelihood of Moral Injury is by demanding that their soldiers treat enemy combatants and local-national civilians with respect. A war zone constitutes the ultimate "us versus them" environment, so it's easy for soldiers to lack empathy for anyone who is not "on their side." This attitude can easily lead to a dehumanization of "the other" which is often reflected in and exacerbated by soldiers' language. Soldiers' usage of pejoratives to describe their enemy has, unfortunately, a long history—for example, "heinies," "nips," "krauts," "chinks," "gooks," "ragheads," "sammies," and "hadjis."[7] Some leaders support the use of dehumanizing terms for enemy combatants, believing that it helps their soldiers overcome their natural aversion to killing and thus enhances their mission effectiveness and safety.

6. Army captain Jonathan Silk suggested this technique in "Making Sense of Killing."

7. Holmes, *Acts of War*, 364–65; Fromm, Pryer, and Cutright, "The Myths We Soldiers Tell Ourselves," 60.

A more professional, morally healthy approach is for leaders to do all they can to help their soldiers acknowledge the humanity of their enemy counterparts. After all, dehumanization holds up for only so long; at some point, soldiers realize that the targets they engage are indeed human beings.[8] When that realization happens, soldiers feel deceived, and if they have already left military service, they may lack ready access to resources that can help them deal with this realization. Rather than perpetuate an unsustainable wartime lie, then, leaders should speak honestly about the humanity of the enemy.

With support from intelligence staffs, leaders should discuss with their soldiers the demographics and motivations of the enemy, who in many cases share much in common with their own soldiers.[9] In truth, the enemy are fathers, sons, and brothers[10]; they too are young, idealistic, and willing to die for a cause they believe in. Leaders should explain that we believe the enemy fighters' cause to be objectively unjust, which is why they must be defeated, but the fighters themselves often do not realize the error of their ways. Leaders should describe enemy combatants as fellow human beings who—whether misguided, malicious, or both—are fighting for an evil cause that must be defeated. Having acknowledged to their own soldiers the humanity of the enemy soldiers, leaders would find it easier to develop soldiers who kill efficiently yet respectfully,[11] who defend the innocent without hating the aggressors, and who ultimately appreciate both the necessity of fighting and the tragedy of war.[12] By not denying the humanity of their enemy, soldiers would retain their own full humanity.[13]

I never heard the term "hadji" used during the 2003 invasion; soldiers referred to "the enemy" and "civilians." The pejorative "hadji" came into use later that summer to refer to insurgents, and then expanded (in many units)

8. Ibid., 368. This point was also made by Doug Pryer in a personal email to the author.

9. In two companies I visited in Iraq in 2007, the commanders had all their soldiers watch and discuss the movie *Red Dawn*, which features young Americans fighting an insurgency against an invading army, to gain an appreciation for the motivations of their enemy.

10. Yes, I realize and appreciate that not all combatants are male. But the great majority of them are, and the emotional impact of this sentence is greater when it refers to fathers and brothers rather than the more accurate but generalized "parents and siblings."

11. Respecting enemy soldiers has a long tradition in the warrior ethos. See, for example, Pressfield, *The Warrior Ethos*, 18.

12. Gray, *The Warriors*, 158–59; also, Sites, *The Things They Cannot Say*, 71.

13. Ibid., 158–60; also, George, "Moral Injury and the Problem of Facing Religious Authority."

to refer as well to unsupportive Iraqi civilians and (in some units) to all Iraqis and even all Muslims. Language shapes attitudes, and attitudes result in behaviors. Leaders who set a good example and demand that their soldiers use respectful language, such as "enemy" and "civilian," emplace a healthy obstacle that blocks the moral slippery slope of attitudes and behaviors that can lead to unjust acts that result in Moral Injury.

Requiring that soldiers use respectful language is a good first step, but much more is required of leaders to influence moral conduct in war. An inherent responsibility of leaders is to establish, embody, and enforce high standards in all areas of professional conduct. A huge challenge, though, is that the conditions that characterize soldiers' experiences in war—fatigue, frustration, fear, grief, and anger (to name only a few)—impose a steady downward pressure on standards. For example, soldiers frustrated by civilians who don't provide information about insurgents may feel justified in smashing or stealing items during a search of their home. Soldiers afraid for their lives may be tempted to shoot first, confirm identification later. Soldiers grief-stricken at the death of a buddy may feel entitled to acquire and abuse alcohol or drugs, or even to rough-up a detainee or two. Behaviors such as these are wrong in themselves, and likely to result in Moral Injury. They are also indicators of leaders who are failing in their duty to serve as moral compasses. I've never seen or studied a unit that maintained moral standards on relatively minor issues (e.g., respectful language, no substance abuse) suffer a major moral breakdown (e.g., beatings, murder). Rather, the typical pattern is for a unit to become "morally worn down" over time by the extraordinary pressures of war, its leaders unintentionally and unreflectively accepting lower and lower standards of behavior until a final step down the slippery slope lands them all in the abyss.

A US Army infantry company commander in Iraq understood the importance of enforcing standards of moral conduct, telling me:

> I keep my soldiers on a tight leash when it comes to the rules of engagement, and they hate me for it. When they're frustrated and angry, especially after we've taken casualties, they want to unleash hell on somebody, anybody, to get some payback. At times like those, any Iraqi who appears at all sketchy looks like an enemy. I don't allow them to engage targets that are at all questionable. This is my third deployment, and I've seen what happens to the guys who kill recklessly. When we go home, they drink too much, beat their wives, get divorced, and kill themselves. I won't let that happen again. My soldiers are angry with me now—thinking I put too many restrictions on them—but

once this deployment is over, they'll be thanking me for the rest of their lives.[14]

Leaders have a duty to maintain high moral standards in their units throughout the course of their wartime deployments, regardless of their own feelings or competing priorities. They should routinely accompany their soldiers on missions, engage with them personally between missions, and conduct inspections to reinforce standards and to identify any aberrant behaviors in their ranks before they take root and spread.[15] Perhaps most importantly, leaders should anticipate and intervene in morally high-risk situations, taking actions to identify and mitigate the risk of soldier misconduct. For example, in the emotional days after a unit has suffered casualties, leaders should ensure that moral standards are reiterated in all mission briefs and should increase their personal supervision of higher-risk situations such as detainee operations.

Leaders are sense-makers.[16] After their soldiers return from war, leaders have the duty and the opportunity to help their soldiers integrate their morally traumatic wartime experiences into meaningful personal narratives of honorable service. Leaders should personally thank their soldiers for performing their duties—for protecting their teammates and contributing to the mission—and then express their own responsibility for putting their soldiers in those situations. Soldiers do not start or conclude wars; nor do they plan patrols. Leaders in their chain of command—from top to bottom—are the ones who make the decisions that bring about soldiers' morally tragic situations. Therefore, a member of that chain of command who personally knows what the soldiers experienced should take responsibility for the requirement that they engaged in violent acts against fellow human beings. The dual nametapes on military uniforms convey a deep moral truth—that soldiers act as individuals (last name) on behalf of the collective (US Army, e.g.). Soldiers in war should be commended often by their leaders for their service, yet also be reminded that they acted as one small element of a national collective body that bears the ultimate responsibility for each mission, each deployment, and the war itself.

Additionally, it is important that combat veterans have the opportunity to talk through their experiences with others who can understand them. After a deployment, leaders should dedicate time on their unit's calendar for

---

14. This statement came from an interview I conducted with an Army captain in Baghdad in May 2007. A very similar point is made in Zabriskie, *The Kill Switch*, Chapter 2.

15. Company Commanders, "Leading our Soldiers to Fight with Honor," 58–62.

16. Drath and Palus, *Making Common Sense*.

their redeployed soldiers to talk deeply with each other about their experiences. Soldiers benefit greatly from reflecting on and talking about their deployment experiences, especially with others who shared those experiences. They also benefit from hearing other soldiers' perspectives on their common experience.

In one army unit,[17] soldiers gathered monthly after returning from war to discuss their experiences. During each session, they focused on only one of the following questions, taking turns sharing their answers:

1. What deployment experience surprised you the most?

2. What deployment experience troubled you the most?

3. What was your best day during the deployment?

4. What was your worst day during the deployment?

5. What did you learn about yourself during the deployment?

6. What has been the most difficult part of coming back from deployment?

The monthly conversations had an enormously positive effect on the soldiers, helping them integrate their wartime experiences into their postwar selves.

Leaders should ensure that such conversations happen in their units by putting them on the training schedule, and they should emphasize their importance by personally participating in them. Just as military units routinely dedicate time and effort to repairing their vehicles and equipment, they should do the same for their hearts and souls.

Many combat veterans who suffer post-traumatic stress disorder eventually enjoy post-traumatic growth.[18] The same can be true of Moral Injury. One way that leaders can facilitate the healing processes is by fostering a unit narrative that acknowledges the moral tragedies of war yet frames their soldiers' experiences as opportunities for increased moral self-awareness and moral growth. After all, a sociopath would not—in fact, could not—experience the grief, shame, anger, moral disillusionment, and other responses that are indicative of Moral Injury.[19] The possibility of Moral Injury presupposes a morally good person—someone who holds and values deep moral commitments. Leaders should remind their soldiers of this fact, encourage them to reflect on their injurious experiences in order to gain greater self-awareness of their moral values, and challenge them to live those values

17. Peter Dissmore, email to author, October 31, 2016.

18. Calhoun and Tedeschi (eds.), *The Handbook of Posttraumatic Growth*. Read more at the *Posttraumatic Growth Research Group*, https://ptgi.uncc.edu.

19. Tick, *Warrior's Return*.

more intentionally in their everyday lives. In this way, the same deeply held moral commitments that created psychological distress can become springboards to happier, more purposeful lives.

Some years ago, an experienced combat leader[20] posed a question to me: "Do you think of your subordinates primarily as soldiers who happen to have personal lives on the side, or as people just like you who happen currently to be soldiers?" I had to admit to myself that I unconsciously held the former attitude. I thought of my soldiers as resources to be developed, trained, and led to accomplish missions. I did genuinely care about their welfare,[21] but I related to them *as soldiers, not as people* who had grown up as civilians and would (God willing) live many more decades as civilians after they'd finished their military service. I don't think that I was unique in my approach, which may explain the military profession's relative inattention to its members' moral concerns.

Military leaders have always been entrusted with the well-being of their soldiers, and that responsibility should extend to them as people, not merely as soldiers. Leaders already prepare their soldiers for war in many ways—tactically, technically, culturally, mentally, physically, legally, administratively, among others. This essay has argued that leaders should also prepare their soldiers morally. After all, even in justified wars, military leaders compel their good people to do normally bad things to accomplish the war's necessary and morally praiseworthy goals. Given that soldiers' experiences in war will likely remain with them for the rest of their lives—for better and worse—leaders should do what they can before, during, and after a deployment to empower their soldiers to act morally while at war and to make peace with their participation in war for the rest of their lives.[22]

20. Army Captain Nate Self, the Ranger platoon leader at the Battle of Takur Ghar in Afghanistan.

21. I supported their efforts to take college classes, wrote them letters of recommendation, and so on.

22. I am very grateful and indebted to many people for their feedback on drafts of this essay, in particular: Kevin Cutright, Nick Ayers, Mike Toler, Peter Dissmore, Chris Douglas, Darrell Fawley, Ken Bolin, David Oclander, David Yebra, Tony Burgess, Dan Fox, and Richard Schoonhoven.

19

PETER FROMM

Cool on Honor

Homer once observed that the presence of weapons makes those near them quick to use them. He used the phrase, "For iron by itself can draw a man to use it."[1] I would like to paraphrase that beautiful observation and say that, "Having power over others makes one quick to use it, and often in a bad way." Making use of this idea, I will explore my experiences as a young soldier and cadet and share how I have come to understand the past.

Most often, cruelty towards the initiates of an institution manifests itself in systemic "violence," such as gender and race discrimination, and in institutional bias that harmfully labels teammates or others as second class. This kind of objectification of others is sometimes referred to as "institutional cruelty." However, this sort of systemic institutional cruelty can also help to foster personal abuse stemming from power and authority in the chain of supervision. An example today is the US Army's effort to change a culture that has allowed sexual harassment to go on for decades. In spite of years of training and indoctrination, the bulk of harassment reports and assaults come from power abuses in the chain of command.

The experience that I describe here took place during the 1970s. In many ways, the Army then was a harbinger of the need to address institutional hypocrisy that continues to some degree today.

---

1. Homer, *Odyssey*, XIX.17–18. The novelist Joe Abercrombie has given perhaps the most poetic rendering of this line: "The blade itself incites to deeds of violence" (Abercrombie, *The Blade Itself*, 12).

Honor Is a Learning Process

Time, December 27, 1976, "Armed Forces: A Barrage Hits West Point's Code":

> Honor is a learning process, but it is being taught badly where it is the most esteemed: West Point. This was the harsh conclusion of two reports issued last week, offering some of the toughest criticism the 174-year-old academy has ever received. Shortly before the studies were made public, the commandant of cadets, Brigadier General Walter Ulmer Jr., was abruptly transferred. The major report was drawn up by a six-man commission appointed by Army Secretary Martin Hoffmann to investigate last spring's cheating scandal (*Time* cover, June 7 [1976]). Wrote Commission Chairman Frank Borman, the former astronaut, in a letter to Hoffmann accompanying the 91-page study: "We believe that education concerning the honor code has been inadequate and the administration of the honor code has been inconsistent and, at times, corrupt. The cadets did cheat, but were not solely at fault. Their culpability must be viewed against the unrestrained growth of the 'cool-on-honor' subculture at the academy, the gross inadequacies in the honor system, the failure of the academy to act decisively with respect to known honor problems, and other academy shortcomings." The report maintained that *too much authority has been given to the cadets to supervise themselves, while the academy's staff has reneged on its responsibility.* [Emphasis mine.]

In April of 1975, exactly a year before this cheating scandal broke at the Military Academy, I was in New Mexico as a machine gunner in Weapons Squad, 1st Platoon, Alpha Company of the 1st Battalion (Ranger), 75th Infantry. The first battalion of the Ranger Regiment was new in those days, a little over a year old from its inception but having just become fully operational in early December of 1974. We parachuted into the desert from C-141 Starlifters out of Savannah, Georgia. After weeks of sand and mountains that April, Alpha Company headed to a small base for a rest. While there, I called my dad. During our conversation, he told me I had received a letter in the mail from West Point. My squad leader, then-Staff Sergeant Victor Aviles, had labored to write letters to request my nomination in the summer and fall of 1974.

Every former cadet from West Point remembers registration day, or "R-Day." Those of us who traveled up from the City de-bused and with our bags filed into the bleachers on the east side of the football stadium. Written instructions that came in the mail said what should and could accompany new cadets to the Academy. The list included only a few items, including a pair of broken-in black leather shoes. The suggestion was a reminder to me that we would be doing a lot of "drill and ceremonies" and copious amounts of shoe shining. Other than the shoes and the clothes we came in, Plebes could bring a bag of toiletries and pretty much nothing else.

I brought a small bottle of Formica floor wax and cotton balls with me. In Airborne School at Fort Benning, I had learned the technique of preserving a spit shine with a Formica over-coating on the toe and heel of my jump boots. Before that, in the hot summer sun at Fort Polk's Infantry School, my spit shines might last only an hour without Formica, something I learned the hard way by trying to buff up my boot toe on the back of my pants leg during an inspection. The Formica would save me some time, I reasoned, in frenetic scrambles to expected inspections and meal formations during cadet basic training. The little bottle made it through my bag's inspection at the stadium.

It never occurred to me that this floor wax might constitute some form of cheating, but at West Point, it became a question mark for me. Honor indoctrination began almost immediately upon arrival, and, perhaps amazingly, the advantage the wax brought made me wonder if I was "cheating" with my shoe shines as the summer progressed. I probably incorrectly reasoned the time savings was something that only a small percentage of others knew about.

During the marching, drilling, yelling, saluting, and bag filling that first day, senior cadets repeatedly asked if I was a "Prepster" (from the US Army West Point Preparatory School) or if I was from Reserve Officers Training Corps (ROTC). Because I had been a soldier, I already knew how to do everything I was being taught. The drill instructor senior cadets, the "Firsties," who we reported to, saw my salute was fairly exact, and it was their job to teach us how to do it. "Did you learn this in ROTC?" they asked me—to which, among the four things we were limited to uttering, "No sir" was the only correct response. The seniors that day and hence forward never solicited a declaration of my history other than if I was a "Prepster" or an "ROTC" product.

This line of questioning continued for weeks, and it later bothered me some, just as the Formica wax did. For us new cadets, the West Point Honor Code possessed a growing presence, and exploiting unfair advantages was part of the formula. Sometimes, as the summer dragged on, I wondered if I could be brought up on honor charges, either for my shoe waxing or for not telling someone I was a soldier. With the deepening indoctrination, I wondered where the line lay.

The first honor case I heard of from my class was about Cadet Steven Verr, a starving plebe who, during "Beast," intimated that his parents had been in an accident to a group of Firsties bullying him over his moistened eyes.[2] The superintendent later in the academic year exonerated Verr (in March 1976) of making a false statement in light of the bullying involved in his grilling. However, some cadets unwilling to accept General Berry's decision threatened Verr's safety. Some actually implied they wanted to kill him. One cadet said he would lie to convict Verr and that he wanted to "bury my snow pick in Verr's head" but that he and others would harass Verr so "he'll wish he quit." This information comes from Verr's hometown newspaper, the May 24, 1976 *Nashua Telegraph*, and from *Time* magazine articles about West Point's growing troubles that year. Cadet William Anderson, the "Honor Captain" and Honor Committee chair, was charged with abusing his position in the inquisition-like bullying of Verr. Significantly, the Academy eventually assigned Verr a bodyguard at the request of Army Secretary Hoffman.

That summer of 1975, when Verr allegedly lied to an upperclassman, a detachment from 1–75 traveled to West Point to train the sophomore class at Camp Buckner. A Ranger from Alpha Company 1–75 named House, who I knew only casually, tracked me down to my room one Sunday and took me for an unauthorized ride out of the garrison in his pick-up truck. We drove out to his hooch near a lake to meet up with mates and have a barbeque. Soon after this, a few others from my own platoon found me in Washington Hall at lunch and asked my cadet commander to let me eat with them. My cadet table commander moved me from my table squad and took me across the great room to sit with the Rangers. After this happened, the senior cadets told me to wear my badges on my cadet uniform. My worries about the honor system effectively ended there, but I think this lunch with my fellow Rangers ultimately led to other problems for me with the senior cadets.

Where It Is Most Esteemed

Near the end of cadet basic training, the Firsties put the Plebes through a week of elementary field training around Lake Frederick. The last event in the bivouac was the bayonet lanes, an event intended to be a training crucible. Before our turn in the lanes, my platoon waited in the bivouac area roughly a couple hundred meters from the wood-line where the training occurred. A first-class cadet in our company trainer cadre called out to

2. The "Beast" or "Beast Barracks" takes place during the first seven weeks a cadet attends West Point. Upon completion, participants officially join the Corps of Cadets.

me, and, with a certain sadistic glee, he told me his roommate was going to put me into the hospital before this event was over. I remember telling one cadet that it was not a big deal—just more "spirit of the bayonet" nonsense. Later, an ambulance sped toward the lanes' training area lights flashing, siren blowing.

When I entered the bayonet lanes, I held onto my pugil stick instead of throwing it over the wall that Plebes had to climb to start the event. The senior cadets had a scheme going on to catch trainees off balance, as usual. Each Plebe cadet had to fight five Firsties in his lane, and the first opponent in line stood behind a wall, roughly six-feet high, poised to pounce as trainees descended to confront him. The idea was that, in each case, the first-class cadet would issue a command to the Plebe to execute a given stroke, and he would counter it and release the trainee to the next opponent in line. In fact, the plan was really a way for some Firsties to pound on the Plebes, turning the training into a hazing event.

In the case of the wall at the first opponent, the seniors had a tradition of telling Plebes to throw their pugil sticks over the wall, as doing so would make it easier to climb over. Plebes foolish enough to believe the advice, and do as they were told, would face the Firstie opponent with no stick to wield in defense and so be pummeled mercilessly.

When I went over the wall, I was psyched-up to fight and forgot I was supposed to wait and execute the stroke ordered to begin the bout. I bounded at my opponent with an unexpected butt-stroke to the left side of his helmet. He was surprised and much maddened, and he came back at me furiously. Trained in the infantry at this drill, I had an easy enough time blocking him. Finally, the senior told me to go on to the next opponent down the lane. As I "range-walked" away, he came hard at me from behind and tried to blindside me. I heard him moving, turned, and blocked and hit him again. He retreated very angry, and, as I was looking over my shoulder, I saw him go to talk to one of the lane controllers. I do not remember much about the next three opponents, except that they seemed to go as advertised: a command to thrust or block, which I obeyed, a stroke from the Firstie, a counter-stroke, some frantic fighting, and off I went to the next senior cadet in the lane.

The fifth and last opponent-trainer in my lane was "A-man," one of the football team's mascots, a former lineman who would dress up in a Superman-type costume at games and stride the sidelines bellowing and flexing his muscles. Later I believed my first opponent had gone to him to mark me out. When I confronted him in the bayonet lanes, he gave me the command to thrust at him. I did so, my left arm fully extended as though I had a bayonet aimed at an enemy's chest. I heard an audible snap and felt my left arm sink. At first, I could not feel anything other than the stick fall. A-man brought the unpadded aluminum part of his stick's pole straight down, aimed at striking my extended forearm at a right angle. He had commanded me into a vulnerable position, as expected, to take a free shot at me—but this went beyond merely whacking a Plebe. I took a metal-on-bone direct hit on my extended forearm.

The aluminum hit the middle of my forearm and broke the left radius and ulna in several different places, shattering them. The strike was hard enough to break the skin in a four-inch abrasion above the bone break. When I looked down to see why my left arm would not come up, I saw it hanging at what looked like a second elbow. Then came the pain. The bones were sticking jaggedly in the skin, threatening to break through. I dropped my stick and went to the ground trying to lift my arm back into normal position to prevent more damage. At the same time, I stretched out by a tree and raised my feet up against it.

A-man snarled something derisive at me but quickly backed off when he saw my arm was hurt. As I lay on the ground trying to keep my arm stable, the senior lane controller—the most senior cadet there—approached and screamed at A-man. That impressed me so much that I remember it in detail now after more than forty years. I thought A-man's cheap shot was revenge for my unintentional misbehavior with the first opponent, and that is probably correct. However, the cadet commander, now in his tirade at A-man, said something like "this is the third time today!" I remember clearly being taken aback with how angry he was at A-man for apparently repeatedly hurting the Plebes.

As a medical specialist from the 82nd Airborne splinted the break at the scene, I cursed at him in my anger. He was viscerally compassionate with me. The pain was making me lash out, he knew it, and I felt ashamed and apologized to him. Later, as other senior cadets gathered, they started to ask in a taunting way if the arm really was broken. The 82nd medic told them it was, and he led me from the woods to a controllers' hut.

At the hut, the specialist turned me over to more Firsties, and the staff there called for a driver who took me on a rough ride to the old cadet hospital maybe a half-hour away near Grant Hall in the garrison at West Point. The surgeon on duty, a Major Kimball, looked me over. After the X-ray tech finished and the doc examined the pictures, he tried to straighten the arm out and set it. The next day, he took me into surgery and attached two six-screw stainless steel plates to help the pieces of bone knit.

After the operation, I went to a bed in the orthopedic ward. There were three others with variously serious broken-arm injuries, all in line in a big room. The nurses called our beds "swan row" because we all were initially dressed in a line with our arms in traction, like a formation, the hand pointed out like a bird's beak over a broad white body of plaster. Fluid soaked through about six inches along on both sides of the cast where my incisions were. Mine was the only one with stains, as I remember.

When someone asked me later to give a statement about why my arm was broken for the medical record, I presumed it was a cheap shot gone unintentionally awry—essentially an accident to the degree that A-man could not have meant to hurt me so badly.

While in the hospital, doped-up in a haze for the first few days or so, I had many visitors. One visitor at this time was A-man. I remember him sitting at the end of my bed with an impatient hangdog look on his face. We said nothing to each other. Significantly, I heard later that the chain of command had ordered him to come and apologize. (Do we apologize for training accidents?) General Ulmer, the Commandant of Cadets, came to visit too, when I was more or less sobering up from the Demerol, about three days after the surgery.

After the first week went by, I was off the traction. Major Kimball decided to have me stay in hospital for a little more than two weeks, but he let me start attending classes so as not to get too far behind in the semester. I brought my books back to my bed. During the first of those two weeks, I had missed "reorganization," a time when plebes endure much harassment and enculturation as they entered their regular academic companies, which in effect were fraternities. My company was Alpha Company, 2nd Regiment— colloquially known as "A2," a fraternity self-conscious of its long bad-ass tradition.

Fostering a Subculture

When I first reported in to A2, I had to report back to the ward nurses each day to have the bloody fluid seeping through my cast graphed and the time checked. The time marked on the cast was, they said, to make sure I was not losing fluid too quickly. The upperclassmen in A2 told me several times they would accuse me of cheating in math if I persisted in having these numbers on my cast.

A month or so after classes started, I received two apologies from first-classmen who had been at Lake Frederick. In one case, a Firstie, who I knew of from my "Beast" company, came to my room when my two roommates were gone. He sat down, and when he saw the pink drainage stains on the sides of my cast, he began to well up. He told me that he should not have let it happen. He had known the attack was coming beforehand, and he knew it was a serious matter. I was literally speechless. Until this time, I could not bring myself to believe A-man had purposely broken my arm.

Another apology very soon came from the cadet who warned me while standing out in the field at Lake Frederick—ostensibly A-man's summertime roommate. He caught me between classes and, less emotionally, told me he did not think it would turn out as bad as it did, the way it did, and that he was sorry. I felt like I was at a loss at what to do. The implicit therapy of the confessions did far more for them than it did for me. I started to think seriously about going back to the Army, certain that legal recourse at West Point was out of the question. I also thought that even if A-man had not really intended to break my arm, there was still something seriously wrong.

Following closely on the heels of these confessions, some anonymous Plebe in our company had the temerity to write his "congressman" complaining that he was not getting enough to eat, and the blame fell to me. Word had come down to the company, but the commander had no idea who it was. Either that same day or the next, I found a green colored official note stuck to the door of my room saying I was to report to General Ulmer in the commandant's office. This coincidence was damning.

During the time between the posting of the note and the time I found it, apparently, several upperclassmen saw it. The note merely said I was to report—nothing else—and the missing reason created the wrong impression. I went to see the commandant at the appointed time in his office unsure of what was happening. However, he only wanted to see how I was doing because I had intimated to his son (also a new cadet) that I was thinking of going back into the regular Army. He encouraged me to hang in there and see out the semester. I said nothing to him about the confessions. When General Ulmer finished, I told him I would finish the semester before making any decision about going back in. When I returned to my room, an upperclassman threatened me with retaliation for squealing to my member of Congress.

Soon after, some of the senior cadets confronted me. I took their ongoing harassment as an indication of the promised retaliation and as cowardice, given the power relationship. As the tenor of my cadet experience continued to worsen, I tried to imagine what it would come to. At one point I contemplated revenge by ambushing one particular senior cadet who had spit in my face. He was a company commander in 1st Regiment, known for his bad temper.

In the late 1980s, as I studied ethics at Indiana University to teach at West Point, the line between the legitimate toughness one would expect in the military and the sadism the cadet leadership system was capable of fostering grew clearer to me. It dawned on me that the cadet system was similar in many ways to the prison system, in that it could foster a psycho-sexual power dynamic of domination that went largely unsupervised.

In my confusion as a cadet in 1975, I tried to articulate it to myself, but I was never sure exactly what to think beyond the sense of moral betrayal I felt. As a cadet, I wanted to reconcile how intentional and gratuitous cruelty fit with the institutional Honor Code and with tough, realistic training. How could the code be about only lying, cheating, stealing, and tolerating it? How could a formal inquisition be conducted for investigating and rooting out a minor lie told under duress in the case of Cadet Verr, but not for addressing known cases of assault with intent to inflict pain on the part of senior cadets? I felt like the honor system was a web for destroying whomever the senior cadets wanted to destroy.

All concerns for developing military toughness aside, tolerating bullying and felony-grade assault had to be worse than Verr's lie, had to be a monumental contradiction of any honor code worth the name, had to be moral dereliction on the part of the senior officers who should have been more engaged. In later years, as I heard of hazing incidents in military units and at colleges, including cases where women were sexually abused, I realized looking back at my cadet experience how overt abuse was tolerated there and at other places in the force during the 1970s.

Eventually, I went to see my cadet company commander to tell him I was not going to play their "Lord of the Flies" fantasy anymore. He asked me to continue at least going through the motions of respecting cadet norms until I had cleared post. In the past, he told me, former soldiers rejecting the system had notoriously thrown in a monkey wrench in some way or another. I had nearly two years left on my enlistment contract, and the Army moved me on to the 82nd Airborne Division where a scarred-up, cynical first sergeant with half his right hand missing suggested I return to New York and break somebody's legs. He surprised me by the anger he felt for what had happened to me, and I had not even related the whole of the experience.

Reneging on Responsibility

The Army of the mid-1970s was a moral mess by today's standards, and perhaps conditions at West Point were only a reflection of those days. However, its special system of company fraternities prepared the ground for especially bad behavior in the Corps of Cadets. I contrasted the betrayal I felt on the part of the officers who failed to control things among the students with the professionalism I had encountered in the 1st Ranger battalion. After finishing my enlistment at the 82nd Airborne Division, I entered ROTC at San Jose State University in 1978. Here the four Army officers and two sergeants running the program were fully engaged with the cadets, and there was zero tolerance for bullying or hazing, as was the case with the Rangers. Before accepting me into the program, they asked me what happened at West Point, and I told them just what is here in this essay. They seemed to have understood what happened to me without prejudice.

However, not many people wanted to hear negative things about the Academy, especially in the Army's West Point community. In 1981, I reencountered General Ulmer again at Fort Hood when I was a new lieutenant fresh out of ROTC. He recognized me one day when I was working in the Secretary of the General Staff's office at the First Cavalry Division's headquarters. He stopped and talked to me a few seconds, and our Assistant Division Commander, a Brigadier General who had a family history at West Point, asked me how the Corps Commander knew me. So I told him what had happened, which led to him telling me I was a liar. This reaction is pretty much what I came to expect if I told anyone this story.

Whenever anyone asked me to talk about my cadet experience after that, I'd get a sick rushing feeling and my heart would pound. I developed a fear and distrust of moral judgment, especially from officers, and though I did well enough as an Army officer, I felt like I had to hide the story as much as I could. Any recounting of my record involved me nervously omitting the five months I spent as a West Point cadet so I wouldn't have to explain my anger and frustration. It took me a long time to realize that it wasn't just anger at moral betrayal making me feel this way, but that the moral dissonance of the situation confused me and forced me to try to shut out that part of my past.

Much later, when I was teaching ethics at West Point in 1990, bringing up the Army of the 1970s and the ethical climate at the Academy that it helped spawn was a professional buzz kill. I learned quickly to keep my mouth shut, not to blaspheme the sacred institution, as some regarded those days as a golden era before women arrived, and some saw my leaving the Academy as somehow a mark of shame that I ought to carry as an Army officer.

However, what happened to me as a cadet deeply informed my experience as a teacher. At first, even though I was a senior captain when I arrived at West Point to teach, the First Class cadets were objects of loathing to me. But, more constructively, I felt like I understood the moral climate in which they navigated. As I got over my hatred for them, it helped me be a better teacher, I think, and I quickly came to see myself as a steward who had the responsibility to introduce them to philosophy. In 1996, I was invited to return to teach there again when I was a lieutenant colonel. Through ironic accident, I was made the secretary of the Superintendent's Honor Review Committee, and I served in that capacity for three years as an additional duty. In that capacity, I came to see my cadet experience there as an invaluable insight into the system.

Less optimistically, as I grew older in the Army I developed a sometimes acute sense of agoraphobia that carried the same panic sensations I would get whenever I was asked about my cadet experience at the Academy or when I imagined I was being scrutinized, socially and professionally. My own assessment is that the visceral aftereffects of moral dissonance (or what is today commonly called "Moral Injury") crippled me as an adult trying to make my way in a conflicted profession. Even now, though I intellectually understand things better, the life habits of being a soldier viscerally resonate inside me, for instance in the writing out of these memories.

The bottom line is that I think the service academies can be wonderful places for developing officers under the right conditions, but the way they have been run at times turned them more into places where healthy psychological perspectives are just accidents of the individual. They are not places that build character, as they claim, but places that reveal it and then magnify what one already is. I think the one great strength of the academies is that they generally recruit some of the best young people in the country in terms of character and intellectual drive, at least when not recruiting for sports teams. This fact alone makes the atmosphere at the academies mutually uplifting. The moral harm comes later, when subjection to an insular military life that functions as an echo chamber for four years can create people like A-man. The same dynamic happens in some units that fail to see outwardly and develop a sloppy sense of professional self-righteousness, which in turn can lead to an unarticulated, unexamined sense of entitlement in power and authority, one where it becomes pretty easy for people inclined to abuse others to indulge themselves. I call it moral sloth, but another word might be cowardice.

20

CHARLES PACELLO

Moral Trauma and Nuclear War

My Moral Trauma in the Air Force

The young man I was when I graduated from the United States Air Force Academy was value-driven and filled with a sense of honor and integrity in all that I did. I had a highly developed sense of social morality, a firmness of character built upon a solid foundation in my Catholic-Italian family roots, traditions, and family values, all of which exemplified extreme loyalty to what's right, good, and noble. Like my dad and grandfather had before me, I had a strong desire to serve my country, to preserve, honor, protect, and defend all life. This included the willingness to sacrifice my own life so that others could go on. My hope was that one day my contributions to the world would lead to an end of war for all men, women, and children, that love and peace would be forever their inheritance. That was who I was—the epitome of the All-American boy who wanted to do good, live well, and make the world a better place for my family, wife, children, and grandchildren. I served in the Air Force as an officer from May 1996 until July 2001.

After my commission, I was assigned to the GPS/NDS program office at Los Angeles Air Force Base (AFB). NDS stands for Nuclear Detonation/Detection Systems, and I served as Chief of the US Nuclear Detonation Detection System (USNDS) Mission Processing. I was responsible in part for the operational readiness and capability of the ground survivable mobile units called GNT (Ground NDS Terminal) that would only be used for Integrated Tactical Warning/Attack Assessment and Nuclear Force Management. In other words, end-to-end nuclear war. Under my leadership, these became operational for the first time. My team and I executed all mission essential testing that resulted in full operational acceptance and turnover of a new system—a first for the NDS survivable ground mission. All the agencies connected to this mission could now use the equipment for first strike capability, mobile operations command during and after all-out nuclear war had been launched, and assessment of the damage inflicted—where we hit them and where they hit us. All this is on my Officer Performance Reports; nothing I have written here is classified.

I remember sitting in one of these mobile units during our testing, looking around and contemplating what my efforts were contributing to. In that agonizing moment, I realized that I was participating in plans to destroy and annihilate humankind from the face of the earth. My mind filled with images of bombs going off. People were using this machine that I and my team had made operational to conduct nuclear war, and it made me nauseous. A great knot formed in my stomach as these and other thoughts consumed my mind. In the core of my being, I felt as if my soul had been pierced through, and I thought to myself, as I looked around in terror and rage at what I was contributing to, *This is not what I signed up for. I wanted to preserve, protect, and defend our nation. Not participate in the planning for the destruction and annihilation of mankind.*

In that pivotal moment, I lost my innocence. I received a deep moral, psychological, and spiritual wound. No longer could I see myself as a good and honorable man, not when I was being asked to do something that violated me to my very core and that I felt was not honorable. To me, it was premeditated mass murder. And there was nothing I could do to change what I believed at the time was the inevitable outcome of the work I contributed my life and talents to. It was against the natural order of things, against the right way, against everything I was raised to believe in: a just, freedom-loving, life-preserving nation and God. I was participating in an extraordinary evil, something no one wanted to talk about, acknowledge, or even face. We were all prisoners to this conspiracy to blow up the world, compelled out of duty to our command to follow these orders, and thus be complicit in the unspeakable horror that would surely come. In my mind, there was no logical reason to prepare for this outcome unless we felt, on some level, that it was inevitable.

I felt betrayed by my country, my leadership, and my God. Entering the collective darkness of humankind, all I could see was immeasurable suffering, death, and destruction on an epic scale. The Apocalypse was no longer just a story in the Bible, but an all-too-real reality. The thought that I was contributing my energy and talents to this end made me sick. We all want to contribute something to this world, to serve a higher purpose, add to the continuity of life, and make life better; but no matter how I looked at it, I couldn't see how what I was doing served any higher purpose. I grew increasingly despondent, angry, depressed, filled with rage and hopelessness for the fate of humanity. I lost my moral compass. The disintegration of my character was not far behind.

My soul revolted. What I was doing and engaged in violated everything I stood for as a human being. My mind and actions were participating in an overall objective my heart told me was wrong. Moral Injury is a crisis within the soul, the seat of our conscience, wounding our hearts and severing our bonds with others and with the Divine. When the soul suffers a wound as epic and profound as this, the disintegration of one's moral character is surely to follow.

No longer could I cloak myself in innocence—the innocence I learned and cultivated in my youth—nor hide behind the safety of serving a higher purpose for the highest benefit of all. Instead, I was betraying all that I stood for. As a consequence, I began to question the rightness of the social order and the institution I belonged to. I didn't know it then, but I know it now, that there had been a fundamental break with the trustworthiness of the world God created, a break that humankind perpetuated. The world was not innocent, good, and filled with beauty. There was evil, and I was a part of it.

Nuclear war broke out inside of me. Nightmares of a futuristic apocalyptic destruction of the human race filled my nights, destruction that I had played an instrumental part in causing. I'd wake up with night sweats, sometimes completely paralyzed in my bed. I grew increasingly, crushingly depressed by the work I was doing, and I lost all hope for myself and for humanity. Life lost all meaning and purpose. Everything seemed pointless. Nothing made any sense to me. What hope was there for a future? What was the point of getting married and having children when we were going to blow each other up anyway? Why curse them with such a horrible existence?

Other questions troubled me at the same time: Why live a moral life? What's the point? And why live honorably when there was no honor in what I was doing, no matter how someone tried to frame it? Everything seemed like a fraud to me. The masks of morality, spirituality, and goodness covered up the terrifying truth that the world God created was amoral, chaotic, violent, cruel, and built upon endless suffering and pain. Hopelessly isolated, depressed, and withdrawn from my coworkers, other officers, and family members, I chose to "numb out" these terrible feelings, thoughts, and nightmares with alcohol first, and then drugs. All I wanted was to forget and feel good.

The unraveling of my character and the trail of wreckage—personal, familial, and professional—that I left behind me devoured ten years of my life. I wanted to die. My life, as I knew it, was over. All that was precious to me had been severely crippled and disaster loomed ahead. I'd left the Air Force with an "Under Other than Honorable Conditions" discharge. My bridges were burned, my future gone, the past a distant and painful memory. All that remained was to live the rest of my life with the guilt, shame, and self-loathing for what I had done and undone. No longer believing in a loving God, having turned my back on him, I was stuck in the Underworld, confronted with demons on all sides, and pursued by the Furies. My life became a dark odyssey filled with drug and alcohol abuse, chronic depression, and suicidal contemplation. I subconsciously sought ways in which to destroy myself (using drugs, hanging out with very dangerous people), and I sabotaged all that was good in me. And all this occurred as a consequence of the moral soul wounding I'd received from being on the frontlines of nuclear warfare.

The Dark Night of My Soul

What I needed at the time was to have some way of expressing the pain I was in without being shamed, punished, or ridiculed for it. I needed spiritual guidance. There was none I was aware of at Los Angeles AFB. What I needed to understand was why we were doing work that went against everything that I had learned in church and Sunday school. Why would God allow this? What moral justification could we use to justify this work? Is there any? Where could I feel safe, safe to speak the horror I felt in my heart and dreamt about, the horror exploding deep inside of me without fear of being written up about it? Where could I find someone to help me make sense of this collective darkness—this evil—that I was a part of? Help me to give it meaning, some higher purpose that served my highest ideals, point me towards some reconciliation with God?

Nothing like this was to be found at my base—no kind of grief work, no help in healing of our moral and spiritual wounds. Perhaps the commanders didn't feel it was necessary at the base because it is not a place where many officers, enlisted, or civilian personnel experience war trauma. Nevertheless, moral guidance, clarity, and spiritual tending to my invisible wounds were all desperately needed. I knew no one to whom I might turn to help me cope with, embrace, and transform my wounds. This war within me was one I was left to fight on my own.

It was to the arts that I turned as a way to start over, to regain some sense of my own humanity, and to find the joy I once knew. This led to some success. I went to study in Oxford, England and met a beautiful woman, fell in love, and ended up recreating with her the very same traumatic bond that I had witnessed between my parents. My father, a Vietnam War veteran, had returned home from that war with the pain, rage, and trauma of having fought in combat for two tours. He, like many of us veterans, drank excessively to drown out his memories, flashbacks, nightmares, disorientation, and disconnection from the civilian world. When he drank, the beast came out, and this caused a lot of violence, abuse, and pain in his relationship with my mother. Being the first-born son, I witnessed and experienced the terror, fright, and suffering playing out between these two wounded souls.

As one traumatized so early on in my life, I've learned that these things don't disappear, don't go away. Our traumas stay with us, and we repeat them over and over again, until we transform them. And so, on an unconscious level, I played out with my girlfriend the same relationship I witnessed between my parents—the distrust, the disloyalty, the cheating, the betrayal of her love. These were the very things I perceived my mother had experienced with my father in the very beginning of their relationship. Then, the roles switched, and I was the one being abused, suffering emotional abuse from my fiancée, until she left me suddenly and unexpectedly, sending me into another crisis point in my life. The night when she left me and I opened the door to our apartment, it was as if a bomb had exploded, deep within me, where she and I had lived together. Now, from that same place, pain, agony, and rage spewed forth, together with everything I had been holding up inside of me my whole life. Now I was in a battle for my very life.

This was the darkest night of my soul, the supreme ordeal in my journey. Most of the time I couldn't sleep, and when I did sleep, I had terrible nightmares. Comatose at work, people would wave their hands in front of my face to see if anyone was home. Each time I opened the door of our apartment I would relive the trauma in all its intensity, over and over again. I would stare at the walls for hours on end and break down into uncontrollable sobs, so deep, so heavy, so painful. I was extremely vulnerable, longing to feel loved and connected to someone, but afraid of getting hurt. On the one hand I wanted protection from more hurt, and on the other I felt sheer rage, wanting to hurt and destroy, wanting revenge—on everyone.

But something inside me said, "You've got to keep going, you can do it, you can face what needs to be faced." Getting down on my hands and knees, I prayed like I never had before. I knew I was in trouble. There was a gaping hole inside me where my soul had been and where I now knew only pain, the most excruciating, unendurable pain that I had ever known, and it never left. In the deepest and darkest moments, I wanted to commit suicide.

The Road Home to Myself and Healing

Fortunately, I did not make that choice. Instead, I chose to struggle and fight my way back from the pit of despair to the morning light of a resurrected life. Faced with nearly insurmountable circumstances—without access to the VA, without medical insurance, without the means to purchase medication—I had to find some other way out of the labyrinth that was my hell. I meditated daily. In the deepest despair, and the sense that my world had ended, I found a spark of hope in *A Course in Miracles*. It offered me a lifeline, and I took it, meditating on each thought for each day as best I could, trying to find my way out, and up.

I naturally tended to my wounds, isolating myself from the rest of the world when I wasn't compelled to go to work. For five months, I endured the agony of being beset by all the memories, traumas, guilt, and shame for my past actions, until I finally met someone who wanted to help me. Sarah Larsen, a medical doctor, recognized I was in trouble. She was someone I could relate to, someone who could hear me and understand my distress. I broke down yet understood and trusted the process, finding that her listening allowed me to discover and embrace what was already in me—wisdom. I began researching all I had to do. I got organized, started learning, started developing, and sought out those who could help me learn more. I got insights through this process, and I developed my own holistic program.

Along my journey I met Dr. Edward Tick, who helped me to confront the dark shadow of nuclear war, the moral wounding it had inflicted on me, and the dire consequences that followed. I mourned the loss of my innocence. I gave meaning to my traumatic experiences and put my story into a narrative. This allowed me to situate my story within the larger context of war trauma. And when I shared my story with other veterans who also had Moral Injury, I discovered I wasn't alone, and I began to heal.

I traveled to Greece with Dr. Tick on a sacred, healing pilgrimage, and connected to the therapeutic traditions of the ancient Greeks. I learned how the guilt and shame of my past kept me a prisoner in my mind, and that it was only by my facing what in me needed to be faced that I would eventually overcome the shadows that haunted me. It was my attitude in the face of external circumstances and a deep desire to heal my invisible wounds that made the difference. I wrote the dreams for my life and knew that if I could dream it, I could achieve it; and this gave me hope.

Other efforts too facilitated my healing. As a part of the purification and cleansing of my soul, I attended Native American sweat lodges, participated in sacred rituals, and shared my story in drama form before the community who stood as my sacred witness. I gave restitution to the community through teaching other veterans the benefits of mindfulness practices, conducting workshops with other experts in the field of trauma, and I started coaching others on how they too could make peace with their past. Ultimately, forgiveness was the key that set me free—forgiving others, forgiving God, and most importantly, forgiving myself.

We all get to choose how we allow the traumas in our lives to influence us. If we suppress them, they come back to us in another form asking for us to look at them. Nothing goes away until we have learned everything we need to learn from them. We can't change what happens to us. However, as I've learned on my return journey home, we can change our relationship to what happens. There is wisdom to be gained even, and especially, from our most excruciating pain, as the Greek playwright Aeschylus reminds us: "In our sleep, pain, which cannot forget, falls drop by drop upon the heart, until, in our own despair, against our will, comes wisdom through the awful grace of God."

21

HAMILTON GREGORY

They Were Called Morons

The Vietnam War, which began in 1955 and ended in 1975, was the longest war in American history. During the war's early years, the US government relied on volunteers to do the fighting, but as the war intensified in the mid-1960s, there were not enough volunteers to fill the ranks. So, the government resorted to conscription, forcing many young men to leave their homes to join the Armed Forces.

Conscription, most often known as the military draft, came with its own set of problems. For instance, President Lyndon Johnson and Secretary of Defense Robert McNamara did not want to anger the vote-powerful middle class by drafting their college-age sons or by sending the National Guard and Reserves to war. McNamara thought he had the solution: in 1966, he lowered mental standards for entrance into the Armed Forces so that thousands of men with low IQs—men who previously had been deemed unsuitable for military duty—could be inducted.

McNamara's program was known as Project 100,000 because it aimed to induct 100,000 men each year. By the end of the war, the program had taken in 354,000 men. Of these, 71 percent were sent to the Army, 10 percent to the Marine Corps, 10 percent to the Navy, and 9 percent to the Air Force. Among the troops, these men were often known as "McNamara's Morons," "the Moron Corps," or "McNamara's Boys."

Military leaders—from William Westmoreland, the commanding general in Vietnam, to lieutenants and sergeants at the platoon level—viewed

McNamara's program as a disaster. Many of the men in Project 100,000 were slow learners who had difficulty absorbing necessary training. They were often incompetent in combat, where they endangered both themselves and their comrades. A total of 5,478 men from Project 100,000 died while in the service, most of them in combat. An estimated 20,270 were wounded, and some were permanently disabled (including an estimated 500 amputees). Statistically, men with low IQs were three times more likely to die than other GIs and twice as likely to be wounded.

I got to know some of McNamara's Boys while serving in the Army from 1967 to 1970, and I spent many years conducting interviews and gathering stories for my book, *McNamara's Folly: The Use of Low-IQ Troops in the Vietnam War*, which was published in 2015. I found that in basic training, many Project 100,000 men failed tests on the rifle range because of their mental limitations. The military wanted to simulate realistic combat conditions, so to qualify with an M-14 rifle, you were supposed to hit pop-up targets at different distances on a brushy hillside. You never knew where the next target would pop up, and it stayed up for only five seconds. This was not enough time for men who were mentally slow to shift their aim and fire.

Such men should have been discharged and sent home. In fact, many company commanders tried to have the men discharged, but they usually failed because both the Army and the Marine Corps were facing serious manpower shortages in Vietnam and were reluctant to discharge anyone.

One of the saddest stories I collected involved Barry Romo and his nephew Robert, who ended up in Vietnam at the same time. Barry said, "I loved Robert like a brother. We grew up together. He was only one month younger."[1]

Barry served as an infantry platoon leader in 1967–1968, and he saw a lot of combat, winning a Bronze Star for his courage on the battlefield. During his tour, he learned that Robert had been drafted and was being trained at Fort Lewis, Washington, to be an infantryman, destined for Vietnam. Barry was alarmed because Robert was "very slow" and had failed the Army's mental test. But then along came Project 100,000, lowering standards and making him subject to the draft. A host of people—his relatives, his comrades at Fort Lewis, his sergeants, his officers—wrote to the commanding general at Fort Lewis, asking that Robert not be sent into combat

1. This story about Barry Romo and his family comes from the following sources: Hunt, *The Turning*, 80; Barry Romo, interviewed by the author, April 7, 2001; Romo, "Veteran's History Project"; Clark et al., "Students, Scholars Debate Military Draft Reinstatement"; Romo, "The Never Ending War," 8. Romo's speech, "The Never Ending War," was delivered at the Bavarian House of Parliament as part of a program about war and its consequences.

because, as one relative put it, "he would die." But the general turned down the request.

When he arrived in Vietnam, Robert was sent to an infantry unit near the border of North Vietnam, one of the most dangerous combat areas. During a patrol, he was shot in the neck while trying to help a wounded friend. He did not die instantly, but heavy gunfire kept a medic from reaching him. Barry said, "He drowned in his own blood."

At the request of the family, Barry was given permission to leave Vietnam and accompany Robert's body home to Rialto, California. The aluminum coffin was sealed and draped with a flag, and the family was not allowed to view the remains. (It was Army policy to discourage or forbid viewing when a body was badly mutilated.)

Looking back, Barry said that Robert "really didn't have much luck. While others were getting deferments, he was drafted. While Congressmen's sons were getting exemptions for braces on their teeth, Robert was drafted as part of Project 100,000."

In a speech delivered forty-two years later, Barry said that the family had never recovered from losing Robert. "His death almost destroyed us with anger and sorrow."[2]

Another case involved a battle for Saigon in May, 1968. Lieutenant Frank Neild had a radioman, James Hewitt (not his real name).[3] Neild called Hewitt "big, dumb, and nice—a nineteen-year-old piece of cannon fodder from rural Pennsylvania," and he said that Hewitt was "nicknamed 'Lurch' because of his glazed expression and half-opened mouth." His superiors "found it hard to believe that anyone as slow as Hewitt could have passed the aptitude tests required for military service, and chalked him up as one of McNamara's 100,000," Neild said.

Hewitt "wanted desperately to do a good job as the team radioman, but could not figure out how to adjust frequencies." Neild "tried to coach him, but nothing stuck." Finally the lieutenant asked his superior to replace Hewitt "with a trooper who actually knew how to operate a radio." Neild said that while Hewitt's "character was impeccable," his "problem was that he couldn't think." While waiting to be replaced, Hewitt was grievously wounded in combat, and he died two weeks later.

Some people think that you don't have to be very bright to be successful in combat, but this is not true. Men who are slow in their thinking are very vulnerable. To survive in combat, you have to be smart and you have to

2. Romo, "The Never Ending War," 8.

3. This story about Frank Neild and James Hewitt comes from Nolan, *House to House*, 63, 274.

think quickly. You have to know how to use your rifle effectively and keep it clean and operable; you have to know how to navigate through jungles and rice paddies without alerting the enemy; and you have to know how to communicate and cooperate with other members of your team.

In 1982, Eliot Cohen said, "The dull-witted soldier does not simply get himself killed—he causes the death of others as well."[4] According to one Vietnam veteran, Chief Warrant Officer William S. Tuttle:

> If you take someone with an IQ of 40 and give him a rifle, he's more dangerous to you than he is to the enemy. I almost got shot twice and had one guy almost nail me with a light anti-armor weapon when he was startled by a sudden noise. If you put [a man with a low IQ] in an infantry patrol, you have to spend most of your time making sure he doesn't kill [a comrade] by accident, and doesn't get himself killed during contact because he's totally unaware of what's going on around him. Imagine sending a five-year-old into combat. That's what Project 100,000 was all about.[5]

G. J. Lau, an Army veteran who served with the 1st Infantry Division in 1969, remembered Jerry, who was a member of "McNamara's 100,000." One night, he recalled:

> Jerry was out on the perimeter standing night guard. A very popular officer had been out setting his men in position and was returning to inside the wire. There is a challenge procedure, just like you see in the movies.
> "Halt, who goes there?"
> "Lt. So-and-So."
> "Advance and be recognized."
> That's not it exactly, but you get the idea. You order the person to halt and then do whatever it takes to identify them as friend or foe, normally not a difficult task given the obvious differences between the average Vietnamese and us Americans.[6]

But for some reason, Lau said, "Jerry saw the officer approaching and shouted out 'Halt,' and then immediately opened fire, killing him on the spot."

---

4. Bailey, *America's Army*, 107. At the time, Eliot Cohen was a Harvard professor. One of the nation's most prominent political scientists, he would go on to serve as a counsellor in the US State Department under Condoleezza Rice from 2007 to 2009.

5. Tuttle, "BillT."

6. Jerry's story comes from Lau, *SitRep Negative*, 89–91.

The killing caused consternation in the camp. "The men under the officer's command immediately made it known to any and all that Jerry was a dead man. Period. End of discussion. Some leader must have taken that threat pretty seriously, because Jerry was transferred by first light. Never saw him again," Lau said.

Most of McNamara's Boys were from low-income families, so they went unnoticed by most of the public and the news media. One journalist who did take note was Joseph Galloway, a war correspondent who won a Bronze Star with Valor in Vietnam for carrying wounded men to safety. He wrote a column shortly after the death of McNamara in 2009 entitled "100,000 Reasons to Shed No Tears for McNamara." Of the men of Project 100,000, he wrote:

> They were, to put it bluntly, mentally deficient. Illiterate. Mostly black and redneck whites, hailing from the mean big city ghettos and the remote Appalachian valleys. By drafting them the Pentagon would not have to draft an equal number of middle class and elite college boys whose mothers could and would raise hell with their representatives in Washington. The young men of Project 100,000 couldn't read. . . . They had to be taught to tie their boots. They often failed [in basic training], and were recycled over and over until they finally reached some low standard and were declared trained and ready. They could not be taught any more demanding job than trigger-pulling, [so most of them] went straight into combat where the learning curve is steep and deadly. The cold, hard statistics say that these almost helpless young men died in action in the jungles at a rate three times higher than the average draftee. . . . The Good Book says we must forgive those who trespass against us—but what about those who trespass against the most helpless among us; those willing to conscript the mentally handicapped, the most innocent, and turn them into cannon fodder?[7]

I share Galloway's anger and rage, especially when I recall a trainee I knew at Fort Benning. I will call him Freddie Hensley (I am not using his real name to protect the privacy of his family). I met him at Special Training Company, a camp for men who had failed basic training. I had been sent there for rehabilitation after I was hospitalized for heat exhaustion.

Freddie was among dozens of men with low IQs at Special Training who could not pass basic training because of mental limitations. One of the events that you were required to pass in order to graduate from basic was

throwing five non-explosive practice grenades. You had to throw each grenade ninety feet onto a huge canvas target that was flat on the ground and
resembled a giant dart board, with a bull's eye and concentric circles. The
scoring was similar to that of a dart board, too—the closer you came to the
bull's eye, the more points you got. In order to simulate combat conditions,
you were required to stay on one knee while throwing. Freddie and most of
the other Special Training men could not even reach the target, much less
the bull's eye. Because of the heaviness of the grenade, they needed to throw
it in a high arc, like a center fielder throwing a baseball to home plate, but
most of the men failed to grasp the concept. They would try to throw the
grenade in a straight line like a pitcher throwing a ball to the catcher, and the
grenade would plop down far short of the target. Despite all the sergeants'
explanations and demonstrations, they could not understand the concept of
a high arc. One evening, I took Freddie and some of the other men to the
PT field and tried to use visualization. "Imagine there is a bird in the sky,"
I said. "Throw the grenade and hit the bird." Unfortunately, the men could
not translate the idea into action.

Freddie was too slow-witted to pass the rifle test. He would see a target
pop up at random, but he couldn't shift his rifle and squeeze off a round in
the five seconds before the target disappeared.

Freddie had a distinctive personal appearance. Even though all his
hair had been shaved off by an Army barber, he was a good-looking young
man, with a fresh, appealing face. One sergeant called him "Pretty Boy." This
was the first impression of Freddie. On second glance, however, there was
something amiss. His eyes were chronically filled with apprehension and
self-doubt. Like some people who are consumed with dread and anxiety, he
was always sighing. If I were sitting on my bunk and he approached from
behind me, I could hear him coming. He was a veritable sighing machine.

After I left Special Training Company, I lost contact with Freddie, but
I did hear that he and other men with low IQs were sent down the path to
Vietnam even though they had failed all the supposedly necessary tests. A
few years after the war ended, I arranged to get a computer printout listing all the names of Americans who died in Vietnam. I skimmed the list,
looking for last names that matched the names of men I had known at Fort
Benning, and I discovered that Freddie had been killed in combat. His death
hit me hard. I remembered how he was always sighing—an indication of the
tremendous anxiety he experienced in Special Training. I remembered how
he lacked the mental quickness to qualify with the M-14 rifle. Learning of
his death made me quiver with rage—a fury that I still feel decades later.

Grasping at straws, I got to thinking that maybe there was another
man named Freddie Hensley who died, so I tried to find his family by

telephoning people in his hometown with the same last name. (This was in the days before the Internet, so finding people was more difficult than it is today.) I eventually made contact with his mother and ascertained that the Freddie I had known was indeed the man who died in Vietnam. I told her that I had been Freddie's friend at Fort Benning. She said that she and the family were proud that Freddie had given his life to defend his country. As we talked, I carefully introduced my belief that Freddie should not have been sent into combat. Before long, she was expressing grief and anger and bewilderment. She told me that when Freddie received his draft notice, she and other family members went to the induction center and explained that Freddie had been in EMR (educable mentally retarded) classes in school and had not been able to drive a car and that it would be a mistake to draft him. In response, a sergeant reassured the family that Freddie would not be put into danger—he would just do menial jobs such as sweeping floors and peeling potatoes.

"He was a good boy," she said. "When he was little, we used to go everywhere together. He was my Little Man." She began to sob, and she lamented, "Why did they have to draft him? I want to know why."[8]

The plaintive cry of Freddie's mother acted as a spur—an incentive—to tell the story of Freddie and the other unfortunates who died because of McNamara's folly. I spent over four decades conducting research and interviewing veterans and family members. In addition to relating the details of the men's needless personal tragedies, I wanted to make a strong argument that America should never again induct low-IQ personnel into the Armed Forces.

Doing research fueled my ongoing anger. I had thought that in helping vets and their relatives to tell their stories, I would experience a catharsis—a purifying cleansing of my negative emotions and thoughts—but the opposite occurred, as I found more and more sad and tragic stories. The extent of the misery endured by low-IQ men (most of them from poor families) was much worse than I had imagined.

Another source of anguish for me was discovering in my research that McNamara's folly had not ended with the winding down of the Vietnam War. It was continuing, year after year. Although the military draft and Project 100,000 were abolished, the Army and Marine Corps had monthly recruiting quotas, and whenever they failed to reach their quotas, they were authorized to induct mentally limited soldiers and Marines. I found reports of abuses and deaths, especially during the drawn-out wars in Iraq and

8. Interview by the author with the mother of the soldier described, March 5, 1977. Her name is withheld to protect her family's privacy.

Afghanistan. In 2008, for example, an Army private named David Dietrich of Perry County, Pennsylvania, was the subject of a *Newsweek* magazine article entitled "He Should Never Have Gone to Iraq." Before and during his Army time, he was considered slow in his thinking, and he had trouble retaining information. In basic training, he couldn't hit targets on the rifle range, even though he was given extra training. His comrades had a nickname for him—Forrest Gump, the name of the low-IQ soldier in the Vietnam War who was portrayed in the movie starring Tom Hanks. One superior campaigned to have Dietrich sent home on grounds that he would pose a danger to himself and others if he was sent to Iraq, but the request was rebuffed by higher-ups. As with Vietnam, there was a big push to get troops into the combat zone. Soon after he arrived in Iraq, he was assigned to act as a scout in an abandoned building, where he was supposed to watch furtively from open windows. A few minutes after he started his duty at one of the windows, he was shot dead.[9]

Such post-Vietnam stories, although nowhere near as numerous as the similar stories in the Vietnam War, filled me with fury and despair. Had we learned nothing from our Vietnam experiences?

Gathering stories from Vietnam and beyond—and deciding which to include in my book—made me sad and heartsick, and I sometimes thought of abandoning the project. But I persevered because my beloved wife Merrell kept encouraging me, reminding me of her belief that I was possibly the only man in America who had the experiences and the commitment to tell the full story—"a story that needs to be told," she would say—and to help make sure the folly is never repeated.

So I soldiered on, and I finally finished my research and published the book in 2015. It became an Amazon best-seller and received praise from Vietnam vets like Four-Star General Anthony Zinni of the US Marine Corps and Jan Scruggs, the vet who led the crusade to build the Vietnam Wall in Washington, DC. I felt gratitude at the book's success because—at long last—I had succeeded in getting the story out to the nation.

My happiness, however, was short-lived. I had thought that publication of the book would cause me to experience catharsis. But psychic relief did not occur, because the book caused me to receive heart-rending emails from people all over the country. One veteran wrote,

> In basic training at Fort Polk, Louisiana, in the fall of 1968, I was assigned to one of McNamara's 100,000 for rifle range training. At the time I couldn't understand how this young man from

9. This story about David Dietrich comes from Ephron, "He Should Never Have Gone to Iraq."

Alabama ever got inducted into the Army because he literally could not understand the concept of firing a rifle, and he endangered others even in training. He did complete basic and went on to Advanced Infantry Training at Fort Polk's Tiger Land, was sent to Nam in April of 1969, and was killed in action in May. He wasn't even there long enough to make any sense of what he was up against. What a sad waste of a young life.[10]

Another veteran wrote that at one training center during the war, he witnessed the following scene: A callous NCO, who was irritated at the large number of illiterate McNamara's Boys under his command, told the men, "I don't care if you can't read or write. Most of you will be dead in six months anyway."[11]

A woman in Arkansas said that her brother, a Project 100,000 draftee whom she described as "mentally deficient," was killed in Vietnam. "Thank God the story is being told," she wrote. "Sending those boys into battle was more than unfair—it was a criminal act!"[12]

Although nothing can equal the anguish felt by parents, spouses, and siblings, I and many other veterans feel anger and rage when we think of the needless deaths of men whom President Lyndon Johnson (in a secret White House tape) referred to as "second-class fellows."[13] When I was interviewed on an Oregon radio show, the interviewer, who was a combat veteran, choked up as he talked about two of his low-IQ platoon mates who were killed in Vietnam. "They shouldn't have been sent into danger," he said.[14]

A half-century after the events at Fort Benning, I discovered a term (new to me) that conveyed the anger and despair that I had experienced (and still experience to this day)—*Moral Injury.* This is a good description of my bruised mind and spirit. My basic beliefs about fairness and justice were violated. My trust in elders, who were supposed to act wisely and humanely on my behalf, was compromised. Sending mentally limited men into combat violated the moral principle of treating vulnerable people with kindness and compassion instead of exploiting them. Although the war ended

10. Mark J. Minger, email to the author, May 26, 2016. Minger served with the US Army in Vietnam from April 1969 to April 1970.

11. Joseph Hudson, email to author, June 6, 2016.

12. Email to author, August 3, 2016. The woman who penned this email prefers not to be identified.

13. Beschloss, *Reaching for Glory*, 140–141. Preserved on these pages is a conversation between President Johnson and Secretary of Defense Robert McNamara that occurred on November 14, 1964.

14. "Veterans Voice Radio Show," hosted by Marvin Simmons, KBOO 90.7 FM, Portland, Oregon, Dec. 18, 2015.

decades ago, I am troubled and depressed when I think about what happened then—and what still happens today. I feel consternation and shame that my country would permit such unjust and immoral policies.

It was *wrong* to induct men with low IQs in the Vietnam War, and it is *wrong* to induct them for today's wars.

22

DOUG ANDERSON

Something Like a Soul

Why should we hear about body bags and deaths? It's not relevant. So why should I waste my beautiful mind on something like that?

—Barbara Bush, March 18, 2003, *Good Morning America*

Boarding the flight to Portland I watched a young man and his wife—or sister—head up the ramp. He looked like somebody had unhooked his nervous system from the right side of his body. His left hand and face showed the mottled layers of several surgeries. What happened on the left side of his body had affected the right. I thought, he must have been driving, or riding in the left rear seat, because he was wounded in areas that would have been exposed to the IED in the window frame on the driver's side of the truck or Humvee. I wondered if the absence of a wheelchair was an indication that he intended to fight, to recover as much as he could. The young woman walked beside him, one arm around his waist, one on his injured arm, steadying him. Once aboard, she settled him slowly in the aisle seat of Row 20, stowed their bags, and climbed over him to the center seat.

I found my seat and settled in. A soldier with desert camo and tan passed me on the way to his. I said, "Thank you for your service," and shook his hand. He looked at me like they all do, as if I'd spoken from some place just outside the reality he was used to. I knew that state of mind. I hated the war. I'd hated the one I was in, too—another ten-year disaster. I thank them for their service, not because of any political sentiment, but because I know what they've seen and that they can bear witness. It doesn't matter much what their politics are because the things they'll tell us are a kind of precise record that will outlast the politics; but this testimony can only be heard at the personal level. You have to get to know them to know what they really think, and that is more than most people are willing to do.

There is nothing new about war. Poor people kill other poor people and those in power become rich. Young men go to war and are permanently changed. So many civilians die that it no longer matters why the war began. Life gets worse for the civilian population of the countries in which we fight our wars under the pretext of freeing them from tyranny. The "freedom" we promise them never comes. We replace one despot with another one more friendly to our national interests. No, there's nothing new, but seldom has there been a time when war was so utterly disconnected from the daily life of most Americans. Orwell's perpetual war is now the norm. The idea is no longer revelatory. Soldiers weave through airports daily along with businessmen talking on cell phones. One way or another, the servicemen and women are working for the same corporations as the businessmen. The briefcase is related to the desert boot but few people make the connection. After all, isn't there a war always going on somewhere?

Our condition of perpetual war has resulted in a professional army that operates independently of everyday life in America. In spite of the hundreds of thousands of mercenaries—euphemized as "civilian contractors"—employed by the US in Iraq and Afghanistan, American servicemen and women remain on the sharp end of the fighting. The mercenaries are employed principally as security for American corporations. They are not subject to the Uniform Code of Military Justice and are not held accountable to the degree the troops are. In most cases, they aren't held accountable at all. They do not do reconnaissance or infantry patrols, and they incur far fewer casualties than regular Army, Air Force, Navy, or Marines. They also make about $100,000 a year, whereas an average infantry grunt makes from $22,000 to $25,000 per year, including combat pay. A former student of mine, who had been an airborne ranger in Iraq, told me the following story. He was on a bus traveling through the "green zone." Aboard with him were Iraqi and American civilian employees, soldiers, and a Halliburton contractor who was demonstrating very poor gun safety, waving his rifle around with his finger inside the trigger guard, posturing, and generally acting like an ass. My student said, "I knew if we got into the shit, I was going to shoot him first." Ostensibly, this was about gun safety; but there was a deeper resentment in play: this guy made too much money and he was accountable to no one.

One of the strategies employed by Bush-Cheney at the beginning of the Iraq and Afghanistan wars was to do an end run around the democratic process. Instead of a draft, National Guard and reserve units were called up and the "stop-loss" program was devised whereby a service member's tour of duty could be extended as much as four or five tours. You can imagine the personal toll. This is old news for anyone with half a brain and some powers of observation, but it has never entered the thoughts of a large number of the electorate.

There are consequences in a long war that differ greatly from, say, World War II, which, for Americans, was over in four years. It was a horrible and catastrophic war, larger in scale than any wars that have followed, but it was over, and a very real justice had been done. However, decade-long wars, like Vietnam, like Afghanistan and Iraq, yield very different consequences. Long wars create a level of depravity among servicemen that is never understood by the public. If you continually expose people to legal murder, it makes them numb and cynical. This depravity is increased if the reasons for the war are murky. Human life becomes worth even less. Bizarre events begin to take place that on their face seem utterly psychotic and for those ignorant of the circumstances, seem to come out of nowhere. Pat Tillman shot dead with a tight group of 5.56 rounds in the center of the forehead. Some of us think it was a hit. In fact, some of us think that it may have had something to do with Tillman, having gone sour on the war, contacting Noam Chomsky. A group of Americans are caught photographing their own acts of sadism inflicted on prisoners at Abu Ghraib. Otherwise decent young men decide to randomly murder Afghan civilians. These things do not come out of nowhere; they are the product of a war that has gone on too long. In the Vietnam War, the slow rot could be found in many units long before the My Lai massacre. The availability and cheapness of Southeast Asian heroin added a grievous pall to the war, and the "fragging" of officers by enlisted men told the story of a war gone bad beyond repair.[1] When I was on my way home from Vietnam in 1968 there was a Marine on the plane, leg and wrist shackled, and flanked by two brig chasers. When I arrived at the barracks at Okinawa, I learned that he had killed his commanding officer. He was one of many whose lives were ruined by things he never expected to happen in a war.

1. Editors' note: "fragging" is the deliberate killing of one soldier by another, often by means of a grenade.

The more politicized the conduct of the war, the more frustrated the men and women on the ground. The longer the war goes on, the more it becomes about surviving and not about its putative patriotic purpose. Reality has a way of rolling right over such sentiments.

My first day in Vietnam in February of 1967, I knew something was wrong. On my first patrol I saw an old man beaten by a squad leader for no other reason than he was Vietnamese. What I saw in my fellow Marines was not the attitude of men who believed they were fighting for a noble cause—protecting the South Vietnamese against communist aggressors. Their behavior was an admission that no one cared what the war was about anymore, and that the civilian population had become the enemy, and the enemy threatened their survival. There was nothing else beyond that, no long view, no strategy. That day was the beginning of my education, and an immense darkness opened under me. What I saw that day in these men was a kind of soul damage.

* * *

What is a *soul*? The word still enjoys strong metaphorical significance in spite of the smirks it attracts in our snarky times. I sometimes think it is a composting of all the provisional selves we create to manage a life. Paracelsus argued that the soul is not inside us, but surrounds us, goes before and behind us. It must therefore be wiser, see more than the "self," which is often so busy justifying its own identity that it has lost touch with *what is*. There is nothing ethereal about the soul: it is worldly in a way the mind will never be. Perhaps the strongest argument for its existence is that you can damage it, imprison it. Lose it. It is important for us to imagine a soul, even if we are not religious, because its spaciousness allows for us life's imponderables, against which a conscious and unconscious seem so utterly lame. A soul is spacious enough to hold our lives. Some faculty, some *something* must be said to collect meaning, to collect experience, and transform it. It must matter to have lived.

I dread being one of those old men who stand by the road and wave their cane at the cars, hair all white fire. One of the last forms of innocence is lost in old age when you realize that no one cares what you know. You can say, *Look, there, it's happening again.* You can say, *No one will win this war, but it doesn't matter to those in power because they'll grow rich from it.* The patriotic cause is the shuck and jive routine that brings the electorate along. You can say, *You may think you're a badass, but there are other things that will test your courage more than the war itself, like those things you have to live with, those things you have done.* When the war is over, few will remember what it was about. Millions will be damaged by the war and no one will remember them.

Williams James called the assumption that things get better simply because time has passed the "meliorative myth." Like many these days, I am a pessimist. I imagine a future of international corporate feudalism protected by armies of mercenaries that, like soccer teams, are composed of men from many countries who are loyal to whomever pays them but who have no personal stake in what happens to one country or another. Such things as "nations" will be merely sentimental.

But where does this leave the people who have incurred the damage from war? What do we do about them? Surely something must be done. Empathy is inconvenient because it makes us shift our consciousness away from being expedient. Most people don't want to go there: it's disruptive, what it reveals might lead to making sacrifices; worse, it may lead to the knowledge that the way we live and the things we condone, are wrong. With the ascendency of the right in this country, we have seen an outright hostility to empathy. In fact, they even admit it. During the Sotomayor confirmation hearings, Republican Senator Jeff Sessions said the following:

> Thank you, Chairman. Judge Sotomayor, let's talk about empathy. I find it shocking that President Obama said that judges should have empathy. I hate empathy. My Republican colleagues hate empathy. In fact, I am proud to say that we've reached an all-time low in the "understands the problems of ordinary people" category.[2]

These "ordinary people"—the same ones who would be impacted by cuts in social programs that the Republicans are continually campaigning for—are the ones who end up fighting wars. We are experiencing a growing sociopathy on the part of power and money that hearkens back to pre-Roosevelt breadline days. It is no accident that it is the profiteers—executives with obscene salaries and bonuses—who are always the most vocal in support of this or that war, resting assured that their children will never have to fight. A cynic might say, *It has always been thus.* I say it is a matter of degree, and that regarding the culture, it is worse than it has ever been.

Let us demand that people who vote for wars should be sharply aware of each individual human being who dies or is maimed in such a war. Let them know their names, see the wounds on their bodies, hear their cries of despair. Let them feel the full weight of each casualty. They should at the very least not try to hide, as did Bush-Cheney, the photos of the coffins coming back.

2. Editors' note: Quoted in Collins, "3 Days of the Sotomayor," *New York Times.*

A soul is not pure luminance; it is rather a bruised light in which we carry all that we have been and all we have seen. When we acknowledge this, we deny nothing, and that way we are whole and responsible. When we arrived in Chicago, I watched the young man struggle to get up and walk, the young woman taking his arm. People behind them were impatient to get off. The young businessman behind me said to someone on the other end of his cell phone that he would see them in an hour if *he could ever get off this plane.* The irritation in his voice was obvious. This vet struggling to get off the plane was just another irritation. And, of course, the guy behind me will never connect the maimed soldier with the health of his stock portfolio.

The young man and woman shuffled into the terminal, the other passengers swimming around them on the way to baggage claim. Soon, they are the only two walking slowly toward the escalator. The rest have gone.

23

CHESTER NEZ with JUDITH SCHIESS AVILA

Code Talker

I boarded a Trailways bus for Albuquerque, New Mexico's largest city, where my older brother Coolidge lived.

En route, I stopped at the federal building in Gallup, New Mexico, to get an identification card, a card that was required for Native Americans at that time. Dressed in my spotless Marine uniform, I entered the building with confidence and approached the desk of a civilian paperpusher. From behind his desk, the man stared at me, the Navajo Marine, and his eyes narrowed.

"You're not a *full* citizen of the United States, you know." Wielding the small power given to him by his position, the man pressed his lips together and raised his brows in a contemptuous expression. "You can't even vote."

"I'm a Marine. I'm on my way home after serving my country in battle," I said. I took a deep breath and told myself to stay calm. This guy didn't know anything. But I didn't much like what the civil servant had to say.

I stared at the smug man. "I wish I had my forty-five with me," I said. I pointed my finger like a gun, aiming at the man's chest. "I'd shoot you right there. Right there." I turned around and walked out, ignoring the protests that followed me out the door.

Although Native Americans were made citizens of the United States in 1924, we weren't finally granted the right to vote in New Mexico until 1948, three years after I finished my service as a Navajo code talker in the Pacific War.

Coolidge met me at the bus stop in Albuquerque.

"Welcome home, brother."

Coolidge was my older brother, but I could see that he was proud of me, his little-brother Marine. We went to Coolidge's small house in the sprawling desert city. Immediately Coolidge's friends began to arrive.

"Let's meet this Marine brother," they'd say. And when I shook their hands, they told me, "Congratulations on returning safe."

Over beers the men always asked, "Well, how was it? What did you do in the war?"

I remembered the Marines' warning. I couldn't mention being a code talker, couldn't say anything about helping to develop the top-secret code. "The Marines issued me a gun and some ammunition and told me to go hunt down and kill some Japanese," I said.

For two and a half weeks, Coolidge, various friends, and I celebrated my return.

After celebrating and then spending several months in Albuquerque, I realized that I missed the rest of my family. Grandmother, Grandfather, Father, and Dora still lived on the Checkerboard.[1] I wanted to see them all and to help Dora with the exhausting task of herding Grandma's sheep. I headed west on a Greyhound bus to Gallup, then walked from there, with my thumb stuck out for a ride.

I stepped from the car that dropped me off at *Chichiltah*. Bright red rocks with splashes of purple shadow greeted me. The mesa glowed white and red. A bold turquoise sky, feathered with clouds, arched above me.

With the familiar beauty of home finally surrounding me, I remembered the Navajo prayer:

> *In beauty I walk.*
> *With beauty before me I walk.*
> *With beauty behind me I walk.*
> *With beauty around me I walk.*
> *With beauty above me I walk.*
> *With beauty below me I walk.*
> *In beauty all is made whole.*
> *In beauty all is restored.*
> *In my youth I am aware of it, and*
> *In old age I shall walk quietly the beautiful trail.*
> *In beauty it is begun.*
> *In beauty it is ended.*

1. Editors' note: The 27,425 square-mile, semi-autonomous territory of the Navajo Nation, comprised of portions of Arizona, Utah, and New Mexico, is often referred to as the "Checkerboard."

A neighbor was holding a "sing" when I first arrived, and my father was helping out. A sing is a ceremony conducted by a medicine man or woman, a person also called a "singer" or *hataathlii*. It is part of the Right Way of life. It puts things back in harmony when something has gone awry.

I stood in the doorway of Grandma's hogan. A figure approached from down the canyon. As it grew larger, I realized it was Uncle, riding a horse. I hadn't ridden a horse since before enlisting back in 1942.

"Climb up," said Uncle when he got near, patting the rump of the horse.

Uncle and I had always been good friends. I swung up behind him, happy to see him and eager to reach the sing and greet my father.

The familiar aroma of juniper smoke announced the gathering, as the smell of popcorn announces a carnival. It reached our noses well before we spotted the site of the ceremonial. Then we gained the top of a piñon-dotted hill and saw hundreds of *Dinè* inhabiting a valley between red mesas.[2] The colorful scene moved like an industrious city, all the activity centering on a special hogan that had been built specifically for the occasion. Women stood about in bright crushed-velvet blouses, their turquoise and silver "squash blossom" necklaces hanging heavy around their necks. They talked to friends while small children clung to their long, full skirts. Men sported heavy silver-and-turquoise belt buckles and multiple turquoise rings on each hand. Dense, handwoven blankets, wrapped around shoulders as protection against the cold, turned the open area into a moving tapestry.

A sing, which can be held anywhere in the vast empty miles of Navajo land, is a huge undertaking. Often the host family saves for years in order to afford the mutton to feed a large crowd. They stockpile firewood for the bonfires and gather poles for the ceremonial hogan. They pay the medicine man or woman who performs the ceremony. Dedicated to helping one person with a specific problem—like an illness—the sing benefits all who attend in good heart.

During the sing, the *hataathlii*, singer, and his assistants create several dry paintings. The intricate designs and multiple colors are prescribed by tradition. Rock, sandstone, and charcoal, as well as other locally available substances, are ground to a fine powder to make the colors, which are dribbled carefully onto the hogan floor by hand. Paintings are usually created by several men working together for four or more hours. The person for whom the sing is being held sits on the sand painting while the medicine man prays. At the end of the short ceremony associated with each specific sandpainting, the painting is destroyed. The traditional design represents

2. Editors' note: *Dinè* is the Navajo word for the Navajo people and language.

the unchanging laws of the Right Way, while the destruction of the painting reminds all attendees of the transience of life.

My father, still tall and lean, approached Uncle and me, his face lit by a hundred-watt smile.

"I am relieved to have you home safely, my son. My daily prayers have been answered."

But we Navajos don't celebrate the accomplishments of one who has done his expected duty, so although the homecoming was joyous, there was no reason to celebrate my bravery. And, of course, I could not tell Father about my service as a Marine code talker.

Father had to stay and assist at the sing, which could go on for as many as nine nights. I knew that participants slept during the day, because ceremonial events would keep them up all night. All night, chanting and singing, punctuated with rattles and drums, would fill the dark, the music pounding on until it became the earth's heartbeat.

But I had been gone a long time, and I wanted to be home, I left the sing and rode back to Grandma's hogan. Father would join us there when his duties were fulfilled.

I think everyone was happy to have me back. For them, now that I was home in the box canyon nicknamed Nez Valley by my family, everything returned to normal. I hoped the quiet would be healing. Back among the sheep and goats, with the people I loved, maybe life would return to normal.

I tried to relax, to return to my past self, but my memories were not peaceful like those of my grandparents, father, siblings, and extended family. And the quiet grew increasingly disturbing and unreal.

The adults on the reservation were careful to never discuss the war in front of young kids. No one wanted our children to glorify war in any way. It was okay to speak to other adults about the conflict, but even so, I stayed pretty quiet. The secrecy that the Marines had imposed upon the code talkers stifled me. It wasn't much help to talk about what I'd done and seen in general terms, as I was allowed to do. My memories were very specific and very disturbing, and I decided that it was better not to say much at all if I couldn't reveal my true story.

I knew that other soldiers returning from war had the solace of talking things out if they wanted to—either with their families, with friends, or with other enlisted troops. Their efforts had not been deemed secret, like ours. We code talkers, forbidden to talk about the realities of our war, were largely denied that solace of getting everything out into the open. Even though I knew my family wanted to learn about what I'd faced, and even though I knew they would help me if they could, I couldn't bring myself to talk about the limited things I was allowed to reveal.

The Japanese enemy populated my dreams, continuing to plague me even when I was awake. Our invasions of hostile islands played like an endless film in my head, with me and my buddies exposed to enemy fire as we struggled toward the beach.

When my time at home had passed the half-year mark, I finally broke down and told my sister Dora about these unwelcome visitors.

Then I told Father, Grandmother, and Grandfather. The dead Japanese wouldn't let me sleep or function normally during the day. All that blood I had walked through had stained my mind. Just as the island fighting had trapped us soldiers, never letting us get away from the battles, keeping us scared twenty-four hours a day, the devil spirits of my dead enemies now trapped me, never letting me enjoy any peace. My family agreed that if things continued as they were, the Japanese would eventually take me away. I needed a ceremony. They would put up an Enemy Way.[3]

A hand-trembler performed a diagnosis. Although I knew it was the Japanese who plagued me, the hand-trembler was part of the ceremonial protocol.

Grandma brought me to the hand-trembler's home.[4] The trembler, who could be either male or female but in my case was male, held an unpolished crystal in his hand while chanting in my presence. He asked questions, which I answered as accurately and as honestly as I could. The trembler concentrated on the crystal until he fell into a trance. His hand began to tremble. He saw the cause of my nightmares revealed in the crystal. This was important, because the trembler would prescribe a specific ceremony, one that would address the causes of my problem, not just the symptoms. His understanding of both my symptoms and of human psychology in general led him to make a diagnosis. He told me which healing ceremony I needed in order to get back in balance.

"I will select a fine singer to perform your ceremony," Father told me. The hand-trembler had diagnosed my problem, but the singer, or medicine man, was the one tasked with fixing it.

The four-day ceremony chosen for me was one of the "Bad Way" ceremonies, one that would rid me of an evil presence.[5] The hand-trembler had determined that the cause of my problem was evil, not good. It involved ghosts, *chindi*, left behind when the Japanese who were haunting me had died. Every person has at least some kernel of evil, and the *chindi* is com-

3. The phrases "put on" and "put up" are both used when referring to a ceremony.

4. Traditionally, an older person accompanied the "patient" when he visited the hand-trembler.

5. We Navajos practice Bad Way ceremonies as remedies for evil and Good Way ceremonies to help to keep people on the Good Way road of life.

posed of everything that was evil in the dead person. The specific ceremony chosen, called a sing, like the ceremony my father was attending when I arrived home from the war, was one often performed for children returning from boarding school or men returning from War, "the Enemy Way."

Originally the Enemy Way ceremony was created to destroy the ghosts of the monsters which had plagued the early *Dinè*, monsters which had been vanquished by Changing Woman's twin sons. In more modem times, the Enemy Way is used to destroy the ghosts of *any* enemy or outsider, consequently restoring balance and allowing a return to the Right Way, the Good Life.

We Navajos see ourselves as composed of two bodies, the physical and the spiritual. The two are inseparable, and life according to the Good Way requires that they be in sync, and that we be in sync with our world. Traditionally we worry more about living life according to the Good Way while we are on this earth than we do about an afterlife. I can't remember any mention of an afterlife in the Navajo Good Way, other than references to the *chindì* left behind by the dead. When someone died, their *chindì* could stay behind in the form of a coyote, or could simply remain in the place where the death occurred.

The diagnosis of the hand-trembler had told me what I would need for the ceremony. The sing would require something personal from a Japanese person. This was called the "scalp" but could be a few hairs from a Japanese head or a scrap of clothing worn by a Japanese person. That kind of thing wasn't easy to find on the reservation, but we were lucky that some of the Navajo soldiers, as I mentioned earlier, had cut hair and clothing from the dead Japanese and sent the items home to be used in ceremonies. The items were purchased by medicine men who utilized them as "scalps" in the Enemy Way ceremonies.

Father asked for advice from friends and neighbors, eventually choosing a medicine man to perform the Enemy Way. Traditional Navajo ceremonies, with their accompanying historical stories, chants, and sandpaintings, are complex. To perform a chant that might last from four to as many as nine nights, a singer must memorize prodigious amounts of material.[6] Although a medicine man or singer might study and learn several ceremonies, many specialized in a specific one. Thus, a specific "sing" or "way" often had a limited number of preferred singers.

It was the medicine man's job to help me figure out why the enemy continued to plague me. Knowing the "why" became the first step to

---

6. Clyde Kluckhohn and Dorothea Leighton, *The Navajo*, 163. Memorizing a nine-night chant is comparable to memorizing an entire Wagnerian opera, including the orchestral score, all vocal parts, and details of staging and costumes.

overcoming the problem. Then my body and mind could be cleansed, leaving me free of my Japanese tormentors and bringing me back to the "Good Life."

Father talked to the medicine man at length, telling him about my problems. The medicine man gave Father questions to ask me, and Father relayed the answers back to the medicine man. He told him how my visions grew stronger at night, until they veiled the rest of my world.

In preparation for the ceremony, my family butchered a goat and several sheep. They would feed the people who came to the sing. Wood was chopped, and the ingredients to make mounds of fry bread and tortillas were purchased. The family hosting or "putting up" a sing never knew how many people would attend. Traditionally, Navajos were supposed to take part in at least four sings during their lifetime, so often people heard of a sing and traveled to find it.[7] Of course, people close to the family came. But many others, even people my family didn't know, heard about me—the returned Navajo Marine—and came to lend support and help me reenter the Good Life. Everyone brought food and news to share. And they brought *hozoji*: kindness, compassion, and goodwill.

On the first night, the ceremony was performed near the home of the medicine man. The last night it was held at Grandma's home, and on the intervening nights at a location between the two. The young woman who led the Squaw Dance portion of the sing rode on horseback, carrying the prayer stick—or rattle stick—from one location to another. Several men and boys, also on horseback, accompanied her.

Squaw Dances, part of the Enemy Way sing, are so named because the young women who participate in the dance pick male partners from the audience. After each dance, the male bargains with the female, arranging a price he must pay to be released from the dancing. The price—always minimal—is paid, and the young woman chooses another partner. The dance is very popular.

At Grandmother's home, a large fire in a shack provided a place for cooking. My female relatives prepared the food, and everyone who attended was welcome to eat. At night, most of my female relatives slept in the cook shack, and the men in the hogan. Other families camped on the ground overnight, sleeping on sheepskins and blankets. No conjugal relations were allowed during the days of the ceremony.[8] Everyone was supposed to concentrate on the purpose of the sing.

7. It is said that a person should attend four sings. Some say it is preferred that the sings all be for the same problem, even if the person attending is not the primary patient in all four.

8. Whether or not this restriction was actually observed is questionable.

The pot drum, an integral part of the sing, was made of pottery and filled with water. Taut buckskin, stretched over the pot, was punched with eye- and mouth-holes. The drum-with-a-face represented the ghosts, who were beaten into the ground as the drum was played for the Squaw Dance songs.

Dry paintings, or sandpaintings, were created on a skin placed on the floor of Grandma's hogan.[9] Several men, over a period of hours, painstakingly created these paintings from various finely ground colored sands, charcoal, and corn pollen. The *hataathlii* supervised their creation. Every line had to be correctly placed.

Each painting was used in a ceremony involving me, then destroyed afterward. The medicine man told me things I needed to know in order to recover from my bad visions. These things were secret, just between him and me, so I can't talk about them here.

The traditional scalp shooter was hired. He fired at the Japanese items—the "scalp"—that the medicine man had provided for the ceremony, using a sling similar to the one I had played with as a boy, except that this sling was made from rubber and buckskin instead of string and the tongue of a shoe.[10]

The sing was a success. *Hozoji* was exhibited toward all who attended the ceremony, just as tradition mandated. I reentered the trail of beauty. For a long time afterward, my dreams and visions of the Japanese subsided.

9. Some families putting on a sing build a ceremonial Hogan, separate from the hogan in which the hosting family lives. This was not done in my case.

10. Scalp shooters often employed a rifle rather than a sling.

Reporters

All sorrows can be borne if you put them into a story
or tell a story about them.

—Isak Dinesen

An enemy is someone whose story you have not heard.

—Jewish proverb

Never think that war, no matter how necessary, nor how justified, is not a
crime.

—Ernest Hemingway

24

ERIC NEWHOUSE

Recovering from Moral Injury

There are some common truths about post-traumatic stress disorder that are generally accepted. Combat causes trauma and intense trauma causes PTSD, which is a natural reaction to unnatural conditions—it's a mechanism designed to keep a soldier alive in a world that's out to kill him.

So, PTSD is a learned behavior by a brain that is molded by the conditions that surround it, which is a condition called *neuroplasticity*. The problem with PTSD is that symptoms like hypervigilance continue even after the warrior leaves the battlefield. Night terrors and flashbacks continue to make the battlefield threats seem current. However, neuroplasticity also dictates that the brain will begin to change again as new conditions are experienced.

How to help vets unlearn those survival tactics is a critical question for our society today, particularly since American soldiers have been in combat around the world virtually nonstop for the past half century.

But that's just half the issue of PTSD, because it only involves what others are trying to do to you. And the other half goes largely unrecognized by the medical community.

Killing violates our inborn moral code, and failing to save our buddies leaves us feeling powerless. Anger, guilt, and depression are common symptoms, as is survivor guilt. Therapists such as Jonathan Shay, a recipient of a MacArthur Foundation "genius" grant, Edward Tick, director of the private group Soldier's Heart, and Brett Litz, a VA psychologist, argue that what happens in war may more accurately be called a Moral Injury—a deep emotional wound that pierces a person's identity, sense of morality, and relationship to society.

Both aspects of PTSD often occur simultaneously.

Let me give you an example: my friend Jack Jager, who was a scout dog handler during the war in Vietnam. That meant he lived in the field, using his dogs like bird dogs to flush out enemy soldiers or to sniff out mines and booby traps. That put him on the cutting edge of combat.

"We got overrun once, and that was my last combat experience," he told me a few years ago. "We ran into a camp of NVA regulars, and our battalion commander told us to withdraw a little. But in the evening, we got surrounded. Later I found out it was called the Easter Massacre because it happened on Easter Sunday. Out of the twenty-one men in our squad, we had eleven killed and six wounded. I remember a guy with his arm blown off asking how the hell he could load his rifle with just one hand. So, we withdrew. We had a river at our backs, and two guys who were mortally wounded tried to do their best to hold them off. We slipped into the river, floated downstream, got out on the riverbank, and spent most of the day eluding them."

Jack came home and tried to live a normal, civilian life, but couldn't. He was nervous about living inside, so he found a wooded area behind his apartment, built a camp, and lived there with his dogs for protection.

His breaking point came when his mom asked him what had happened to him over there. But he couldn't tell her. Instead, he fled to Montana, got an isolated job as a long-haul trucker, drank heavily, and fell in and out of four marriages.

"I felt very guilty," Jack told me. "There are things I did that I feel very guilty about. I was brought up right, brought up to do right, but in war the compassion is not there. Human beings were not made to kill each other. I saw some soldiers who just could not pull the trigger on an adversary face to face, and they died. After all the depravity of war was over, I was afraid people would know what I was, so I just ran away from it."

Cutting-edge researchers in the field consider any act that violates deeply held moral values to be a potential source of Moral Injury. They also say that, if Moral Injury occurs, this violation can be experienced by the perpetrator, victim, or even a witness. So, it involves more than just the victim. Non-life-threatening rape or incest are potential examples of Moral Injury; either the victim, the rapist, or a witness could lose complete faith in their own goodness, the goodness of others, and/or the goodness of God and believe that they are powerless to prevent a repeat of such evil in the future.

Jennifer Sluga, six-year veteran of the Wisconsin National Guard, says her ordeal made her a strong advocate for others who had have experienced sexual assault, a crime that can cause Moral Injury if it violates an individual's moral code and if it is perceived to be unjustified.

Now a psychotherapist at the Vet Center in Madison, Sluga estimates that 90 percent of her patient caseload also suffers from Military Sexual Trauma (MST).

Her ordeal started in boot camp when she and her "battle buddy" both reported to sick call. Her buddy was sent to the hospital, and that left her alone with the doctor.

"He had lot of rank on his chest and expected me do anything he said," Sluga said. "He wanted me to get undressed, then he began touching me, and it became pretty obvious that this was nothing in the realm of anything medical."

Sluga finally managed to push him away and ran to her barracks, only partially dressed.

"I ran to our barracks because I wanted to shower and cry, but another woman saw the marks on my body, asked about them, and then called the drill sergeant," she said. "He ran over to sick call, and I thought he was going to kill the medic. It was really cool to be validated like that."

But it didn't stop there.

Several members of Sluga's unit also reported sexual abuse during their deployment, and she began advocating for them.

Finally, the medic was charged with sexually assaulting his patients, and Sluga, her battle buddy, and her drill sergeant were all required to testify at his court martial. "He finally admitted to sexually assaulting more than seventy soldiers and excused it by saying he had been raped as a child," she said.

No wonder Sluga was severely traumatized. But she didn't realize it until after she had left the National Guard and returned to college. "I didn't recognize that I wasn't doing well until I went from an A student and I was failing all my classes, not attending classes, sleeping twenty hours a day. I just wanted to go hide."

Her breaking point came after she and her classmates got an exam back, and one of the girls was complaining about a bad grade.

"She said, 'It really raped me,'" Sluga remembered. "And I just wanted to jump over the chairs and scream at her, *Did it really rape you? Did it make you feel completely out of control? Did it actually hurt you?*"

That led to counseling and therapy. And it led Sluga to a career helping others as a psychotherapist.

Now look at Sluga's ordeal in light of our previous discussions on Moral Injury. She was betrayed by virtually everyone in her chain of command: the medical officer who sexually assaulted her, the officers who let such conduct go unchecked. Those fellow soldiers—who are supposed to save your life if necessary and have your back—should be the last individuals anyone should need to protect themselves against. Failure of your authorities to protect you from harm is a form of betrayal that often leads to Moral Injury.

Ed Tick argues (persuasively, in my opinion) that America has failed its veterans. Not just the government—all of us.[1]

Soldiers should only be asked to fight in just wars to protect our country, he says. And since they are being asked to kill, there should be social rituals to protect them emotionally before they do. When they return home, there should be purification ceremonies.

"Countless Americans who served in our politically and economically motivated wars feel broken because they betrayed the warrior's purpose and code, because the war was not unquestionably and purely defensive, because society and the government refused their tending tasks and judged and blamed veterans for their psychological problems afterward, and because both government and citizenry refuted collective responsibility." Tick wrote in his newest book, *Warrior's Return: Restoring the Soul after War.*[2]

After the war, vets feel isolated. They don't talk about what they did (or didn't do) because they feel they've violated our moral code. And we don't ask them what they did (or didn't do) because we're afraid of what we might learn. As Tick writes, "It is the utmost betrayal for any country to send its sons and daughters into slaughter for unjust reasons and afterward abandon, neglect, and mistreat them, and then leave them in a bereft and condemned condition for the rest of their lives."[3]

I remember talking with the grieving family of a young Marine killed in Iraq. As we stood in the cemetery, a snow-swept knoll in northeastern Montana, his mom recalled her son's last visit home a few months before and how devastated he'd been by an incident in Iraq. The twenty-year-old had told his family that he and his friends had been tossing candy to a bunch of Iraqi kids when one pressed too close. Warned to stay away, one kid kept advancing. And finally, remembering the stories of bad guys who carried knives or guns or bombs strapped across their chests, this young Marine shot the kid.

---

1. Unless otherwise noted, all quotes from Edward Tick are from personal conversations at different times (dates not available).

2. Tick, *Warriors Return*, 136.

3. Ibid., xiv.

When they checked the kid's body, he was unarmed. "Mom, I killed an innocent Iraqi goatherd," her son had said over and over again.

Killing goes against the moral code of virtually every society, so what a soldier does in a combat situation redefines him in his own mind. He knows he has crossed a moral line. And he knows that having done it once, he can always do it again. Worse, he knows that his family and friends will also know that about him.

As a Christian, there's only one thing that's worse. I believe that God handed down a set of laws written in stone that say very explicitly: "Thou shalt not murder." Later, that commandment was imprinted on our hearts, hard-wired into our psyche, as it were. So, breaking that law also separates me from my Creator, providing a triple whammy.

"A chaplain at Walter Reed (Medical Center in Washington, DC) told me once that healing involves renegotiating your covenant with God," Tick related to me, adding that conventional medicine doesn't take that aspect into account. "I've talked with a number of vets who say they are treated as victims, but that they know they were the perpetrators," he said.

Treating Moral Injury

Atonement

Drawing on Native American culture, Tick also counsels a path of atonement to healing. He noted to me that the Lakota Sioux have a term for combat stress that can be translated as "his spirit has left him" or "his spirit has been emptied." And he cited a Flathead Indian "victory song" in which a returning warrior asks forgiveness for the damage he has done to the cosmos.

War creates an identity crisis for returning vets, Tick told me; they initially transform from civilians to warriors, but they never can return to being only civilians again. So, healing involves making atonement for what they have done, creating a new post-warrior identity for themselves, and sharing their experiences with the community. That lifelong journey can lead to acceptance and spiritual peace again. Failure to do that leads to nightmares and flashbacks as the suppressed combat experiences struggle to be recognized. "Holistic medicine looks for true healing, not just symptom management," said Tick.

My friend Mike Orban is a 'Nam vet who never really recovered from losing his soul in combat. His book, *Souled Out*, examined his years of pain with searing detail and unflinching honesty. It also detailed his struggle for atonement.

Mike wrote about his year-long fight in 1971 to stay alive on the killing fields of Tay Ninh Province in the Central Highlands, with every sense on high alert to protect him from ever-present danger. He wrote about how empty it made him feel when he realized there was no legitimate purpose to his mission, that he was merely killing others so they wouldn't kill him. And he wrote about the anger he felt toward the Washington bureaucrats who so needlessly sacrificed the lives of young American soldiers that they deemed expendable. These were classical signs of Moral Injury.

But unlike so many war books, this part of his is designed merely to give us a taste of what Mike went through. Most of *Souled Out* is about the aftermath of war and how he no longer fit in. Mike compared himself to an abandoned house with a leaking roof, sagging floors, dirt-smeared windows, and rotting furniture on the inside, but with a lush garden and freshly painted, lovely exterior.[4] All his energy for the next five years went to keeping up that facade.[5]

But it wasn't until 1976 when he volunteered to go to Africa with the Peace Corps that he noticed a huge positive change. Part of it was the beauty of the jungles of Gabon, and part of it was living among rural natives so close to nature. But finally, he realized that he simply needed to help others to make up for the harm he had inflicted in combat. It felt so good that after three years in Gabon, he joined USAID for another two years in Cameroon.

Returning to America in 1980, he began a long slide downward, working just enough to pay for food and alcohol as he scrounged off his brothers and sisters and did his best to avoid facing the major problems in his life.

At the end of that long road, Mike faced a grim choice: suicide or recovery. And recovery meant facing the demons that he had worked so hard to avoid. But in 2001, he committed himself to a ninety-day inpatient PTSD program at the VA hospital in Tomah, Wisconsin, to begin that process.

In some respects, *Souled Out* is just one of many books detailing the odyssey of a warrior coming home from war. But it's much more than that because at the end of the day, Mike summoned up the courage, energy, and resolve to fix the roof and the floor, pitch out the rotting furniture, clean the place up, and slap a fresh coat of paint on the walls inside so he could live again in that once-abandoned house.

Like every restored home, there are always new problems and fresh additions to the maintenance list. But there's a real joy in seeing fresh life in this house . . . and in my friend Mike.

4. Orban, *Souled Out*, 45–46.
5. Ibid.

Forgiveness

The late Hardie Higgins, an Army chaplain for many years and author of *To Make the Wounded Whole: Healing the Spiritual Wounds of PTSD*, argued that the battlefield strips away the belief system that soldiers grew up with, leaving them empty: "The key to recovery for victims of PTSD is, I believe, to assist them in discovering the redemptive meaning of their suffering and . . . how to use that suffering to add meaning to their future life."[6]

One of the vets he has been counseling was crippled emotionally for decades by the memory of clubbing a Vietnamese boy to death with a rifle butt. Higgins reached out for healing by setting two chairs in a room, then asking the vet to sit in one and explain why he clubbed the boy, then move to the other chair to let the boy talk with the soldier. "He explained to the kid that he was just a soldier doing his job and he was sorry," Higgins told me. "Then I put him in the other chair and said, 'Now you're the little kid. What do you want to say to the soldier?' And it was amazing how much more forgiving that little kid was. He said, 'I know you were just a soldier and you didn't know what you were doing.' When you hear that kid talking about forgiveness, there's some real healing going on."

Higgins also uses the Bible to help vets lift their levels of guilt. He reminds them of that familiar verse in the Lord's Prayer: "Forgive us our trespasses as we forgive those who trespass against us." That's a deceptively simple phrase, but it really means that God will forgive me if I forgive others. And if God forgives me, I have to forgive myself, too.

Exercise as Therapy

Self-forgiveness leads to giving yourself permission to enjoy life again, and one of the best things you can do is find recreation that's fun. But it should also be something physical. That's because exercise is therapeutic in helping produce new brain cells, which reduces the anxiety and depression that are the hallmarks of moral injuries.

There are some fascinating medical studies that link heightened anxiety levels to deficits in new brain cell development.

"This realization could lead to novel approaches to treating a variety of anxiety disorders, including post-traumatic stress disorder (PTSD), because people who suffer from such conditions have trouble telling the difference between situations that merit fear and those that are innocuous," wrote two

---

6. Higgins, *To Make the Wounded Whole*, 86.

Columbia University neurology professors, Mazen A. Kheirbek and Rene Hen.[7]

For years, scientists believed that adult humans stopped producing new neurons, but then about twenty years ago, evidence from the brains of adult rodents, monkeys, and even humans showed that new neurons are being produced continuously in two areas of the brain, one of which is involved with smell and the other involved in learning, memory, and emotion.

According to Kheirbek and Hen, one of the learning and memory functions that appear to involve new neurons involves pattern completion, which is laying a memory down so that it can be retrieved. The other involves pattern separation, which is recording details of an event so that it can be distinguished from other events.

The neurologists tested their theory in lab mice by shutting down neurogenesis, or the production of new neurons, in some mice and boosting it in others. Then they took the mice from their safe home cage and put them in another cage in which they got a mild electric shock.

"Animals lacking new neurons remained overly skittish, reacting in alarm in both environments, even after repeated trips to the harmless box proceeded without incident," they report.[8] But that didn't happen with mice with an increased number of new brain cells. Several other studies have also shown that mice lacking in new neurons have been unable to distinguish between safety and danger, the neurologists write.[9]

They add that there's potential in these findings for greater understanding of PTSD:

> If neurogenesis is, in fact, involved in pattern separation in humans, the finding could offer insights into the cause of anxiety disorders such as PTSD. Psychologists have long suspected that the overgeneralization of memory contributes to anxiety disorders, which are marked by an exaggerated, sometimes crippling, fear response, even when the environment holds no immediate threat. Such inappropriate generalization could be the result of a diminished ability to distinguish between a past trauma and an innocuous event that shares some similarity with the traumatic event—for example, a picnic that is interrupted by an unexpected loud noise. Individuals with a normal capacity for pattern separation might flinch at the sudden boom but quickly realize that the park is not a war zone and continue with their lunch. A veteran with impaired ability to carry out pattern separation,

7. Kheirbek and Hen, "Add Neurons, Subtract Anxiety," 63.

8. Ibid., 64.

9. Ibid., 65.

on the other hand, may be unable to separate the sound of a car backfiring from the memory of a battlefield—a mistake that could precipitate a full-blown panic attack.[10]

Researchers, they point out, have found that most humans continue to add about 1,400 new brain cells per day to the hippocampus well into old age.[11] While the authors suggest that veterans may suffer from a deficit in neuron production, they suggest no reason why so many vets would be experiencing this disorder.

They do however, explain what cures the condition: exercise. Mice running on a wheel in their cages showed increased rates of neurogenesis.[12]

And that may well explain why vets who are kayaking, whitewater rafting, hiking, and mountain climbing can alleviate the symptoms of PTSD. They're producing more new brain cells and reducing their anxiety levels.

Out on a Raging River

Exercise does not have to be in a gym. In fact, it may be better if it's not. One terrific example of healing exercise is whitewater rafting down the Lochsa River, a twenty-mile stretch of wild and scenic river in western Idaho that boasts twenty-five Class III, IV, and V rapids. I floated the Lochsa a few years ago, and it was a once-in-a-lifetime thrill for me. Now vets are floating it together as part of the X Sports 4 Vets program.

"When I got out on the river, it was like team building," Brandon Bryant, an Air Force vet, told me. "It was exciting without the inherent danger of going out in the field."

During five and a half years in the Air Force, Bryant fought the war from a cubicle in Las Vegas, where he was the co-pilot of a UAV (unmanned aerial vehicle) Predator. "When we shot missiles, I was the one who guided them into the target," he said.

But the first deaths he witnessed were American soldiers returning from a mission in Iraq just after dawn.

"We saw something that looked like a buried IED (improvised explosive device) in the road, but we couldn't stop them. The first vehicle went over it. Then the second went over it. It exploded, and everyone died," he said. "I was nineteen at the time and I felt guilty, as though I was responsible

10. Ibid., 66.
11. Ibid., 64.
12. Ibid., 66.

for the deaths of our military members. That's when I knew I would never be the same again."

In one sense, it was like being a bombardier in Vietnam. In another, it was a lot worse.

"We flew the Predator by satellite in Iraq and Afghanistan, gathering intelligence for a week or so unless our guys were under attack," he said. "Then we found out where the bad guys were shooting from, and we would drop bombs on them. I could see the aftermath of every strike."

When Bryant returned home, he was diagnosed with 100 percent PTSD. He carried a lot of guilt and a lot of anger at people who had little regard for their own lives or the lives of others, which suggests a clear case of Moral Injury. And he isolated himself from most civilians, including his own family, who couldn't understand what he'd been through.

That changed on the river.

"Being in combat, that adrenaline rush comes with worry," said Bryant. "Deep in your gut, you're not sure if something bad is going to happen until it's all over. But out on the river, you know that if something bad happens, you've got a lot of guys around to help you. So there's no risk of dying."

I'm with Bryant to a point, but when I floated the Lochsa, I knew there was a risk of death. I felt we were challenging a huge natural element, something that was dangerous but not malevolent, something that could kill you but didn't necessarily want to.

There was a lot of teamwork involved in pulling the oars together strongly so we could power the raft over a curl of boiling whitewater without it flipping backward and dumping us into the frigid water.

And when one of my friends, sitting in the seat directly in front of me, got washed into the river, I jumped to my feet, pushed an oar at him, pulled him over to the side of the raft, grabbed the shoulder pads of his life vest, lifted him as high as I could, and then fell backward, dragging him on top of me into the raft. What a rush that was!

Adrenaline is a huge part of floating the Lochsa River, just as it's a huge part of surviving combat. But we now know that adrenaline also plays a large role in enhancing memory for emotional events, so that voluntary exercise that involves an adrenaline rush may facilitate the "learning" of safety and the consolidation of new, positive memories.

Paul Gasser, a neuroscientist at Marquette University in Milwaukee, said that just the exercise from extreme sports reduces stress. "Exercise is at least as effective an antidepressant as any of the pharmaceutical treatments," he told me recently.

Gasser and his colleagues have been tracking adrenaline and a hormone called cortisol in both humans and laboratory animals. Adrenaline is secreted into the bloodstream instantly by the adrenal gland during "fight-or-flight" situations, because it enhances quick bursts of energy for survival purposes, heightened memory function, and a lower sensitivity to pain. Cortisol, an important stress hormone also secreted by the adrenal gland, acts more slowly to facilitate adaption and recovery after stress.

Neurologists have found that PTSD patients appear to have lower baseline cortisol levels and a decreased cortisol response to stress. This means that these patients appear to have lower levels of the hormone that is critical for relaxing after stress. They say that this may be a risk factor for PTSD, and increasing that cortisol response could facilitate recovery.

Both adrenaline and cortisol are produced during periods of voluntary exercise. Elevating the adrenaline levels during voluntary exercise, which leads to an increase in the cortisol levels after exercise, appears to help the body recover better after stress, said Gasser. And alleviating the depression alleviates one of the major symptoms of Moral Injury.

Steve Hale, who deployed to Iraq in 2004–2005 with the Washington National Guard, can speak first-hand about the benefits of the X Sports 4 Vets program in Missoula, Montana. "I gave it a shot and really saw the value of it," he told me. "I got a connection between me and the experience and between me and the other guys. It was almost like being born again."

Combat had changed his perspective. "I really believed in the mission until the first bullet skipped across the hood of the vehicle," he said. "Then it was all about self-preservation and helping your buddy get home too."

When he got home, he wasn't exactly sure who he was, except that he wasn't the same person he had been before Iraq. Like Bryant, Hale was depressed and tended to isolate himself from others. But that made it hard for him to understand that he wasn't alone with his problems. Working and bonding with other vets has given him a chance to see how they are resolving their common problems, said Hale.

And then there's that adrenaline rush that Gasser talks about.

"You're on the edge to where it could be dangerous, but it's not," Hale told me. "People talk about numbing, but this makes you feel again. It's good to have a pucker factor and your heart race. It's a good positive outlet, not like getting drunk and getting into fights, which is how we used to cope. But you can't sustain that morally or legally. This is constructive versus destructive.

"Every time I get out on the river, I come home with stories and big pleasant memories," Hale said. "It does me a lot more good than the pills they've been throwing at me."

25

JOSHUA E. S. PHILLIPS

Torturing Torments the Soul

In May 2006, Jonathan Millantz phoned me to describe his wartime experiences in the Iraq war. I was reporting on the problems that US soldiers faced in trying to report on abuse and misconduct during the Iraq war, and Millantz contacted me to tell me his story.

He served as an Army medic and was attached to a tank battalion during 2003–2004. He mumbled as he spoke, making it difficult to understand him. Millantz talked with a drawl that was native to western Pennsylvania, but he seemed to bury his words and speak under his breath about the troubling things he had seen and done.

He wasn't traumatized by firefights or blasts from bombs. In fact, the members of the tank battalion that Millantz served with, Battalion 1/68 of the 4th Infantry Division, saw relatively little conventional warfare. After US forces drove Saddam Hussein from power, American soldiers were soon fighting a guerrilla insurgency. It was a different kind of war than the one they'd trained for.

Battalion 1/68 served in Iraq's "Sunni Triangle"—a violent, chaotic area at the time. There, 1/68 troops were ordered to capture insurgents in house raids. They kicked in doors, raided houses, and captured Iraqis suspected of supporting the insurgent groups who fought coalition forces. Then soldiers were tasked with guarding their captives in a makeshift jail on their forward operating base in Balad, Iraq. And that's when things went bad.

At first, Millantz maintained that he was just a medic tending to wounded prisoners and checking their vitals.

"From my point of view, keeping a person alive while doing these so-called 'interrogation techniques' . . . definitely burns an image in your brain that you'll never forget," said Millantz.

Years later, he cautiously admitted he was abusing prisoners at the jail. After several years of interviews, it became clear that Millantz and other soldiers from Battalion 1/68 were deeply troubled by the violence they had witnessed being inflicted, and had themselves inflicted on their prisoners. They described keeping prisoners up all night by blasting loud music next to their ears. Others forced Iraqi to hold straining positions for hours, and some admitted they had performed water torture by pinning down prisoners while pouring water over their mouths and noses to make them feel like they were drowning.

They said that, at first, they mistreated Iraqi prisoners for many reasons: anger, frustration, boredom. Then the abuse worsened when they helped question prisoners. "I think any human being in that situation would have done similar things," said Millantz.

It had a ruinous impact on the soldiers who engaged in or witnessed the abuse.

Like other men in his unit, Millantz was diagnosed with post-traumatic stress disorder (PTSD). He periodically sought counseling and passed through the Veteran Administration's drug rehab program as he battled substance abuse. Some of his former unit members had trouble managing their anger, and they dealt with serious depression and anxiety. Sergeant Adam Gray was one of Millantz's fellow unit members. Gray's friends and family described how deeply troubled he was by the prisoner abuse. Military medical records show Gray attempted suicide months after his deployment; shortly thereafter, he died of an accidental overdose.

All the therapists and social scientists I interviewed said that service members who had traumatic experience like Gray and Millantz needed to get prompt treatment. Yet the researchers and clinicians whom I spoke to also said that PTSD seemed like an inadequate way to capture the traumatic experience associated with these kinds of wartime experiences.

The service members I interviewed made it clear that it was difficult for them to openly discuss their involvement in prisoner abuse and torture.

"It's been hard over the years coming to terms with what actually happened over there," said Millantz. "I don't know if I'll ever have closure. I feel uncomfortable even talking about it with myself or another veteran."

Many of them felt that the stigma attached to torture was shameful and made it difficult to seek help. But they also feared recrimination from investigations and courts martial, and their concerns were justified. In 2006, the Department of Defense issued a directive that required military medical staff to report any prisoner mistreatment that they learn about, even if it comes out of consultations between service members and therapists.[1] That means service members who seek mental health treatment because they were troubled by prisoner abuse, and discuss such events with military medical staff, can ultimately be investigated because of what they described in therapy. That might make troops even more reluctant to confide in military therapists about wartime experiences like prisoner abuse.

Because most perpetrators suppressed their experiences and rarely shared it with anyone, there are few studies on how prisoner abuse and torture traumatizes the person who commits it.

Still, there is at least one longitudinal study that revealed the effects of prisoner abuse on American veterans. In 1983, the US Congress set up the National Vietnam Veterans Readjustment Study (NVVRS) to research PTSD and other psychological problems that Vietnam veterans suffered because of the war.

The NVVRS took four years to research and included over 3,000 interviews with Vietnam veterans. The researchers found a strong correlation between increased exposure to combat and psychological trauma, and they also found that "abusive violence had the strongest correlation with PTSD" for Vietnam veterans. Dr. Richard Kulka, the chief author of the NVVRS told me, while citing at times from the study, that abusive violence included, but wasn't exclusive to, the "degree of involvement in torturing, wounding, or killing hostages or POWs."[2]

"We can go into long philosophical discussions of torture—Is it effective? Is it justifiable?—but the one thing the research has shown is that . . . it's not good for the people doing it," Dr. Kulka, told me.

Kulka and the NVVRS examined the impact of prisoner abuse and torture through the prism of "abusive violence." But others viewed it through another lens. Some of those I interviewed referred to "moral conflict" or a kind of inner conflict during wartime that they defined as a "spiritual injury."

1. Department of Defense Instruction Number 2310.08E, 4.

2. These words come from an interview with Richard Kulka on July 27, 2009. The authors of the NVVRS took ninety-seven war experiences and clustered them into five categories: Exposure to Combat; Exposure to Abusive Violence and Related Conflicts; Deprivation (general discomfort during war); Loss of Meaning and Control; and Prisoner of War. Exposure to Abusive Violence and Related Conflicts included these criteria (for men): "degree of involvement in torturing, wounding, or killing hostages or POWs; involvement in mutilation of bodies of enemy or civilians; witnessed or involved in situations where women, children, or old people were injured or killed by Americans or South Vietnamese soldiers" (Kulka, *Trauma and the Vietnam War Generation*).

While the definition of "Moral Injury" is relatively new, the concept of it has been around for some time. Dr. Jonathan Shay eloquently unpacked the idea of Moral Injury in his landmark books, *Achilles in Vietnam* and *Odysseus in America*, where he uses the Homeric stories of the Iliad and the Odyssey to illustrate the history and complexity of this phenomenon. Shay contends that three conditions need to be present for there to be Moral Injury: "(a) a betrayal of 'what's right'; (b) either by a person in legitimate authority (my definition), or by one's self . . . ; (c) in a high stakes situation."[3]

That "betrayal of 'what's right'" can cover a lot of ground. It might even become a nebulous idea for those who grapple to understand how Moral Injury is best defined and how it applies to describing a particular traumatic response. According to researchers and clinicians, Moral Injury is unlike other wartime trauma in that it falls outside of the fear responses that are associated with post-traumatic stress.

If the stories I covered intersected with Moral Injury, they seemed do so when they connected to what some have deemed "transgressive behavior" or, as Kulka and others put it, "abusive violence."

But not all the troops I interviewed who mistreated prisoners were psychologically traumatized; some of them weren't upset by prisoner abuse and even defended what they had done as being necessary. Studies on abuse-related trauma show that guilt is one of the factors that determines the extent to which people are psychologically affected by their experience.

For some of the soldiers I interviewed, those feelings of guilt weren't just a response to "a betrayal of 'what's right'"—they were also rooted in a sense of helplessness in correcting it. Millantz told me how he and other soldiers spoke out about the prisoner abuse but were ignored or rebuffed by their superiors. His friends and family said he often despaired that he was unable to halt the abuse and torture. At one point, he told his sister, Roslyn Millantz, about how he was plagued by those feeling of guilt from a hospital bed.

"He would mumble things to me when he was in an out of consciousness in the hospital after taking numerous pills," his sister recalled. "He mumbled things to me like, 'I tried so hard, Roslyn, to fix what I did . . . the tortures, the jails.'"

Twice in the three years I knew him, Millantz nearly died from drug overdose, although they might have even been suicide attempts. He was cryptic whenever he talked about it. Yet Millantz also seemed hopeful, and pledged to keep "soldiering on" and that he was "not going to give up."

---

3. Shay, "Moral Injury," 182.

"I consider myself very fortunate," he said, pointing to veterans he knew who committed suicide. "I know people [who had] guns pulled out of their mouth. I know people who can't get out of bed every day without being on fifteen different types of medication [from] the VA."

Just one week after my last conversation with Millantz, on April 3, 2009, Millantz's mother discovered her son dead in his bed. The coroner determined that he died of an accidental overdose, just like his fellow unit member, Adam Gray.

Millantz belonged to a group of soldiers who said that their experiences with prisoner abuse and torture was the main source of their wartime trauma. And yet, their diagnosis with post-traumatic stress didn't quite align with the kind of wartime trauma they described. The soldiers I interviewed never applied the term Moral Injury to their situation. But instead of referencing fear-based responses associated with the battlefield, many of them said they were plagued by feelings of guilt and shame resulting from their experiences with prisoners.

These service members also felt that they had to stomach the pain: they feared that discussing prisoner abuse could lead to recriminations, and they were afraid of betraying their friends. The stigma associated with prisoner abuse made it especially tough for them to open up with therapists and chaplains, and many of the service members I interviewed hid their experiences from friends and family.

All told, this had a devastating impact on the service members and veterans I interviewed. Even if they didn't have any knowledge of Moral Injury as a concept, they seemed to be grappling with the destructive, sometimes tragic, effects it had on their lives. That seemed especially true for former soldiers Gray and Millantz.

26

MICHAEL PUTZEL

Survivors' Guilt and Recompense

On August 4, 2005, Ricky Miller sat up all night writing a long email to the officers who had led him in Vietnam.

"Thirty-five years ago today I flew into a place called Three Rivers," he began, as he set out to describe an incident that would dog him probably for the rest of his life.[1] Miller was the crew chief aboard Gunky, a battered black Huey helicopter he regarded as his personal pet. He recounted a mission to extract a reconnaissance team from his unit's "Blues" platoon, a small, quick-reaction infantry force. Miller and the Blues were part of C Troop, 2/17 Cavalry, made up mostly of flight crews for scout, gunship, and transport helicopters flying armed reconnaissance for the 101st Airborne Division. They called themselves the Condors.

The grunts on the ground that day were surrounded by North Vietnamese regulars in the notoriously hostile jungle valley called the A Shau. The enemy used the valley as a supply route from the Ho Chi Minh Trail in Laos through the mountains to the populous coastal plains of South Vietnam. They fought to protect that lifeline throughout the war.

The American soldiers, three of them already severely wounded, were under attack from all sides. The first two Hueys got in and out without serious

---

1. Email message from Former Specialist 5 Ricky Miller to Major General (Ret.) Benjamin L. Harrison, Major (Ret.) James T. Newman, Major (Ret.) Malcolm Jones, and former C Troop Warrant Officer scout pilot Steve Karschner, August 5, 2005, used by permission.

damage and extracted most of the team, but the third took several hits from small arms and .51-caliber heavy machine guns. Gunky was number four, the last ship in. Miller saw enemy soldiers climbing the hillside toward the small clearing where Gunky's pilot was trying to land. The Huey's machine guns rattled off streams of fire left and right to buy the Blues precious moments to reach the aircraft as it set down.

Miller saw that one of three Americans shooting back at the North Vietnamese was only a few feet from the aircraft but was blinded by blood covering his face and couldn't see to aim his rifle.

The crew chief abandoned his machine gun, grabbed a pistol, and jumped off his helicopter to help pull people aboard. He recognized the closest of the wounded as Private First Class Ed Long, who had been hit back and front by mortar shells and was crawling toward the ship, feeling for the skids with outstretched arms. Miller scooped him up with one arm and boosted him onto the floor of the chopper. He turned and saw another familiar soldier from the Blues platoon and ran toward him, zigzagging to dodge enemy fire. It was Larry Bandon, a short, stocky, blond corporal. Miller dragged him toward Gunky and hoisted him aboard. Banton landed on top of Long, who told Miller years later he thought it was a dead body that fell on him. At the edge of the landing zone, perhaps thirty yards away, Miller saw the unit's radioman struggling to pick up another fallen soldier. He ran through the incoming fire to help and glanced over his shoulder to see enemy soldiers firing their AK-47 assault rifles in his direction. When he reached the wounded soldier, he looked down and recognized twenty-two-year-old Paul A. Johnson, the acting platoon sergeant and Miller's best friend.

"He had been hit directly in his back, and there was a hole so big that you could see all of his insides—his lungs, everything," Miller wrote. He shouted at the radioman to run for the chopper, saying he would carry Johnson. "From then on my world went quiet. . . . I got down on my knees, held Paul up. He opened his eyes but didn't say anything but gave me a big grin. . . . I tried to keep the tears down as much as I could as I didn't want Paul to think he was that badly wounded. It was hard though. . . . I told him I was going to carry him back and for him to just try and relax so the bleeding would slow down. Paul was a pale white. . . I stumbled one foot in front of the other trying to keep my wobbly knees locked in place so as not to fall down with Paul on my back. All I could think of was, 'Why, God? Why my friend? Why did you get me to come here today?'"

He remembered being knocked down by the concussion of a mortar round exploding nearby, getting up, and going on, then being knocked down again. As he approached the helicopter, he could see the co-pilot, Warrant

Officer Mark "Mighty Mouth" Minear, watching him from the cockpit. He stumbled and went down again, exhausted. He thought he would die there with his friend and started to signal Minear to take off without them. Then he heard Sergeant Johnson speak, just enough to tell him to save himself and leave Johnson behind.

"My back was killing me, and I could feel my heart beating so hard that I could feel my heart hitting my chicken plate" body armor, Miller's email recounted. "I remember back in high school when I ran the five-mile, I think it was, the taste I would get in my mouth about three-fourths of the way through the run. I had that taste in my mouth now, and I knew then I was pushing myself to my fullest."

Eventually, they reached the chopper, boosted Johnson's limp body aboard, and Miller told the aircraft commander—too soon—to take off. The ship shot upward, and Miller just managed to grab the skid with one arm to keep from being left behind. With the aircraft rising out of the trees, he swung his body over the skid, reached for the barrel of the mounted machine gun, and grabbed a solid metal canister on the Huey's floor. He knew it held two thousand rounds of ammunition for the M-60 machine gun and wasn't going anywhere. Miller pulled himself on board as Gunky headed for Phu Bai and the Army's 85th Evacuation Hospital.

He opened the craft's first-aid kit, took out a couple rolls of gauze, and stuck them in Johnson's gaping wound without bothering to unwrap them first. The sergeant opened his eyes, motioned for Miller to bend toward him, "and he told me to make sure that his mom and dad and brothers and sisters knew that he loved them all and he had thought of them in his last moments. I told him to shut up. 'You're not going to die on me.'"

Gunky was flying so fast the whole aircraft began to shake as the crew raced its cargo of wounded to the hospital.

"Paul again woke up and pulled my head down again. 'Promise me, Rick, that you will tell my family I loved them and I thought of them. . . .' I told him I would but that he could tell them himself because he wasn't going to die now. . . ," Miller wrote. Tears swelled in the crew chief's eyes, and he pulled the dark sun visor on his flight helmet down to hide his face from his friend.

"I stroked his hair, tried to clean up his face somewhat," and in minutes the helicopter landed at 85th Evac. Johnson clutched Miller's hand as the orderlies loaded him onto a gurney, and as Miller freed his grip, the sergeant told him, "Bye, my friend. We were the best, weren't we?"

The crew chief's Army green flight suit was so soaked in blood that medics tried to put him on a gurney, too, but he pulled away and sent them after the other wounded. Johnson died a couple of hours later on the operating table.[2]

Minear told Miller afterward that he would put the crew chief in for a Medal of Honor for the heroics he had shown during the rescue mission, but the paperwork never got completed. Twenty-five days later, on August 29, Minear, who had been promoted to aircraft commander in the interim, was flying a mission to insert a team of five Rangers into the jungle not far from where the earlier incident had occurred. The North Vietnamese were waiting for them, and as the Huey set down, a blast of fire from a .51-caliber machine gun ripped through the cockpit and killed both pilots, Minear and his co-pilot, First Lieutenant John Frederick Shiefer, and two of the Rangers. Only three Rangers and two crewmen seated in the back of the aircraft survived.

Ricky Miller kept Gunky flying for another year, extending his Vietnam tour to twenty-two months, most of that time with C Troop, 2/17 Cavalry. The Army eventually awarded him a Bronze Star with V for his actions in rescuing the Blues riflemen that day. He tried several times to get it upgraded, if not to the Medal of Honor, at least to a Distinguished Flying Cross that would recognize his service in aviation. In the fall of 1971, he went home to Texas and was stationed at Fort Hood, but he couldn't find the excitement and pride he had felt during the war. He talked to some shadowy recruiters about flying black operations in Central America, but nothing came of it, and he decided to leave the Army. After his discharge, Miller "just sort of disappeared," as he put it. He left friends and family behind, ignoring attempts to contact him and hung around an abandoned airfield outside the West Texas town of Big Spring, where he took up dirt-track car racing to get his adrenaline pumping. He said he was trying to emulate the exhilaration he got from combat. He also drank a lot.

Miller eventually settled down and took a job with a large discount jewelry chain. But he couldn't bring himself to keep his promise to tell Sergeant Johnson's family about his friend's final thoughts of home. Johnson's last wish hung over him for years. After the company he worked for was sold, he traveled through the South doing consulting work for smaller jewelers. At Christmastime, about twenty years after Johnson was killed, Miller found himself in Nashville, Tennessee, and realized he was less than two hundred miles south of Johnson's family home near the village of New

2. Details of the battle, in addition to those in Miller's email, came from interviews with Ricky Miller, Ed Long, Major (Ret.) Malcolm Jones, former WO Harvey Rients, and Trina Judson, the unpublished book *Four Condors* compiled by Jones, and incidental accounts by other members of C Troop, 2/17 Cavalry, 101st Airborne Division.

Haven, Kentucky. On Christmas Day, he drove north to find the family at last and fulfill his obligation. He didn't know the way, however, and pulled into the wrong driveway, where he encountered a bunch of bootleggers, who came toward his car carrying rifles and shotguns. He explained who he was looking for, and they sent him off with directions to a family named Johnson. When he arrived, three generations of Johnsons were gathered for the holiday and welcomed him in to talk about his friend. They had never known what happened, only that their soldier was killed in action.

Miller showed them pictures of the platoon sergeant in uniform from a C Troop photo book he had with him and gave them the printed sheet he carried from a memorial service that the troop held for Johnson at its headquarters in Phu Bai the week he was killed. Then he asked if their mother was around. No, he was told, she had died the year before. He felt awful that she never heard the story of her son's last hours and his final thoughts of love for his parents and siblings. Despite his guilt, however, Miller simply hadn't been able to summon the strength earlier.

Perhaps because they didn't know Miller or why he had come to them, or maybe because they didn't question the snapshots they saw or the different first name, no one told Miller he was talking to the family of the wrong Sergeant Johnson.

On his way to the house, he had tried to find his friend's gravestone in the local cemetery, but without a map or identifier, he didn't know where to look. He stopped at one small graveyard he came to on the road and saw a Vietnam veteran's grave marker with a similar name, but the date of death was August 13, 1970, and Miller concluded it had to be someone else. Indeed, it was. On the Vietnam Veterans Memorial in Washington, the name of another Sergeant Johnson from the same tiny town in Kentucky is carved into the same polished black stone panel where Paul Johnson's name appears among more than 58,000 others. He was Staff Sergeant Nicholas G. Johnson, killed in the Mekong Delta, far to the south, just nine days after Paul Johnson was mortally wounded up north in the A Shau. The two men even shared a birthday, October 1.

The family Miller visited gave him directions to their soldier's burial site, and on his way out, Miller pulled off the road at the cemetery where he had stopped earlier that day. He sat in the car for quite a while but didn't get out. He was too emotionally wrought to go see. Nor did he realize that his whole visit involved a case of mistaken identity.

Early in 2013, twenty or more years after that visit to New Haven, Miller received a tip that someone had posted a note on an enhanced, Internet version of the Vietnam Veterans Memorial in Washington. A young woman was asking for information about Paul Johnson from anyone who knew him in Vietnam. It was from Trina Judson, who identified herself as Johnson's niece.

"I am looking for any servicemen that had served with Paul," the posting said. "Myself and his family would be forever grateful if someone could reach me that knew of Paul. Please contact me anytime via email. Also, just want to say thank you so much to Ed Long whom posted such a beautiful piece about Paul. Unfortunately, there was no contact information so I could reach him. Please Please contact me if you have any information at all regarding Paul. Again, I would be forever grateful. Bless to all that had served."

She knew about Long, who was severely wounded in the firefight in which Johnson was killed, because eleven years earlier, he had added his own post to the web page for Johnson on the same site.[3] In a remembrance entitled "my sgt.," Long said, "I just wanted to give a long overdue salute of respect to my sgt. paul Johnson. He was only 22 and I was 19. I often think of him and of that fateful day as I was injured and sent to a hospital in Japan. Fortunately for me I survived but the memories continue to be difficult. I was there that day. If any family member wishes to contact me I would be honored to speak with you and perhaps answer some questions that have remained unanswered for so many years. Rest assured he was indeed a hero in every description of the word and for that you can be proud. Respectfully, edward long." He probably didn't realize that he hadn't attached an email address or any contact information to his remembrance.

Trina Judson wasn't the only relative to post a message on the remembrance page. Three years earlier, her aunt, Paul's kid sister Maggie Jackson, put up a note under the heading "Gone but not forgotten."

"Paul was my older brother," she wrote. "We created lots of memories throughout our childhood. He is most definitely a hero and will always be in my heart. If anyone that knew him has any information that they would like to share, please email me." She did include an email address, but she never received a response.

When Miller saw Trina Judson's appeal, he contacted her to tell her about her uncle's death and pass along contact information for Ed Long, whom he hadn't seen since he heaved the wounded rifleman onto his Huey under fire. Long was living in Maryland, only about an hour's drive from Washington, and Judson was in Virginia, also not far from the capital. She hastily arranged to meet Long at The Wall on Memorial Day the following week, and they persuaded Miller to fly up from Texas to join them. They met at the Metro subway station on the National Mall, Miller wearing his

3. http://www.vvmf.org/Wall-of-Faces/26322/PAUL-A-JOHNSON.

beloved black Stetson Cav hat and Long a floppy "boonie hat," favored by grunts such as those in the Blues Platoon. He also wore his old Army field jacket. Long's gray hair and nearly white mustache made him instantly recognizable as a vet from the Vietnam era. As they walked the well-trodden dirt paths to The Wall, nearly everyone they passed expressed the now-standard gratitude the troops always felt was denied them when they came home: "Thank you for your service."

They stopped to be interviewed by a crew from a local television station, and Trina Judson presented each of them with an American flag, flowers, and an angel statuette she said would keep watch over them. Both men told her they still felt terrible guilt that her uncle had died and they had survived.

Long also told Miller, his long-ago buddy, "I want to say thank you for my life." He had been quietly grateful to his aging Army buddy for forty-two years.

The three then approached The Wall to find Paul Johnson's name on Panel 8W, Line 82. They brushed their fingers over the polished black stone and felt the depression of the capital letters etched deeply into the slab. A volunteer helped them make rubbings of the name to take home.

Miller recounted for Trina Judson his attempt to save and comfort her uncle.

"'I know I'm gonna die, Rick,'" the platoon sergeant told his friend. "I said, 'No, you're not. Be quiet. Think about Kentucky. Think about something nice at home.' He said something, and I couldn't hear him. He grabbed hold of my shirt, and he said, 'I want you to do something for me.' I said, 'Sure, buddy. What?' He said, 'When you go home, if you make it back, I want you to go by my parents' house in New Haven and tell them I love them.'"

Miller's voice broke, and the big West Texas cowboy began to cry, but he forced himself to finish his confession: "I told him I would. I got back. They asked me if I would escort Paul back, and I said, 'I don't think I can.' I felt like I let Paul down. He died. It was my fault, I thought. I couldn't do it. Twenty years later I did make it up there. His mother was already passed away. That's it."

Trina Judson tried to comfort them. "I beg each of you to let any guilt you feel go," she told both men. "There was nothing you could have done. . . . You are truly heroes in our eyes. You have our undying gratitude, and you'll always be the heroes in our lives. And there's no way we can repay you for not only going beyond the call of duty, but also spending the last few moments of Paul's life and making sure that he was comfortable and that he knew that he had friends around and someone there with him. That means more to us than anything. And we can never repay you guys for everything."

"He was wounded pretty bad, and I don't think he was in pain," Miller offered. "We gave him morphine."

"I know he wasn't in pain when he died," Long added. "When he was taking his last breath and just letting it out, he was not in any pain. He seemed to be at peace. And the nurses and the doctor that was on the floor with him worked, I mean, like, you know, banshees to try to save Paul. And, when he passed away, it was no pain, no crying or yelling out. It was just peace, like he went to sleep."

Miller and Long left The Wall in fine spirits. Just seeing each other after all those years gave them a big boost, and Trina Judson calling them heroes in the Johnson family's eyes helped a lot. But Ricky Miller still felt he had some unfinished business in New Haven, Kentucky; he wanted to visit Paul Johnson's grave and say his farewell. It ate at his gut.

Sometime after her meeting, Trina Judson told her Aunt Maggie about it and put her in touch with Miller on Facebook. She got him to promise he would return to Kentucky.

Worrying about going back wasn't as bad as the aftermath of his first visit, when he left the cemetery without getting out of his car. That experience—and his anxiety about it—had drained him terribly. The buildup of stress about the trip to visit his friend's family was so intense that he developed Bell's palsy a day or two afterward, and the paralysis of the facial muscles it caused made the left side of his face sag dramatically for months.

He didn't realize until August 2015 that the family members he saw on that first trip were related to a different soldier with a similar name. Miller had never actually met any of his friend's ten brothers and sisters.

He has now, but even all these years later, it wasn't easy.

Miller, sixty-five, and battling several serious health problems traceable to his combat experience, vowed to return to Kentucky to visit his lost friend's grave and meet with any of Paul Johnson's family members who wanted to see him. Maggie Jackson, three years younger than Paul and still devoted to the memory of her big brother, rounded up all but one of her nine surviving siblings to welcome him.

Miller and his wife Ruby drove nearly 1,000 miles from their home in Clyde, Texas, to meet Paul's family on the forty-sixth anniversary of that awful day in the A Shau. Without Ruby's encouragement and support, Miller said, he would not have been able to go through with it. In his hotel room before going to meet the family, he lay on the bed, struggling with his torn feelings, doubting he was capable of getting up and going to the restaurant where Paul's relatives would be waiting. Ruby helped him get there.

"They were very appreciative," Miller said afterward. "I was thinking they'd be mad at me. The reason I never went back: I thought it was my fault that he died." But instead, the Johnson family greeted him as a hero, the warrior who wouldn't abandon his friend and got their brother back to be buried at home and not left behind as missing in action. Maggie Jackson, the sister who had posted her unrequited appeal on the web all those years before, escorted the couple to BJ's Steakhouse in nearby Bardstown for a celebratory dinner and hours of exchanging memories.

There were presents and pictures and plenty of talk. Brother Jesse makes wine and gave the Millers two bottles of his best. His wife made a batch of her special salsa. Maggie was proudest of her present, a period box that she found with her granddaughter at Goodwill. The granddaughter thought it contained a French harp and asked if she could see it. When the box was opened, they found a Vietnam War commemorative knife with a Huey helicopter emblazoned across the yellow field and three red stripes of the South Vietnamese flag and Vietnam veterans' service ribbon.

"It melted my heart," the kid sister said.

The next day, Maggie and Ruby accompanied Miller to the cemetery and showed him where Paul Johnson was buried. Then they left him alone to be with his friend.

27

PETER MARIN

Living in Moral Pain

Two years ago I was asked by a magazine editor to write an essay on the Vietnam films that were then beginning to appear. Searching for a way to measure the quality and accuracy of the films, I began to talk to Vietnam veterans. What I found both astonished and moved me: a world of moral pain and seriousness that put to shame not only the films in question but also the way most Americans deal with their moral relation to the world around them. The films I was supposedly concerned with ceased to concern me; what became important, and what I eventually wrote about, was the vets themselves. They absorbed me not only in themselves but also for the questions their difficulties raised about the capacity of our society to deal with the psychological and ethical problems that beset them.[1]

Those questions are not easily exhausted, and I have found them again on my mind these days as America's attention has turned back, grudgingly, to the vets. The veterans, still angered by the way they are treated, have grown increasingly vocal, increasingly visible, refusing to vanish into the past with the war.

---

1. Editors' note: This groundbreaking essay by journalist Peter Marin is reprinted here as it was first published in 1981 and as it has been reprinted multiple times since. While it addressed veterans of a war that "ended" over four decades ago, it remains enlightening and foundational at its core. While not using the term "Moral Injury," Marin spoke pointedly and with deep wisdom and compassion to the moral wounds inflicted and spiritual wreckage left by war.

Their public complaints are varied and familiar: the paucity of their benefits; the weakness in the programs designed for them; the ingratitude and indifference of their fellow citizens; the red tape and bureaucratic foul-ups in VA assistance; the unwillingness of the government to recognize its responsibility for many of their problems, including the effects of Agent Orange and what psychologists now label the "delayed-stress syndrome."

All of those complaints have validity. But something about them, and about the response being made to them, seems to me as inadequate as the films I was asked to review. *Time* magazine's cover story on the vets this past summer is typical of the response. It portrayed the vets as victims of the society that sent them to war, and said that the solution to their problems was increased acceptance and gratitude here at home. Left unsaid in such analyses are two crucial aspects of the vets' suffering that no one seems to want to confront. The first seems to me to be the unacknowledged source of much of the vets' pain and anger: profound moral distress, arising from the realization that one has committed acts with real and terrible consequences. And the second is the inadequacy of the prevailing cultural wisdom, models of human nature, and modes of therapy to explain moral pain or provide ways of dealing with it. Of course, many vets have problems directly traceable to other sources, and no doubt there are vets who are not disturbed in any way by their participation in the war.

Yet the fact remains that in private conversations with many disturbed vets, one begins to sense beneath the surface of their resentment the deep and unacknowledged roots of their anger. That is not only my experience. In the past several months a number of men and women who work with vets in clinics and rap groups have told me that both the war stories related by the vets and their explicit concerns have begun to change, revealing more and more clearly their moral distress.

Shad Meshad, western coordinator for the veterans' Outreach Program, put it this way: "We aren't just counselors; we're almost priests. They come to us for absolution as well as help."

A psychologist put it more explicitly: "Day in and day out, now, we hear stories about atrocities and slaughter, things we didn't hear before. Why men were silent before and now speak remains a mystery to me. But something has changed, and sometimes you hear almost more than you can stand. It is, I swear, like being in Germany after World War II."

It is no accident that the war in Vietnam, by far the most morally suspect war America has fought in modern times, has raised the most problems for those who fought it. Some of the problems can be ascribed to the vets' youthfulness, to the unfamiliar horrors of a guerrilla war, and to the fact that the ambiguity of American attitudes toward the war has indeed denied the vets gratitude and help they feel they deserve.

But none of these considerations should obscure the fact that what they now suffer is essentially the result of the bitter reality that caused the schisms here at home—the very nature of the war: what the veterans saw and did in Vietnam, the war's excessive brutality and cruelty, and the arbitrary violence with which we fought it. True, stories similar to those that have emerged from Vietnam occasionally surfaced after World War II and the Korean War. But one would probably have to go back to the American Indian wars to find something similar to the treatment of the civilian populations in Vietnam, and even then the extent of gratuitous violence might not be comparable.

There were two fundamental kinds of violence:

The first was programmatic, large-scale, widespread, and intentional—policies established at various levels of command. It included the conscious and wholesale slaughter of civilian populations, something that other nations (and war critics at home) perceived as genocide. The precedent for this kind of violence was set decades ago, during the World War II fire-bombing of Dresden, when civilian, not military sites became targets. In Vietnam, the policy was extended further; in the name of ending the war and protecting "innocent" soldiers, the administration punished "guilty" civilians, choosing as a conscious strategy the murder of noncombatants. Of course, that did not happen everywhere. Many of the US commanders and troops attempted to distinguish between civilians and combatants—as difficult as such a task is in the midst of guerrilla warfare—and to observe the ordinary "rules" of war. But far more often than Americans like to realize, those rules were broken, and the war literature indicates they were broken more often by the Americans than by the Vietnamese; as a nation, we were guilty of acts that would have appeared to most Americans, had they been committed by others, as barbaric.

The second kind of violence was more sporadic, arbitrary, and individualized, ranging from large-scale but apparently spontaneous massacres, such as those at My Lai, to the kinds of "recreational" violence in which a GI, just for the fun of it, might gun down a woman crossing a field or a child at the side of the road. How much of that went on is not clear, and we will probably never have an accurate picture of it, but stories abound. One cannot read through books like Gloria Emerson's *Winners and Losers* or the interviews in Mark Baker's *Nam* without coming upon several examples every few pages. Most veterans have stories of this sort. Few of them talk about their own actions, but there is always something they have seen, something a buddy described. What the stories reveal is that many of our soldiers acted as if they had been granted an implicit permission to act out at will, upon an entire population, gratuitous acts of violence.

One cannot tell how many soldiers were involved, nor how many now suffer psychological and emotional disturbances from their involvement. Even the number of Americans who served in Vietnam remains in doubt. Whereas the figure was once estimated as 2.5 million, it has now been revised upward to 4 million. Studies suggest that one out of five veterans has been severely affected by stress, which would put the figure at 800,000, and researchers and therapists seem to agree that perhaps 50,000 need immediate help. But whatever the figures, no one who speaks to many distressed vets can doubt that their involvement in the excessive violence of Vietnam is a fundamental source of their inner turmoil, and that it expresses not just psychological stress but moral pain.

It is here that our collective wisdom fails the vets, here that our dominant approaches to human nature and our prevailing modes of therapy prove inadequate. We seem as a society to have few useful ways to approach moral pain or guilt; it remains for us a form of neurosis or a pathological symptom, something to escape rather than something to learn from, a disease rather than—as it may well be for the vets—an appropriate if painful response to the past. As if he were reading my thoughts, a VA psychologist told me that he and his colleagues never dealt with problems of guilt. Nor did they raise the question of what the vets did in the war: "We treat the vets' difficulties as problems in adjustment."

That is true, I suspect, of most of the help the vets receive, save for what they and the therapists closest to them have begun to develop in their own rap groups and clinics, where they have been struggling for a decade to discover and describe the nature of their problems. Yet even within that struggle there are difficulties.

By now, a rather extensive body of written work pertaining to the vets exists: at least fifteen new papers were presented just at the American Psychological Association convention last August [1981]. Most of the literature hinges on the notion of what is called the "delayed-stress syndrome," a term whose widespread use arose in connection with the Vietnam veterans: the psychological and emotional disturbances that, well after the war's end, emerge in men who previously seemed unscathed. The concept is an important and useful one; no doubt there is a syndrome of symptoms and behaviors that appears several months or years after the war and that can be attributed, retrospectively, to its stresses. Such symptoms, all observers agree, include flashbacks, nightmares, uncontrollable anger, paranoia, anxiety, and depression.

But many researchers also extend the range of symptoms to include a variety of cither emotional states—among them, feelings of guilt, perception of oneself as a scapegoat, alienation from one's feelings, an inability to trust or love. It is there that the trouble begins, for such symptoms are less persuasively attributable directly to the war, especially when they appear individually and not as a set of interrelated symptoms; one suspects that in many cases their classification as delayed stress obfuscates the real nature of the veterans' experience.

Let me give an example. Imagine (as is often the case) a particular vet who has seen close up not only the horrors of war but forms of human desperation, suffering, and tenacity that are altogether different from what he had seen before. He comes home sensing a relation between the nation's policies and the complex reality he has witnessed, between our privilege here and the suffering elsewhere in thc world. Is it surprising that such a man, having seen his own comrades senselessly killed and reflecting upon the moral illegitimacy of the killing he himself has done, would find it increasingly difficult to come to terms with the "normal" life he left behind? How would the moral smugness and obliviousness of American life strike him? How would expensive restaurants strike him, the talk about interest rates, or even TV commercials?

No doubt such a man would be "irritable," would be angry, would find himself at odds with things, unable to resume his previous job, pursuits, or relationships. But to call all such problems "delayed stress" or to see them as explicable only in terms of the war would be to misstate the condition entirely; it would in effect avoid the real significance of the vet's condition, would void it in some way. Similarly, seemingly precise analytic terms for repressed guilt—"impacted grief," for one—and theories about psychological denial become systems of denial, a massive, unconscious cover-up in which both those who fought and those who did not hide from themselves the true nature of the experience the terms are supposedly identifying.

Reading through the literature on the vets, one notices again and again the ways in which various phrases and terms are used to empty the vets' experience of moral content, to defuse and bowdlerize it. Particularly in the early literature, one feels a kind of madness at work. Repugnance toward killing and the refusal to kill are routinely called "acute combat reaction," and the effects of slaughter and atrocity are called "stress," as if the clinicians describing the vets are talking about an executive's overwork or a hysterical housewife's blood pressure. Nowhere in the literature is one allowed to glimpse what is actually occurring: the real horror of the war and its effect on those who fought it. Much of this masking seems to have its root in the war itself, when the army psychiatrists charged with keeping the troops in the mood for killing treated as a pathology any rebellion against orders or the refusal to kill.

Such attitudes persist. Some VA therapists are now talking about the need to "deresponsibilize" their patients—that is, get the Vietnam vets to attribute their actions to external causes rather than moral choice. Those who mention guilt usually describe it as "survivor's" guilt—shame not for what was done, but for having outlived one's comrades—or hurriedly attribute guilt to "the expression of aggressive impulses," by which one can only assume they mean the slaughter of innocents. Even a sympathetic observer like John A. Wilson, a psychologist whose perceptive and sensitive work on stress was put into my hands by vets who found it important, manages to render the moral aspect of the war less important than it is. Wilson ascribes most of the vets' pain to the truncation of the "normal" development of the ego; drawing on the work of Erik Erikson, he uses a table that connects stressful experiences to "qualities of ego-development and personality integration," listing eleven stress-producing events. The eighth reads, in its entirety, "Death of Buddies and Atrocities." A single entry treats the death of one's friends and performing or witnessing atrocities as if they were all more or less the same thing or had the same moral or psychological impact.

There are, of course, several worthy authors who go beyond such thinking. Robert Jay Lifton's work comes first to mind, if only because his book *Home from the War* (1974), published relatively early, has had a more powerful impact on other therapists than any other work. Lifton has been largely responsible for the idea of the vets as victims, and there is no doubt that he radically changed the way others saw the veterans' experiences.

There are others, too, who come to mind: Chaim Shatan, B. W. Gault, Arthur Egendorf, Arthur Blank, Bill Mahedy, Robert Laufer, and Jack Smith. These men have either written about the war or worked extensively with vets; often, they have done both. One can see in their work a moral deepening that seeks but has not yet found a completed form, a language and perception that will do justice to the realities of moral experience.

Why has most psychological thinking about Vietnam avoided the issue of judgment? There are several reasons. Much of the research on Vietnam veterans has been funded by government agencies or by veterans' organizations. Several psychiatrists who work with the vets have told me that in this area as in any other, researchers tend to look for results and frame findings that will keep their funding sources happy. Then, too, many of those writing about the vets are devoted to them; they want to see them get whatever they need from the government, and they feel that the best way to get such help is to portray the vets as victims, by locating the source of their troubles in the war itself. One also suspects that many shy away from the question of moral pain simply because it is likely to open up areas of pain for which there is really nothing like a "cure." As one therapist told me regarding the atrocities and attendant shame that were sometimes discussed in his rap group: "That, my friend, is the hardest thing to deal with. When somebody brings it up, we all fall silent. Nobody knows how in hell to handle it."

Beyond those reasons lies perhaps the most significant one of all: that of the limits of the discipline itself, the inadequacy of psychological categories and language in describing the nature and pain of human conscience. The truth is, much of our confusion in regard to therapy and moral pain stems from the therapeutic tradition itself.

A strain of moral sensibility and conscience was always present in the work of Freud. But it is also true that two elements combined in his work to separate considerations of psychological health from moral or social concerns. The first was the need to isolate the self in the therapeutic process from its complex familial or social connections in order to see it clearly and deal effectively with it. What began as a useful fiction gradually hardened into a central motif or approach: the self in therapy is characteristically seen as separate and discrete from what surrounds it—an isolated unit complete in itself, relatively unaffected by anything but inner or familial experience. Secondly, morality itself was often treated in Freud's work as a form of social intervention or outside imposition, something fundamentally alien to the individual ego. There were good reasons for his view, of course—most notably the heavy and oppressive German morality of the times and the obviously destructive dissonance between inner human life and the regulated social order established around it. Nonetheless, in its justifiable accent upon human need as opposed to social obligation, psychoanalysis established habits of thought that have now been honed in America into a morally vacuous view of human nature.

Our great therapeutic dream in America is that the past is escapable, that suffering can be avoided, that happiness is always possible, and that insight inevitably leads to joy. But life's lessons—so much more apparent in literature than in therapy—teach us something else again, something that is both true of, and applicable to, the experience of the vets. Try as they do to escape it, the past pursues them; the closer they come to the truth of their acts, the more troubled they are, the more apart they find themselves, and the more tragic becomes their view of life.

The veterans' situation is Oedipus' situation—not for the reasons Freud chose, but because it reveals to us the irreversibility of certain kinds of knowledge, the power of certain actions and perceptions to change an individual's life beyond any effort to change it back. Oedipus saw and was blinded, came close to the truth and lost the world of men, and once in exile he suffered not so much because of what he had done, but because of what he learned he had done: the terrible and tragic knowledge deprived him of the company both of men and of gods.

Such knowledge has come to many vets too. What they know is this: The world is real; the suffering of others is real; one's actions can sometimes irrevocably determine the destiny of others; the mistakes one makes are often transmuted directly into others' pain; there is sometimes no way to undo that pain—the dead remain dead, the maimed are forever maimed, and there is no way to deny one's responsibility or culpability, for those mistakes are written, forever and as if in fire, in others' flesh.

Though this is perhaps a terrible and demanding wisdom, it is no more and no less than what all men should know; it is the ethical lesson life teaches those who attend to the consequences of their actions. But because our age is what it is and because most Americans flee from such knowledge, this wisdom is especially hard for the vets to bear. Though it ought to bring them deeper into the human community, it isolates them instead, sets them irrevocably apart, locks them simultaneously into a seriousness and a silence that are as much a cause of pain as are their past actions. They become suffering pariahs not only because of what they have done but because of the questions it raises for them—questions that their countrymen do not want to confront, questions for which, as a society, we have no answers.

A few months ago, after I had talked about guilt and the war to a group of vets, professors, and students, a vet came up to me.

"I left in the middle of your talk," he said angrily. "What you were saying didn't make sense. I feel no guilt. There was no right or wrong over there. All of that is nonsense. It was a dream. That's how I leave it behind. I don't let it bother me. I couldn't understand what you were saying."

Yet he had returned to register his complaint, and as he spoke to me, his eyes filled with tears. There was a grief revealed by his gaze that he could not admit to me, nor perhaps even to himself, possibly because he had little hope of finding a useful way to deal with it. I suspect that its release, or at least its acknowledgment, would have radically changed him, radically changed his relation to the world; but it made itself felt instead as a refusal to consider the past in any moral way at all. I have now talked to enough vets to know that for many of them— though by no means for all—hopelessness lay behind the tears that neither one of us mentioned.

So, in responding, I chose to broaden the question of responsibility, arguing that, yes, the vets were guilty, but many of us had been guilty also, and that we were guilty not only for the war, but for countless public and private acts whose consequences had been pain or suffering for others. It was all of us, I tried to say, who ought to struggle to come to terms with human fallibility and culpability. The vets were not alone in that, or ought not to be alone in that. It was a struggle all men should share. At that, he relaxed. The tears were still there, but more obvious now, less masked. His voice was softer and less truculent.

"I see what you mean," he said, "but you didn't say that before. I can understand what you're saying now." I had said it before, but I had said it in a way that made it impossible for him to listen, for in making the guilt his alone, or in making it sound as if it were his alone, I had deprived him of precisely the kind of community and good company that make it possible for people to see themselves clearly. What he needed, as do all the vets, was not only a way of thinking and speaking about his life, but the willingness of others to consider their lives in the same way.

This is precisely the point at which the failure of therapy becomes tragic, and it is at this point that the future task of therapy becomes clear: to see life once again in a context that includes the reality of moral experience and assigns a moral significance to human action. It may be that certain acts and certain kinds of guilt set men irrevocably apart from their fellows: Oedipus, after all, entered a realm in which the common wisdom was of no use to him. But one cannot help feeling that this is not the case with the vets, and that the isolation they feel has as much to do with our corrupt view of human nature as it does with their past actions. The moral anguish they feel, as intense as it gets, is in many cases simply an extreme form of certain painful experiences that would be entirely familiar to us if we paid as much attention to moral life in our therapies as we do to other forms of behavior.

What the problems of the vets ought to point toward are several categories of moral experience ignored in therapy but applicable to all men and women, and familiar to many of them. Those categories, if we could bring them to bear on the problems of the vets, would be of immense use in illuminating their torment. Beyond that, it would educate us all about the psychological consequences of the moral pain that their problems reveal.

The first category of moral pain is the common notion of "bad conscience," a person's reaction to past actions he or she finds inexcusable or inexplicable. Bad conscience causes the individual pain, shame, and guilt, and demands a way of setting right what has been done. But it goes beyond this reaction, approximating what Sartre, in Being and Nothingness, called "bad faith": the underlying and general sense of having betrayed what you feel you ought to have been.

We are familiar with that feeling in the emotional realm; we know how those who settle for emotional or sexual lives that do not satisfy them, or those who sacrifice desire to fear, can feel humiliated and depleted or experience an almost organic shame. In some way, at some level, they know their lives to be a lie. The same apprehension can be true in the moral realm; we can experience in the present a pain engendered by past actions that seem to us reprehensible, and to the extent that we merely try to outlive such events, forgetting or ignoring them, we may indeed feel ourselves to be guilty of a kind of bad faith—of breaking a covenant not only with others or with God, but with our own nature.

It seems to me that is the experience of many Americans who cannot help measuring in their minds their privileged condition and the way they choose to spend their lives against the varieties of need, deprivation, and pain they see around them. Many of us suffer a vague, inchoate sense of betrayal, of having somehow taken a wrong turning, of having somehow said yes or no at the wrong time and to the wrong things, of having somehow taken upon ourselves a peculiar and general kind of guilt, having two coats while others have none, or just having too much while others have too little—and yet proceeding, nonetheless, with our lives as they are.

How much more painful, then, are such feelings for the vets, for in Vietnam, the consequences of their actions were irreversible and concrete suffering or death. Any response to those events save one that arises from an individual's deepest sense of debt or justice is likely to leave a person mired in bad faith.

The second category of moral pain has to do with what might be called "the world's pain"—the way we internalize and experience as our own the disorder, suffering, and brutality around us. Some people take on the pain of others as a personal burden; external suffering mixes with their own immediate emotional experience in a way that often makes it difficult to sort out what has been produced by one and what by the other. We can call it empathy if we want to, but it goes well beyond a specific response to a particular person's particular misfortune. It can take the form of a pervasive sense of suffering, injustice, and evil—a response to the world's condition that produces a feeling of despair, disgust, or even a sort of radical species-shame, in which one is simultaneously ashamed of oneself and one's kind.

Who can forget the images of John F. Kennedy falling in the open car or of the young female student at Kent State kneeling above her fallen comrade, her mouth open in a scream? And who cannot remember the televised images from Saigon of South Vietnamese soldiers crowding into the last planes to leave, the women and children clinging to them and falling through the air as they took off? The horror one feels in relation to such sights can be traumatic and perhaps permanent; it works in ways we do not understand, depriving us not of self-esteem but of something equally important to the ego's health: a sense of a habitable world and of trustworthy human connections.

Often this response to suffering is hidden away, repressed, or ignored; it eats at people from the inside out, but because they feel helpless in the face of what causes it, they try as best they can to ignore it or try to solve it in ways that have nothing to do with its causes. Much of the apparent "selfishness" at work in America, the tendency to turn inward toward self, is not a function of greed; it is instead an attempt to alleviate pain and guilt by turning away, by giving up the world—at least in terms of conscience.

Time and again one hears vets say about the war and its issues: "It don't mean nothin." They struggle to empty the past of meaning—not because they are hardened to what happened or because it does mean nothing, but because it is the only way they can preserve sanity in its shadow.

The veterans have seen in themselves and in their comrades behavior that visits upon them truths about human nature and human suffering that will (and should) remain with them for the rest of their lives, calling into question the thin surface of orderliness they see around them. They suffer now, in a bitter way for which we have no words, the brute condition of the human world, which is for them neither an abstraction nor an idea; it is, rather, what they know, how they feel, who they are. Their grief, akin to Oedipus', or to Buddha's at the sight of suffering, or to Christ's at human evil, is far more than a therapeutic problem; it raises instead, for each of them, the fundamental questions of how to live, who to be.

Here we come to the third category of moral pain: the way most of us suffer when we cannot act out in the world our response to the suffering we have seen in it.

In the past several decades, therapy has concentrated on analyzing individual pain or frustration in terms of loss and deprivation: how needs for warmth or love have gone unanswered. The therapeutic answer to that condition, which makes a certain sense, has been to teach us how to get what we want.

But in concentrating on that aspect of pain we have underestimated the ways in which we suffer when we cannot find how to express our love, to give back to the world in some generous way what it is we feel toward it. Morality, argued Kropotkin, is simply "an overflow of vitality." He meant that it is a natural and unconscious response to the world, a sort of natural gratitude engendered by the interplay of private energies and the surrounding reality. In such a view, there is no such thing as feeling separate from action; each response to the world naturally becomes and demands a gesture. But when the process is not fully completed, when it is truncated, we experience a sense of loss and humiliation, a sense of depletion akin to what we feel when rejected in love or frustrated in desire.

A few months ago, I attended a meeting of vets, academics, and therapists in which we were supposedly discussing "the healing process." The discussion had been rather dry and constrained until one vet began to speak. He had been in the war, he said, though not in combat. Coming back from it had been hard, and his feelings about it had grown stronger since its end; nothing had seemed right, he was unable to settle down or come to terms with life, but he seemed unable to explain why.

"I'm an artist," he said. "A sculptor. At least that's what I've been doing lately. Coming home from the war, I saw huge piles of shell-casings. And a couple of years ago I realized that I wanted to use them to make a gigantic sculpture. Something to commemorate the dead, to let people know what the war had been like. For years I tried to get those casings. But they wouldn't let me have them. They were being recycled, they said, to make new shells. . . ."

And suddenly he was shaking and weeping, unable to go on, crying, as vets will, at the impossibility of explaining to others what drives them.

Later he came over to talk to me. "I don't know how to explain it," he said. "I keep thinking that if I could do this one thing, if I could just get it, if I could make this one thing, then somehow it would be all right, they'd see, they'd know, and then it wouldn't happen again."

This impulse is, in essence, what one finds unacknowledged in many of the vets, and the inability to act upon it drives them deeper into distress than they were when they first emerged from the war. We know how imprisonment affects animals, how they are affected by the loss of space and freedom. Often they sicken and die. The same things happen to men and women, but we are far more complicated creatures, inhabiting history as well as nature. When we cannot act in history, when our response to the world around us cannot be spoken or acted on, we suffer inside—as do the vets—a set of experiences for which we have no psychological name.

Most good therapy, Paul Goodman once said, cutting pragmatically to the heart of the matter, is a combination of a whorehouse and an employment agency. What he meant is that if it did not teach people how to make lives for themselves embracing useful work and good loving, it did no one much good. The same thing can be said in relation to the vets. Somewhere along the line, therapy must enter those areas in which the therapist and patient become comrades, where what has been discovered about one's own experience and its related pain raises questions not only about psychological wholeness but also about moral responsibility: What to do, what to be, how to love? Though no one can solve these problems for another, it is safe to say that no one will be much use to the vets without taking these questions seriously and understanding that at the heart of each life and satisfaction lie fundamental moral questions about choice, responsibility, and the doing of good that must be answered with action that comes from one's deepest commitments.

There is one last point that must be made not only about the encounter between therapists and patients but also about any contemporary "helping" relationship (teacher and student, for example) that involves the shared re-definition of reality. For decades now, we have considered Buber's "I-thou" relationship the ideal model: a respectful intimacy in which the integrity of the other is not violated as the other's nature is fully perceived, understood, and embraced. No doubt all of that is necessary and good. But it is also mor-ally insufficient. It is incomplete. For it does not fully take into account the inevitable presence of the invisible others, the distant witnesses: those who have suffered our past acts and those who may suffer them in the future.

The proper consideration for therapists and vets, for all therapists and all Americans, is "I-thou-they": the recognition that whatever we do or do not do in our encounters, whatever we forget or remember, whatever truths we keep alive or lies we fabricate will help form a world inhabited by others. Our actions will play a significant part in defining not only the social and moral life of our own people, but the future of countless and distant others as well, whose names we will not know and whose faces we will not see until perhaps, a decade from now, other American children view them through the sights of guns. The responsibility of the therapist, then, neither begins nor ends with the individual client; and the client's responsibility neither begins nor ends with himself or herself. Both extend far outward, from the past into the future, to countless other lives.

Whether a consideration of all these elements will make a difference to the vets is not at all clear. It may well be that many of them will be forced to live with certain kinds of pain and regret for the rest of their lives, though one can hope that they will be successful enough to turn the truths of the past to some use, becoming the keepers and bearers of those truths rather than the victims. What is clear is that their psychic well-being will depend in large part upon their capacity to resolve the issues of conscience that haunt them. Whatever skills or comfort they manage to salvage from tradi-tional therapy, they will have to see through to the end, and largely on their own, the moral journey that they began in Vietnam.

One can hope that the rest of us will accompany them when we can and follow them when we should; and that perhaps out on the edges of acknowledged experience, in those regions of the self into which the vets have been led and for which we have few words and little wisdom, therapy will regain a part of the seriousness that has so far eluded it and move a bit closer to coming of age.

Chaplains

The Colonels or Commanding officers of each regiment are directed to procure Chaplains accordingly; persons of good Characters and exemplary lives—To see that all inferior officers and soldiers pay them a suitable respect and attend carefully upon religious exercises. The blessing and protection of Heaven are at all times necessary but especially so in times of public distress and danger—The General hopes and trusts, that every officer and man, will endeavor so to live, and act, as becomes a Christian Soldier defending the dearest Rights and Liberties of his country.

—George Washington, Headquarters, New York, July 9, 1776

A chaplain is the minister of the Prince of Peace serving the host of the God of War—Mars. As such, he is as incongruous as a musket would be on the altar at Christmas. Why, then, is he there? Because he indirectly subserves the purpose attested by the cannon; because too he lends the sanction of the religion of the meek to that which practically is the abrogation of everything but brute Force.
—Herman Melville

28

TOM FRAME

Moral Injury and the Influence of Christian Religious Conviction

Despite the decline of religious conviction in many Western nations over the past thirty years, Christian moral theology has had a continuing influence on attitudes toward armed conflict and military service, the responsibilities of the state, and the duties of individuals. While surveys continue to show remarkably high levels of Christian affiliation but remarkably low levels of Christian adherence, I would contend that the majority of Westerners would assent to the existence of a being they would readily refer to as God. What they do with or about that belief is uncertain. But I would assert that belief in a transcendent being whose existence is relevant to the way the world is ordered has a bearing on the construction of value systems and the exercise of moral judgments. I would also argue that most Western uniformed personnel have embraced a form of Christian anthropology (a religious vision of the human person) and, whether or not they are conscious of their religious commitments or spiritual sensitivities, they retain the capacity for their soul (their capacity to experience the numinous, the transcendent, the eternal, and the divine) to suffer injuries that will leave them with unseen wounds.

Of the many other unseen wounds sustained by uniformed personnel during deployments, interest has naturally returned to the incidence of Moral Injury. I use the word "returned," because there is evidence in ancient texts that war was considered a morally alienating experience, irrespective of whether it was an offensive or defensive campaign, and that returning warriors needed to undergo a moral cleansing after their experience to recover their moral self ahead of re-entering a moral community. The thought that deploying personnel might incur some form of Moral Injury is unsurprising. In fact, it is rather obvious. The thought that someone might be unaffected by killing other human beings and destroying their property, that someone would be indifferent to a personal encounter with civil chaos and endemic poverty (such as in Somalia), political violence and political "gangsterism" (such as in Cambodia), is actually more surprising. In fact, it is worrying. The idea that observing the outcomes of genocide and ethnic cleansing might not distort a person's faith in humanity is almost impossible to believe. But a person can be affected by these experiences without suffering from a mental disorder in need of treatment. Our society expects them to be affected. The interpretation of their experiences and their integration into a personal narrative has become critical to our understanding and appreciation of Moral Injury. It may be, for instance, that the effects of their experiences become the foundations not just for personal maturing but a fuller and more candid account of what it means to be human in the twenty-first century. We need to consider the possibility that some returning personnel may have a better developed sense of what is important in life and why, than those who send them or welcome them home.

This essay outlines the place and importance of religious convictions in considering why and how uniformed personnel may suffer Moral Injury in the course of their service. It contends that theology can contribute to understanding Moral Injury in terms of interpreting its causes, distilling its essence, and resolving its consequences.

From Advocacy to Opposition

In contrast to the World Wars of 1914–1918 and 1939–1945 when most churches and many theologians lent their support to the Allied cause, by 1950 there was a distinct shift in mood and mindset drawn from a new attitude to the nation-state, namely that nationalism needed to be overcome or, at least transcended, because its expression was so destructive. This led to the rise of institutions like the United Nations and the World Council of Churches. The theologians who had once found ways of justifying, if not promoting, wars now struggled to give any account of human life in which war could be rationalized. Discussion of war and military service became more nuanced and complicated as theologians questioned the moral authority of the state and the enduring moral obligations of uniformed individuals. The near universal support for collective defense before 1945 changed with the rise of nationalist movements in former European colonies, doubts about whether Communism was intrinsically evil, and uncertainty about the Soviet Union's actual intentions in Europe and in Asia. This created the space for churches to contribute to community forums and political debates on the moral quality of Western diplomacy and the ethical character of armed conflict. The suspicion that the political parties of all persuasions were using the armed forces for political expediency and economic advantage gained momentum throughout the 1960s.

The escalation of Western involvement in the Vietnam Conflict after 1962 was coupled with the rise of individualism and the decline of reliance upon institutions, including the churches, to give guidance on ethical questions and moral dilemmas. Now individuals would decide for themselves what was right. People no longer needed to rely on the corporate conscience; they could determine their own moral values and decide on their own moral conventions. Churches were deemed unworthy of the trust placed in them because they were patriarchal, authoritarian, and puritanical. This trend in thinking worried many Western militaries who responded by introducing character guidance training and, later, character leadership training, devised and delivered by chaplains. Morals and ethics were tied closely to religious convictions. Men with strong religious foundations and clear Christian convictions would be better able to resist indoctrination should they be captured and become prisoners of communist regimes.[1]

The other major aim of character training was to reinforce the moral quality of uniformed service. At a time when armed forces found it difficult to recruit young men—mostly because there was full employment in the civilian sector and service wages were poor, but also because peacetime uniformed service was less appealing to potential recruits—many militaries believed they needed to restate and reinforce traditional messages about the worthiness of military service. This need became acute in countries like Australia and the United States after 1965, when community campaigns against conscription and Western involvement in the Vietnam Conflict had the potential to destabilize the armed forces by encouraging dissent and eroding morale.[2] Uniformed chaplains played a vital role in providing a set of theological constructs that attempted to lift the conversation from political dispute to moral virtue. As the level of formal religious adherence began to decline in the 1960s, there were demonstrable departures from

1. Gladwin, *Captains of the Soul*, 235–37.

2. See Forward and Reece, eds., *Conscription in Australia*, and J. M. Main, ed., *Conscription: The Australian Debate.*

some elements of Christian social teaching (such as those regulating relationships), but the values and virtues that were associated with character, and the attributes and aspirations connected to personality, remained intact over the next three decades.

Ironically, throughout the same period (1960–1990) the churches moved from being the most vehement advocates of armed conflict and supporters of military service to being the most strident opponents of the use of force in any political or diplomatic setting. There was also a growing reluctance to provide clergy for service as chaplains. By the time Iraq invaded Kuwait in August 1990, the churches were hosting the most vocal critics of any armed response to unprovoked Iraqi aggression.[3] The institution that had once played a vital role in imparting moral legitimacy to war was at the forefront of denouncing its inherent immorality.

In this context military leaders were caught in a bind. They could not comment publicly on political opposition to operations in places like Afghanistan and Iraq because such commentary would have attracted complaints of political partisanship. The moral condemnation of the churches and others was essentially ignored on two grounds. First, the inculcation of moral principles for the express purpose of rebutting moral opposition would have resembled indoctrination and proved controversial. Second, because morals were now deemed to be personal and, therefore, private matters, they could not be prescribed or mandated by any government agency. This left a reliance on legality as a guide to morality. If it was legal it was probably moral or, at least, possibly not immoral. But legality is a very poor guide to morality, partly because it does not deal with the moral conscience and partly because it does not contend with human feelings. An action can be legal but immoral, and the fact of an action being deemed legal does not help a person who feels, or worse knows, that they have acted immorally either by their own standards or by a consensus of their peers. This observation points to the difficulty of defining and dealing with Moral Injury in a post-Christian, secular society: there are so many unanswered questions, and so many answers that are highly problematic, because they are essentially polemic.

---

3. *Church Scene*, a national Australian Anglican newspaper, and *The Record*, a Perth-based Roman Catholic publication, contained denunciations of any use of force in Kuwait by an international coalition. See for example the editorial and contributor articles in *Church Scene*, 2 November 1990.

Morality and Its Subject Matter Experts

When the armed forces accept they have a responsibility for the moral well-being of their members, what does that actually mean beyond an overarching duty of care? And if military leadership accepts that uniformed personnel possess moral principles that inhabit a moral self that acts with a moral framework directed by a moral compass, who has responsibility for this component of their well-being? These are not straightforward matters because they presuppose answers to a series of questions that continue to occupy the minds of philosophers and theologians. These questions include: What is morality and what are its origins? Is moral sensitivity innate to a person or is it acquired? Who is entitled to prescribe morality and on what authority does their prescription stand? Is there a difference between conscientious beliefs and moral principles? To claim that a uniformed person can be morally injured is to presume they have a moral self to injure. And the notion of a moral self is not a value-neutral concept, and this moral self is not without content either. Values and virtues, convictions and aspirations originate from somewhere. The idea of value-neutral morality is absurd.

All morality has a pedigree. To ask the disciplines of behavioral science to exceed their self-imposed limits by postulating the contents of a moral code or prescribing the features of a moral framework is misguided and mistaken. As a discipline, psychology is not in a position to define what is morally right or wrong. It can deal with an individual's reactions to their actions, but it is not competent to make pronouncements about their intrinsic moral quality. As a value-neutral discipline, psychology needs to rely on disciplines like philosophy and theology for a descriptive narrative that includes moral judgments about an attitude or action. In any event, when an individual claims that a certain conflict was unjust, that a specific mission was opportunistic, or that a particular operation was immoral, they are drawing on ideas and insights that have evolved and developed through interactions with a range of competing visions of what it means to be human.

These ideas and insights about right and wrong are the products of political, social, cultural, and spiritual reflections. They may be inconsistent and incoherent when taken together, but they are sufficiently organized and operative to lead a person to make judgments about whether something accords or conflicts with what they deem to be moral or immoral acts. If a person is directed to act in a manner that conflicts with their sense of right and wrong; if they find themselves compelled to act in the face of wrongdoing but do nothing; if they acted with the best of intentions but find their actions led to the worst of outcomes, it is very likely that the individual's sense of themselves will be adversely affected. Why? Because the principles that gave point and purpose, and meaning and direction, to their life, have been denied or violated in such a manner and to such a degree that the person is alienated from themselves and estranged from the world. When a person finds they are living with a stranger in an alien environment, they need to be reconciled with themselves and relocated in the world. In so doing, they become someone new and the earth is effectively recreated. These are some of the causes and consequences of Moral Injury.

Death, Destruction, and the Divine Character

That people are morally injured in the course of their service should come as no surprise given that uniformed people are mandated to use lethal force and to deny adversaries material support. A deployed person does not need to see "guts and gore" to be deeply wounded when they believe they have been manipulated or mistreated by those they trusted; they do not need to observe first-hand atrocities like genocide or ethnic cleansing to have their sense of right and wrong disrupted and their conscience badly injured. Meeting those who have committed such acts, and encountering their victims, is sometimes enough to lead a person to decide that the world is evil and humanity is corrupt, and to lose trust and abandon hope. They might conclude: such a world is not worth defending; such a species is not worth protecting. Conversely, they could persuade themselves that the world is the venue for a cosmic struggle between good and evil in which the cause of good was specially entrusted to them and the persistence of evil is evidence they failed. If only they had done more; if only they had been more diligent. For others, a different kind of realization dawns: the people I am told to protect are neither my family nor my friends. I do not know their names and their faces are unfamiliar. This is not my country and will never be my home. Why should I die for them and for this place? One of the reasons that Moral Injury may be more prevalent in the modern era is that deployments are a long way from home and it is difficult to see the connection between these activities and the defense of one's own family and home. Indeed, some deployed personnel may see themselves as nothing more than state-sponsored mercenaries being paid to fight a war that has little to do with them or what they value in life.

Because most Westerners have been molded by the Christian story—a story that includes strong injunctions against killing others and destroying their property—when they are involved in activities ranging from armed conflict to humanitarian aid, both their value system and their sense of self will be affected in some way. Deployed personnel are obliged to see, hear, smell, and sometimes do what they were not designed to see, hear, smell, or do, evidenced by the involuntary revulsions that some sights, sounds, smells, and deeds elicit. This evidence would also include the theological claim that human beings are made in the image of God. Given theology's claim that God is the creator and sustainer of life and living, death and destruction are contrary to the divine character and concomitantly the source of deep disturbance for human beings. Consequently, human beings have a natural reluctance to damage and destroy because, in being fashioned in the divine image, human nature is to create and sustain. This theological claim has entered popular consciousness in the form of social commentators and judicial officials exclaiming that someone should have "known," by which they mean instinctively sensed or intuitively realized, that what they were doing was wrong when they killed a person or destroyed their property. Their sense of right and of wrong should have guided their actions because it didn't "feel right."

Human beings recoil in horror when they see their own species suffering. They wince at images of corporal and capital punishment. Television presenters issue warnings that the following report "contains images of a graphic nature." I do not think this is simply a case of *not* having become accustomed to seeing images of death and destruction. What is seen offends against a proper sense of self and human life. There is, then, general agreement with theology's injunction against murder because it destroys life and produces a murderer. There are echoes of this agreement in campaigns against capital punishment. While this outlook can be attributed to nurture or evolution or conditioning, a universality about the principle of not harming others transcends and in some cases even defies cultural conventions.

It may be, then, that when individuals are placed in environments where the values and virtues that ordered their world are absent, or when they observe actions and attitudes that are contrary to that ordering, they can be adversely affected by challenges to the story that animates their own life and that accounts for the world as it is—or should be. In effect, an environment containing toxic ideas and poisonous imperatives injures them morally. The experience is not unlike ingesting foul air—it damages everything it touches, including a person's moral conscience and spiritual well-being. It does not matter whether the person observes, for instance, cruelty and callousness and does either something or nothing, that they have observed these things is enough for their worldview to be shaken if not shattered. Where a society has lost the ability to make sound moral judgments and there are no restraints on what is considered evil; when human life is not accorded dignity and people are treated as commodities; when expectations of civilized conduct are ignored and the imposition of political will becomes paramount, the likelihood of Moral Injury is increased substantially in each instance. The extent of the injury, and the degree to which it debilitates an individual, will be influenced by whether that individual believed they did something when they should have done nothing, or did nothing when they should have done something. In other words, sins of commission and omission can exacerbate the extent and the severity of the wound.

In sum, while no one is unaffected by witnessing violence and observing evil, the experience is deeply internalized when a person feels a moral obligation to act and is not convinced their own conduct was either moral in itself, or sufficient to restore the moral order that previously made their own life predictable and acceptable. Internally, the morally injured person has a disordered values system that produces either contradictory or condemning attitudes towards self and others. Externally, the morally injured person concludes the world has no ordered values and is, therefore, without point or purpose. I would put the combined effect in Platonic terms: the injury produces a personal narrative in which truth, goodness, and beauty have lost their appeal. Without these things, human life turns into mere existence.

The situations in which Moral Injury occurs do not have to be traumatic. But the cogency and the coherence of the individual's moral outlook will be critical to determining whether the experience produces turmoil or despondency, or whether it leads to a more reasoned and nuanced framework for dealing with a world that, at times, makes no sense and which often discloses no point or purpose. I do not believe asking questions about life and living are indicators of mental health *per se*. Every person has a moral sense that can be fledgling or mature. Age is not always a determinant either. This makes me uncomfortable with any depiction of the human person that subsumes morality—that part of us which ponders the rightness and wrongness of an action and struggles to give expression to truth, beauty, and goodness—into something else.

Moral Consensus and Moral Incoherence

My account of Moral Injury relies upon the existence of moral content. There is a range of sources for moral content, and I have argued that religion is one source, since Christianity continues to have a pervasive and powerful influence on the moral being of Western uniformed personnel. But the armed forces are relying on a moral consensus that is declining, as the Christian metanarrative loses its prominence in popular culture. In addition to religious indifference, the churches have foregone much of their entitlement to speak about moral values as a result of clergy abuse scandals as well as their often uninformed and simplistic responses to the complexity of modern diplomacy and international relations. Other than chaplains, who have earned the right to speak and gained sufficient respect to be heard, uniformed personnel do not seek church counsel on any matter of morals relating to their service. If this trend continues, the existing moral consensus could be supplanted by moral incoherence. It will be difficult to generalize about Moral Injury in the absence of a common language or a shared grammar to articulate the whole realm of the inner life—including its moral dimensions. I have not mentioned, of course, the spiritual dimension, which is an integral part of religious experience and the capacity of human beings to sense the numinous, the transcendent, and the divine.

As the decline of institutionalized religion and organized spirituality continues there has been a resurgence of interest in commemorative ceremonies associated with military service. These are very ambiguous occasions. Ministers of religion often preside, but the "preacher" is a spokesman for universal (usually meaning secular) values. There are the forms of religion but little of its substance. God is mentioned but under the veil of music. There is talk of transcendence but no reassurance of resurrection. The significance of suffering and sacrifice, the redeeming features of war, is given prominence while futility and waste, the constant elements of armed conflict, are virtually ignored. The motivating desire is to ennoble what remains irretrievably ignoble: state-sanctioned murder and orchestrated savagery. The absence of opportunities for confession and absolution in government-sponsored commemorative events may eventually render them vacuous.

The notion that religion might play some part in healing people afflicted by Moral Injury will be as repugnant to some as the notion that it is a clinical condition that can be treated is to others. My contention is that Moral Injury is a human wound rather than a religious one, but inasmuch as many in uniform profess affiliation with a faith community, it would be unreasonable and unwise to deny a place for religious perspectives on the nature of the wound and the process of recovery alongside other perspectives which claim an insight in this area. The field of Moral Injury has plainly been "colonized" by psychology, and some mistakenly think that one discipline can answer every question and resolve every dilemma in addressing unseen wounds. This is certainly not the outlook of those who have contributed to this book. It would be a mistake to interpret this essay as a criticism of psychology and its practitioners, nevertheless it notes that psychology naturally has its disciplinary limits. Reducing emotions and feelings to signs or symbols of mental health is crude reductionism, and restricting one's concerns to mere "functioning" is to take an impoverished view of human potential. I am addressing this mistake in the hope that Western military establishments will take a holistic approach to Moral Injury.

29

D. WILLIAM ALEXANDER

Gregory Is My Friend

Opening note: Because the subject of this essay is so complex, because it occurs so relatively rarely, because it is so difficult—in my experience—to obtain free consent to share the stories of veterans experiencing this form of disorientation, and because it is so important for caregivers to protect intimacy gained in current and former relationships with these veterans at all costs, I am not able to provide a single illustrative vignette for discussion, as I would prefer to do. The individual whom I will call "Gregory" below is mostly based on a single veteran with whom I worked for more than seventy-five sessions, but his name and some very significant details of his story have been changed. I still write in the hope that readers will find "Gregory's" story valuable, as it is related here, because all of the commentary on my personal relationship with him is quite accurate, and is shared as something that I treasure deeply—and which has changed my life and work in important ways.

I first met Gregory while working as a psychosocial consultant near a major military installation, and I will likely never be able to forget the elusive and ethereal quality of his presence when he entered the room.[1] His long hair and beard were in disarray, his clothing hung loosely from an emaciated frame, his hands were tense and clawed, and his eyes—hung under

---

1. Gregory's name and some very significant details of his story have been changed. This has been done in order to provide both a robust illustration for discussion and protection for his identity.

arched eyebrows as if he were perpetually surprised—were at the same time intense and hollow. At first he simply stood in the doorway as if he had seen a ghost—or rather as if he had long been seeing ghosts. He stood as if a third of him had remained in the parking lot, a third wished to come in and sit down, and another third was somewhere quite far away.

By the time I met him Gregory he had been unable to maintain almost any kind of relationship since his service during the Vietnam War. He had suffered from chronic insomnia, had not worked steadily during all of that time, and had carried a diagnosis of post-traumatic stress disorder (PTSD) with accompanying psychopharmacological prescriptions and various forms of psychotherapy in various settings for nearly thirty years. His most recent psychiatrist—assigned by a government agency—had discussed with him the concept of "Moral Injury" after seeing him for a few months, and suggested that he work concurrently with someone who could explore the moral dimensions of both his experiences in the war and his homecoming. I became the recipient of that referral, being a combat veteran myself and having worked with a number of complexly disoriented combat veterans in psychotherapy and psychosocial support in previous years.

Gregory and I met almost weekly over the following two years, and there is no possibility of summarizing the work that we did together in the scope of an essay such as this. There is also no magic formula to be provided, no complete cure to relate, and no set of techniques to offer for "manualiza-tion." Because of the increasingly clear tendency for theorists and caregivers to interpret and analyze the aspects of their client's most complex forms of trauma-related disorientation in a way that corresponds with their central theoretical presuppositions, it will not be helpful for me to lead with mine, lest I alienate readers whose presuppositions differ.[2] Rather, I will privilege Gregory's description of his own suffering to set the stage for a few sugges-tions in caring for persons experiencing one of the most unusual features of disorientation among combat veterans. In any case, the love itself which knits the lives of two people together for so many hours is theoretically neu-tral, and there was only (for one of us) the persistent love of self-offering which suffered many attacks but which struggled constantly to refrain from retaliation, and (for the other) an eventual expansion of the ability to re-spond to the call of loving friendship that makes the bearing of responsibil-ity for one's part in the hell of war more possible.

2. Susan Johnson has added some helpful commentary on this caregiver phe-nomenon in her 2005 work *Emotionally Focused Couple Therapy with Trauma Survi-vors*, noticing that creative collaborations across theoretical lines begin organically in trauma work once caregivers see the limits of their orientation in caring for the most disoriented clients.

A Sight Picture on a Living Hell[3]

When we met, Gregory was experiencing each of the five most complex features of combat-related distress among contemporary veterans that I have seen over the course of my work and that cannot be easily approached by the dominant psychiatric discourse in trauma care: (1) a conscious loss or disconnection from emotion, inner vitality, and bodily sensation, while retaining memory of what it was once like to feel alive and embodied; (2) persistent, socially debilitating mistrust of people in authority and precious others, often combined with an intense longing to want to relate again; (3) a radical dissolution of moral intuition and narrative coherence, interrupting meaning-attribution and severely impeding a veteran's ability to relate to societal norms; (4) occasional moments of uncontrollable, lustful, exhilarating rage in which no humanity or compassion is accessible, and which seem to be activated with little or no warning; and (5) self-horror after the perceived absorption of evil present on the battlefield, usually accelerated by the veteran's actions.[4] None of these five features represent a new discovery, and in fact caregivers working with veteran populations will undoubtedly recognize some or all of them from work with their own clients. Some of these five features are commonly discussed within the Moral Injury discourse, with varying levels of success. I will briefly address Gregory's experience with just one of these five features, as it is the one that, in my experience, is the rarest and most inadequately addressed of the five.

Gregory lived with the constant sense that there was a personal form of evil within him, which he had absorbed either during or soon after killing another human being. He did not claim to be constantly in contact with this evil entity, but claimed that he always had a sense that it was "lurking" within, ready to emerge at a moment's notice.[5] He had no sense of what triggers might accompany its emergence, and at the time we met, previous exercises in journaling had not revealed any potential triggers. This evil presence within, as he understood it, would emerge both in social situations and when he was alone, both at home and when he was traveling, when he was otherwise feeling better or feeling worse. The most painful aspect of its emergence was the feeling of overwhelming hatred towards himself and anything living, and violent urges to harm himself and other living things,

---

3. Editors' note: A "sight picture" is what is seen through a sniper rifle scope.

4. This five-point formulation was originally designed as a part of my Doctor of Philosophy dissertation at the Centre for Trauma, Asylum, and Refugees at the University of Essex, and the list is taken from chapter 2 of that work, Alexander, "Combat-Activated Thymic Disorientation."

5. The quotations from Gregory may not have captured his exact words.

with very palpable suggestions that he experienced as coming from outside of his mind. He felt that he "coupled" with something evil during his service, and described his connection with this evil as a sort of "dark marriage" that took place when he pulled the trigger of his weapon all of those decades ago.[6]

Gregory and I first discussed his sense of this "dark marriage" while exploring a more common form of disorientation—what I noted at the time as a surprisingly incomplete ability to make coherent and cohesive meaning of his life's experiences both during and after Vietnam. This did seem to be strongly connected with his description of faith in God. Gregory had believed deeply in God as a boy, and had been taught by his father that God is very active in the world, and that God's energies are active in every area of life. For some of Gregory's life this deeply-held belief stood as a monument in his inner landscape. In contrast, his years in Vietnam contain only confused language about God—at times he wondered aloud where God was when his comrades were injured or killed, and how sometimes "you just can't blame God, because all of the problems of the world are not his problems." At times he spoke about his singular act of killing in the war as the moment when he lost God, "as if I lost hold of the hand I'd been holding all my life, and kept feeling around without finding it again." And on at least one occasion he mentioned that God never came too close to Vietnam.

After the war, Gregory's understandings of the safety of the world, the dependability of the world, and the activities of God in the world were chaotic and difficult to follow. This confusion of the meaning of life and its relative structure and safety was not a simple difficulty with meaning-attribution. Gregory would often display paranoid behavior and bizarre thinking in the moments that he believed God was not watching or involved. He was more erratic with friends and neighbors, and occasionally crossed social norms in seemingly unwitting but striking ways. After these occasions he would demonstrate surprise at being confronted by fellow citizens or the authorities—sometimes as surprised with them for being offended as they were at his offense.

6. I comment on this phenomenon at length in my dissertation, "Combat-Activated Thymic Disorientation," citing work with three of my own clients and similar first- and second-person accounts from the writings of Amaya Muruzábal ("The Monster as a Victim of War"); Robert McLay (*At War with PTSD*); Leah Wizelman (*When the War Never Ends*); D. C. Hoop (*PTSD: The Strugle Within, from Saigon to Baghdad*); Arthur Egendorf (*Healing from the War*); John Wilson, Matthew Friedman, and Jacob Lindy, eds. (*Treating Psychological Trauma and PTSD*); Victoria Beckner and John Arden (*Conquering Post-Traumatic Stress Disorder*); Scott Blake (*A Journey with P.T.S.D*); Tim Segrest (*Reflections of PTSD*); and Michael Boal ("Death and Dishonor").

Before I comment further on our exploration of this phenomenon and its surprising opening into a discussion on a sense of evil lurking within him, it may be helpful to some readers to note that I often make use of certain mindful techniques in my work with complexly disoriented veterans and persons who have endured extreme forms of adversity. In simple terms, I find that this allows us to begin and end sessions in a more embodied way, allowing thoughts and bodily sensations to be experienced together and accepted as they are, and preparing us for a real encounter with each other at a pace and in a manner that can be examined in the context of living relationship in "real time." If my clients can relate to themselves and to me in a more integrated way when we are together, then our friendship can become a part of a new possibility for them in every other area of life. More to the point, however, the simple practices of inner attention with which we begin and end sessions can bring us the added benefit of a point of return when our time together reached a place of extreme intensity—especially when this intensity is unexpected and threatens a state of diffuse physiological arousal, which will interrupt our ability to relate to one another for the rest of the session.

Keeping this simple explanation in mind, there came a time when Gregory and I were relating about how his sense of the predictability of God's presence changed during the war, and we came close to the moment when he had the enemy combatant he killed in the sights of his assault rifle. His body clearly changed and he quickly entered such a place of "extreme intensity" as described above, and we returned to one of our simple practices for a few minutes, which as I mentioned was our practice together in such times. When we opened our eyes and looked at each other, he told me, still breathing a little heavier than usual, and with a grim expression, something to this effect: "If I tell you what happened when I pulled that trigger, I will be pulling my trigger on you too." I cannot relate here how grateful I was that he was able to speak to me so clearly, and to be capable of such care for me after all that he had endured over so many years. In my experience, people who have endured acute forms of adversity, and especially those who have been perpetrators or empowered actors within the adversity, often give their caregivers warnings before allowing them to tread into the depths of the hell that remain within them, but these warnings are rarely so direct. In the next few weeks, Gregory began to painfully relate to me his decades-long experience of feeling as if an evil presence resided within him, often dormant but always present. It was a very sobering experience for both of us to connect around this reality, as any reader could imagine.

In essence, however, my work with Gregory over the next year centered not on his experiences of evil *per se*, but rather on his sense of what had allowed the "absorption" of this evil to occur—a single action, which was both the central experience of his life and the apparent underlying trauma of almost all of the various forms of disorientation he had experienced for forty years: the killing of another human being. After he had killed another person in combat—which had been justified according to the rules of engagement, which he felt had been tactically necessary, and which contained no obviously complicating factors such as a subsequent desecration of the body of an enemy—he had, according to his own conscience, engaged in fratricide, because of the humanity of the enemy. More than this, or perhaps intrinsically linked with this, his act of fratricide had been for him an act of existential suicide. After killing another human person, he had not been able, in his own words, to "feel any damned thing at all" for God or for anyone else. And in this act, which had opened for him this void of inner vitality, he had also experienced something very uncommon. He felt that God had left him, that evil had entered him, and that afterwards the times he felt anything strongly for other people, it was an evil impulse to hurt them or to damage their property.

The psychiatric paradigm cannot adequately account for the complexity, uniqueness, and totality of this most painful feature of Gregory's disorientation, and no criterion in either the DSM-5 or the ICD-10 approaches his experiences in an organized and manner.[7] Gregory's experiences do not fit cleanly within the scope of criteria for psychiatric delusions, which might otherwise make him a candidate for diagnosis in the Schizophrenia Spectrum according to the DSM-5.

Perhaps equally important, especially given the topic of this book, is that the Moral Injury paradigm and its public discourse has not often attempted to engage with and to give an adequate account of this phenomenon, beginning with the earliest work of Jonathan Shay. In *Achilles in Vietnam*, Shay does make mention of a soldier who sensed that a "monster" had entered him in combat and remained afterwards, acting suddenly within him outside of his consent.[8] He mentions a second soldier

7. Here DSM-5 refers to the latest edition of the *Diagnostic and Statistical Manual of Mental Disorders* published by the American Psychiatric Association, and ICD-10 refers to the psychiatric section of the latest edition of the *International Statistical Classification of Diseases and Related Health Problems* published by the World Health Organization. Please note that I owe a key formulation in this sentence (uniqueness, complexity, and totality) to my teacher and supervisor in both systemic family psychotherapy and psychosocial support to traumatized populations, Dr. Renos Papadopoulos, with whom I studied at the Tavistock Clinic in London and the Centre for Trauma, Asylum, and Refugees in Essex, United Kingdom.

8. Shay, *Achilles in Vietnam*, 95.

that described a time when "evil entered into him."[9] Another soldier he quotes describes "evil" as an entity that came into his life and that made him "turn into something" he wasn't before.[10] Shay does not treat any of these accounts directly, even while taking seriously his clients' own language in reporting their own experiences of complex suffering. This is perhaps most remarkable because of his extraordinary openness to exploring philosophical and literary ideas outside of the psychiatric paradigm in order to better account for the extreme and unusual features he was seeing in his work with veterans.[11] Although much good has been accomplished in development of the Moral Injury paradigm since Shay's earliest writings, I do not believe that there exists within this paradigm today an organized response to this most rare of disorienting features among veterans—many of whom also suffer from disorienting features more commonly discussed within the paradigm.

There are probably many reasons for this, but in my estimation they probably include (1) a sensitivity to language of the supernatural, and relatedly a sense of hesitation to engage in discussing veterans' accounts of "evil" that seem to exceed the abstract, necessitating a serious epistemological formulation in response, and (2) the now very wide number of different professionals from the disciplines of psychology, philosophy, theology, and social work engaging the Moral Injury discourse—each with a unique set of presuppositions about the nature of evil and the limitations of the human experience—which limits the collective ability to discuss the phenomenon in a helpful and coherent way as a part of the larger discourse. Indeed, for these very reasons, I will not now move into a principled discussion of the phenomenology of the suffering of veterans like Gregory who are experiencing this disorienting feature, informed by my own ontological and existential presuppositions. I will, however, offer what I think can be offered in spite of the realities contained in the reasons listed above. I will offer three suggestions for caregivers, friends, neighbors, and family members of veterans experiencing this feature, in the hope that it may impact their attempts to love these veterans, no matter their own ontological and existential presuppositions underlying the offering that love.

9. Ibid., 33.

10. Ibid., 95.

11. I discuss this tendency at length in Chapter 4 of "Combat-Activated Thymic Disorientation."

In Hell, But without Despair

First, I would like to suggest that it is possible for veterans experiencing this presence of evil in and around them to begin to relate to someone in a loving way *before* they experience a sense that the evil within them has left or has been reduced in influence. This is something that veterans in Gregory's situation often assume is impossible, and they will often in fact sabotage relationships and potential relationships from this place of assumption. A sage in the Eastern Orthodox contemplative tradition once received this guidance, in his own spiritual life: "Keep thy mind in hell, but despair not."[12] Although this statement may have myriad applications, one certainly may be that it is possible to begin to bear the worst hell that we have perpetrated, or that has been perpetrated against us, without being crushed under its weight. In essence, this hints at the possibility of experiencing a change not to what has happened in our lives, but how we are able to relate to what has happened in our lives. This change is most likely never possible without loving relationships to support such inner movement, and so for many long-disorientated and essentially isolated veterans, these relationships must be developed from the ground up. They can be. For Gregory, they were.

Second, it follows that in order to develop a loving relationship with a veteran who believes that a relationship of love is impossible for him, a painful reality must be borne by the person offering him love, which may be considered an action of co-suffering with the veteran: a veteran in this position will most likely *attack before accepting* any energies of love from anyone, and for the veteran, this is an almost inevitable act of defensiveness. To ever accept that he is still lovable after what he did in combat, Gregory had no choice but to attack me in many ways as I tried to become his friend, including constantly questioning my motives, belittling my professional work, and even insulting me personally. In addition, as Gregory grew closer to becoming my friend, he attacked to keep me at a distance so that I would not be "contaminated" by the evil he sensed within himself. Nevertheless, however it may be framed, attacks are difficult for caregivers, and it is impossible not to feel spurned and rejected on some level in these moments. However, I do not know of a way in which a caregiver can avoid these feelings and still offer the kind of relational love that such veterans need to heal. What a caregiver or friend *can* do is to expect these attacks, and when they come, to keep loving in humility and to try never to retaliate. The person who can love through the attacks, who can be wounded by the wounded

---

12. This quote comes from the life of Saint Silouan the Athonite, and it can be found in many places. Chief among them, perhaps, is Archimandrite Sophrony Sakharov's *Saint Silouan the Athonite*.

and can keep loving—this person can become a living and new possibility for veterans like Gregory.

Third, here is an important epistemological reality that is especially important for caregivers, but also should probably be heard by theorists within the Moral Injury paradigm: It is quite important, in my perspective, to allow these veterans to describe their disorientation in the way that they experience it—even if their language makes us uncomfortable, or challenges our presuppositions. For psychotherapists, this often means maintaining discipline against the systemic or personal pressure to professionally convert our veterans' spiritual or metaphysical language to psychological language when they speak of such a phenomenon as being inhabited by "evil." For some theorists, it would mean maintaining discipline against the pressure to quickly convert veterans' spiritual language into the language pertaining to their own theoretical milieu.

For this very reason, incidentally, I have often wondered why the Moral Injury discourse has maintained the label of "Moral Injury." Is it not somewhat reductive, and does it not in some way at least implicitly encourage all caregivers and theorists interacting with its ideas to place maximum emphasize on the moral dimension of the suffering of veterans? I believe that adding the moral dimension has been an advantage in veteran care, which before was often locked into a pattern of reducing the suffering of complexly disoriented veterans to its psychological, behavioral, and social dimensions. However, could it be that simply adding the moral dimension of veteran suffering has completed the epistemological demands of encountering such complexly disoriented people and trying to aid in their healing?[13] This addition certainly does not help to fully account for the feature of disorientation under consideration in this essay, although that feature certainly does have a moral dimension. Gregory experienced an evil within, and he could not conceive of it in any other way.

13. I would encourage a renaming of the "Moral Injury" discourse to something much wider in its epistemological foundations, perhaps along the lines of the admittedly unwieldy title "combat-activated onto-ecological disorientation." The idea of onto-ecological disorientation was developed at the Tavistock Institute in London by Renos Papadopoulos to engage in caring for traumatized persons, accounting for (1) all of the many and various dimensions of a person's being which may be affected by adversity, including but not limited to a person's psychological, social, physiological, emotional, behavioral, cultural, spiritual, and meaning-attributive dimensions, and (2) all of the various elements of a person's environment, which may include but which is not limited to language, surrounding architecture, rhythms of life, familiar sounds, smells, and faces, geographical locations, familiar climate, and so on. For more, see his 2002 work *Therapeutic Care for Refugees: No Place like Home*, and his "Failure and Success in Forms of Involuntary Dislocation: Trauma, Resilience, and Adversity-Activated Development," in *The Crucible of Failure* (2015).

Doing Together and Becoming Together

It would seem terrifyingly simplistic to say that "love is the answer" in aiding veterans like Gregory toward healing, who have experienced a connection with or absorption of evil in combat that has contributed to such personal and relational devastation in the aftermath. And yet that love is the answer is my very suggestion, with the caveat that loving veterans like Gregory will certainly mean co-suffering. In my experience, co-suffering is in fact a part of all of our healing, as none of us can be healed from anything alone. I went into two intense years with Gregory, armed with many therapeutic tools, and some experience as a caregiver, and with my own exposure to combat. However, in the end, the three things I have offered to readers here are the only things I had that made any difference—and of course the way that I "had" them changed along the way.

Gregory still suffers today, a few years after concluding our work together. He still struggles to make new friendships and to relate to his family, although he has grown in both areas. He still has moments of rage that he does not anticipate in time for him to engage them in the way that he would like, and he still has difficulties trusting people in authority—or for that matter, anyone with a gregarious, ingratiating persona. On the other hand, his ability to bear the reality of what he has done in killing another person has grown, and with it his sense of God's presence has become more steady and his sense of an evil within himself has diminished. He has also been able to begin a small work of repentance that has helped him in many ways, and which has stretched him in terms of relating to others—and this could not have been possible without first more fully bearing his act of killing and its impact on the entirety of his own being.

However, this all began with love: a loving caregiver, with many faults and many failures—but with good supervision and spiritual direction!—trying to offer a call to him and looking for a response, and enduring his attacks as much as possible, with love and attention. And I grew also, especially seeing his capacity to respond to love with love of his own, after so many years enduring so many adversities. His resilience was a miracle to me, and was a source of wonder and challenge.

On our last day together, just before I was to move to another town, I remember seeing Gregory walk in to my office with a warm smile and sit down as if he owned the place. Our time together that day was emotional and difficult, even though—especially given his particular form of suffering—we had spent a lot of time preparing for our parting of ways. As he left the door and walked out to the parking lot I thought to myself—and my notes read—"I am leaving Gregory not as a client, but as a friend, and what have we *done* together that has been so important as what we have *become* together?"

30

DAVID W. PETERS

Sin Eater

Since I've been home from Iraq, I have learned to live with some seriously mixed emotions. Serving in Iraq as a chaplain was the high point of my life. It redefined everything I believed, it birthed my closest friendship on this planet, and my service there is forever proof that I am tough, that I am a man. I'm also terribly ashamed of my enthusiasm for the war, for the way I encouraged young women and men to die over there, for blessing a war with my words and presence, and for what I and my colleagues did to destroy the Iraqi people. Pride and shame flash on the screen of my mind during the day and in the night. During the evil hours, they become a bitter cocktail of brutal fantasies and self-destructive compassion. The fear at the bottom of all this is that I am not good.

And I was only a chaplain, a non-combatant, wandering around the battle space with words of encouragement and a cross on my helmet. Now, I think I am not at all like the man who hung on that cross, five hundred miles west of Baghdad. I am one of the Romans who put him there.

When I came home from Iraq I did very little reflection on my time there. I was numb to most of my feelings, and I trusted fewer and fewer people with my story every day. I was also optimistic about my future, since Iraq was in the rearview mirror. But then things started to fall apart. I found out my wife was having an affair. No doubt this was, in part, connected to my numbness. I moved to another duty station, I started drinking, and I lost about thirty pounds.

During that slide of self-destruction, I participated in a writing group at Walter Reed Army Medical Center in Washington, DC. What I wrote for the group eventually became my first book, *Death Letter: God, Sex, and War.*

In those dark days I never heard the term "Moral Injury." I probably would not have been interested, even if I attended a class on it. I did not want to think about my deployment or my current mental and spiritual state. I was shattered, and that seemed normal and familiar to me.

Ten years later I began to examine my deployment and my homecoming. I read about Moral Injury and began asking questions of my former, shattered self. I wondered if I could have some of it, even though I was a non-combatant.

From these questions I conclude that I do indeed have Moral Injury. Some of it comes from being the "sin eater," that person from old England and Appalachia who eats the food for the dead, thus allowing their souls to pass on. Like that chosen person of old, I took in the evil around me. I heard confessions and admissions of cruelty and disdain. I ate all those stories, and they gave me strength, sustenance, and a purpose for living. It also made me sick and injured, morally and emotionally.

Baghdad, Iraq: During the Deployment

Soldiers are superstitious, and they all carry at least one charm to ward off their own death. They carry handkerchiefs with the words from Psalm 91 printed on them. There's an Internet myth circulating about a unit in World War II that prayed this same psalm and not one of their men died. Someone printed the psalm on camouflage bandanas and handed them out by the thousands. At first they were desert camo, then they switched to the Army Combat Uniform (ACU) pattern. This pattern is a gray and white checkered pattern, and it's meant to camouflage us in the desert, or in a gray, urban environment. For a while, during the transition from one combat uniform to another, we wear a mix of camouflage, desert, and ACU. We can tell how long a unit has been in Iraq by the camo pattern. This is part of the secret knowledge of combat.

We fold the Psalm 91 bandanas in quarters and place them in our helmets, on top of the pictures of our trucks or lovers. Maybe the psalm will protect our heads from death or a traumatic brain injury. Maybe they'll just absorb our blood.

Psalm 91 says "a thousand shall fall at thy side, and ten thousand at thy right hand" but it won't kill you. Because the people in the psalm trust in the

Lord, they won't die suddenly and unaware. Psalm 91 says "thou shalt tread upon the lion and adder," and no harm shall come to you.

The devil quotes this same psalm to Jesus in Matthew 4 when he tempts Jesus. In this story, the devil takes Jesus up on the highest part of the temple and dares him to jump. The devil says that if he jumps, the angels will catch him in their arms. The devil supports his claim by quoting Psalm 91. The devil says that if Jesus jumps the angels will "Bear him up in their arms, lest you dash your foot against a stone." The devil dares Jesus to be a daredevil. But Jesus doesn't jump. He just stands there and tells the devil to shut up. A few years later when Jesus hangs on the cross, God turns his face away from his bleeding son. He cries out, "My God, my God, why have you forsaken me?" No one comes to his rescue. A thousand stand on that day in Jerusalem, watching him die slowly. Only one man falls and not one angel comes to save him.

Before a night mission, we gather in a circle and talk through the route and the objective. We go over contingency plans and rollover procedures. We make sure the radios work and that everyone has a map and plenty of ammo.

When the pre-combat checks are over, most of the team lights cigarettes in the darkness. The low growl of diesel engines fills the night and the headlights of our trucks cast their beams through the cloud of cigarette smoke.

In these moments, I see the holy incense going up before an ancient altar made of uncut gravel. The warriors invoke the god of the road, the god of love, and the god of war to favor them over the enemy in the unlucky lottery of death. The incense goes up and then I say my prayer. I pray that we will all have courage for this mission. I pray that those we love will be safe at home. I thank God for our lives. I thank God that this war came to us, on our watch, so our children and grandchildren can have the fruits of peace and security. We walk to the vehicles. Our boots crunch through the rough gravel, and we squeeze our armored bodies into our vehicles and roll out.

Iraq is like Las Vegas. It's hot, and the dining facility stays open all night. Everything in Iraq runs 24/7 and there are few clocks. The twisted jackpot is death and nobody beats the house. The unlucky winner is a dentist one day and an infantryman the next. He could even be a chaplain. As I stand in the circle of warriors night after night, I whisper into the darkness, "Burn your incense. Call on your gods. We can use all the help we can get."

I write to my wife Anna and call her every day. When I'm in the backseat of a Humvee rolling down a Baghdad street I think of her. She is the happy place I go when I can't stand the heat, the exhaustion, or the boredom. Every day when I kneel down to pray in my room, I think of the ways I have not been a good husband to her. I think of my failures big and small. When I return, I'll buy her the minivan she has been saying we needed for three years. She has the most thankless job of war. It's her responsibility to tell the world how I'm doing when they call her. I know we will emerge from this war with a passion for one another that will be worthy of the World War II couples that are memorialized forever for their long-distance relationships.

I call her when I come in from a mission and I'm exhausted. She is just going to bed and the sun is coming up in my war world. She tells me about the boys and how her friends are cooking dinner together. I miss her. I ache for her. We call several times a week, but we rarely laugh together. The work we must do on the phone is too serious. There's always the shadow of death creeping into the edges of the phone call.

After a vehicle is blown up, medics, engineers, and carpenters drive out and clean up the blast site. They walk around slowly scanning the ground for the fingers, hands, or anything they can put in a plastic bag. They pick up the remains and put them in special bags. They look for clothing and dog tags. They tow the damaged vehicle back to the base to a restricted area where all the blown-up vehicles await transport to Kuwait. In this high-walled parking lot, they scrub out the inside of the blood-and-explosive-stained vehicle with powerful cleaning compounds. They hose away the blood and bits and pieces of the men and women who died in the twisted, burned steel. The medics do this with great joy. They are not happy they are called to the scene of death. They are happy they can endure it, and their special gifts are of some use in this world.

My medics enjoy their exclusive priesthood at the altar of blood and death. They have passed the initiation of seeing and smelling dead blood and flesh. They will carry these images and smells with them until they turn forty or fifty years old and can't fall asleep at night anymore. They can't sleep because they see the images they've filed away in the back folders of their mind. They will not be able to avoid the blank stares of the dead or the severed hand that still has a wedding ring on its finger.

The Soldiers who are called to clean up a blast always find the helmets and the boots. There's usually little left of the boots but burned leather and rubber. The helmets have bits of hair on the inside with sticky blood. The recovery team takes the helmets and boots and makes a display in the front of the chapel for the memorial ceremony. They take a rifle, fix a bayonet to its muzzle, and stick the barrel down in a wooden stand. On the butt of the rifle they perch the helmet. In front of the rifle, they place the empty boots, heels together, in the position of attention. This is the symbol of a dead warrior. Somewhere between a man's helmet and boots he has marked his brief, twenty-three-year-old passage on this planet. He was only part of this world for a moment, and that moment was one of war.

Washington, DC: After Redeployment

After the divorce, I drive up to my ex-wife's apartment to pick up the boys. They are wearing jeans and sweaters, and I adjust the rearview mirror so I can look at them while I drive. My oldest son asks me, "Why is Mom is so mad at you all the time?" I ask him, "Are you sad we aren't together right now?" He says he's sad and that he doesn't like living in two houses. I tell them I don't like it either, but that's the way it is.

I put them to bed in my apartment. They ask for a monster story, and I ask them which monster story they want. They want to hear about Medusa. So I tell them the story and they hang on every word. I say how Perseus used his mirrored shield to look at Medusa. They get excited as I tell them more about how her mythical powers would turn him into stone if he looked directly into her eyes. The boys love mirrors and the Gorgon's snaky hair, so the story is perfect. We kneel and recite the "Our Father," and I sing them a song I wrote for my oldest son's fifth birthday. He likes his song and asks me to play it again. I play it one more time, and I kiss them both. Their soft cheeks are divine. They say I have cactus cheeks and that mommy doesn't. I tell them this is a good thing and shut the door. I remember my own dad kissing me goodnight and thinking the same thing.

On the balcony of the apartment, I look out into the night. Cars drive by on the road below. Each one is headed somewhere. Only the parked cars lack a destination. Like Abram in the Old Testament, I look up at the sky and question the God who promised me a good marriage. I tell him I had damn near done everything I was supposed to do and now everything is a fucking mess. My voice rises from the whisper of my mind and I speak. I yell at the Master of the Universe and tell him I don't like what happened. I taunt him for how he turned his Almighty back on me when I needed him most. I rail on, "Don't you care that she left me? Don't you want us together?" There is nothing but silence. I know the answer, but I can't believe it. I know that God loves my ex-wife as much as he loves me. I feel most betrayed by this thought. Whose side is God on in a war? Whose side is he on in a divorce? Whose side is he on in the Super Bowl?

Then the questions break. I whimper, sob, then burst into a full-on ugly cry. I weep at the silent stars and the fingernail-shaped moon. I hope all the clocks will stop and die with my soul. When I stop weeping, I hear a voice. The voice is silence. It is the stillness of the unconditioned. It is a voice unconditioned, like a horse standing still. There is Kierkegaard's royal coachman seated above him with a whip, poised to strike at the slightest movement of the horse. It is the Universe or God or the Ground of Being herself that has a message for me. The voice says, "You can leave her now." The voice is not my own. My weeping has been heard, but God has surprised me in the worst way imaginable. I don't believe him and walk back inside.

I think about the story of Jacob in the book of Genesis on the shores of the Jabbok Creek wrestling with a man. The man is strong, but Jacob doesn't give up. He puts the man in an arm lock and puts his knee into the man's side. The man can't move. Jacob pins him there for almost an hour and the man begs to be let go. Jacob says, "I won't let you go until you bless me." Jacob waits for the blessing of the wrestler as the pre-nautical twilight begins to lighten the sky. Faces are now becoming distinguishable. Now is the time when armies attack. The wrestler does not bless him, but with a sorcerer's magic, he shrinks Jacob's leg muscle and he howls in pain. Jacob lets the man go. He lies on the ground and holds his leg with both hands. The man walks away.

Jacob rises in pain. He looks down the path to where the man disappeared. He begins to follow and realizes that his leg still hurts. He can only limp. Jacob remembers with satisfaction that he pinned the man down until he pulled this trick on him. Jacob limps home and the blessing is his hurt leg. I know how Jacob feels. I wrestle with this man every night, and I can barely walk in the morning.

God doesn't care about Jacob's conflict with his brother. God doesn't care that Jacob has two wives and eleven children who might die when the sun comes up. God only cares about one thing—winning the wrestling match. God tests Jacob's resolve just as he's about to lose everything. I realize this is the only challenge in the universe. God loves the world and the humans that make it spin. God loves the stories we live out, unaware we are on the great stage of the Almighty. When I wrestle God on the banks of my own Jabbock Creek, I know he is an old god and he doesn't care about my marriage. God doesn't care about my war. He only cares about me. Of all the revelations in the universe, this one truth shocks everyone who hears it.

The next evening, I'm in a supermarket wandering the aisles. I put some things in my cart I think might impress a sophisticated city girl. I stop in the wine aisle and look down the twenty meters of wine. I stand in front of what I call the "Odd Bottle" section. I glance at the bottles of port, sherry, vermouth, and Manischewitz. There's even a small bottle of plum wine waiting respectfully for a successful Japanese man. I know this is my section. I spot a well-dressed couple, a breeding pair in matching black wool coats, compare bottles of Sauvignon Blanc for a party. They would never come down to where I stand. I'm like these bottles. I take a bottle of Manischewitz off the shelf and open it. I take a drink and look over at the couple. They look back at me in a mix of shock and pity. I take another drink and slowly push the cart towards the register, pausing only long enough to put a bag of pita bread in the cart.

Even though I've been back from Iraq for over two years, I'm still there. I'm alive there, dead here. I'm myself there. I'm scared there. Over there, there's always a golden day before me when I will see my family again. Now there's nothing hopeful on the horizon. There's no magic day where all manner of things will be well. It's just an endless succession of seconds that will one day stop.

Baghdad, Iraq: During Deployment

My war is full of contradictions. I think of the laser beams we use. About halfway into my tour, they give us laser pointers. The Soldiers in the turrets use them to ward off approaching vehicles when we are on a convoy. They shine them into the cars that come too close and the cars veer away. The Iraqi drivers believe they are lasers from weapon scopes or something. I think, but I'm not sure, that they can see they are just handheld laser pointers. This is, after all, a country where many homes have cable TV and indoor plumbing. They have cell phones but unreliable electrical service. These are the contradictions of a nation too long at war with her neighbors and the world.

My Soldiers shine their laser beams into the cars and no one dies. Shortly after that I'm on a convoy, and I notice that all the Humvees have sirens and police lights on them. The order came down from division to equip each vehicle with police equipment. I look for the box of donuts in the cab of the vehicle. Now, when we roll down the roads of Baghdad, the noise of our sirens precedes us. Cars pull over to the side of the road while their drivers give us dirty looks.

I only drive one mission in Baghdad. To my knowledge only a few chaplains drive Humvees during 2006 in Iraq. Chaplains are different from the rest of the Soldiers. Since we are non-combatants, we don't carry weapons. Even though the Geneva Convention states that we can, we have chosen not to. During the Vietnam War, some magazine put a picture of a chaplain on the front cover draped in machine gun bullets. Since then, we stay away from carrying weapons.

I drive a Humvee with a .50 caliber machine gun on the roof. We have intercom headsets and my Chaplain Assistant, Sandy, is my TC (Tank

Commander). Non-tankers like us borrow the cool names. We are the third vehicle in the convoy. We are a gun truck that is supposed to protect the Logistics Convoy (Log Pack) that is carrying supplies to a distant FOB (Forward Operating Base). We drive south on Route Tampa. On one side of the road, there's a wasted and burned tractor trailer that has flipped on its side. It was blown up by an IED the night before. Its cargo of bottled water is blasted across the shoulder and embankment of the highway. Bottles are everywhere. The cab is charred. It doesn't look like the driver survived. He was more than likely Indian, Pakistani, or another of the third-country nationals who do the real dangerous work here. Most of them make the minimum wage for their country, and many of their recruiters keep most of their income for themselves. We rarely interact with them on the FOB unless they are doing our laundry.

Our convoy survives the trip to the distant FOB and we turn around and go home. We slow down and roll through an Iraqi checkpoint. I'm driving and my assistant is in the passenger seat. She is looking for IEDs. At the checkpoint, there's an Iraqi man in his late sixties standing there arguing with the Iraqi soldiers. He's waving his hands wildly, which may not necessarily mean he is angry. As we approach this exchange, the young Soldier who is arguing with him looks at me. Then he looks at my female assistant. He gets a look on his face that can only mean he wants to impress this American woman. He makes a fist and punches the old man in the stomach. The old man is wearing a long white robe and the young Soldier's fist causes the robe to billow. Then the fist connects with the old man's stomach. The old man doubles over in pain and we leave the checkpoint. In this moment, as I witness the least serious attack of the war, God dies. The God of my childhood, with His right and His wrong, drifts away like the air that billowed out of the old man's robe. All that's left is the dust and the heat and the war. As the God of my childhood floats off, another takes His place.

This new God can't possibly care if people have sex or if they kill each other. This new God of love and war only cares about humans being themselves. His glory is the human person fully alive, and He knows that war is the only place where warriors feel fully alive. This new God of love and war doesn't believe in good and evil but allows civilians to believe in such things. Warriors and lovers never believe in either. All is fair in love and war and, although this is often said, it's rarely believed by those who are afraid to inflict pain on another person. All the lovers who have left husbands and wives are convinced it was the right thing to do. The consequences, be they harsh words or the Scarlet Letter, are worth it.

All the warriors know that when a nineteen-year-old man has to shoot a nine-year-old girl because she's being used as a human shield, that there is no real morality in the world. The warrior knows the right thing is always right, but it will haunt him forever. One second after the Soldier's thumbs depress the triggers on the side of the .50 caliber machine gun, the girl is cut in half. The bullets are six inches long. One second after the girl dies, the Soldier knows there's no right or wrong, only war. He'll see this girl in his nightmares for the rest of his life. Her life is now connected to his.

One such Soldier tells me about her on a summer afternoon at Walter Reed. I listen to his story. I spend the next day trying to help him embrace this girl. He's running from her, but she keeps following. He wants to take a shotgun from his gun cabinet, put the barrel in his mouth, and pull the trigger. He knows how easy it was to pull the trigger and kill the girl. He's tried it once before.

I try to help him look at the girl and not run from her. He can see himself turning towards the little girl who is following him. When she's close, he hugs her. They are one now and always will be.

Fort Hood, Texas: Months before Deployment

They come and get me one morning at 4:15 a.m. when I'm still at Fort Hood, Texas before I deploy to Iraq. I report to the Casualty Notification Office and get the file of the family I will tell about a death in Iraq. I'm notifying an ex-wife and her son that an ex-husband and father died in combat.

I get in the van with the Sergeant First Class (SFC) who is the Notification Officer. It's his task to be the first to ask the question at the door. He will ask if he is speaking with Jane Smith and if he can come inside. When two men show up at an apartment at 6:00 a.m. on a Saturday with their shiny brass buttons and green suits, it can mean only one thing—that death has come to call. All the wives and parents are told that the death notifications only happen between 6:00 a.m. and 10:00 p.m. at night. My wife told me that while I was deployed, she would look at the clock at 10:00 p.m. and breathe a sigh of relief. Every other knock on the door before 10:00 p.m. could be the angel in green with those shiny buttons.

I stand at the door of the apartment. We knock. The sergeant rehearses his lines. "The Secretary of the Army has asked me to express his deepest regrets that your husband, Staff Sergeant John Smith, was killed in action on 19 August 2005 in Baghdad, Iraq." After knocking for twenty minutes, we leave and get a coffee at McDonald's, to wait for their return. The sergeant keeps saying his lines out loud. He's scared. We bide our time. We won't give our position away. We will, like Death himself, show up when the family least expects it.

In a military community our task can't be any less private. We sit in the McDonald's and drink coffee to stay awake. We weren't sleeping well with the duty phone before it rang. Then we were up before the sun and fatigue is setting in. We sit in our uniforms and everyone looks at us with pity and understanding. The kind eyes take some of the edge off the morning and then it becomes too much. We leave and sit in the government van in front of the apartment building. It's always a van and it's always an apartment building.

At 9:00 a.m. we go back to the house and knock on the door. This time a woman comes to the door and she screams, "Oh, my God!" when she sees us. She knows and the sergeant feels guilty. I can see this by looking at the sergeant's face. It's a look of disgust and panic. He's faced many things, including the enemy, but now he's the enemy. He's face to face with a woman who has just lost something in war. She turns abruptly and we follow her in. She sits at the small glass-topped kitchen table and the sergeant and I sit across from her.

When we sit down, the sergeant mumbles his lines and the woman listens. When the sergeant is finished, we look at her. Her eyes are fixed on the basket of small gourds that is the centerpiece of the table. All three of us stare at the gourds. Then she picks one up and throws it across the table at us. It misses us and hits the living room wall a few inches from the large plasma screened TV. Then she weeps. She weeps in angry sobs. She says that she doesn't want to tell her son. Then she stops and looks up and says, "My son, our son, is developmentally disabled and, even though he's seven, he might not understand."

The sergeant is eyeing the door. I ask her if there is someone I can call to come over to the house. She says she'll take care of that. I hug her and say nothing because there is nothing to say. I think she might feel the buttons on my jacket. Maybe it will remind her of an embrace in better times with her Soldier who captured her heart but couldn't keep it.

Something happened between then and now. It was only for a time. Something changed between them. Now, all that exists is a child that might not understand his own father's death. There's also more than $400,000 of Serviceman's Group Life Insurance that she will keep in trust for her son's eighteenth or twenty-first birthday, depending on the box the Soldier checked only days before he went to Iraq.

The sergeant and I drive back to the Casualty Notification Office. I thank the sergeant for doing such a good job with this notification. The chaplain isn't there to comfort the bereaved. The chaplain is there to comfort the one who makes the notification. The sergeant shakes his head and sighs. We both stare at the road knowing we're on call for six more days. This could happen again and again. We both wonder what kind of men we will be when it's over.

I do more of these visits in the years following this visit, but I never remember any of them. I only remember this one notification because of the gourd she threw when words were not enough. I will always know it was in autumn.

31

SEAN LEVINE

Legal War, Sin, and "Moral Injury" in the Age of Modern Warfare

The question is this: Why do warriors return from justified wars feeling sinful and alienated, and what are we to do about it? As we have come to understand, post-traumatic stress disorder (PTSD) does not, as a category of long-term post-war maladaptation, fully encompass the experience of many warriors who have returned from a combat deployment. In fact, the connection between return from war, PTSD, and the staggering suicide rate among America's warriors has not been clearly defined, and one could argue that such a connection does not exist at nearly the rate that many assume.[1] Although it is possible to imagine that someone suffering from PTSD could commit suicide, nothing specifically ties the suicide rate in the military to PTSD caused by war. Those who go to war experience trauma. By nature,

---

1. Junger, *Tribe*, 83. Junger makes this important point: "Suicide is often seen as an extreme expression of PTSD, but researchers have not yet found any relationship between suicide and combat. Combat veterans are, statistically, no more likely to kill themselves than veterans who were never under fire." He goes on to explain that the much-discussed suicide rate of twenty-two veterans killing themselves each day, while tragic, can be misunderstood. Statistically, the majority of that number come from among the Vietnam era veterans, not from among the veterans of Iraq and Afghanistan. So, many warrior suicides—not all, but the majority—are happening long after the end of their involvement in war, and they may not be connected to PTSD at all. Which is not to say that the suicidal behaviors have nothing to do with war trauma, but they may not be directly relatable to actual PTSD.

the battlefield contains traumatic experiences, and the warrior on the battle-field encounters all sorts traumatic moments at various levels of intensity. Upon return from the battlefield, normal response patterns formed in an abnormal and traumatic environment can persist for a short time lasting for several weeks to several months. However, for most people, such persistent patterns of response (increased startle response, hypervigilance, sleep dis-turbances, flashbacks, nightmares, etc.) wane naturally over a span of time, usually not longer than about six months. When they persist beyond about six months, it generally means that proper treatment has not been sought out and that acute trauma responses are becoming chronic. Still, if proper treatment can be found, PTSD can be relatively easy to treat in a short-term, solution-focused therapeutic context in which a trained trauma therapist administers time-tested trauma protocols. Actual PTSD, once identified, can be treated.

PTSD can also be misdiagnosed and overmedicated. The medical mod-el currently in dominance within the military and veterans' affairs medical systems has tried to resolve mental health issues by attacking—sometimes vigorously—symptoms, and, almost every other day, a news story breaks about overmedicating in both medical systems. When one focuses on symptoms, "treatment" attempts to reduce suffering and increase comfort by masking symptoms, so the medication begins to flow. Even worse, in many cases, doctors and therapists, in an attempt to ensure that warriors get all that they deserve and are not deprived of benefits, too quickly call any post-war "maladaptations" PTSD, and then they begin medicating what they perceive to be the symptoms of PTSD. Yet, as has been noted repeat-edly in literature of late, many warriors who return from war with mental health issues suffer from a complex web of mental, emotional, spiritual, and existential sensibilities and concerns. Many of these sensibilities and con-cerns fall well outside the actual criteria for PTSD, even though the surface symptoms may look like PTSD. It is the existential issues that do not fall within the diagnostic criteria for PTSD that have gained the notorious title "Moral Injury."

Moral Injury may seem to be a dubious category. How can one be in-jured morally? At what "place" in the human being can such an "injury" be located? How does that "place" receive injury, and by what mechanism is the injury inflicted? Such questions could be multiplied, and, although some can be answered, not all of them can be answered satisfactorily, which makes the idea of "Moral Injury" somewhat troublesome. Still, it is the best description we have been able to craft in order to describe a phenomenon that appears to be more prevalent that actual PTSD. That is to say, far more warriors have been afflicted with a persistent existential crisis that erodes the very fabric of their sense of self in the wake of deployment to war than actually have the psychiatric disorder brought on by the stress of post-trauma adaptation to "normal" life. A vast number of warriors who have trouble re-adapting to life back home, if you listen closely to their stories, experience a spiritual and existential ambivalence that leads to a deep identity crisis due to the fact that they have perpetrated, witnessed, or failed to prevent battlefield events that run against the grain of identified or unidentified, but viscerally felt and "known," personal moral or ethical views and commitments. This we call Moral Injury, for lack of a better term.

This raises the question to which this essay seeks to offer an answer: Why do warriors who fight in legal wars feel that they have transgressed morally? How is it possible, given the legal sanction of the State in defense of the State's interests around the world, for a warrior fighting for a just cause as defined by a legal authority, to feel sinful? Why would a good man or woman fighting with all the support of the Nation and engaging according to laws of war and rules of engagement, return home and say to a chaplain, a priest, a pastor, a counselor, a therapist, or a friend, "I have lost my soul: I know right where it is, but I cannot get it back and I feel totally dead inside," even when that warrior has not broken the law or committed a war crime? If a war is a good and just thing, why are so many warriors on the modern battlefield damaged spiritually by war?

The answer to those questions, for me, centers on the fact that war is inherently evil. Not only is war "not good," and not "a necessary evil," more often than not, war is an unnecessary evil, and there are other ways to address the global crises that often lead too quickly to the deployment of hundreds of thousands of warriors into the den of sorrow, sin, and trauma that war always is. Some would argue that war can be virtuous because such a painful crucible often brings out the virtues of the warriors who fight in it. Courage, honor, self-sacrifice, just to name a few, emerge in the context of the great contest of war. As an Eastern Orthodox chaplain, I agree that warriors often demonstrate great virtue on the battlefield, and I could tell story after story of such heroic behavior.

Yet the heroism of warriors, in my view, says nothing at all about the inherent nature of war itself. Rather, it describes the potential greatness of the human person. A tornado, a hurricane, a flood, a plague, a famine, and a foreign invasion all share this same characteristic: while not good in and of themselves, they create contexts in which the goodness of the people experiencing them might emerge in powerfully demonstrative ways at undeniably heroic levels. This is the goodness of humankind coming to the fore in trying circumstances. War focuses human energy on the destruction of other human beings and the systems that keep human beings alive. War has always been, in the modern era, indiscriminate, and remains so today despite "smart bombs." The only thing smart about a bomb is the mechanism that allows a human being, remotely located, to place it on a desired target, but I have witnessed and also heard of countless times that precision munitions have been poorly placed by people who did not fully grasp the context, since they were sitting in front of screens hundreds of miles away from or several miles over the battlefield. War focuses on destruction, and such destruction simply cannot be called "good."

Standing directly in the way of our ability and our willingness, as a culture, to encounter Moral Injury in our returning warriors is the philosophical juggernaut of the Western commitment to Just War Theory. (Just War Theory spawned in time Just War Doctrine within the Roman Catholic Christian Tradition.) This theory suggests the possibility of killing in a morally acceptable fashion for the good of stopping evil and preserving social order. However, this fails to adequately address the reality of what war actually is. Certainly, philosophers and theologians can construct a make-believe world of ideas and ethical equations wherein war looks like other human endeavors of competition, and these thinkers can suggest rules that set the killing of other human beings and the destruction of the world into neatly carved categories that delineate "right and wrong" ways of going about it. Yet none of this deals with the reality of war. In fact, war represents the quintessential dehumanizing evil that threatens to annihilate our species and to destroy the world in which we live.

The human heart's response to war and killing hearkens not to philosophy, but rather to the ontological reality that to strike out at another human being is tantamount to striking a blow against one's own being and existence. To kill another human being is to kill a brother or sister, and this killing of a brother or sister is, ultimately, a suicidal gesture. War is not a game with rules, but we try to convince warriors that it is. We need them to believe this so that they will engage in war at least long enough for our national interests to remain intact around the globe. The famed quip, "War is hell," has been watered down to mean only "War is difficult, painful, unpleasant, or otherwise inconvenient." But war really is hell—it is literally hell on earth—and war does not contain, inherently, anything good. Anything good and noble that takes place in war does not come from the ontology of war itself but from the goodness that resides in the human beings who must go to war, and this goodness is squandered and wasted on the battlefield. To any attempt to make war an inherently "good" thing, such as the attempt by Webster and Cole in *The Virtue of War*,[2] I respond with the counterargu-

2. Webster and Cole, *The Virtue of War*. This is perhaps the most definitive attempt,

ment that there exists no virtue in war. In and of itself, war lacks virtue, and, in fact, is the ultimate "anti-virtue."[3] The fact that many men and women bring virtue with them to war says much about the virtue inherent to the warriors but nothing about any virtue inherent in an act of war itself. Further, no good intention can override or set aside, even temporarily, the evil that war is.

The Eastern and Western Christian notions of war contrast powerfully, and it is from the Western philosophy of the world, war, and the Kingdom of God that Just War Theory emerged from an idea, to a theory, to an accepted doctrine within the Roman Catholic Church and in most of Catholicism's Protestant Reformation "children." While the Western Christian tradition, following Ambrose of Milan and his disciple Augustine of Hippo, stands upon the notion of a justified killing of enemy combatants, the East never sought to justify this killing, even if it recognized a difference in moral category between killing in combat and cold-blooded killing. Killing has never been categorically accepted as "right and good" in any circumstance within the Eastern Christian Tradition.

Despite the fact that a few Orthodox writers in the Christian East have attempted to demonstrate a clear acceptance of Just War Theory, these arguments run clearly contrary to the traditional Orthodox rejection of just war, and have received only cautious skepticism among most Orthodox historians and experts in Byzantine studies.[4] Far more prevalent are the voices like those of Dr. Timothy Patitsas and Dr. James Skedros. These professors teach at Holy Cross (Orthodox) School of Theology, and both represent the preponderance of voices within the Orthodox Christian Tradition, both historic and present-day. As well, one may also look to the writings and the work of Jim Forest, an Orthodox Christian peace advocate and prolific writer.

---

but, again, it has not received the status of wide acceptance.

3. Dr. Timothy Patitsas, in his presentation at the Orthodox Christian Association of Medicine, Psychology, and Religion (OCAMPR) 2015 Conference, called war the "anti-Theophany," a vision of death and destruction that can be countered only by first beholding "Theophany," a vision of the beautiful and the good.

4. I have not attempted to find other sources like Webster and Cole's text cited above, so that side of the argument may not be adequately represented. When it comes to Orthodox writers who defend Just War Theory, Webster's is the view most often discussed. Perhaps it would be worth locating other pro-Just War Theory Orthodox voices, which would be another project for another time. It is not my point to give equal air time to these opposed voices, though that may, I understand, weaken my argument here. I stand confidently within the camp of those who see no place for Just War Theory within truly Orthodox theology.

Just War Theory, though created at a time in Christian history when the Christian community remained one, came into existence within the cultural context unique to the Western Christian section of the Roman Empire. Granted, the impetus for such a theological underpinning for Christian imperial conquest emerged from the conversion of the Roman Empire from pagan to Christian under the influence of Christian emperors governing the whole of Christendom. Yet, clearly, Just War Theory was coined and minted in the West and never achieved sound philosophical or theological footing in the Christian East. As Jim Forest, the lead figure within the Orthodox Peace Fellowship, states, "The Just War doctrine is chiefly associated with Western Christianity," and he goes on to substantiate this claim by quoting at length the detailed study of patristic sources that Father Stanley Harakas conducted in his search for answers in this area.[5] In his research, Harakas noted the absence of anything resembling an intentionally crafted justification for war in the Christian East. Likewise, when Dr. Patitsas describes the contrast between Eastern and Western Christian views on war he explains:

> For the West by the time of the Crusades, war might in certain cases not be morally ambiguous. A blessed cause for war makes the war an unqualified good, and therefore participating in it is not a sin. Even killing in war is not a sin, but can in fact be part of a holy service that absolves you of your sins. What the Orthodox Byzantines retained was an older Greek notion that war inevitably damages the soul. Even in a just cause, in self-defense or to protect innocents, participation in war still harms the soul in some measure.[6]

In like manner, Dr. Skedros asserts when summarizing the Orthodox Christian approach to war and killing:

> Military service is not inherently evil, but I would not say, therefore, that the veneration of military saints in Byzantium glorified war and glorified killing, or that the Orthodox Church had a notion of just war. The Byzantines didn't occupy themselves with such questions. They were pragmatists, they were realists.

5. Forest, "War and Peace." Fr. Harakas' conclusions find full expression in his article, "No Just War in the Fathers." He asserts: "As I searched the sources of Eastern Orthodox tradition for material regarding war, I began to see that these contained none of the traditional components of the western just-war theory. The West, beginning with Saint Augustine, had developed a set of ethical prescriptions and proscriptions concerning entrance into war (*jus ad bellum*) and behavior during war (*jus in bello*). I couldn't find such ethical reasoning in the Greek Fathers or in the canonical tradition of the Orthodox Church."

6. Patitsas, "The Opposite of War Is Not Peace," 28.

War was a part of their reality and they had to deal with it accordingly. It didn't mean it was right to kill people, but in some contexts it was appropriate.[7]

Along with the Orthodox Christian voices that decry the ugly legacy of Just War Theory, one can find a growing number of dissenting voices among Western Christians and also many non-Christians. In a masterful address delivered to the 14th World Summit of Nobel Peace Laureates, Mairead Maguire calls upon His Holiness Pope Francis to officially repudiate Just War Theory and replace it with a "Theology of Peace, Nonkilling, and Nonviolence."[8] In the address, the Nobel Laureate states:

Here, in Rome, conscious that we are meeting in one of the most important Christian centers in the World, I would like to address a message to His Holiness the Pope. I thank Pope Francis for his love and work for the poor, his opposition to the death penalty, the crime of torture, and his recent interfaith initiative to end modern slavery. However, I would like to make a special appeal to His Holiness Pope Francis to replace the "Just War" Theory with a Theology of Peace, Nonkilling and Nonviolence. Our Christian roots are steeped in Jesus's nonviolence and in the words of the late US Theologian Fr. John L. McKenzie, "you cannot read the scriptures and not know that Jesus was totally nonviolent" and that the "Just War Theory is a phony piece of morality." I believe there is a self-delusion at the heart of humanity which says we have a right to kill each other, [and] the longstanding defect in our Christian just war theology feeds this myth of justified violence, militarism, and war. How much the world needs a clear unambiguous message from Pope Francis, and all our World's Spiritual Leaders, that violence is not the way, violence is never justified, violence is always wrong, and there are many ways of peaceful resistance to injustice as His Holiness pointed to with his call for a justice without revenge.[9]

Maguire appeals to the one man who can, *ex cathedra*, end the long history of religiously justified killing in order to facilitate the process of reshaping the world away from unmitigated militarism toward a true and lasting peace.

---

7. Skedros, "War, Byzantium, and Military Saints," 13.

8. Maguire, "Appeal to His Holiness Pope Francis." It was delivered at the Summit gathered in Rome, Italy from December 12–14, 2014.

9. Ibid.

As well, Dr. Robert Meagher calls for an end to the idea of justified killing and justified war, and his appeal, like that of a growing number of voices, finds its *raison d'être* in the ever-growing
tidal wave of Moral Injury accounts among war veterans.[10]
He asserts: Lawyers, like the theologians that preceded them,
are often quick to believe that the distinctions and rules they
inscribe in their documents will have any ordering or taming
effect on the chaos of war. What must be said again and again
until it sinks in is that war has its own rules, and they have little
or nothing to do with serving justice or preserving humanity.[11]

While Just War Theory appears to make for a good argument, the
legacy thus far imprinted on the pages of human history shows that it does
not play out well on the battlefield or in the aftermath of war. What started
out as a "promise" that war could be waged without sin and Moral Injury,
without guilt or shame, without risk to one's very soul, and without the inherent criminality evidenced in Cain's slaying of his brother, Abel, in Genesis 4:1–16, has become an unfulfilled promise. As Meagher states,

Whether or not these promises were first or ever made in good
faith is something we can never know, and it doesn't matter.
What we can know is that they have not been kept. We know
this from experience, the experience of war, the killing lab in
which the theory of just war has been tested for sixteen centuries. It is time to declare its death and to write the autopsy.[12]

War hurts the human soul because war is evil. Some would seek to
refute this assertion, but I argue that Just War Theory in service to blind
patriotism has done inestimable damage to the souls of thousands of our returning warriors. Far better would be the adherence to the ancient Christian

10. Meagher, *Killing from the Inside Out*, xii–xxi. I mention this to stress the point
that Meagher argues from the existential experience of countless warriors rather than
from a disconnected philosophical position. The start point, then, finds roots in the
spiritual, psychological, emotional, and physiological experience of moral guilt among
warriors. Meagher aims at resolving this affliction by means of the honest assessment
that killing hurts the soul. Just War Theory stands in the way of progress toward this
resolution. I have included here several pages in the book that directly point to that
start point in Meagher's argument, but really, the entire book repeatedly brings one
back to this. For example, on page 131: "Better to make a fresh start and to listen to
those who know firsthand what they are talking about. When the reality in question
is war, this means that we would do best to listen long and hard to combat veterans,
as well as the correspondents who take notes at their side." Any "theory" of war must
answer for and to these stories.

11. Ibid., 133.

12. Ibid., 129.

view that war damages the human soul because war and killing are inherently evil, and that the proper response to winning at war is not celebration but mourning. Mourning tells the dastardly and ugly truth of war and allows the warriors to quietly acknowledge that, despite heroic behaviors exhibited in war, war has no heroes and has no real victories. This view aligns with the wounded souls of thousands of warriors who, although glad for having survived and for having prevailed in battle, still grieve the destruction they have witnessed and perpetrated. There exists little to celebrate in the aftermath of war, but much, rather, to mourn. As decorated combat veteran and author Karl Marlantes eloquently states:

> There is a correct way to welcome our warriors back. Returning veterans don't need ticker-tape parades or yellow ribbons stretching across Texas. Cheering is inappropriate and immature. Combat veterans, more than anyone else, know how much pain and evil have been wrought. To cheer them for what they've just done would be like cheering the surgeon when he amputates a leg to save someone's life. It's childish, and it's demeaning to those who have fallen on both sides. A quiet grateful handshake is what you give the surgeon, while you mourn the lost leg. There should be parades, but they should be solemn processionals, rifles upside down, symbol of the sword sheathed once again. They should be conducted with all the dignity of a military funeral, mourning for the lost on both sides, giving thanks for those returned. Afterward, at home or in small groups, let the champagne flow and celebrate life and even victory if you were so lucky—afterward.[13]

While describing the positive impact of a "shared public meaning" of war within the context of a culture wherein most of the citizens understand and bear the burdens of war (Israel being a modern example), noted war journalist and documentary filmmaker Sebastian Junger makes a similar point to Marlantes' when he says about American society the following:

> Such public meaning is probably not generated by the kinds of formulaic phrase, such as "Thank you for your service," that many Americans now feel compelled to offer soldiers and vets. Neither is it generated by honoring vets at sporting events, allowing them to board planes first, or giving them minor discounts at stores. If anything, these token acts only deepen the chasm between the military and civilian populations by highlighting the fact that some people serve their country but the

13. Marlantes, *What It Is Like to Go to War*, 95.

vast majority don't. In Israel, where around half of the population serve in the military, reflexively thanking someone for their
service makes as little sense as thanking them for paying their
taxes. It doesn't cross anyone's mind.[14]

Offering some sort of token celebrity status to warriors in an attempt to
somehow assuage societal awkwardness in the presence of war veterans
does nothing to help war veterans come home. Granted, neither did the
open contempt received by many Vietnam War veterans. But celebrating
war veterans does as much damage as hating them but in a different way. In
both cases, society fails to jointly bear the burdens of war that weigh down
the souls of our veterans, because society, filled as it is with a majority that
has no clue about war experiences, must deny the trauma of its warriors lest
that trauma radically redefine our understanding of war causing immense
discomfort, guilt, sorrow, mourning, and grief—all of which our culture
seeks to avoid at all cost, even the cost of living in the real world of our
morally injured warriors.

   Moral Injury cannot be healed without the truthful telling of what has
been done by and what has happened to the war veteran. Killing, in any
circumstance, violates a deep moral sensibility situated in the human heart,
and this "heart alarm" sounds because war and killing represent profound
evils that wound, fragment, and dissipate the very core of the human person. Feeling guilty about war and killing is neither pathological nor irrational, and Orthodox Christian theological anthropology speaks profoundly
to both the cause of post-war Moral Injury and to the characteristics of an
effective methodology of treatment—namely, confessing one's sin before a
benevolent moral authority and discovering forgiveness. Moral Injury, like
a warning light on the dashboard of a vehicle, signals damage, impairment,
tarnishing, and more, to the image of God residing in each person, and
the symptoms present an opportunity to restore the reflection of that image
through hard work to full brightness. That is a worthy task and aim.

   By way of concluding these reflections, let me suggest a contrast between what our warriors get when they return from war and what they actually need. For the last several decades, our warriors have been returning
from the horrors of war to an increasingly fragmented society that no longer
coheres along any of the important lines of possible connection that held
ancient cultures together. To quote Sebastian Junger again, "Given the profound alienation of modern society, when combat vets say that they miss the
war, they might be having an entirely healthy response to life back home."[15]

14. Junger, *Tribe*, 99.

15. Ibid., 78.

Warriors leave a "brotherhood of pain" and a "community of sufferers" upon return from war and enter a culture emaciated by individualistic self-preoccupation.[16] Warriors come home tainted by the stain of blood, guilt, existential crisis, identity confusion, and rage at a government and a society that so quickly commits its sons and daughters to dangerous ventures for spurious reasons, and in that state they encounter a culture that neither shares their combat experience nor truly wants to. Warriors leave the cohesive "bands of brothers and sisters at arms" and attempt to enter a distracted, "every man for himself" culture of individualistic consumption-for-pleasure, and from that culture, warriors receive "Thanks for your service" almost as an afterthought, and what crosses the warrior's mind at that moment is, "What the hell do you know about my service?" The answer, of course, is "nothing," which renders the thanks banal, vacuous, and meaningless at best. At worst, such unthought greetings represent deeply offensive and hateful reminders of how uncaring a culture the American society can be. We all know, if we think about it for just a minute, that "thanks for your service" is more for the person saying it than for the person to whom it is said. But we do not take a moment to think about it, and that is what angers so many vets.

War requires a collective culture. Unit cohesion becomes a must when every person in a unit will either pull together or be broken apart and attrited. The outcry from warriors has been that society has no place for them. Some vets find their place, or perhaps more accurately, they carve it out with hard work. Yet many never find a place to reconnect, and it is to this reality that many "veterans' organizations" attempt to respond by creating contexts for veterans to come together and "belong." Still, this is nowhere near the same thing as the society at large taking its eyes off of all the self-preoccupying narcissistic hobbies of individualistic pleasure-seeking that distract most people so that the society can truly attend to the war burdens of its veterans. Warriors need that, but they do not get it. I have already quoted Sebastian Junger several times in this essay, and I concur totally with his premise that social isolation—at present, a palpable epidemic in America—calcifies war trauma into a cement-hard crust around the hearts of our warriors. We wonder why PTSD and Moral Injury and other like trauma responses seem so absent in some warring cultures, and the very simple answer is that those cultures received their warriors back into a cohesive band of caring human beings who were willing to ritually and practically carry the burdens of their warriors. American culture breeds the opposite, and there exists no shared cultural meaning to war, deployment, coming home, and reintegrating. Without this culture of shared meaning, warriors'

---

16. Ibid., 55.

experiences, rather than being part of a cultural story, become isolated and atomized, without honored expression and without honorable reception by the wider culture.

What do we need? We need rituals in which war veterans and civilian citizens work together to mutually own war trauma. We need contexts in which war veterans can tell their stories without the risk of being "shut down" because those listening will not hear them out to the bitter, painful end. We need citizens, pastors, priests, therapists, and others who will not argue with a warrior's sense of moral guilt, spiritual taint, soul-death, emotional numbness, and emotional rage by waving flags, spouting patriotic nonsense, and appealing to just causes and justified killing in order to deflect the moral evil of America's wars. We need an American society that looks down at its collective hands and sees blood; not only on the warriors, but on the hands of every citizen and non-citizen living within the protection of America's military. We need social circles small enough to be truly social but large enough to end isolation wherein warriors can meaningfully belong; not just to "vet groups" that meet isolated from the social network, but entire social networks of warriors and civilians including one another. We need to stop telling our warriors they have nothing to be ashamed of and start listening to their shame, their guilt, their loss, their inner emptiness. We do not listen to such tales because they threaten our illusions and assault our easy-won comfort, but we should listen, and in listening, we should help carry, own, share, and grieve rather than deny the burdens of war. Rather than medicating and then ignoring our warriors, we must find ways to bring them to the center of the "village" and give them full voice, and, together, we must appeal for, give, and receive forgiveness. Unfortunately, our culture is unlikely to experience the kind of shift that will make this possible without some sort of national crisis, but that does not mean that movements within our culture cannot begin to actively pursue changes in how we incorporate our warriors back into our lives in meaningful and healing ways.

32

MICHAEL LAPSLEY
with STEPHEN KARAKASHIAN

Owning the Past, Healing the Future

War damages all who wage it. Even among those who return physically unharmed, elevated rates of suicide, automobile accidents, domestic violence, and abuse of drugs are among the visible indicators of war's toll, and there are hidden costs as well. Many of these remain locked up in the veteran's heart and mind unspoken, emerging only years later, if at all. My father was a soldier in World War II, and my mother once told me that the man who went to war was not the man who came back. In Aotearoa, or New Zealand, the country where I grew up, the day that we remember the war dead is called ANZAC Day. It originated as a commemoration of those who fought and died in World War I, and has now become a time when we remember those who fell in the wars we have fought since.[1] There are parades, laying of wreathes, and other ceremonies. My father never participated in the events of ANZAC Day because he wanted to forget his war experiences. He kept silent about them for fifty years. But when he was dying, he began to talk about the war, and in the end, he asked that his funeral be one for a returned soldier. Though he tried to forget, he failed, so he began at the last moment to face the past.

1. Editors' note: Anzac Day commemorates the first major military action of the combined Australian and New Zealand forces in World War I. ANZAC is an acronym for the Australian and New Zealand Army Corps.

In the United States, the Institute for Healing of Memories–North America that I lead works with war veterans in Minnesota and Arizona. Quite a few of the veterans that we work with there are homeless, some from as long ago as the Vietnam War. We know that, much to our shame, Minnesota and Arizona are not unique. Nationwide, a disproportionate number of war veterans are homeless. They are held prisoner in part by their unspoken memories.

We bring veterans together in weekend-long groups in a safe and secure space, and we call these Healing of Memories workshops. In one such workshop in Arizona, an older veteran told me, "I've waited forty-two years to tell my story." He had never felt permission to speak about it before, nor been given the safe and confidential space where this might be possible. In Healing of Memories work, we do just that. Above all we allow veterans to be themselves. For some, the most pressing pain has to do with antecedent pain from childhood; for others, it is their current situation—homelessness, a desperate family problem, unemployment, drug addiction—some of which may indeed be a reflection of their war service. In either case, we let it emerge gradually as the story unfolds. Others may need to begin with stories of war, stories that cover anger, shame, and grief, and these stories implicitly give encouragement to others who are more reticent.

The truth is that if a war is unpopular, veterans are all too often given the message that they should go away, integrate themselves into civilian life, and disappear. On the other hand, if the war is popular, we hold parades honoring them, write articles about their bravery, and bestow symbolic perks on them like moving to the head of an airport line. But in neither case do we actually want to sit down and listen to the raw truth and the nightmares of what they have experienced. In a veteran's family, this can become the elephant in the room that no one wants to talk about, either because they fear they will not be able to handle the destructive emotions that emerge or they don't know how to begin. Is it any wonder that veterans feel isolated and misunderstood?

But talk about it we must. It is my own belief that the soul of the United States has been infected by endless war, and the nation's unwillingness to talk about what war is really like perpetuates the problem. What would it mean for the American people to engage in courageous conversations about war? In a recent article in the *New York Times*, Roy Scranton, a returned Iraq veteran and author, makes a public contribution to that conversation. He writes about the film *Star Wars*, coming as it did soon after the fall of Saigon, and how it reinforced American mythology about war at a time when it was being questioned:

> [*Star Wars*] recasts for Americans the mythic story so central to our sense of ourselves as a nation. In this story, war is a terrible thing we do only because we have to. In this story, the violence of war has a power that unifies and enlightens. In this story, war is how we show ourselves that we're heroes. Whom we're fighting against or why doesn't matter as much as the violence itself, our stoic willingness to shed blood, the promise that it might renew the body politic.[2]

He then goes on to say:

> The real gap [in our understanding] is between the fantasy of American heroism and the reality of what the American military does, between the myth of violence and the truth of war. The real gap is between our subconscious belief that righteous violence can redeem us, even ennoble us, and the chastening truth that violence debases and corrupts.[3]

There has been much attention recently in the press about the damage done to veterans who suffer from conditions that bear acronyms like PTSD, CTE, and TBI (post-traumatic stress disorder, chronic traumatic encephalopathy, traumatic brain injury). In one sense this is a welcome development, because at long last it is a recognition that there is, in fact, damage from war. However, the acronyms serve another important, less desirable function. Designating them as a syndrome distances us from the everyday lived reality that these men and women are now tragically experiencing. They are also an attempt to medicalize an outcome of war and thus to render it curable, if not now, then in the near future, through the boundless US faith in the power of American technology—in this case, medical advances. Surely, we think, there must be a pill, a sophisticated procedure, or a machine with some sort of healing rays, something yet to be discovered, that will heal the traumatized brain and thus erase the toll of war.

Years ago, when I was chaplain at Cape Town's Centre for Survivors of Violence and Torture, I ministered to those who had lived through apartheid's violence and torture. I gradually came to the conclusion that we often over-pathologize people's reaction to trauma. Some people do indeed have serious psychological and emotional issues, in some cases pre-dating the trauma, and they need to be seen by mental health professionals. But others need a different form of care that takes questions of human agency and moral values into account.

---

2. Scranton, "'Star Wars' and the Fantasy of American Violence."
3. Ibid.

As a person of faith, I look at the matter with a rather different set of spectacles. What has been left out of the clinical perspective is the matter of moral agency. Apart from the physical damage that is the loss of life and limbs, war creates damage at three other levels—the emotional, the moral, and the spiritual. Damage at the emotional level is now widely recognized as PTSD and is seen as a mental health issue. So, we send those suffering from it to psychiatrists. But what is left out of this perspective is that a soldier's emotional reaction is often intertwined with her moral angst, and that cannot be treated with medication.

We teach our children that it is wrong to kill another human being. We imprison and ironically, in the United States, even put to death those in civilian life who kill. At the same time we expose children to a barrage of violent movies and video games that we call entertainment and which, as Roy Scranton has pointed out, make heroes of those who use violence. Emerging out of this contradictory moral brew, we send our young men and women off to boot camp where they are given permission to kill and are taught that obedience is not only a virtue, but that their very survival and that of their fellow soldiers depends on it. So when they go to war they do as they are told and what the situation seems to require. Then, when they return to civilian life, we withdraw permission to kill and again condemn it as a deep moral wrong, yet we are surprised that they are afflicted with what we call post-traumatic stress disorder.

War presents soldiers with impossible moral choices akin to that in the film *Sophie's Choice*. Sophie, interned in a German concentration camp with her two children, must choose which of them will be sent to a work camp and which will be gassed to death. In the end, Sophie finds living with the responsibility for the choice she has made impossible to bear and she commits suicide as many returned soldiers do.

There is another kind of damage to human beings that is spiritual in nature. The great Abrahamic faiths of Islam, Christianity, and Judaism share a fundamental belief that all human beings are made in God's image and likeness. Accordingly, there is something of the divine in all of us. Christians often express this by saying we are all children of God. So in war, we are attacking the divine in the other, and the attacker is also morally transgressing the divine in him or herself. This is spiritual injury.

From this perspective, an important part of healing involves restoring the moral and spiritual order, which is a redemptive act, an act of spiritual and moral alchemy that brings good out of evil and life out of death. In traditional Christian theology, a sinner's relationship to God can be restored through confession and penance and ends with God's forgiveness. In a more secular or non-Christian context we might say that healing requires accepting responsibility for one's actions, which might well include apology and some form of making amends to those harmed when this is possible. Some Vietnam veterans, for example, have found healing and self-forgiveness by returning to Vietnam and working with its people in some way. Moral and spiritual healing to be complete needs to culminate in forgiving oneself—not by minimizing or forgetting what was done, but by accepting the transgression and expiating it in some way. This is not a quick or easy process. It can take a very long time and for some, it may never be complete. What is important is to be on the journey. Much of the work of the Institute for Healing of Memories is about helping people through storytelling and sharing to discover a personal alchemy by which they can transform their past acts or their failures to act into a life-giving force that allows them to heal their memories and fully rejoin the human family.

I would like to suggest that Moral Injury also affects nations, and healing at this level requires a communal process that calls for courageous conversations. Nations, like individuals, avoid facing the consequences of their choices. One of the reasons why the United States has managed to avoid a national conversation about its endless wars is because it has discontinued the draft. After the debacle of the Vietnam War there was pressure to end conscription. While the impetus for this came partly from the peace movement, the military readily supported it because they realized that without a draft, there was much less likely to be a national conversation about future wars. Individuals were no longer forced into the position of making a choice to go or not to go to war. During the Vietnam War, it was precisely that dilemma that provoked a prolonged national conversation about the war. A similar conversation in the United States is now long overdue. Let us hope for the sake of the country's soul that it soon begins.

33

WILLIAM P. MAHEDY

Excerpts from a Chaplain's Notebooks

July 25, 2008

He told me very calmly, "I am going to kill myself. I deserve to die and go to hell."

"Why?" I asked.

"Because I not only killed enemy soldiers in combat, but I murdered lots of innocent civilians as well." Knowing I had been a chaplain, he went on: "You have spent your entire life working for God, and I have done all this evil, so where does that leave me?"

"You get the party and I don't," I replied.

"What are you taking about?" he asked.

So I did a quick paraphrase of the story of the Prodigal Son in Luke's Gospel. I pointed out that I was like the older son, while he, with all his guilt—which amounted to real sorrow and repentance—was like the younger son, the one who gets the party. I threw in the story of the lost sheep, with me being among the ninety-nine left alone by the shepherd who goes out and finds him. "It leaves me feeling jealous of you," I said. "Because you're getting all this attention from God." He had never looked at it that way before, so he decided to stay alive long enough to ponder these things.

At our next session, I told him about Saul of Tarsus, a man with blood on his hands, on another murder mission, who was converted and became the great apostle. Subsequent meetings introduced him to assorted biblical characters, and also to John Newton, the slave ship captain who, after his conversion became a priest and the author of the great hymn "Amazing Grace." We got around to Ignatius Loyola, a soldier, recovering from wounds, who decided to become a soldier for God and then founded the Jesuits.

After several sessions, I introduced the conclusion to all this: "Compared to a lot of people God has used to accomplish great good in this world, you really are kind of a Sunday school kid. So quit wallowing in guilt and do some good for other people." He decided to do just that.

In the two or three years remaining in his life, he became a friend, counselor, benefactor, and mentor to a great many people. When he finally died of the liver disease that his many years of drinking had caused, we celebrated his life at a funeral attended by hundreds of people he had helped and who were inspired because they knew the history of his life. As the preacher on that occasion, I was able to add his name to the list of those in whom God's grace had accomplished much. Because he was doubtless enjoying the feast prepared for him in heaven, we had one in his honor right after the funeral. It was quite a party.

April 23, 2008

A friend who is an Episcopal priest, a woman who served in Iraq as a US Army chaplain, spoke of her experience there. As she said very succinctly: "In combat we embrace evil." To which I, recalling Vietnam, replied: "Yes, and evil embraces us." War brings about a rapid and radical conversion from one belief system to another. It is a conversion from a world of innocence to a realm of mindless and massive violence. Combat calls into question a benevolent God and leads to nihilism. For countless soldiers the religious beliefs of childhood become impossible. Though they may continue to believe in God and practice religion, faith is most often filtered through a deeper, darker prism. The altered state of being that results from war is a "new faith." It is a kind of religious experience that grasps Reality as partially hidden and partially known.

The knowledge of violence is a revelation, an initiation into the unspeakable—the unthinkable—mystery of good and evil. Like all revelation, it is only partial, for it promises further disclosure, deeper understanding, and more power. The veteran continues to search for that which remains hidden beneath the veil of this transcendent experience, while hoping somehow that further revelation might include a restoration to innocence, a return to the garden. As life unfolds for former soldiers, it becomes clear that no return is possible—but the quest for peace of soul continues.

No one knows better than the soldier that war has irrevocable and enduring consequences. People are dead and maimed, homes and villages destroyed. Personal responsibility for such actions cannot and should not be denied. The great moral discovery in a combat zone is of one's own limitless capacity for malice, and, by extrapolation, the unsuspected depths and pervasive nature of human depravity. A veteran must live with this knowledge for a lifetime.

The attributes of violence are authentic and enticing, but the effects of violence, both upon society and upon the soul, are clearly evil—evil beyond anything else in human experience. And yet there is a stubborn refusal to accept evil of this magnitude as the final reality. The human spirit both demands and understands that there be some reality beyond violence. This realization is the beginning of spiritual healing.

Propensities of nature and grace assert themselves so that conscience, wisdom, weariness, religious impulses, and a desire for healing—all conspire in a struggle to dethrone violence from its primacy. In this pursuit of peace the subtle contour of another revelation emerges: a disclosure that violence may be only penultimate, that another reality might instead be definitive. At this point the issue becomes truly religious, amounting to a clash between two contenders for ultimacy. There takes place within the soul a practical testing of these two alternative and contradictory religious hypotheses.

Psychotherapy provides a formidable critique of violence. It allows the veteran to revisit the brutality of the original event in a benign and supportive context. It discloses the futility and destructiveness of clinging to combat survival mechanisms. Psychiatry offers remedies for the biochemical residue of violence. Therapy is an essential step in healing the wounds of war for a great many veterans. Therapy loosens the grip of violence upon the soul but is unable finally to dislodge it. The final displacement of war's violence requires a transforming experience that exceeds in magnitude and significance the original transformation into that realm.

This new transformation must be more infectious, compelling, transcendent, and transforming than is violence. It must be expressed in a liturgy. It must be a community experience. The second transformation requires a peace that transforms violence itself, a peace that passes understanding. John Fergueson, a Marine combat veteran of Vietnam and also an Episcopal priest, is convinced that some combat events create a transcendent experience of evil. The experience is one of true *ekstasis* (ecstasy) in the classic sense. In ecstasy, one seems to transcend oneself. The other self is created in what is often a dissociative state.

A person then must live in both selves, but sometimes there is insufficient energy. The person goes back and lives in the evil self, by continually reliving the experience, by going back over it again and again. . . . It is what he or she does in order to be empowered to deal with his or her fragmentation. Regardless, the residue of war remains entrenched and often intractable, because it was etched upon the soul through an event that took a person outside of himself or herself in a moment of massive violence. Another self was created in a moment of *ekstasis* that bore the semblance of a religious transformation. It was a conversion experience, an introduction into a new realm wherein goodness was subverted. The only effective remedy is a counter-transformation, a second and more powerful *ekstasis* than the first. There must be an experience of transcendent good that is more powerful than the evil experience. This is a lifelong journey.

Combat creates a dark night of the soul. This is a classic religious term. Veterans come very close to experiencing a state of soul that is described throughout the literature of Christian mysticism. The spirit enters a period of bleakness, a night of the soul. God is grasped only as if in a cloud—a cloud of unknowing. Religious good feelings, joy, and enthusiasm all disappear. This experience of the mystics is the biblical experience lived to its fullest extent. Christians, in following Christ, also must cry out with him on the Cross: "My God, my God, why have you abandoned me?" Veterans can get to that spiritual place very rapidly and at a very young age.

For the mystics, God is found in the depths of one's soul only after a period of apparent absence (a state commonly described as the "dark night," or "cloud of unknowing").[1] The dark night experience shatters shallow religious images and practices. Religious enthusiasm disappears. God no longer seems to be present either in one's own life or in the world. Often one is almost overwhelmed by a sense of inadequacy and even of sin and guilt. Eventually, through a very painful process, one becomes aware again of God's presence. Now, however, the presence arises from the midst of a deep and abiding "cloud." The emptiness and desolation of life, the sense of personal inadequacy and sin, can become points of contact with God. But this takes a good bit of understanding, lots of guidance, and some very hard work.

Vets understand these concepts through personal experience. Understanding the relationship between the veteran's journey and that of the Christian mystics has been helpful to many. Vets have undergone a journey of the spirit not unlike that described by the mystics. They have had

1. Editors' note: A reference to the Spanish sixteenth-century *Dark Night of the Soul* by the mystic Saint John of the Cross and the anonymous Middle English *The Cloud of Unknowing*.

consciousness-altering experiences. Our modern world offers a number of these: war, holocaust, genocide, massive starvation, nuclear awareness.

To make this journey a fruitful one, we must first unmask a religious underpinning that is most detrimental to veterans' spiritual health. This is the myth of American innocence, the belief in American Exceptionalism. It is a form of civil religion that goes back to seventeenth-century England and was transported to the American colonies. I recall it was best expressed in a veterans group by a Vietnam helicopter door gunner. "Before I went to Vietnam," he said, "I believed in Jesus Christ and John Wayne, but in Vietnam both went down the tubes."

The John Wayne and Jesus Christ connection amounts to a national myth. According to this myth, our nation is incapable of fighting an immoral war. The myth goes even further. We believe that the wars we fight must not merely be just, but they must be waged on behalf of a holy cause. For us war must be a crusade. In a holy war, we tell ourselves, the nasty business of killing is really God's work. Get on with it and God smiles on you. In Vietnam and again in the present wars in Iraq and Afghanistan, that myth is unmasked.

The Jesus Christ and John Wayne myth is pervasive. It lies at the heart of American self-definition as an article of religious faith. Our pilgrim forebears felt that they had been called to a religious destiny unique in human history. John Winthrop (1588–1649), who was to become the first governor of the Massachusetts Bay Colony, set a tone and direction to American life that remains almost unaltered to this day. Before disembarking in Salem Harbor in 1630, Winthrop reminded the settlers: "[We] must consider that we shall be as a City set upon a Hill, the [eyes] of all people are [upon] us."[2] In that moment the myth was born. America was to be a chosen people among the nations of the earth. It was to be a moral example to the rest of the world. The corollary was also implied by Winthrop: the rest of the world must keep its eyes upon us and follow our lead, for "the God of Israel is among us, when ten of us shall be able to resist a thousand of our enemies, when he shall make us a praise and glory."[3]

Scholars call the mythology of a nation its "civil religion." Every tribe, people, and nation has some sort of civil religion. What distinguishes the American version from others is its dependence on the Hebrew and Christian Scriptures for its language and concepts. Though the United States owes its cultural origins as much to the philosophy, laws, and ideas of ancient

2. Editors' note: A reference to the often quoted 1630 speech of John Winthrop. See Parker, *John Winthrop*, 42.

3. Ibid.

Greece and Rome as it does to biblical religion, we have never acknowledged this fact. We prefer to express our self-understanding in terms of the traditional biblical faith. Civil religion in America seems to resemble biblical religion, but in fact it is very different. Our civil religion convinces us that our national goals are transcendent and beyond question. It diminishes other nations and inverts religion, constructing its own model of God.

While sometimes war is the lesser of two evils, and combat sometimes a necessity, we don't usually discuss war in these terms—the terms of the classic Just War tradition. We usually revert to our civil religion. There has never been a greater need for a public conversation about religion and war than there is now.

Returning veterans are aware of the disjuncture between battlefield realities and this religious belief system. The journey out of the night becomes possible, when civil religion is laid to rest. Liturgies, retreats, sacramental ministry, conferences, various approaches to prayer, scripture study, spiritual reading, and use of the various religious and spiritual traditions are more fruitful without the impediment of civil religion. This new awareness gradually becomes one of God's pervasive and gracious presence. A far more profound faith has replaced the one that was lost. Through the grace of God, one comes to perceive the Easter experience of the risen Christ emerging from the darkest corners of the soul.

Twelve Steps to Spiritual Recovery: Twelve Activities of the Spiritual Boot Camp

1. We admit that we are powerless over the memories, emotions, attitudes, thoughts, bodily reactions, and spiritual pain resulting from combat.

2. Having undergone a "conversion experience" into a world of violence, we come to believe that a Power greater than ourselves can restore us to peace of soul, peace with others, and peace with God as I understand him.

3. We make a decision to turn our anger, guilt, resentments, shame, and fear over to God and to commit ourselves entirely to God's loving care.

4. We make a searching and fearless moral inventory of ourselves, including all we have done in combat, leaving out nothing we have done personally but not accepting responsibility for what we did not do personally.

5. We admit to ourselves and to one other person the exact nature of our past wrongs and our present tendencies to do evil, asking God to forgive our past sins and remove our defects of character.

6. We make a list of all persons we have harmed and become willing to make amends to them all, either directly or indirectly, insofar as this is possible without harming others or ourselves.

7. Having admitted our tendency to "play God" in our judgments of others and of ourselves, and now submitting our judgments to those of God, we forgive all others any offenses they may have committed against us, we forgive ourselves and accept God's forgiveness of us.

8. Having entered into a deeper spiritual state, we surrender ourselves completely to God, letting go of our hidden hatreds and desires for revenge and also of our guilt over the unintended consequences of acts we performed in good faith or in ignorance.

9. We begin to exercise a specific and detailed "discipline of trust," whereby we gradually come to trust ourselves, trust others, and trust that God will restore to us our power to rejoice, to give thanks, to praise, and to enjoy.

10. We begin to enter into the silence and the still waters of our souls in peace rather than in the isolation and loneliness of fear, spending time in quiet prayer and in sharing what we have discovered within ourselves in prayer and worship together with others.

11. We commit ourselves to completing the final mission of combat soldiers: becoming bearers of peace, prayerfulness, happiness, and rejoicing, resolving to go behind the "enemy lines" of fear, mistrust, selfishness, greed, and hatred that surround us in our culture, confident that, as warriors of peace, we will overcome these barriers using the weapons of peace, mercy, and kindness that we have been given.

12. Where before we were infected with the contagion of violence, we will now spread to others the contagion of peace that we have received, planning our mission carefully, including all those within the ambit of our lives.

Scholars

We read to know we are not alone.

—C. S. LEWIS

When everybody is swept away unthinkingly by what everybody else does and believes in, those who think are drawn out of hiding because their refusal is conspicuous and therefore becomes a kind of action. . . . The manifestation of the wind of thought is no knowledge; it is the ability to tell right from wrong, beautiful from ugly. And this indeed may prevent catastrophes.

—HANNAH ARENDT

34

KRISTEN J. LESLIE

Betrayal by Friendly Fire

She stopped me in the woman's restroom at the end of a conference on Moral Injury. She wanted to talk about my presentation on Military Sexual Trauma (MST). Early in basic training her drill instructor made sexually explicit comments that made her cringe. At her graduation party, her drill instructor followed her to the restroom and raped her. The cuts and bruises lasted a few weeks and then healed. The psychological, spiritual, and professional wounds lasted far longer. She did not report the rape because she knew it would not help. The rape was bad, but she knew that reporting it would make her life hell. She had seen how other victims had experienced retaliation by those in their chain of command. Regardless, she was not a complainer and she hoped she could get on with her life.

This had not proven to be the case. In fact, her sense of self changed to a bifurcated before- and after-the-rape existence. Before the rape, she had loved being in uniform. Serving had given her a sense of purpose, new skills, and a community of sisters and brothers she had never known. After the rape, she felt uncomfortable in her body. She lost the sense of confidence that had always been central to her identity. She was on edge around new people and in new places. She spent too many nights getting lost in a bottle. Because she knew she was not fun to be around, she removed herself from social situations. One year after the rape, she was separated from service with a mental health disorder.[1] She now wonders if getting some help

1. For more on administrative discharges and MST, see Darehshon, "Booted,"

could have salvaged her military career. She misses her battle buddies and yearns for her pre-rape self. She wants to know what "greater good" her sacrifice has served.

She came to the conference on Moral Injury looking for some answers to her Military Sexual Trauma. Why did she feel so on-edge in the world? Why couldn't she trust people anymore? How could she live in her polluted body, when "God don't like ugly"? And, how could she relate to people— even her friends—who (she was sure) saw her as damaged goods? In this essay, we will explore some of the connections between Moral Injury and MST with the goal of providing some insights for MST survivors as they work toward resilience and healing. To do this I will begin by exploring definitions of Military Sexual Trauma and its prevalence. I will discuss the morally injurious nature of MST and its effects on survivors. I will explore why survivors rarely report MST, and then end with actions that survivors can take to strengthen their resilience and actively work toward the "restoration of a life worth living."[2]

Military Sexual Trauma: Definitions and Prevalence

Military Sexual Trauma (MST) is the traumatic and debilitating physical, psychological, and spiritual effects that follow a sexual assault while serving in the military. Sexual assault is the "intentional sexual contact characterized by use of force, threats, intimidation, or abuse of authority, or when the victim does not or cannot consent."[3] This includes completed or attempted rape, forcible anal or oral sex, and assaults with intent to commit these acts. This can be assault by physical force or "constructive force" (threats, intimidation, or abuse of one's rank to coerce).[4] The perpetrators of MST on male victims use it as a definitive method of emasculation, and on women, as a

---

Human Rights Watch.

2. Judith Herman names the goal of healing from complex trauma as "the restoration of a life worth living" (Herman, *Trauma and Recovery*, 268).

3. Department of Defense, "Fiscal Year 2014 Annual Report on Sexual Assault in the Military." For a fuller discussion on defining MST, see Morris et al., "Unseen Battles," 94.

4. The Veterans Administration (VA) definition of MST includes both sexual harassment and sexual assault. The Department of Defense (DoD) definition includes only sexual assault and more closely resembles civilian definitions. In this essay I will use the DoD definition of sexual assault. For more on this distinction, see Stander and Thomsen, "Sexual Harassment and Assault in the US Military," 20.

way of "putting them in their place."[5] Central to understanding the impact of MST is the high rates of sexual assault and the low rates of reporting.

The prevalence of sexual assault within the military is staggering. In 2013 alone, an estimated 10,600 male (1 percent of men) and 9,600 female (4.9 percent of women) active component service members (6.5 percent of total serving) were sexually assaulted. Nearly all of these assaults (90 percent) took place within a military setting or were perpetrated by military personnel.[6] Men and women serving in the reserve component experienced significantly lower rates (0.4 percent of men and 3.1 percent of women). As with active-duty service members, a majority of the assailants of reserve-component members were military personnel (81 percent), and a majority of the assaults occurred in a military setting (63 percent).[7]

Sexual assaults against servicemen often involve repeated and physically violent assaults that occur in a context of bullying, abuse, or hazing. The perpetrator's intent is to humiliate, abuse, or emasculate the male victim, rather than to have a sexual encounter. The assaults are more often perpetrated by multiple coworkers at work, during work hours, and generally do not involve the use of alcohol.[8] Assaults against servicewomen are more likely to be committed by an individual male service member after the workday, away from duty responsibilities, and are more likely to involve the use of alcohol. In this context, alcohol is often used as a means to groom the victim, making her less able to resist the assault. Women are less likely to describe the attack as intended to abuse or humiliate them and more likely to perceive the intent as sexual.[9] Women who deploy to combat environments are more likely to experience both sexual harassment and sexual assaults than those not deployed.[10]

A precursor to many cases of MST is sexual harassment. In 2013, 22 percent of active-component women and 7 percent of active-component men (making a total of 116,600 service members) were sexually harassed. This is significant in understanding MST because those who experience sexual harassment experience far higher rates of sexual assault. One third of those who were sexually assaulted say the offender sexually harassed them before the assault.[11]

5. Herman, *Trauma and Recovery*, 253.

6. Morral et al., *Sexual Assault and Sexual Harassment*, xvii.

7. Ibid., xxiii.

8. Ibid., xix.

9. Ibid., 90.

10. LeardMann et al., "Combat Deployment," 219.

11. Morral et al., *Sexual Assault and Sexual Harassment*, 92.

The Morally Injurious Nature of Military Sexual Trauma

Service members know that from the start of their service they will be called to make sacrifices for a greater good. MST survivors are forced to confront the notion that the "sacrifice" they endured (and continue to endure) serves no greater good and is, in fact, disruptive to any benevolent outcome. MST is morally injurious when the sexual assault (and subsequent public responses) violates a survivor's essential assumptions about the world and their place in it. Moral values give order and meaning to our lives. When a service member's core moral beliefs are violated, they experience a destabilizing of their core beliefs about self, other, and God. The morally injurious nature of MST can leave a survivor questioning their grounding sense of fairness and justice in the world. For religious service members, this can result in crises of faith and feelings of divine abandonment. As a survivor once reported, "What happened to me made me ugly, and God don't like ugly." The betrayal at the core of Military Sexual Trauma devastates a survivor's ability to trust others and the military culture that committed to honoring them. This increased sense of vulnerability can be jarring and morally abhorrent to a service member who has been told that vulnerability is a sign of weakness and failure.

At the heart of a morally injurious experience is the violation of what Jonathan Haidt and Fredik Bjorklund call "moral intuitions," the unconscious evaluative feelings about the character or actions of a person.[12] When a service member is sexually assaulted, they experience the disruption of moral intuitions in relational and embodied ways. This can happen when they have to report to someone in their chain of command who assaulted them, or failed to hold their assailant accountable. Being on duty with or failing to report a repeating offender can be demoralizing. Living at a distance from family, especially children, when the environment no longer merits self-sacrifice can feel less like honorable service and more like abandonment of those they love. The embodied nature of a morally injurious assault can leave men and women with a sense of alienation from their bodies. Having worked hard to meet the physical standards of a warrior, MST can force a survivor to struggle with the very sacredness of their body. Sexual intimacy can become confusing or a source of harm. A significant part of combat training is learning emotional control. The emotional upheaval related to MST can cause service members to feel that they are not in control emotionally, and in turn, not worthy to serve.[13]

12. Haidt and Bjorklund, "Social Intuitionists," 188.
13. Hoyt et al., "Military Sexual Trauma in Men," 255.

Reporting: The Rape Was Bad, But Everything That Followed Was Worse

Reporting MST to a military authority or organization is an important way for survivors to have access to restorative care and services. It also allows the larger system to hold assailants accountable for their crimes.[14] Unfortunately, many MST survivors are reluctant to report because it can lead to professional and social retaliation. Of the active-duty women who filed formal reports, over half (52 percent) experienced professional or social retaliation.[15] If they do accuse a fellow shipmate, soldier, airman, or Marine, they know they likely will be ostracized and subjected to harsh treatment by their peers. They can be accused of malingering in order to cover up other problematic behaviors (e.g., drinking, fraternizing, missing duty) and contaminating the cohesion of their unit. For anyone outside majority demographics (LGBTQ, racial, ethnic, and religious minorities), the retaliation can be even more damaging. For all survivors who seek redress through their chain of command, they can quickly discover how little they are valued. Reporting can harm one's promotion and ability to remain active duty. In other words, "the rape was bad, but everything that followed was worse."[16]

In addition to MST, of those who were victims of sexual harassment, 44 percent were encouraged to drop the issue, while 41 percent said that the person to whom they reported took no action.[17] When commanders are responsible for maintaining the health and mission readiness of their units, assault and harassment charges (rather than the assaults themselves) are too often labeled as the disruptive forces that detract from the mission. Because responding to reports takes time, limited resources, and is typically very complicated, commanders feel pressure to encourage victims to drop charges or too often dismiss the charges altogether.

Even when reporting provides viable avenues of justice, many service members would rather avoid making waves, using their previously established coping mechanisms to deal with the fall out. They joined the military with the belief that the training would make them tough. Reporting an assault could be perceived as a personal weakness. For male survivors, stigma and gender stereotypes are significant barriers to seeking help. Being perceived as weak can be almost as traumatizing as the actual experience

14. DoD, "Fiscal Year 2014 Annual Report on Sexual Assault in the Military," 6.

15. Morral et al., *Sexual Assault and Sexual Harassment*, xxiv.

16. *The Invisible War.*

17. Ibid., 94.

of violence. This is especially true in a hypermasculine environment, where physical strength and control of one's body is directly related to success. Any sign of being out of control is seen as a weakness, and for a man, a threat to their core identity. When this exists, repairing this damage to a man's reputation can take priority in healing, even over deeper emotional and spiritual wounds.[18]

For many women serving in the military, they are warriors first and women second. Captain Amy McGrath, an F-18 back-seater, said she worked hard to establish her niche among aviators in a male-dominated fighter squadron. She did not want to stand out.[19] For many, it is the sexual assault that turns the unit's focus on them as women. When Major Tammy Duckworth, presently a senator from Illinois, was recovering from life-threatening combat wounds in Walter Reed Medical Center, she was asked to speak to a group of female legislators on how she felt about a ban on women in combat. She told them that she thought it was stupid and unrealistic under the conditions of modern warfare. Women are fighting and dying as warriors, not as women.[20] Women join the military not to be female Marines, female soldiers, female airmen, female sailors, or female warriors. They join to be warriors. Military Sexual Trauma changes the narrative about them from warriors to women.

Failure to report sexual assault and harassment can exasperate a victim's experience of trauma and yet, fear of retaliation is not regularly cited as the primary reason that men and women do not report the violations. Most indicate that they did not report MST because they wanted to forget about it and move on, or because they thought it was not serious enough to report.[21] High rates of sexual assault accompanied by low rates of reporting leave too many women and men suffering in silence and living in the fear that it will happen again.

Survivors' Traumatic Responses to Assault

All women and men have a fundamental right to determine how their bodies interact with others. Men and women who were sexually assaulted while serving in the military experience a violation that assaults both this embodied right and the fundamental premise of a military unit. Good order and discipline, unit cohesion, mission readiness, and the charge to never

18. O'Malley, "Military Sexual Trauma in Male Survivors," 18.
19. Holmstedt, *Band of Sisters*, xiv.
20. Duckworth, "Introduction," viii.
21. O'Malley, "Military Sexual Trauma in Male Survivors," 94.

leave a comrade behind are core mandates for anyone wearing a uniform. Honorable and selfless service is central to this moral code. From early in basic training, service members are conditioned to understand how essential these mandates are to their membership in this community and to their very identities. Sexual assault by a service member is a form of "friendly fire" that contradicts this basic notion and shatters the moral framework of the environment. Assault by someone who swore to uphold the Constitution, follow orders, and protect the lives of their comrades can leave a victim feeling disoriented and morally betrayed. To understand an MST survivor's experience, it is helpful to frame the assault as incest, where the assailant is known, trusted, and tasked with attending to the welfare of others. As with Moral Injury, both incest survivors and MST survivors can subjectively struggle with their allegiance to a person or system that has been both protector and betrayer.

Survivors of MST live with scars that are physical, cognitive, emotional, spiritual, and social. Sexual assault is an attack on a person's body that can leave bruises, cuts, and scars. Because this involves parts of the body that the victim deems as personal, private, and for some sacred, it can be difficult to discuss the specifics of the harm without violating one's own personal, social, and moral code. Many would rather keep silent than tell a friend, family member, or helping professional about the physical harm done to them. In the period after the assaultive event, a victim can experience classic signs of trauma—an inability to concentrate, a hyperalertness to their surroundings, and a sensitivity to physical touch. Cognitively, sexual assault by a known assailant (as is most often the case in the military) can leave one struggling to make sense of the comrade-as-assailant, and consequently, the nature of the violence itself.

The thinking goes, a known and trusted colleague cannot, by definition, violate someone they call sister/brother. As such, "the event" gets interpreted as something other than violence. This cognitive dissonance leaves a victim questioning their own ability to make sense of the interaction and can leave them questioning their own intuitive sense about whom they may now trust. This can even lead to counterfactual thinking—a process of questioning decisions and actions that took place around the assault, while looking for alternative outcomes based on hindsight knowledge rather than what was actually known in real time.[22] It is a way of making sense of the violence, even when the assault did not follow a logical course of cause and effect. Counterfactual thinking can leave a victim second-guessing all of

---

22. Litz et al., *Adaptive Disclosure*, xii.

their actions and relationships. Social connections, the very things that can help a traumatized survivor, can feel too demanding and threatening to risk.

Central to an MST survivor's response to the violence are the emotionally condemning experiences of shame, embarrassment, and self-blame— for not confronting the earlier harassment, for their decision to use alcohol, for not being in control enough to stop the assault, and so on. Some experience trauma-induced fear of their surroundings. Some of these emotional responses can be life-threatening. Men who live with MST often experience an assault at the core of their gendered identity. Historically, rape has been used as a torturous tool of war and a way to emasculate or "feminize" the enemy. This feminizing of the enemy is so culturally recognized that it shows up in video games like Call of Duty, where "tea bagging" (hanging one's scrotum in the face of a defeated enemy) is the way to show superiority. In a military culture that values hyper-heterosexual and heteronormative standards of strength and power, male survivors of sexual assault can feel disempowered to the point of feeling dehumanized and emasculated. For many males, healing from this emasculation becomes the primary concern in their healing process.[23]

MST can leave survivors with existential and spiritual questions, starting with questions about the benevolence of the universe or a loving God. This can follow the form of wondering about living in a just world, or being protected by a just and benevolent God. Survivors who are religious may struggle with whether the assault was an act of retribution by God for sins they have committed. For those who understand their bodies to be sacred or temples of the holy, sexual assault can leave them feeling desecrated and impure. The combination of a fear of divine retribution and a sense of desecration can leave a survivor believing that they deserve to be shunned by family, friends, and their religious community. This can contribute to their loss of hope in the present and future. In some religious traditions, forgiveness is the means of making amends for sinful actions and reconciling with a person or community. Forgiveness can be a complex thing for survivors. Forgiveness can be a healing action if the survivor understands that they are not responsible for the assault, that righteous anger can be an important part of their healing, and that forgiveness is not a means to exorcise painful feelings.[24] All of these physical, emotional, and spiritual wounds too often contribute to a loss of trust in one's community and those who want to help. The "friendly fire" nature of MST damages the very grounds on which one may seek to find support and healing.

23. O'Malley, "Military Sexual Trauma in Male Survivors," 18.
24. Leslie, When Violence is No Stranger, 129.

Healing Actions in Response to MST: Words to Survivors

Healing from MST begins with establishing safety in the present and actively attending to the needs of your body.[25] Connect with a supportive community and build friendships. Your inclination may be to isolate yourself from friends and family for a variety of reasons: fear that they will judge your actions before, during, and after the assault; frustration that they believe you but critique the military system that gives you life; and many other reasons. Isolating yourself from potential supportive people will not help you. It will not help your families. Look for people you trust and who will believe your suffering: friends, coworkers, religious professionals, doctors, and counselors. Not everyone is willing or able to support MST survivors. If they cannot, recognize it is their failing and find others who will.

Safety always begins with the body. If you do not feel safe in your body, you will not feel safe anywhere. Remember your military training and PT—physical training. Find ways to be serious about physical activity, including working out, walking, and practicing yoga. Judith Herman, MD, tells her students that the two most important phrases in yoga are "notice that" and "what happens next?" Things begin to shift when you start approaching your body with curiosity rather than fear.[26] Limit your use of alcohol and self-prescribed drugs, because they can isolate you even more.

Once you have begun to attend to the safety needs of your body, find ways and relationships in which you can both talk about the assault and mourn your losses. When you decide to tell the details of your story, find someone who will believe you. When you feel heard and believed, your grieving will be less complicated. Being believed helps your grieving process, which helps your healing process. Find a friend, counselor, or religious professional who will say, "Someone did this to you and caused you to suffer. You did not bring this upon yourself. Neither did you deserve it. It was wrong and should not have happened. You did not fail the mission. I believe you." When you feel believed, you are more able to heal.

When you find a caring professional who is willing to receive your story, it is important that they willingly meet the following standards of care:

- understand your assault as violence and not bad sex;
- keep confidences;
- assess for your safety (and possibly that of your family);

---

25. This model draws on Herman's model of healing from complex trauma, which includes establishing safety, remembering and mourning, and connecting. For more on this, see Herman, *Trauma and Recovery*, 2015.

26. Herman, *Trauma and Recovery*, 269.

· believe that what you tell them is real and causes you to suffer;

· affirm that the violence was not your fault;

· discuss reporting options and accept your decision;

· work with you to find networks of support (MST support group, VA, friends, etc.);

· affirm that you did not fail the mission;

· see your strengths, courage, and points of resilience.

A professional counselor, medical professional, or religious professional should never:

· blame you for the assault;

· judge you or the decisions you made before, during, or after the assault;

· suggest that you need to move on more quickly;

· suggest that forgiveness is easy or even necessary;

· if a religious professional, use religious resources in a coercive manner;

· over-share about their own trauma experiences;

· ask you to do things for them physically or sexually.

If the doctor, religious professional, or counselor is not able to meet these standards of care, it is reasonable for you to stop seeing him or her and find another caring professional from whom to seek help.

And finally, healing from MST involves building resilience with the help of a community. You cannot get over pain, trauma, and suffering; you can only get through it. If this is true, healing from MST, like Moral Injury, involves resilience. Resilience is the ability to survive threat or injury while engaging healthy coping strategies that move you toward health. For survivors of MST, this involves working to incorporate the experiences of suffering into a wider and more accepting sense of self. Healing from MST involves building resilience. And resilience is an outcome of caring relationships that help people spiritually and morally integrate moral stress.[27] The key to resilience is not to get over or forget (amnesia or exorcism) but to find or create a community that allows your sense of shame and guilt to have a larger environment of goodness, compassion, and honor.

---

27. Doehring, "Resilience," 635.

Conclusion

Women and men join the military with the promise that they will become part of a larger community that bands together and serves a greater good. Military Sexual Trauma serves no greater good. It devastates the core values of survivors and drives them away from their community. The morally injurious nature of MST complicates a survivor's grieving and healing process as it disrupts their faith and trust in the world. Healing from MST entails establishing safety in the present, finding safe ways to tell the story and grieve, and connect with people and activities that allow a survivor to live honorable lives in the present. In doing this, a survivor can strengthen their resilience and actively work toward the "restoration of a life worth living."[28]

---

28. As mentioned earlier, Herman names the goal of healing from complex trauma as "the restoration of a life worth living" (*Trauma and Recovery*, 268).

35

BRAD ALLENBY

Respecting Moral Injury

It was the winter of 1973 at the point in the training cycle for 50th Company, OC3–73, Infantry Officer Candidate School (OCS) at Fort Benning, when those who hadn't quickly washed out were beginning to feel their oats. We were used to jogging everywhere by that time, and early one morning, a few candidates launched a cadence that we spontaneously took up, thinking it far more demonstrative of our aggressive spirit than the routine "I don't know but I've been told . . ." It began, "I want to rape, kill, pillage, and burn . . ." Our TAC officers[1] immediately stopped us in our tracks, and in a rapid, and obviously powerful intervention, made it very clear that such values were unacceptable in an American military officer. This was not just a particularly sensitive point in Infantry OCS because of the My Lai massacre, Lt. Calley's subsequent court-martial in 1970, and the fact that Lt. Calley had been a 1967 OCS graduate. It was also an important part of the much broader mission to turn new, and fairly naïve, college graduates into American military officers. Moreover, the TAC officers were clearly effective: I remembered that incident serving as a young officer in the Corps of Engineer with the 43rd Engineering Battalion at Fort Benning, and I remember it now.

Simple as that incident was, it resonates with me today in part because it illustrates several things that are relevant to a contemporary consideration

1. "TAC officer" is an expression employed for teachers and advisors at several cadet programs, including West Point and Officer Candidate School.

of Moral Injury. To begin with, it is a reminder that the very process of joining a military organization requires creating a new identity: young civilians with widely varying backgrounds, experiences, and beliefs must be turned into warriors. The homogenous haircut, the assembly-line medical and paperwork processing system, the lack of privacy in the barracks and bathrooms, the regimented day, the well-thought-out psychological structure of boot camp—all reinforce the conversion of individualistic civilians from many different backgrounds into dependable components of a unit where achievement of mission, not individual fulfillment, is the primary value, even at the cost of human life. The transition from civilian to military requires building a new identity for the trainee.

But the identity cannot be entirely new. The military mission, and the warrior identity that it requires, are not secret, and every military creates identities that align with the broader values of its society. Moreover, no military is free to shape a warrior identity from a blank slate; rather, if the warrior identity is going to be effective, it must draw on the identities already common in its incoming civilians. Even non-state actors such as ISIS are constrained by the cultures that they draw their warriors from. More than that, there are always normative choices involved in shaping the warriors that a particular culture or state wants to represent it. Our TAC officers could have let us go on, but if they had, we might have incorporated different values into our idea of an officer, and thus become very different officers, with very different perspectives on our duties and obligations. But they didn't: they intervened, and in doing so, implemented a choice regarding the values that represented what the Infantry School, the Army, and the United States wanted in an officer.

So what that single experience continues to illustrate for me today is that the warrior identity, built as it is from so many different personal and institutional influences, is a design space. It is a constrained design space—constrained by what warriors will accept as authentic given their background, by a network of international laws and norms, by national culture, by the prevailing types of conflict and the technologies with which they are fought—but it is a design space nonetheless. This has always been true, of course, but it is especially relevant today for three main reasons. First, the dramatic increase in mission, technological, cultural, and ethical complexity is putting new and challenging stresses on warriors, some of which inevitably threaten the strong identity that supports them. Second, the importance of identity is magnified today because it is in critical ways becoming a battlespace in itself: both the Crimea invasion and the conflict with ISIS, for example, can be better understood if we recognize that part of their challenges arise from how "identity" in those conflicts has been weaponized by our adversaries. Third, identity and Moral Injury are linked, in that Moral Injury arises when warriors are exposed to, or participate in, acts and conditions that transgress deeply held beliefs—which, of course, are core to identity (both personal identity and warrior identity, which co-exist in the individual warrior).[2] Mitigating Moral Injury, therefore, implies more explicit consideration, and perhaps better design and management, of warrior identity.

Consider a second narrative, this one fictional. In the 1985 science fiction novel *Ender's Game* by Orson Scott Card, the young hero moves through a series of ever-harder space war games, ending with a cataclysmic battlegame in which he finally wins the game by destroying the enemy's home planet. Only afterwards is he told that the game was actually real, and that the ships he was destroying had real humans in them that he had ordered to their deaths, and that he is really responsible for destroying an entire planet, an entire species of conscious entities. Ender, shattered by sudden guilt, collapses into dysfunction, endless sleep, and depression. One of his friends tries to wake him at one point: "The way Mazer talks about it, you were becoming a vegetable," to which Ender responds, "I was trying to."[3] At the end of the book, Ender is turning to religion and attempting to atone for his guilt. Several subsequent books are based on his efforts to mitigate his Moral Injury.

In 1986, Card's story was just a story, but today one has room to wonder. When the US military began to adopt unmanned aerial vehicles (UAVs) and use them for combat missions, some were quick to argue that the technology reduced war and the warrior to video game superficiality. Experience has demonstrated, however, that UAV pilots are, if anything, far more like Ender, the hero of the sci-fi book: that the sudden shift from combat to driving home to dinner with the family can be deeply disorienting psychologically, as the civilian and military worlds—two very different psychological spaces—collide with each other in daily routines of cognitive dissonance. The warrior identity may align with deeper civilian social identities and narratives, but it is fundamentally different in important ways, and the conflict between the two worlds can be brutal when they are brought that close in time and space.

2. See, for example, Pryer, "Moral Injury and the American Soldier."

3. Card, *Ender's Game*, 332. I do not mean to imply that a science fiction treatment of such a profound human condition is in any way equivalent to the reality that a warrior suffers, but only to suggest that the possibility of Moral Injury is a universal human attribute, seen not just in our veterans, but in our novels and stories. Those who want a stronger and more personal nonfiction perspective from a Marine who served in Vietnam should read Karl Marlantes, *What It Is Like to Go to War*.

A different media presentation of the challenges veterans face has been famously presented in Garry Trudeau's *Doonesbury* comic strip, where various characters have had to deal with the challenges of physical and mental injury in combat upon their return to civilian life. Although the difference between PTSD and Moral Injury isn't explicitly recognized in the comic, it is apparent in the experiences of one of the heroes, BD. When BD's leg is blown off in the battle for Fallujah, that physical trauma leads to PTSD. But BD's most repressed memory is when, trapped in an ambush, he gives orders to his convoy to drive at high speed through an urban civilian crowd to escape, with the implication that civilian casualties resulted. Such an event is not a physical trauma, but a moral trauma.[4]

Neither Moral Injury nor warrior identity issues are new, but, arguably, they are increasing in frequency and importance. Accordingly, this essay will examine why Moral Injury may be increasing today, and why this trend matters. It will end with six starting points for the country to consider if it is adequately to address both its own security and the growing challenge of Moral Injury.

A New Strategic Environment: Asymmetry in Weapons and Values

There are several reasons why Moral Injury is so difficult, and why it may be increasing today.

1. A purely combat role is difficult enough, but today's warrior is often faced with multiple missions. This is not just professionally but psychologically challenging. Fighting and killing in combat is profoundly different from policing, which in turn is different from nation-building, and each requires not just different techniques, training, and technology, but also a very different personal psychology and culture. The different psychologies and cultures required by these varied missions can be learned, but they conflict with each other—especially if, as in the case of the UAV pilots mentioned above, the roles are jammed together so that the same person must rapidly shift between them.

---

4. See Trudeau, *The War Within*. Trudeau's efforts to educate civilians about the challenges of returning from combat through his comic strip have earned him significant recognition from the military, including the Commander's Award for Public Service by the Department of Army, the Commander's Award from Disabled American Veterans, the President's Award for Excellence in the Arts from Vietnam Veterans of America, the Distinguished Public Service Award from the American Academy of Physical Medicine and Rehabilitation, and a special citation from the Vet Centers.

2. A hegemonic power in an increasingly multicultural and polarized world, with a military performing many functions with allies and partners who may well have fundamentally different norms and values, and where identity and the narratives that support it are increasingly an explicit dimension of adversaries' strategies, necessarily will put its warriors at higher risk of Moral Injury. The question is how to build warriors with an ethical and supportive identity, but who can function in a world where they must be able to understand, and work with, profoundly different identities, cultures, and narratives to achieve a common goal.

3. Moral influence is increasingly recognized as being an important dimension of "soft power," which in turn is increasingly recognized as an important part of many long-term conflicts in today's world (such as, for example, the competition between Russia and the United States, China and the United States, and fundamentalist Islam and many states).[5] This can lead to weaponization of values: examples might include "lawfare," the practice of turning the laws of armed conflict against military forces that are committed to following them, and Russia's use of Snowden's leaks to fuel European, and especially German, anti-Americanism during the Crimea invasion, thus weakening any potential NATO response.

An important contributor to these trends is the shift in conflict patterns as American dominance in conventional force and technology has forced its potential adversaries towards alternative strategies generally grouped under the classification of "asymmetric warfare." While the general ideas and techniques are rarely new, in many cases such conflict appears in different guises because of emerging technologies. Thus, for example, Russia's Crimean invasion was not a conventional military operation: American and NATO analysts have called it "Hybrid Warfare," while Russian military authorities have used the term "New Generation Warfare." In his seminal article on this form of conflict, General Gerasimov, Chief of the General Staff of the Russian Federation, emphasized that modern warfare exhibited "a tendency toward blurring the lines between the states of war and peace," so that

> The very "rules of war" have changed. The role of nonmilitary
> means of achieving political and strategic goals has grown,
> and, in many cases, they have exceeded the power of weapons

---

5. "Soft power"—the sum of American values as expressed in its culture and behavior, private institutions, laws and institutions, and governance system—is increasingly understood to be a significant pillar of American global strength. See, for example, Nye, *Soft Power*.

in their effectiveness. The focus of applied methods of conflict has altered in the direction of the broad use of political, economic, informational, humanitarian, and other nonmilitary measures—applied in coordination with the protest potential of the population."[6]

The open use of force, often in the guise of peacekeeping and policing, is resorted to only if necessary at the end of the successful hybrid warfare campaign. This is predominantly a campaign of narrative, of identity, not of conventional combat; that's one reason Russia resuscitated the "Novorossiya" meme in Crimea.[7] As Valery Korovin, a Russian theorist, put it in 2008, "In the postmodern age, the most important weapon in conquering a state and establishing control over it has become its own society."[8]

Chinese thinking goes even further towards a substitution of conflict across all cultural domains for conventional force, in an approach called "Unrestricted Warfare":

> [T]here is reason for us to maintain that the financial attack by George Soros on East Asia, the terrorist attack on the US embassy by Usama Bin Laden, the gas attack on the Tokyo subway by the disciples of the Aum Shinri Kyo, and the havoc wreaked by the likes of Morris, Jr. on the Internet, in which the degree of destruction is by no means second to that of a war, represent semi-warfare, quasi-warfare, and sub-warfare, that is, the embryonic form of another kind of warfare.[9]

Unrestricted warfare contemplates developing a deliberate, strategically integrated process of long-term, intentional, coordinated conflict across all aspects of a culture. As Liang and Xiangsui note, "warfare is in the process of transcending the domains of soldiers, military units, and military affairs,

6. Gerasimov, "The Value of Science in Prediction."

7. "Novorossiya" is an historical term denoting southern Ukraine and Crimea as part of the pre-Soviet Russian empire. It was revived by Alexander Dugin, a powerful Russian idealogue with significant influence on President Putin, as a narrative supporting invasion of Ukraine and Crimea by Russia by tying the identity of much of Ukraine and Crimea back to Greater Russia. See Clover, *Black Wind, White Snow,* 12–13, 330.

8. Quoted in Clover, *Black Wind, White Snow,* 282.

9. Robert Morris wrote one of the first computer worms to gain widespread notoriety; it was launched in 1988 and resulted in his felony conviction under the 1986 Computer Fraud and Abuse Act, 18 USC. Sec. 1030 et seq. This quote is from Liang and Xiangsui, *Unrestricted Warfare,* 3. The CIA version at C4I.org is highly preferable to other versions that distort the original content, such as the book version entitled *Unrestricted Warfare: China's Master Plan to Destroy America,* which on its surface takes a rational analysis of the US from a Chinese perspective, and tries to sensationalize it.

and is increasingly becoming a matter for politicians, scientists, and even bankers.... If those such as Morris, Bin Laden, and Soros can be considered soldiers in the wars of tomorrow, then who isn't a soldier?"[10]

Finally, of course, there is the example of IS and, more broadly, Jihadist Islam, which in some ways is the most radical challenge to established norms and legal structures. After all, both Russia and China are successful states within a supportive Westphalian, state-based, world order.[11] Indeed, in some ways, Russia and China are perhaps more comfortable with the traditional Westphalian perspective than the Europeans or Americans, since they reject more recent doctrines such as the "Responsibility to Protect," which erode absolute state sovereignty under certain conditions such as genocide.[12]

Jihadist Islam, on the other hand, rejects entirely the validity of secular authority and thus the state-based system upon which international law, and the norms underlying it, are founded. This is not a case of a sophisticated redefinition of conflict in terms of asymmetric power and opportunity; rather, it is a complete rejection of modernity itself. Such a rejection of world order, not surprisingly, is strongest in the complex mixture of failed states, religious and tribal jostling, and constantly shifting networks of authority that extends across much of sub-Saharan Africa and the Middle East, sometimes referred to as "neo-medievalism" or, in Sean McFate's evocative phrase, "durable disorder."[13] A focus on IS in the short term to avoid serious destabilization in the region requires, among other things, deployment of traditional military force; but it is generally understood that force alone will be inadequate to address the complex factors supporting the rise of neo-medievalism in this region.

For purposes of understanding Moral Injury, these cases suggest three themes. First, the scope, scale, institutional order, and technological dimensions of conflict are expanding. The complexity and new conditions that these interacting shifts create generate more opportunity for Moral Injury among more individuals, including civilians. For example, the privatization of war through increased use of contractors of all types, and the injection of intelligence agencies into conflict zones, puts individuals who are not operating under military law, and not trained warriors, into combat environments. Similarly, the different laws and codes that individuals performing

10. Ibid., 118–19.

11. "Westphalian sovereignty"—a term derived from the 1648 peace treaty ending the Thirty Years' War—refers to the legal notions that each nation has sovereignty over its own territory and domestic affairs and that all states are equal in importance.

12. See, for example, Office of the Special Advisor, "Responsibility to Protect."

13. See, for example, McFate, *The Modern Mercenary*.

the same function might fall under introduce a moral ambiguity that in combat environments can easily enhance Moral Injury. For example, the same drone in the same airspace might be operating under different norms and laws depending on whether it is being operated by a traditional military force, an intelligence agency, or a private contractor who, in turn, might represent different institutional interests with different values.

Second, these cases illustrate an increasing challenge to the norms, principles, and associated legal and regulatory structures that Western Europeans and Americans have long taken to be universal and global. Some, such as ISIS, may categorically reject such values. Others might accept a Westphalian world order but still question the applicability of Western values: China's Central Committee recently released "Document 9," which states in part that "[p]romoting 'universal values'" is actually "an attempt to weaken the theoretical foundations of the Party's leadership" and to use "the West's value systems to supplant the core values of Socialism."[14] Russia under President Vladimir Putin has, especially since 2012, harshly criticized liberalism and Western values, developing instead a narrative of Russia as a "Eurasian" empire reflecting the traditional Orthodox Church and Russian nationalism. The result is that values that are core to European and American identity, and which their warriors tend to regard as universal, are increasingly questioned by others. This increases the risk of Moral Injury among US service members when they find themselves working alongside soldiers and citizens from other cultures with different core values.

The third theme arises from the dynamics of technological evolution: significant changes in military and security technologies often lead not just to the evolution of technological counters, but to new institutions, strategies, and narratives that challenge existing ideas of identity and what constitutes acceptable, "ethical" behavior. Development of advanced cannon, personal guns, and corned gunpowder created a need for large-scale military bureaucracies and the states that could support them—and destroyed the viability of values based on the chivalric knight. It wasn't Morgan le Fey and Mordred that destroyed the values of the Arthurian Knights, but instead, it was the democratization of warfare by musketry. A more recent example is, of course, nuclear weapons, which introduced a technology that, after a period of technological and strategic evolution, is now generally considered by most states to be so terrible as to be essentially unusable in actual combat. The result was not just a technological response but a strategic and institutional innovation, the doctrine of Mutually Assured Destruction (MAD).

14. Central Committee of the Communist Party of China, "Communique."

The overwhelming technological dominance of European military power, combined with the post-World War II anti-colonial independence movements, led to the growth of guerilla warfare into the complex mixture of military, policing, and civil development initiatives that it is today. Counterinsurgency and counterterrorism operations became a rich source of Moral Injury, because insurgents and terrorist organizations adopted very different values from the forces they opposed. The implications of this evolution for Moral Injury are powerful. An excellent example is provided by the French experience in Algeria in the 1950s and 1960s, where officers such as Roger Trinquier provided a comprehensive and sophisticated analysis of the terrorist organization Front de Liberation Nationale (FLN), and a roadmap for successful counterterrorism activities—which included torture and summary executions. This tactical-level analysis was vindicated: by the summer of 1957 the French had won the Battle of Algiers and the FLN was in ruins. But the soft power and Moral Injury blowback from the techniques used by the French undermined the legitimacy of French rule in Algeria, and domestically, the government of the Fourth Republic fell.

Were the French held to a different standard than the FLN? Yes—just as NATO and the Americans are held to a different standard than IS, the Taliban, or militias in sub-Saharan Africa. This is neither surprising nor unfair, but rather represents a profound recognition of the strength of culture, narrative, and identity itself: a French citizen and warrior is not an FLN terrorist, and to go too far in that direction will not just destroy the warrior through Moral Injury, but the civil culture in whose name the warrior serves. The ongoing debate in the United States about torture is so charged precisely because it is not really about torture: it is about culture and identity. "We don't do that" remains one of the most powerful red lines for any American warrior. Violate those core values too deeply, and Moral Injury to the individual—and if it is systematic, the culture—will follow. Relativism fails as an option not because it is unethical (although it might well be), but because it simply doesn't work. Humans, their institutions, and their states, are not built that way.

Indeed, it is at least a defensible hypothesis that any pretender to world power, whether state or IS caliphate, must develop a narrative of exceptionalism that is incorporated into identity and can become a source of Moral Injury. American has its self-image as the "City upon a Hill," inspiring other nations;[15] Russia sees itself as the Eurasian Empire, the Sacred Mother Russia;[16] China views itself as the core civilization, the center of All-under-

15. See, for example, Calabresi, "A Shining City on a Hill."
16. See, for example, Clover, *Black Wind, White Snow*.

Heaven, with 5,000 years of a peaceful, harmonious, and learned culture contrasting sharply with the immature brutalism of the West;[17] IS sees itself as the only true Islamic society on Earth.[18] Each of these narratives in turn shapes and is shaped by, and constrains and is constrained by, the identity of its citizens and adherents. Any program that purports to develop an identity for a modern warrior must begin by recognizing that identity is heavily constrained: it can be shaped, but it cannot be treated as if it were entirely plastic.

Emerging Technologies: The Warrior as Design Space

No one who has been following military and security issues in today's world fails to appreciate the profound changes being generated by the accelerating evolution of technology across the entire technological frontier. Rapid and unpredictable developments involving the core technology domains of nanotechnology, biotechnology, information and communications technologies, robotics, and applied cognitive science change the opportunity and threat environments in unpredictable and sometimes fundamental ways. Familiar examples might include the targeted software weapon Stuxnet, directed energy weapons such as the US Army's truck-mounted millimeter Active Denial System, or the increasing use of artificial intelligence software in weapon systems.

Relevant to Moral Injury, perhaps the most difficult looming challenges arise because this wave of technological evolution is making the human warrior a design space in ways that were never before possible. Of course, humans have always enhanced themselves—think of coffee or ethanol, or more recently, vaccines and pharmaceuticals—but the direct interventions that emerging technologies are making possible today are far more powerful. Drugs to improve physical performance or mental concentration, or to dramatically reduce the need for sleep, are increasingly potent. Drugs in development may lead to the manipulation of memory, enhancing some and reducing or eliminating others, so that PTSD or Moral Injury might be directly treated. Other pharmaceuticals that change attitudes towards risk are under development.

MIT researchers and others have used localized magnetic or electric pulses to change moral and ethical judgments. Increasingly powerful computer-to-brain interfaces, combined with research that enables direct coupling of biological and hardware components are not only revolutionizing

17. See, for example, Wang, "The Myth of Chinese Exceptionalism."
18. See, for example, Graeme Wood, "What ISIS Really Wants."

prosthetics but raise scenarios where humans can be "remotely present" in military robots or weapon systems. Indeed, research that someday may enable telepathic technologies (greatly benefitting small unit operations) and remote operation of robots and mechanical systems directly wired into human brains is ongoing. Integration of AI technologies into many military and security technologies, combined with massive data flows, data mining, and big data analytics, is leading to new cognitive patterns on the battlefield (or across global virtual battlefield spaces, given nongeographic, networked challenges such as Jihadist Islam). Even today, militaries are a leader in developing "augmented cognition," or "augcog," technologies, where cognition does not occur at the individual level, but emerges from integrated techno-human networks. One example of this is the US Defense Advanced Research Projects Agency (DARPA) XDATA program, which funds research on integrated techno-human systems that can process the increasing information streams generated in modern combat far better than either human analysts or computers operating alone. Such trends will accelerate substantially if existing research into developing an implantable brain chip begins to come to fruition. Imagine, for example, if part of your cognitive process were uploaded into the cloud, there to become part of a learning, meta-human cognitive process. This is a scenario rather than a prediction at this point, but the enabling technologies are being researched.

Humans and their institutions are among many other things information-processing mechanisms, and these technologies are being developed in a larger context, one in which the velocity, volume, and variety of information has increased dramatically. Eric Schmidt, the ex-CEO of Google, famously noted in 2010 that every two days humans create as much information as they did in all of history up until 2003.[19] Others have estimated that 250 days of Google processing of web information is equivalent to all the words ever spoken by humanity.[20] Facebook was founded twelve years ago and has over 1.6 billion active monthly users; Twitter was founded ten years ago; the Siri AI app was introduced on the Apple 4S iPhone in 2011. Watson, a very sophisticated expert AI system, beat the humans at Jeopardy in 2011; AlphaGo using a more general technology and self-learning capabilities beat the world champion in Go, Lee Sedol, in 2016. Even experts had not expected the latter result for another decade or so. It blinks reality not to recognize that such profound changes across virtually all information environments and technologies will not also change human cognition, identity, culture, and institutions, just as it is already changing conflict.

19. Schmidt, "Keynote Speech."
20. See, for example, Chartier, "Understanding Big Data."

Such foundational changes in information volume and velocity have significant implications for Moral Injury, because Moral Injury is in important ways an information disease. It arises when the framework that is a warrior's identity is overwhelmed with contradictory information, eventually leading not just to confusion, but to destruction of the framework. With that, the warrior loses identity, meaning, and a narrative that makes order out of conflict, combat, and death. The warrior suffers Moral Injury. Indeed, this equivalent phenomenon can be seen in civil society, where accelerating technological, social, and cultural change is a major stressor for those with lower educational achievement, or who aren't from high-technology, modernist environments. As change and information overload undermine cultural beliefs, social practices, and institutions, we see an accelerating retreat to more fundamentalist belief systems, whether they are cultural, religious, or ideological. Mythic cultural stereotypes and "golden ages" of the past, no matter how unrealistic or fantastic, become refuges and sources of strength. It is no coincidence that the current retreat from complexity is not limited to any particular region, state, or belief system, but is widespread and growing around the world, and appears to be doing so in direct proportion to the rate of change that is endemic to our era.

Understanding and managing issues of narrative and identity, therefore, become critical military capabilities—not just to mitigate Moral Injury and maintain an effective fighting force, but more subtly to successfully manage new modes of conflict supported by new technologies. Some countries may be able to avoid having to grapple with these challenges, at least for a while, but the United States, as the world's greatest hegemonic power, cannot.

What Is to Be Done? Identity and the Warrior as Problem-Solver

A brief discussion cannot hope to outline a systemic response to the challenges of Moral Injury in today's rapidly changing geopolitical and technological environment. Nonetheless, a few salient closing observations may be helpful.

1. Realities, narratives, and identities are not fixed but, especially in today's information environment, are contingent and subject to manipulation and weaponization. This is not a new observation, but the tools, techniques, contexts, and complexities of current conflicts have combined to create challenges for military and security organizations

and personnel that are different in kind, not just degree, from past conditions.

2. Moral injury is not just a serious issue requiring respect and treatment; it is also a systemic challenge. Inability to adapt to profoundly different value systems on the part of individual warriors is not just a personal weakness; it is an exploitable military weakness and a long-term deficiency in American power.

3. Identity needs to be an explicit military design space for military recruitment, training, and operations. It is as strategic as any other element of military and security operations. It must be done within the constraints of, and align with, current US culture and western values. Moreover, those values and their expression in American culture, life, and behavior are themselves an important component of American power.

4. Within the practical constraints of the military mission and environment, civilians entering service must be trained to become more psychologically flexible and adaptive warriors, without lowering ethical standards or condoning simplistic relativism. Warriors need strong values given the tasks, such as killing other human beings, that they are asked to do, but inflexible psychologies are more prone to break, rather than adapt, when challenged at the limits.

5. One way to square this circle is to train warriors to think of themselves in the dual role of warrior and problem-solver. The "problem-solver" identity can enable individuals to maintain strong personal values and the warrior identity, while also being able to work with very different, often conflicting, perspectives. Because other worldviews become a part of an external problem that warriors need to solve, rather than an implicit challenge to identity, they can be objectified and treated and considered in a less stressful way. Moreover, being able to adopt a problem-solving persona not only enables warriors to reduce the chances of Moral Injury but also prepares them for the many, often conflicting roles they are expected to perform in today's conflict environments.

6. Identity and Moral Injury domains are not static, especially nowadays. Accordingly, the strong tendency within military and security communities not to discuss such topics because they are perceived as indicating weakness is not just obsolete but increasingly dysfunctional. Rather, continuing and effective communication regarding these issues at the individual and institutional level should be regarded as an

absolute necessity, both for prophylactic purposes (e.g., to help individuals cope when faced with disturbing situations), and for strategic purposes (e.g., are narratives and identity domains being weaponized by adversaries, and if so how may they best be countered?).[21]

It is unlikely that Moral Injury in war will ever be completely avoided, and taking that as a goal might even be undesirable if the result is to evade the deep moral questions that any commitment of lethal force by a society should raise. But it is also apparent that many individuals and their families, and the military as a whole, are unnecessarily damaged by Moral Injury today, and that there may well be prophylactic or mitigating actions that could, and should, be taken against this growing problem.

21. The effectiveness of communication in mitigating and alleviating Moral Injury is emphasized by, among others, Marlantes to Trudeau. In this regard, some veterans have founded organizations, such as Gallant Few, that encourage discussion among veterans, especially those who have served in elite units and/or seen combat, and between veterans and civilian organizations. See, for example, Knodell, "A Network of Special Ops Veterans."

36

SHANNON E. FRENCH and ANTHONY I. JACK

Connecting Neuroethics and Military Ethics to Help Prevent Moral Injury

How do you teach troops to kill without losing control of exactly whom they kill, how, when, and in what way? It is such an ancient question that some may wonder why we continue to ask it. After all, the vast majority of modern, professional combat troops never commit atrocities. For every My Lai, Haditha, or Kandahar massacre, there are thousands of military engagements that are conducted fully within the restraints of the Law of Armed Conflict.

Of course, the fact that such crimes are rare is cold comfort to the victims of atrocities, their loved ones, and their communities. And those aberrations from proper military conduct are costly in other ways. Public support for the military and its missions temporarily wanes in the wake of atrocities, while more lasting harm is done to efforts to win the "hearts and minds" of the enemy. At the same time, dangers to troops increase as new enemies are recruited on the strength of popular revulsion at the crimes committed.

An additional cost that must not be overlooked is the psychological harm suffered by the perpetrators of war crimes. The idea of perpetration-induced trauma is not new.[1] While some atrocities are the isolated acts of disturbed individuals who would probably commit similar crimes in a non-

---

1. See especially MacNair, *Perpetration-Induced Traumatic Stress.*

combat setting, most violations of the laws of war cannot be traced to some preexisting pathology. Certain conditions of war create war criminals, and the risk is highest for troops fighting in counterinsurgencies and unconventional warfare.[2] That grim reality places the burden firmly with military leaders to do everything in their power to reduce the chances of their young men and women crossing lines that cannot be uncrossed and committing acts that may scar their minds and mar their souls.[3]

Astute scholars from several academic disciplines have begun tackling this problem. We wish to build on their important work and add new insights from the field of neuroscience. In particular, neuroimaging has provided novel insights into the structure of human thought that are highly relevant to how troops relate to their enemies in combat. These insights suggest ways to improve combat training so that our troops have the best possible chance of accomplishing their missions while protecting civilians and their own psychological health.

The Psychology of Harm

There are several key psychological factors that influence our willingness to harm fellow humans. First, it is worth considering notable cases in which individuals have demonstrated a surprising willingness to harm others. In the 1960s, Stanley Milgram conducted a series of infamous but enlightening experiments concerning the willingness of individuals to inflict pain on an innocent person out of obedience to a perceived authority. He found that about two-thirds of the population can be led quite easily to harm others.

Milgram set up an experiment in which subjects were asked to flick switches to deliver increasingly strong jolts of electricity to a person in another room who was supposedly being given a memory quiz. The person taking the quiz was actually an actor (as was the "scientist" telling the subjects when to administer the shocks) and the electrocutions were faked. As the number of imaginary volts went up, the actor in the other room would scream as if in terrible pain, demand to be let go, and even complain about a

2. See Rockel and Halpern, *Inventing Collateral Damage.*

3. The reader should not interpret the use of the word "soul" as a commitment to a dualistic metaphysics. Rather, this is intended as a metaphorical use of language. It is our view that certain types of moral sentiment, which can be scientifically studied and which we believe have real and measurable effects on mental health, are difficult to capture using purely secular language, and can be more readily grasped by most people (including the nonreligious) when theistic language is used. For a careful discussion of empirical evidence that has encouraged us to this view, the reader might examine Jack et al., "More Than a Feeling."

potentially deadly heart condition. Then he would fall completely silent, as if having collapsed or died. Still, the subjects would continue to respond to the authority figure's commands.

Milgram found that the odds that his subjects would resist authority rose significantly when he introduced variations into the experiment, such as having an apparent peer rebel against the authority's commands (which seemed to give the subjects courage to resist the authority), or having a second authority challenge the first (which left the subjects unsure which authority to obey and shattered the subjects' illusion that they were not responsible for their own decisions).[4]

Christopher R. Browning's excellent work, *Ordinary Men: Reserve Police Battalion 101 and the Final Solution in Poland*, provides compelling real-world evidence for Milgram's conclusions. Browning describes how members of the Nazi police battalion 101 were led to commit the mass murder of Jewish women, children, and elders:

> The largest group within the battalion did whatever they were asked to do, without ever risking the onus of confronting authority or appearing weak, but they did not volunteer for or celebrate the killing. Increasingly numb and brutalized, they felt more pity for themselves because of the "unpleasant" work they had been assigned than they did for their dehumanized victims. For the most part, they did not think what they were doing was wrong or immoral, because the killing was sanctioned by legitimate authority. Indeed, for the most part they did not try to think, period.[5]

Most of the "ordinary men" Browning studied were not eager killers, and they suffered a wide range of negative psychological effects as a result.

While both Browning and Milgram point to the important role of authority, Browning's study indicates this cannot have been the only factor. The members of police battalion 101 could have resisted but chose not to do so. Browning notes that there were "nonshooters" in the battalion who asked and were permitted to be exempted from the killing.[6] Browning argues that pressure from authority and peers would likely not have been enough to push the members of police battalion 101 past their moral qualms

4. Milgram, *Obedience to Authority*, 107, 118.

5. Browning, *Ordinary Men*, 215–16.

6. Although somewhat less blameworthy than their peers, these men are certainly not laudable. For while they did not participate directly in the killings, they also did nothing to stop or even protest them. As Browning clarifies, "they did not make principled objections against the regime and its murderous policies, [and] they did not reproach their comrades" (ibid., 215).

without the broader context of a Nazi society that was awash in propaganda calculated to dehumanize the Jewish people.[7]

Next, it is worth considering cases in which people proved surprisingly resistant to harming others, even in the face of grave danger. As Lt. Col. Dave Grossman illuminated in his groundbreaking book, *On Killing: The Psychological Costs of Learning to Kill in War and Society*, it is actually not that easy to train troops to kill enemy combatants, let alone to mass-murder civilians. This is so despite self-preservation being a strong instinct. Grossman notes that in the Civil War, 90 percent of the muskets recovered from the Gettysburg battlefield were still loaded, and some 50 percent of these had been reloaded multiple times without being fired—one was found with twenty-three rounds jammed into its barrel.[8] Even in the face of enemy fire, most soldiers would reload over and over again, unwilling or unable to fire upon their enemy. Grossman also cites the well-known post-WWII study by Brigadier General S. L. A. Marshall, *Men Against Fire*, which concluded that only 15 to 20 percent of soldiers attempted to shoot to kill.[9] While Marshall's methodology has been challenged, there remains significant support for his general conclusions.[10]

Dehumanization and Trauma

David Livingstone Smith discusses some of the implications and effects of the Marshall study in his insightful book, *Less Than Human: Why We Demean, Enslave, and Exterminate Others*:

> Although it sounds very nasty, and Marshall never put it quite this way, his observations imply that military training should concentrate on overriding the recruit's moral integrity, so that he or she will have no scruples about killing on command. Moral reservations are—in Marshall's words—a "handicap" that prevents the soldier from doing his job. . . . The US armed forces overhauled their system of military training to try to solve the problems that Marshall identified. . . . Apparently as a result, US soldiers' ratio of fire increased during the Korean conflict, and by the time the Vietnam War rolled around, American troops had become much more efficient killers. But this solution created a whole new problem. The troops did better in battle, and

---

7. Ibid., 216

8. Grossman, *On Killing*, 23.

9. Marshall, *Men against Fire*, 4, quoted in Grossman, *On Killing*, 3.

10. See Jordan, "Right for the Wrong Reasons."

the ratio of fire skyrocketed, but so did the incidence of combat-related psychological disorders.[11]

We believe that dehumanization can play a more nuanced role in military training. Hence, we do not join with Livingstone Smith's view that effective military training involves a wholesale overriding of the recruit's moral integrity. Instead, we think that their moral sentiments need to be preserved and carefully directed. Recruits need to learn how to put aside temporarily some very natural and powerful human responses, if they are to be effective in combat. This puts our troops in some moral peril, yet we believe that recruits can achieve a stable balance.

Grossman illuminates some of the methods that have been adopted over the years to help troops achieve emotional distance from their enemies. Troops have been drilled to fire on human-shaped targets but not to think about the act of killing itself. The focus has been placed on the mechanics of aiming and firing and responding quickly to changing scenarios. Troops have been taught to "neutralize targets" as efficiently as possible and the word "kill" has been carefully avoided.

Livingstone Smith cogently points out that modern society seems to support this approach and itself fails to confront the reality that waging war involves authorizing the intentional killing of human beings:

> [W]e (contemporary Americans) go to great lengths to avoid acknowledging the simple and obvious truth that war is all about killing people. Read the newspapers and listen to the speeches of our politicians. Young men and women are called to "serve their country" by going to war. When they're killed, we're told that they "gave their life for their country" (a foolish idea: soldiers' lives are taken, not given). But how often do you hear young people asked to go to war to *kill people* for their country?[12]

In other words, we persuade people to kill on our behalf by describing the actions of war in terms that sound wholesome and inspiring. Where this is not possible, we use neutral terms that cloak the emotional impact of these actions. A positive impact of this is to emphasize the warrior virtues, such as loyalty, discipline, honor, courage, and sacrifice. An unfortunate consequence, though, is that this language downplays the negative effects of war on those who kill. It is a cruel bait-and-switch, made worse by the lack of sustained support for veterans who are living with those effects. As the novelist C. S. Harris laments: "We don't take good care of the men we ask to

11. Smith, *Less Than Human*, 230.

12. Smith, *Less Than Human*, 225.

risk their lives and health for us, do we? We use them, and then when they're no longer of value, we toss them away."[13]

Propaganda is not only employed to recruit troops. It is also applied to maintain the aggressive stance of troops against an enemy with whom they are already engaged. Propaganda that tries to deny the humanity of enemies and associate them with subhuman animals is a common and effective tool for increasing aggression and breaking down the resistance to killing. This dehumanization can be achieved through the use of animal imagery and abusive language. As Grossman explains:

> It is so much easier to kill someone if they look distinctly different than you. If your propaganda machine can convince your soldiers that their opponents are not really human but are "inferior forms of life," then their natural resistance to killing their own species will be reduced. Often the enemy's humanity is denied by referring to him as a "gook," "Kraut," or "Nip."[14]

This enemy-as-subhuman approach plays off of what psychologists call "in-group bias." In other words, humans are basically tribal or clannish. We tend to fear and devalue those who are not members of our "tribe." This type of dehumanization is one of the key factors that Browning highlights in the transformation of the members of police battalion 101 into efficient mass-murderers. Milgram notes, "Systematic devaluation of the victim provides a measure of psychological justification for brutal treatment of the victim and has been the constant accompaniment of massacres, pogroms, and wars."[15]

Given that dehumanization plays such an important role in enabling murder and other atrocities, one response would be to suggest that all forms of dehumanization should be resisted rather than incorporated into military training. However, this view is problematic for anyone who is not a pacifist. If we endorse the view that violent military force is sometimes required in defense of a just cause, then we are cornered by the reality that troops do need to be trained to kill. Indeed, for justified military actions, there is a strong moral argument that military training should be directed at enabling our troops to kill in the most effective and efficient manner possible. We doubt this can be accomplished without allowing some form of dehumanization of the enemy (although, as we will later note, this should be coupled with equally intentional re-humanization). The central question now becomes, is there a form of dehumanization that is less morally

---

13. Harris, *What Darkness Brings*, 349.

14. Grossman, *On Killing*, 161.

15. Milgram, *Obedience to Authority*, 9.

perilous than others and mitigates the psychological cost of war while still promoting military effectiveness?

The act of dehumanizing is strongly associated with psychological trauma. Research indicates that the mere act of ostracizing others, such as excluding someone from a simple game of catch when instructed to do so by the experimenter, induces a variety of negative psychological effects in the ostracizer, including increased negative "affect" (or emotion) and decreased senses of personal autonomy and social connectedness.[16] It is little wonder, then, that the much more extreme and visceral actions that follow from dehumanizing an enemy have often been anecdotally cited as an important factor in the psychological adjustment of troops returning from conflict.

While more work is needed to establish direct links between dehumanization and diagnoses such as post-traumatic stress disorder in veterans, recent scholarship makes a compelling case that the horror, shame, and guilt that veterans associate with having participated in actions that they cannot reconcile with their "civilian" sense of self represent major factors that determine their physical and psychological health. Amazingly, for instance, recent research indicates that negative affect[17] and a perceived sense of social disconnection[18] have more powerful effects on physical and psychological health than physical or external conditions, such as economic circumstances, safety, hunger, and homelessness.[19] When we consider why troops have often been unwilling or unable to shoot at the enemy, it is worth considering that they are indeed engaged in a form of self-defense: their unconscious motivation is not so much to protect the integrity of their bodies but rather the integrity of their sense of self.[20]

16. See Legate et al., "Hurting You Hurts Me Too."

17. See Pressman et al., "Is the Emotion-Health Connection a 'First-World' Problem'?"

18. See Hawkley and Cacioppo, "Loneliness Matters."

19. See Pressman, et al.

20. While this claim may seem surprising to readers who aren't familiar with research in social psychology, the authors intend this to be a quite uncontroversial statement. A great deal of research in social psychology, including but not limited to the citations already made, can be summarized as showing that we are very powerfully motivated to preserve our self-image. Indeed, this can be seen as the primary function of offering rationalizations (reasons and justifications for our actions). Rationalizations are a ubiquitous feature of human behavior, and scientific research has shown they frequently fail to hold up to close scrutiny. See, for example, Nisbet and Wilson, "Telling More Than We Can Know," and Haidt, *The Righteous Mind.*

Optimal Cognitive Function

Ideal troops should not just be reconciled to their military actions in a manner that allows them to return to a well-adjusted civilian life, they should also have a high degree of mental flexibility in the field. They should be trained in a way that optimizes their ability to fluidly switch among roles such as active combatant, peacekeeper, and military escort or trainer. However, the psychological demands associated with switching between such dissimilar roles should not be underestimated. Our research demonstrates that there is a fundamental tension between the brain areas used to understand the experiential viewpoint of others and the areas used for emotionally disengaged analytic thinking, focused visual attention, and motor planning.[21] In general, when we turn on one of these networks of brain regions, then we suppress activity in the other. The mutually antagonistic relationship between these networks is a fundamental feature of our brain—it is a very marked neurophysiological effect involving much of the human cortex, and it was observed long before we understood its cognitive significance.[22] It can be detected in the brain even when participants are not engaged in any task.[23] It is also a marker of healthy brain function and an inescapable feature of our evolutionary heritage. Disruptions in the mutually suppressive relationship between these brain networks has been clearly linked to a variety of major mental disorders and to poor performance on tasks.[24]

On the modern battlefield, our troops are asked on the one hand to fight an enemy with clear-sighted and dispassionate efficiency, and, on the other hand, to be sensitive to the mores of a foreign culture, enabling them to win hearts and minds while forming strong and mutually trusting working relationships with military partners and locals. In other words, we ask them to be simultaneously highly analytic and highly empathetic. Hence, it might appear that the demands of the modern battlefield are bound to drive our troops insane. Fortunately, the psychological demands of modern warfare can be accommodated within the bounds of healthy human function.

First, while we cannot be both analytic and empathetic at the same time, a key feature of our neural function is that we are constantly cycling between these two networks. This natural cycling between analytic and empathetic mental modes is part of what is disrupted in individuals with mental disorders. Tasks temporarily and partially disrupt this natural

---

21. See Jack et al., "fMRI Reveals Reciprocal Inhibition."
22. See Raichle et al., "A Default Mode of Brain Function."
23. See Fox et al., "The Human Brain Is Intrinsically Organized."
24. See Broyd et al., "Default-Mode Brain Dysfunction."

cycling, pushing us more into one mode or the other for sustained periods. However, we know that when a task is used to push healthy participants into one mode and they are then given a task-free break, they tend to compensate by cycling deeper into the opposing mode.[25] Therefore, no obstacle is presented by the fact that individuals are required to make use of both modes. In fact, provided the switching between modes is well managed, this is likely to be healthier and less fatiguing than a work environment that only calls on one of these cognitive modes. The trick is managing the switching between modes—ensuring that one is in the appropriate cognitive mode to effectively tackle the task at hand. This requires attending to appropriate cues and the possession of a broader cognitive model that allows us to make good use of those cues.[26]

Surgeons face a tension between analytic and empathetic thinking that is similar in some respects to that faced by the modern combatant.[27] When surgeons wield their scalpels, empathetic thinking can be an outright hindrance. There is no use in surgeons contemplating the emotional significance of their actions as they cut into their patients. Hospitals thus take steps to help their surgeons avoid the distracting effects of inappropriately engaging empathetic thinking at these moments: the patient's face is usually hidden, and there is generally a prohibition against performing surgery on close friends and relatives. Yet the surgeon's job is rarely accomplished in the operating room alone. Surgeons usually meet the patient and family members before and after the surgery—moments when a more empathetic approach is essential for securing fully informed consent for the procedure and for encouraging the patient's recovery.

Clearly, it can be hard to reconcile the adoption of these two very different cognitive modes towards the very same person. Hence, there is considerable concern about physicians' bedside manners and the prevalence of dehumanization in medical practice. Nonetheless, these two modes are effectively reconciled by able physicians every day, and work in social

25. See Pyka et al., "Impact of Working Memory."

26. The research shows that these two modes, corresponding to different "hardwired" neural systems, can be flexibly deployed and that there are individual differences in our propensity to adopt one cognitive mode or the other. For instance, males who evidence more hostile sexism towards women show less activity in empathetic brain regions when they are shown sexualized images of attractive women (see Cikara et al., "From Agents to Objects"). Similarly, humanizing and dehumanizing narratives influence which mode one adopts when viewing depictions of others. Adopting one mode or the other would not usually be a conscious choice, but it is influenced by culture, personality, and training.

27. Glenn, "Why It's So Difficult."

psychology suggests a number of concrete steps that are likely to facilitate their reconciliation in general medical practice.[28]

The tension faced by modern troops is even harder to reconcile. Physicians may reflect that their immediately harmful actions are aimed at healing patients. However, no such luxury is afforded to combatants, who cannot miss the fact that the harm they inflict can never be reconciled for the person at whom it is directed. Instead, they must offset their harmful acts by justifying it in a broader moral framework that includes the harm they prevent to their fellow troops and appeals to more abstract notions of honor, service, duty, and just cause.

The profound psychological dissonance provoked by killing can only be offset by the possession of a very strongly embedded cognitive model that allows this harmful act to be reconciled. If this positive cognitive model is not reinforced, some troops are bound to resolve the intolerable dissonance by adopting a cognitive model that is destructive, both to their military performance and to their own long-term emotional well-being.

Dehumanization and the Brain

It is critical to consider how the two distinct neural systems, described above as being involved in analytic and empathic reasoning, relate to the phenomenon of dehumanization. Recent work in psychology suggests there are broadly two types of dehumanization.[29] One form equates people with inanimate objects or machines (in a military context, this is reflected by the use of expressions such as "neutralizing targets"); the other form equates people with animate but "lesser" beings, that is, nonhuman, dangerous animals, or imaginary monsters (virtually all propaganda about the enemy involves this form, the most notorious example being the Nazi propaganda film, "The Eternal Jew," which equated Jews with vermin).[30] The distinction between these two forms of dehumanization is supported by behavioral work. For instance, objectifying people is associated with indifference on the part of the dehumanizer and feelings of sadness and anger in the dehumanized, and animalistic dehumanization is associated with disgust on the part of the dehumanizer and feelings of shame and guilt in the dehumanized.[31]

We recently conducted a study that examines what happens in the brain when ordinary participants of a wide range of ages view social narratives

28. See Haque and Waytz, "Dehumanization in Medicine."
29. See Haslam, "Dehumanization."
30. Taubert, writer, and Hippler, director, "The Eternal Jew."
31. See Bastian and Haslam, "Experiencing Dehumanization."

similar to dehumanizing propaganda.[32] We identified four broad cognitive modes that humans use to think about other people: (1) When we think of people as objects, we barely engage cognitive processing. We remain indifferent, including to their suffering, and have cognitive resources to spare. (2) When we think about people as biological machines, as a doctor or neuroscientist does, we engage analytic but not empathetic reasoning areas. (3) When we humanize people (i.e., when we think about their experiential point of view), we engage empathetic but not analytic reasoning areas. (4) When we animalistically dehumanize people, we engage both networks. In this mode we think about the person as an agent driven by beliefs and desires, but we refuse to recognize the other as a feeling being like ourselves. We recognize suffering, but we do not feel concern about it. We may even take sadistic pleasure in it. Not only is this last mode the most cognitively demanding, as it requires both analytic and empathetic cognitive resources, but it also breaks with our tendency to suppress one network when activating the other. This cognitive mode has greater similarity to the typical pattern seen in individuals with mental disorders than it does to the typical pattern seen in healthy individuals.

We call this fourth mode a blended cognitive mode, because it involves aspects of both analytic and empathetic thinking. It is often useful. It undoubtedly represents an important aspect of healthy human thinking, but it is also limited and unstable. It is engaged when we think creatively, which sometimes yields important insights but also often bizarre, illogical, and unhelpful ideas. It is useful when needing to think politically or respond to someone who has malevolent intentions, yet it involves a failure to fully appreciate the other's experiential world. It also occurs more frequently when people are chronically fatigued or sleep deprived. While it is no doubt perfectly healthy to cycle between this and other cognitive modes, it is plausible that individuals who chronically adopt this cognitive mode are putting their psychological integrity at risk.

Dehumanizing in a Military Context

To ask our troops to consider the humanity of an individual at the very moment they are killing that person is simply to ask too much. An empathetic stance would hinder their ability to think in a clear, logical, and efficient manner, putting themselves and their fellow combatants at risk. Yet, we must not allow our troops to animalistically dehumanize the enemy. This stance may provide them with a motivation to kill, but it is neither

32. See Jack et al., "Seeing Human."

a desirable motivation nor a cognitively efficient state. Instead, we should train our troops to objectify the enemy in a measured manner that is specific to when they are engaged in combat. This is the only mode that frees cognitive resources to deal with the demands of combat.

Objectification should be linked to particular combat-related tasks and in response to specific actions or threats, not to a people. Troops need to be trained to recognize concrete cues and move rapidly into the appropriate cognitive mode in response. Ultimately, it may be possible to test for this ability and use these tests to determine fitness for combat.

All forms of dehumanization are toxic to some degree, and both animalistic and mechanistic dehumanization can be pressed into service by those constructing conditions for the commission of atrocities. Although our troops need to objectify their enemies in order to achieve the emotional distance needed to engage in effective combat, in moments when they reflect upon their actions, they cannot escape the reality that they have killed another human. Even drone pilots, who operate at a safe distance using an interface that is nearly as removed as playing a video game, have been reported to suffer from post-traumatic stress disorder.[33] Similar belated realizations of horror have been reported by the crews of World War II bombers. Only psychopaths can permanently block a reexamination of their actions from an empathetic perspective. Objectification is a necessary, albeit temporary, fix. Indeed, if we want our troops to maintain the capacity to question clearly immoral or illegal orders, then we would not want it any other way. So, there is no avoiding the need for a larger moral framework that allows troops to reconcile their actions with the perspectives that are afforded by both analytic and empathetic modes of thought. If we fail to reinforce this broader framework, then animalistic dehumanization is bound to rear its head.

When normal people are told that their in-group has perpetrated violence against an out-group, their sense of collective responsibility often causes them to animalistically dehumanize the out-group.[34] We can only imagine how much more powerful this effect is when combatants learn of atrocities committed by their fellow troops. Psychological research indicates that witnessing such examples leads to a lowering of the ethical bar for the witnesses, unless the perpetrators are shunned for them.[35]

33. Dao, "Drone Pilots Are Found to Get Stress Disorders Much as Those in Combat Do."

34. See Castano and Giner-Sorolla, "Not Quite Human."

35. See Gino et al., "Contagion and Differentiation in Unethical Behavior."

This brings us to the importance of the warrior's code.[36] This code insists on bright lines demarking honorable and dishonorable behavior and motivates troops to maintain these lines as a sacred obligation. This code demands that warriors show as much courage in preventing war *crimes* as they do in prosecuting legal warfare. Via this code, the process of social identification that is so essential to the psychological integrity of the combatant serves to help the warrior shun perpetrators and actively guard against what is otherwise a very natural and powerful human tendency to animalistically dehumanize the enemy. A deeply felt identification with the warrior's code therefore not only provides the most effective means to prevent atrocity, but also helps preserve the individual's sense of self and honor. This in turn makes it easier for individuals to avoid the vicious cycle of dehumanizing to justify the prior actions of one's in-group, and better allows them to rehumanize the enemy when combat conditions have passed.

Psychiatrist Dr. Jonathan Shay, in his deeply perceptive work, *Achilles in Vietnam: Combat Trauma and the Undoing of Character*, stresses how important it is to the warrior to have the conviction that he participated in an *honorable* endeavor:

> Restoring honor to the enemy is an essential step in recovery from combat PTSD. While other things are obviously needed as well, the veteran's self-respect never fully recovers so long as he is unable to see the enemy as worthy. In the words of one of our patients, a war against subhuman vermin "has no honor."[37]

Training to support the process of "re-humanization" of the enemy must be given the same attention as the training that allows troops to achieve the necessary psychological distance to be able to kill. This would support and strengthen troops' ability to appropriately shift between empathetic and analytic stances so that they "learn to take only certain lives in certain ways, at certain times, and for certain reasons."[38] Modern conflict frequently requires troops to be able to switch flexibly between collaborating with friendly civilians and engaging in combat with enemies who are hidden amongst them. Given the high psychological demands imposed by these conditions, we believe that combat-related objectification strategies and re-humanizing strategies need to be reinforced consistently within operational units. This is essential both to provide adequate psychological support and because the

---

36. See French, "Why Warriors Need a Code," *The Code of the Warrior*.
37. Shay, *Achilles in Vietnam*, 115.
38. French, "Why Warriors Need a Code," 3.

appropriate contexts for adopting one attitude versus another may need to be updated as conditions change and enemy tactics evolve.

By upholding standards, maintaining discipline, accepting certain restraints, and respecting their enemies, warriors can create a lifeline that they can use to pull themselves out of the hell of war and reintegrate into their society. That is the purpose of the warrior's code of honor. It is a shield that guards the warrior's humanity.[39]

Conclusion

All forms of dehumanization are morally perilous. Hence, it is tempting to hope that we might be able to train our troops to fight without ever dehumanizing the enemy.[40] To give in to this temptation, however, is naïve, even dangerous. Any attempt to square empathy for an individual with committing acts of extreme violence against that person condones a mindset that is too tortured and dysfunctional to condone. To push troops to inflict suffering and death on those they love is to promote the mindset of an abuser, not a mindset we wish to encourage in troops who will return to civilian life.

Violence should be seen as a last resort, but those who must engage in it have no better option than to temporarily place consideration of their targets' humanity to one side, using the psychological technique of objectification. Objectification is a necessary psychological strategy that can both allow troops to perform their duties well and safeguard them from the perils of psychological disintegration. In our view, it is entirely consistent with military honor that troops should be enabled to practice a degree of psychological distance towards the enemy when the situation demands it. Such a carefully controlled and limited degree of interpersonal coldness need not be viewed as wrong. Indeed, when properly exercised, it may be viewed as a virtue. It is similar to the notion, which translates well from our analogy with healthcare, of clinical efficiency.

The best military leaders acknowledge and understand the full range of emotions that combat troops may experience, but make it clear that intentional deviations from the warrior's code will not be tolerated. They understand that it takes psychological agility to switch rapidly between different cognitive modes; to go from seeing someone as a "target to be neutralized" to seeing that person as a disarmed and wounded prisoner to

39. Ibid.

40. Nancy Sherman suggests in *Stoic Warriors* and elsewhere that troops could practice building empathy with their enemies by "trading places in imagination" and fully embracing their shared humanity, 172.

whom one must render aid. Yet that agility is what morality, martial honor, and military effectiveness demand. It is crucial in the performance of the one mission upon which everyone can agree: that of bringing our troops safely home—their bodies and, no less important, their moral souls.

37

ERIK D. MASICK

A Moral Injury Primer for Military Commanders and Lawyers

Military education is thin on the psychological dynamics of combat. This is something [that as] a judge advocate and an advisor to a commander . . . you can emphasize.[1]

—LIEUTENANT GENERAL H. R. MCMASTER

Understanding "Moral Injury" is a critical task for commanders and their legal advisors. A growing community of scholars, practitioners, and providers link the problem of Moral Injury in service members to negative behavioral outcomes and potential impacts to good order and discipline. For commanders and their legal advisors, the notion of an underlying invisible wound informing legal issues is a familiar one, and Moral Injury is an emerging chapter in that book. My intent here is to orient those charged with ensuring good order and discipline and the health, welfare, and combat-readiness of service members to the concept of Moral Injury.

---

1. McMaster, "Lecture to the US Army 58th Judge Advocate Officer Graduate Course," 40.

In doing so, I offer a three-part framework for understanding Moral Injury's causes and impacts within the ranks.[2]

Military legal practitioners could contemplate countless scenarios where a condition impacting moral decision-making capacity might apply to legal proceedings, from administrative separation to criminal litigation. Just such a condition is Moral Injury. As ancient as the written word, all that is really new about Moral Injury is the term itself—a term that continues to inspire much debate.[3] Multiple and competing definitions of Moral Injury now emanate from various disciplines.[4] For the military legal practitioner seeking to understand, apply, or contextualize this concept for a commander, navigating the sea of definitions is a challenge, to say the least. From the research community, three salient themes emerge: Moral Injury results from (1) an act, (2) of transgression, (3) that causes harm to the soldier. The presence of these three components means that a soldier is at heightened risk for Moral Injury.

The first component is an act, of transgression. Versions of the "act" component vary across the disciplines and include things done and left undone, by oneself or another, with varying degrees of personal knowledge required.[5] Consider, for example, one of the definitions in use by the US Department of Veterans Affairs (VA): Moral Injury "is perpetrating, failing to prevent, bearing witness to, or learning about acts that transgress deeply held moral beliefs and expectations."[6] In other words, a variety of situations can cause Moral Injury.

The second component is the "transgression" that is caused by the act.[7] According to Rita Nakashima Brock and Gabriella Lettina, "It comes from having transgressed one's basic moral identity and violated core moral beliefs."[8] Definitions of this component vary significantly as to what the "basic moral identity" and "core moral beliefs" actually or should mean. Some definitions focus on transgressions against a personally embedded moral code, while others focus on transgressions against the organization's

---

2. This analysis does not purport to offer medical, psychological, or therapeutic advice, and is not intended as a substitute for medical, psychological, or therapeutic care.

3. Pryer, "Moral Injury and the American Service Member," 10.

4. Copland, "Staff Perspective."

5. Copland, "Staff Perspective"; Litz, et al., "Moral Injury and Moral Repair in War Veterans," 700.

6. Copland, "Staff Perspective"; Drescher, "Moral Injury and Clergy."

7. Copland, "Staff Perspective."

8. Brock and Lettini, Soul Repair, xiv.

moral code or some combination of the two.[9] Given the spectrum, it's best to think of the second component simply as a violation of deeply held beliefs of some kind (the transgression).[10] Most definitions focus more generally on "betrayals of 'what's right'" or acts "that transgress deeply held beliefs and expectations."[11]

The third component is the harm that is caused by the act of transgression. Here the opinions of experts vary widely on what is actually damaged. Some definitions describe the harm as a "disruption of the self on a number of different levels" or a transgression that "leads to serious inner conflict."[12] Other experts think of the "harm" more specifically as harm to moral and ethical expectations, spiritual harm, emotional harm, psychological harm, or some devastating combination of the above.[13] This component is probably best defined broadly, as the damage caused by an act of transgression that causes substantial inner conflict can manifest in a variety of ways.

Numerous scholars believe that combat can increase the risk-exposure to Moral Injury, most notably from proximity to violence and bearing witness to killing.[14] Other scholars focus more on the aftermath of combat regardless of whether the service member was a participant.[15] Interestingly, specific to the first component, the risk exists even when a service member was in an unavoidable situation.[16] Jonathan Shay, the psychiatrist who popularized the term Moral Injury, poignantly illustrates this point with the example of a "Marine who acted on orders to shoot a sniper who was using an infant serving as a human shield," knowing that he could kill the baby.[17]

9. Des Moines University, "Moral Injury from Sexual Abuse and War"; Copland, "Staff Perspective"; Nash, et al., "Psychometric Evaluation of the Moral Injury Events Scale," 647.

10. Litz, et al., "Moral Injury and Moral Repair in War Veterans," 700; Copland, "Staff Perspective."

11. Nash et al., "Psychometric Evaluation of the Moral Injury Events Scale," 647; Litz et al., "Moral Injury and Moral Repair in War Veterans," 700.

12. Farnsworth, "Dialogical Tensions in Heroic Military and Military-Related Moral Injury," 22; Maguen and Litz, "Moral Injury in Veterans of War," 1.

13. Willis, "Moral Injury"; Des Moines University, "Moral Injury from Sexual Abuse and War"; Litz, et al., "Moral Injury and Moral Repair in War Veterans," 698.

14. Maguen and Litz, "Moral Injury in the Context of War"; email from Dr. Brett T. Litz to author (May 10, 2015). Litz states that exposure to violence is not inherently traumatic. Rather, such exposure is a potentially morally injurious event (or PMIE). A serious transgression must also occur for a PMIE to become Moral Injury.

15. See, for example, Bryan, et al., "Measuring Moral Injury."

16. Brooker, et al., "Beyond 'TBD,'" 254.

17. Shay, "Moral Injury," 185.

So, with these three components presents, what does Moral Injury look like? Many scholars assert that the resultant trauma can lead to negative behavioral outcomes (which matter because of their impact on good order and discipline), a heightened risk for self-harm, and most catastrophically, a heightened risk of suicide.[18] They also assert that Moral Injury can lead to a "shrunken moral and social horizon" if left unnoticed or unchecked.[19] This notion of a shrunken moral and social horizon is a potential intersection between Moral Injury and the law that is crucial for commanders and their legal advisors to understand.

What scholars are really saying here is that when a service member is morally injured, their very notions of right and wrong can change and diminish.[20] This diminishment causes the loss of "a person's ideals and attachments and ambitions" and the subsequent "regressive over-accommodation of moral violation, culpability, or expectations of injustice."[21] One Navy psychotherapist calls this "an erosion of moral certainty, or the confidence in their sense of right and wrong," and "the transformative capacity of what happens when we send our children into a war zone and say, 'Kill like a champion.'"[22] Under this umbrella of outcomes, there are limitless possible manifestations that "can result in behavior that is simultaneously symptomatic and criminal."[23] One preeminent expert thinks of this as "trouble pumping the brakes" in the moral decision-making process.[24]

Further, the shrinking of the social horizon leads to an inability to connect with comrades, diminishment of trust, and withdrawal.[25] As Jonathan Shay writes, "Veterans who experience Moral Injury may experience a reluctance to get close to other people, difficulty trusting others or themselves."[26] Withdrawing in silence with a Moral Injury means that festering turmoil and pain can "work their way out in dysfunctional behaviors."[27] This list includes not just risky behavioral outcomes but also "self-harming behaviors,"

---

18. See generally Masick, "Moral Injury and Preventive Law," part II(C).

19. Shay, "Moral Leadership Prevents Moral Injury," 314. Editors' note: This essay is also collected here, in selection 39.

20. See generally Masick, "Moral Injury and Preventive Law," part II(C).

21. Litz, et al., "Moral Injury and Moral Repair in War Veterans," 701.

22. David Wood, "The Recruits."

23. Seamone, "Dismantling America's Largest Sleeper Cell," 490.

24. Author's telephonic interview with Dr. William Nash (Nov. 13, 2015).

25. Brock, Soul Repair, xv–vi; Shay, "No More Sugar Coating," 64.

26. Shay, "No More Sugar Coating," 64.

27. Willis, "Moral Injury."

"self-handicapping behaviors," or even suicide.[28] Diminished trust and confidence is also catastrophic to any practical application of the philosophy of "mission command," where trust is the bedrock principle.[29]

So what role can the military legal practitioner play in helping commanders navigate the problem of Moral Injury? In their capacity as legal advisors, attorneys must be sufficiently aware of the problem to help the commander make fully informed decisions, an awareness that goes well beyond black letter law.[30] Consider the example of a routine administrative separation for misconduct, where a soldier is also facing possible medical separation. As a foundational matter, the separation authority (commander) must first decide if the soldier will be processed through medical channels or pursuant to an administrative separation from the Army. Secondly, and key in this analysis, the commander must decide if the underlying condition caused, contributed to, or mitigated the misconduct that led to an administrative separation in some way.[31]

Attorneys must be crystal clear not to purport to give medical advice of any kind, while still providing commanders with all the information required to make a fully informed decision. Whether or not a potential Moral Injury impacted the soldier's decision-making would be a fact-dependent but crucial part of the equation that easily could be missed. For the attorney that identifies the potential Moral Injury, there are important questions to keep in mind when reviewing the evidence.

For one, since Moral Injury isn't yet defined in the "textbook," are medical personnel going to notice it at a medical evaluation board? Is it possible for the components of Moral Injury to be revealed during a standard post-traumatic stress disorder (PTSD) screening? What if the soldier meets some of the criteria for PTSD: Do those criteria bunched together, if significant enough, constitute a "sub-threshold" condition that might still satisfy Moral Injury's criteria? If the Moral Injury is evident, did it cause, contribute, or mitigate the misconduct in some way? These are highly nuanced and fact-based determinations that are critical for the advisor and counselor to the commander to highlight and contextualize.

From a purely black letter law perspective, this nuanced analysis has potentially long-term implications. Let's say the commander decides that since the medical evaluation board determined that the textbook criteria for

28. Litz, et al., "Moral Injury and Moral Repair in War Veterans," 701; Shay, "No More Sugar Coating," 62.

29. US Department of Army, *Army Doctrinal Publication* (ADP) 6-0, 2.

30. US Department of Army, *Army Regulation* (AR) 27-26, 17.

31. US Department of Army, AR 635-200, 14-15; US Department of Army, AR 635-40, 15.

PTSD was not satisfied, the administrative separation will proceed and the characterization of the discharge will be Other than Honorable. What happens if the soldier appeals the separation? The Secretary of Defense recently directed service secretaries to consider discharge upgrade applications for veterans with Other than Honorable discharges claiming an underlying PTSD or "PTSD-related" condition.[32] In this directive, Military Boards for Correction of Military/Naval Records are to give "liberal consideration" for discharge upgrades where the medical record can "document one or more symptoms which meet the diagnostic construct of Post-Traumatic Stress Disorder (PTSD) or related conditions."[33] Think back to the attorney-advisor highlighting Moral Injury as a potential sub-threshold or "PTSD-related" condition.

The directive goes on to say that "special consideration will be given to VA determinations which document PTSD or PTSD-related conditions connected to military service."[34] As discussed above, the VA lays claims to definitions of Moral Injury, so what then is the long-term impact of a service member who claims Moral Injury under a VA definition and is undergoing an administrative separation? What if a service member meets the criteria for Moral Injury but not PTSD under the VA construct—is that a "PTSD-related" condition for discharge upgrade purposes? There are strong arguments to be made here that it could be.

What about the countless civilian disciplines that lay claim to a definition? The directive says, "Liberal consideration will also be given in cases where civilian providers confer diagnoses of PTSD or PTSD-related conditions," and it contemplates "narratives that support symptomatology at the time of service which may reasonably indicate that a PTSD or a PTSD-related disorder existed at the time of service which might have mitigated the misconduct."[35] Operative terms like "reasonably indicate" and "might have mitigated" suggest that the secretary's intent is for conditions like Moral Injury (as a possible "PTSD-related," or sub-threshold phenomena) to be given "liberal consideration."

So in our hypothetical, the commander has decided that since the textbook definition of PTSD is not satisfied, the service member will be separated administratively with an Other than Honorable discharge, as no underlying conditions exist to mitigate the misconduct. We know now

---

32. US Department of Army, *Review Boards Agency*, "'NEW' Discharge Upgrades and PTSD."

33. Ibid.

34. Ibid.

35. Ibid.

that on review this separation might be an uphill battle if Moral Injury or sub-threshold conditions are demonstrated. On the other hand, if the commander affirmatively *considers* the potential of Moral Injury and documents that it had no impact on the separation decision, does that then protect the integrity of the separation and the commander's ultimate decision on review? There are strong arguments to be made here that it does. Either way, one can see how the long-term success or failure of even a routine administrative separation under certain conditions might turn on how and when Moral Injury is considered by the commander.

Hopefully, my illustrations of how Moral Injury could impact the most routine of legal scenarios (such as an administrative separation) demonstrates why commanders and their legal advisors must be knowledgeable about this invisible wound. Beyond sheer legal efficacy, any phenomenon that could impact the moral decision-making capacity of a service member should be of great concern to those charged with leading troops and winning our nations wars. My purpose has *not* been to create a new "designer-defense" that absolves liability, but rather to draw attention to a condition that could be a key part, even a controlling part, of legal equations in certain circumstances. The components of Moral Injury, as explored here, can help attorneys seeking to conceptualize Moral Injury, inform legal strategies, develop creative arguments, and establish effective preventive law strategies for commanders.

38

STEFAN J. MALECEK

The Moral Inversion of War

Combat Is Totally Immersive and Inversive

Combat is totally immersive. One either has or has not experienced it. It is so purely personal and so excruciatingly real as to approach the surreal. It might best be described as a cascading rape of the senses. It does not matter that after repeated exposure, many men (and now women) come to develop a hard shell of emotional armor and act as if they are untouched; embrace the thrill and dopamine rush of war ("high on war"); or describe it in glowing terms as the most intense experience of their lives. The initial experience is completely shattering. In one tiny fraction of a moment, everything that one might have held sacred is washed away in a flash flood of overwhelming, sensually, and emotionally imprinting power that obliterates the entire encyclopedia of all previous knowledge.

From that moment, you are exposed to the intimate possibility that you could die, or be forced to kill another human being. You will be defined by experiences that relatively few ever have, that may drive you the rest of your life. The shielding may become stronger. You may learn to pass traumatic incidents off as inconsequential, even enjoyable—creating some of the darkest humor ever heard.

Combat is also inversive—where wrong is right; where killing and cruelty is condoned, even rewarded, with medals and promotions; where those who survive can lose something of greater value than their lives. They can lose their souls.

The Source of My Moral Injury

I served in Vietnam from March of 1968 until May of 1969 as an enlisted Social Work/Clinical Psychology Specialist. I had daily contact with combat warriors needing immediate mental health counseling and an opportunity to release intense emotions. I dealt with every sort of psychiatric injury, to include Cotard's delusion (the belief that one is dead).

I was responsible for the preliminary assessment of all enlisted personnel referred either by doctors, commanders, or sick call. I would take a rudimentary social, military, and criminal justice history and tender a provisional diagnosis. Military culture dictated that I assess the following: Can the individual function in his job, and, if he can, how quickly can he be returned to duty? A man's larger psychological and emotional issues were not considered relevant unless the presenting symptoms were so persistent and detrimental as to warrant attention. Our primary concern was keeping individuals on duty.

Routine complaints of "combat stress" or "burnout" were punished by military authorities as "malingering" to avoid duty. Many of these men had been penalized with Article 15s (minor), even Court Martials, to "inspire" them. Before anyone could be "eliminated for the good of the service" (Undesirable Discharge), clients required a psychiatric evaluation that pinned the onus of behaviors as "existing prior to service." At that time, any soldier who was unwilling or unable to perform was, by definition, "unfit for duty."[1]

Unless extraordinary circumstances could be proven (e.g., letters from commanders or field reports attesting to valor), almost everyone referred for psychiatric evaluation was eliminated from military service so that the military could blithely dismiss individuals without any claim to the GI Bill or other benefits.

Retrospectively, I believe I was morally injured long before I went to Vietnam by the constant betrayals of my parents and the caustic environment in which I had been reared. My fragile personality was fractured through decades of exposure to the violent behaviors of my father, a WWII combat vet. This led me to develop many of the same defenses he had exhibited, including extreme shame and self-repudiation, especially pertaining to my failing to prevent some psychologically injured clients from returning to combat. Instead, I just "rucked up," pretending as if nothing extraordinary

---

1. These phrases are common military expressions.

was happening to me, while memories and loathing ate at me like a slow drip of acid.

By destroying my every belief and forcing me to be part of an immoral system in an unjust war, Vietnam changed me radically. I learned to never take anyone at face value, especially officers and FNGs ("fucking new guys"). I questioned every order, frequently arguing with Division psychiatrists about conditions that were routinely attributed to "exist prior to service." I became grimmer, dour even. My reliance on marijuana, amphetamines, and eventually opium (plus three to five packs of cigarettes a day) was an attempt to stanch feelings of tremendous negativity about the military culture that daily betrayed my core values and that lied about essential aspects of the war and why we were there—feelings that were especially intense when I saw friends neglectfully sacrificed to attain vague and often specious "military objectives."

Although Dong Ap Bia ("Hamburger Hill") occurred soon after I left, I had had contact with numerous combat troops who had been sent repeatedly into the A Shau Valley and whose units had incurred up to 70 percent casualties. They described scenes similar to Hamburger Hill, wherein they were ordered to take an enemy's position, only to abandon it almost immediately afterward—and then be ordered to re-secure it again. I became quite shut down and inured of such experiences. I felt wounded, over and over, despite never being eligible to receive a Purple Heart.

The Aftermath of My Moral Injury

I came home from Vietnam shorn of all that I had previously believed in, my old values system destroyed forever. I was severely opposed to the war in which I had participated. I made allegiances with anti-war groups such as the Vietnam Veterans against the War and the Student Non-Violent Coordinating Committee. I joined peace rallies, and even led a veterans' contingent in an anti-war march (during which I ran from the police, who were dispersing tear gas and beating people). I did not intend to become an anti-government "radical," but I received absolutely no support from any military or governmental agency. They all seemed to feel that I no longer mattered since I was now a civilian.

Attempting to make some kind of sense of the magnitude of my experiences, I extensively investigated the history of Southeast Asia. This led me to explore the history of colonialist political manipulation and the nature and psychology of social movements. This deepened into a lifelong aversion to "mainstream" politics and other forms of government manipulation of populations to support without examination these governments' hidden agendas for power and control.

I have now been clean from cocaine for thirty-four years and marijuana for twenty-eight years. I have also managed, after eleven years without alcohol, to be able to have a very occasional drink without repercussions. This latter makes of me somewhat of a heretic with the Twelve Step crowd, who insist this is not possible. My experience is that you can come to peace with yourself to the extent that you no longer need the soul-ravaging protection that serious addictions demand.

The decades of emotional instability, severe depression, irritability, mood swings, and flashbacks still occasionally surface. My emotional recovery has been helped by many types of psychotherapy, the net result of which has been a continuing expurgation of my bitterness and twisted emotions. I managed to attain a PhD in psychology in 2006, and in 2009, I was finally approved for PTSD veterans' benefits.

I am not on medications and, in fact, refuse to take them. I do participate in, and pay for, alternative therapy. I do not believe it is possible to "think away" one's emotionally rooted psychological symptoms, as is the focus of most VA-approved therapy.

Moral Injury and War

A group of cutting-edge medical experts working on "Moral Injury" define the condition as "perpetrating, failing to prevent, bearing witness to, or learning about actions that transgress deeply held moral beliefs and expectations."[2] This framework also suggests that Moral Injury has unique specifiers, including shame, guilt, demoralization, self-handicapping behaviors (e.g., self-sabotaging relationships), and self-harm (e.g., parasuicidal behaviors).[3] Haunted by dissonance and internal conflicts, harmful beliefs and attributions cause guilt, shame, and self-condemnation.

What this misses is the larger context in which Moral Injury occurs. Within this context, there is a very critical factor that is often overlooked— what Bowlby called "Attachment" and the concomitant "Disorganized Attachment."[4]

Essentially this theory describes a child's need for security and safety in the physical and emotional presence of the mother. Barring the consistent availability of this presence due to work, mental health issues, addictions,

2. Litz et al., "Moral Injury and Moral Repair in War Veterans," 696.

3. Ibid.

4. See Bowlby, *Separation*.

and other competing demands on a mother's energy and attention, a child might react in any number of oppositional or avoidant ways. This peri-traumatic experience might be described as a kind of Moral Injury. Since the conditions of the dominant contemporary culture often demand that mothers be unavailable, individuals grow up in a society that depends upon such dysfunction for continued economic growth. The vast majority of people find ways to adapt to the emotional vacuum. However, even the well-adapted may take into combat a predilection for Moral Injury.

Another underlying cause of Moral Injury may be rooted in our society's willingness to fight unnecessary, unjust wars for material reasons. America's base defense budget for fiscal year 2016 is $523.9 billion, not counting the "black budget" that funds covert CIA, NSA, and other such agencies without reference or accountability.[5] Most of the official budget is balanced by the $445 billion that will accrue from defense-related industries. The need to justify this vast expenditure makes unjust wars a near certainty, leading the United States to conduct eighty-six military interventions since World War II.[6]

This is not to say that all moral injuries are preexisting or due to poorly chosen wars. Even "just" wars create Moral Injury. In training for war and participating in it, recruits learn to transgress the most sacred of moral considerations: Do not kill. Thomas Jones, a retired Marine major general, has pointed out that actions that involve moral transgressions "are part and parcel" of combat.[7] Litz noted, "Service members have to follow orders, and if ordered to do something, it is by definition legal and [considered] moral."[8] As Wood writes, boot camp indoctrination is "a rigid moral code of honor, courage, and commitment with the goal of producing young Marines thoroughly indoctrinated in love of Corps and Country."[9] The actual experience of combat runs completely counter to all of the ideas and pseudo-morality imposed by military training. Although one may often act "heroically," it is most often done out of a desire to survive and protect one's comrades-in-arms, not for any grand ideals of nationalism. I have spoken to dozens of men who committed acts of heroism, many of whom had been awarded medals of valor for their actions. None of them has ever cited love

5. Trading Economics, "United States Gross National Product."

6. Zoltan Grossman, "From Wounded Knee to Syria." Grossman's list ranges from major wars to drone strikes.

7. Quoted in Wood, "The Grunts," from his own conversation with Jones.

8. Quoted in Wood, "The Grunts," from his own conversation with Litz.

9. Wood, "The Recruits."

of country as the basis for their actions, except perhaps sardonically when referring to "Mom, apple pie, and baseball."

In 1996, then-Commandant of the Marine Corps, General Charles Krulak, issued a standing order: "There is no room in the Marine Corps for either situational ethics or situational morality."[10] The code is unyielding. The military's entire values system, Jonathan Shay writes, is designed according to a moral construct that is "so great that it can motivate men to get up out of a trench, and step into enemy machine-gun fire."[11]

Dr. Bill Nash, one of the foremost experts on Moral Injury, has said: "There is an inherent contradiction between the warrior code, how these guys define themselves, what they expect of themselves—to be heroes, the selfless servants who fight for the rest of us—and the impossibility in war of ever living up to those ideals. It cannot be done. Not by anybody there."[12] He went on to rhetorically ask, "So how do they forgive themselves, forgive others, for failing to live up to the ideals without abandoning the ideals?"[13] That inner conflict is the very crux of Moral Injury.

Approaches to Healing Moral Injury

The Importance of Emotionally True Narrative

My status as a combat veteran has stood me in good stead through the last five decades of providing psychotherapy. I am frequently requested because many vets refuse to speak to a non-vet. The primary approach I have taken is to be present and actively listen. I generally allow my clients to "unpack" their memories as they can, and in a manner that works for them.

Cathartic work has been an essential aspect of my personal recovery, though I have come to see that it has the potential to re-traumatize a client. I agree with Shay that this type of work is best done after "safety, self-care, and sobriety" have been firmly established.[14] I also agree with Shay when he writes about the importance of having the right kind of listeners:

> Narrative heals personality changes only if the survivor finds or creates a community of listeners for it. . . . The listeners must be strong enough to hear the story without injury. . . . The listeners

10. Office of the Commandant of the Marine Corps, quoted in Wood, "The Recruits."

11. Shay, *Achilles in Vietnam*, 6.

12. Quoted in Wood, "The Recruits," from Wood's conversation with Nash.

13. Ibid.

14. Shay, *Achilles in Vietnam*, 187.

must also be strong enough to hear the story without having
to deny the reality of the experience or to blame the victim. . . .
To be trustworthy, a listener must be ready to experience some
of the terror, grief, and rage that the victim did. . . . To achieve
trust, listeners must respect the narrator. . . . Respect also means
refraining from judgment.[15]

My writing has always been my "sympathetic witness," which Alice
Miller describes as a person or process that has the property of confirming
one's perceptions.[16] I started writing out of a desperate desire to communicate on my own level, to feel "heard," and to taste the hidden, invisible
world, the kingdom that lay beyond the senses. Writing has always been my
primary technique to express myself without being judged or ridiculed. It
has literally saved my life. It has been my sacred haven, the destination for
my deepest fears and shame, where I allow these feelings to unfold freely
within myself and be released like a flock of wild, caged birds.

The Importance of Forgiveness

I have found it extremely beneficial to focus on forgiveness in treatment.
Forgiving yourself for allowing the original injuries (adopting "victim
stance") and for not wreaking vengeance upon the pathogenic people involved is essential. To not forgive severely retards your ability to be more
devoted to your personal growth. Only forgiveness allows space for new
ideas, new inspiration, and a fresh reality to be born in your heart, creating
the seeds of new purpose. Forgiving yourself, and eventually others, is also
an important mediator of outcome with Moral Injury, in that the emotional
release frees you from carrying the burdens of the past—burdens that require copious healing tears (see next section) that, in turn, allow you to
adopt more personal responsibility for your actions. You may eventually
come to embrace a deeper level of awareness of the never-ending journey of
the soul into the infinite universal embrace from which we originated, and
to which we will return.

Many men view resistance to authority—even healers—as a badge of
honor for their separate and unique selves. Much media attention is paid to
praising various attributes of separate identity, especially in business, sports,
and politics. Such attention actually reinforces egotism and retards spiritual
development. Under the sway of such massive pressure, it is easy to be held
hostage by this belief in a separate self that must fight all others. Killing

15. Ibid., 188–89
16. Miller, *The Untouched Key*, 50.

someone in combat (or witnessing this killing) is the ultimate repudiation of another's reality and a vainglorious attempt to reinforce the sanctity of your own life. All such injuries leave a huge vacuum of regret and shadow to be grieved, which in turn can create what Shay calls an "indignant rage."[17] Thus, what truly lies at the heart of Moral Injury is egotism, grief, and rage stemming from the failure to fully recognize the humanity of others—and, simultaneously, from the denial of a vital part of one's own humanity.

Unexpurgated grief and shame contribute heavily to addictions and every form of "mental illness." I completely repudiate the media and the highly-paid pundits touting and promoting the specious value of various pharmaceuticals to "fix the broken brain."[18] Healing is a deeply personal matter, arising from the accumulated stresses of being forced to live a false life out of tune with one's own actual and natural emotions.

The Importance of Transformative Tears

Crying is one of the most highly shame-based arenas for men, completely at odds with culturally-approved images. "American military culture in Vietnam regarded tears as dangerous but above all as demeaning, the sign of a weakling, a loser," Shay writes. "To weep was to lose one's dignity among soldiers in Vietnam."[19] This was totally in keeping with the culturally approved image of a "real man," who was emotionally unavailable and impervious. This attitude reinforced the idea of "corporately inspired warfare," which judged the value of combat soldiers only by their continuous production of body count and which was fueled by an utter lack of empathy and disallowed emotions.

Crying and releasing emotion is tremendously beneficial for healing, especially when appropriately linked to pernicious memories. These tears are richer in released toxins than normally occurring basal lubricating tears or tears provoked by irritants.[20]

Rosemarie Anderson lists nine categories of benefits to be derived from weeping, summarizing what may be most essential as follows: "One of the most unique aspects of the characteristics of transformative weeping

17. Shay, *Achilles in Vietnam*, 21. Here, Shay discusses the best English translation of the Greek word *menis*, which he believes to be "indignant rage." *Menis*, he suggests, is a form of Moral Injury.

18. See, for example, Andreasen, *The Broken Brain*.

19. Shay, *Achilles in Vietnam*, 63.

20. Frey and Desota-Johnson, "Effect of Stimulus on the Chemical Composition of Human Tears," 560.

is the explicit descriptions of physical/mental/spiritual integration taking place in the context of sacred tears. Integration, re-integration, unification, reclaiming, and healing of the Self, are phrases commonly used by both historical writers and interviewees."[21]

Even before I understood the deeper ramifications of emotional release, I sought the refuge of deep release of dysphoric emotions, fear, and shame, through crying. I have generally cried alone, though I have found the experience of being emotionally vulnerable in the presence of others in a safe environment to be amazingly powerful in deepening my trust of both myself and others. It is the ability to utterly release stagnant or archaic emotions that opens the doorway to deeper refreshment and healing.

Closing Thought

My personal experience is that aberrant, high-risk behaviors such as drug and alcohol abuse change when the protective role these behaviors perform is no longer needed. To eliminate your dependence on such protection, you must allow yourself to feel what you really feel, and release these feelings. Psychotherapies and the approaches described above have proven extremely powerful, both in my treatment and the treatment of my clients. However, healing approaches for the individual is not the most important way that we can combat Moral Injury. The most crucial way would be improving our society by reducing the preconditions for Moral Injury and by ensuring that the unnecessary wars that enflame this grave condition no longer flourish.

21. Anderson, "Nine Psycho-Spiritual Characteristics of Spontaneous and Involuntary Weeping," 172.

39

JONATHAN SHAY

Moral Leadership Prevents Moral Injury

W ho I am: I am a psychiatrist by trade, whose whole clinical career of twenty-plus years in the VA was working with combat veterans with severe psychological and moral injuries. These veterans turned me into their missionary to the Armed Forces on prevention of psychological and Moral Injury in military service. *They don't want other good American kids wrecked the way they were wrecked.*[1]

This is *force protection in the mind and spirit*. For years I have been pushing the veterans' message that three things keep you sane in the insanity of war: Cohesion, Leadership, and Training to protect those we send into harm's way for our sakes.

Cohesion: that is, positive qualities of community in the face-to-face unit—and *stability* is an indispensable part of this: train Soldiers together, send them into danger together and bring them home together. This is not rocket science. But actually making it happen involves a multitude of changes in policy, practice, and culture; it's really heavy lifting for the Services to make these changes. And not one of these recommendations is new with me.

Leadership: that spells out as *expert, ethical,* and *properly supported leadership.*

---

1. Editors' note: This text contains Dr. Shay's remarks "as prepared" for his presentation at the US Army's Command and General Staff College Ethics Symposium, November 16, 2010.

Training: that spells out as *prolonged, cumulative,* and *highly realistic training for what soldiers actually have to do* and *face.*

All three of these are very sensitive—for good or ill—to policy, practice, and culture. That's what I have worked at for more than twenty years as the veterans' missionary. The two books, which people here have been kind enough to tell me were of use to them—*Achilles in Vietnam: Combat Trauma and the Undoing of Character* and *Odysseus in America: Combat Trauma and the Trials of Homecoming*—both carry the prevention message. All of Part 3 and Appendix 3 of the latter book are specifically devoted to prevention, and have got to be the *only* reason that Senators McCain and Cleland would have taken the time to write a Foreword to the book, *together.* These two military veterans certainly "saw the elephant" and "paid their dues."

Well, these three—Cohesion, Leadership, Training—are also combat-strength multipliers so it's win-win. If you get these right, you get *both* combat effectiveness *and* force protection. So it's an easy sell to line leaders and trainers.

In this talk, I concentrate of course on leadership, specifically the ethical dimension of leadership, but I wanted you to see the context of my whole missionary pitch at the start.

At the end, I plan to ambush you with something *way* off the beaten track—the physiology of ethics. You heard me correctly: the physiology of ethics. Hmmm, what can he mean by that? Is he pushing a virtue pill? Stay tuned.

In the last couple years, there are now two meanings of this resonant phrase, "Moral Injury," in circulation. Supposedly, I coined the phrase—I find that hard to believe—but whoever coined it, here's how I use it:

Moral injury is the sum total of the psychological, social, and physiological[2] consequences that a person undergoes, when *all three* of the following are present:

1. Betrayal of what's right (the code of what is praiseworthy and blameworthy, part of the culture);

2. By someone who holds legitimate authority (legitimacy and authority are phenomena of the social system);

3. In a high-stakes situation (what's at stake clearly has links to the culture and social system, but must be present in the *mind* of the person suffering the injury). The stakes never get higher than in war, whether one's own death or maiming, or often even more important, the death or maiming of beloved comrades.

2. The body codes Moral Injury as physical attack!

We see the whole human critter here: culture, social system, mind, and brain/body. I don't have to tell an audience of line leaders that military training and military functioning comprises *all* of these. This is a serious audience here—the Command and General Staff College students aspire to be and are eligible to become battalion commanders. I am not sugar-coating the critical element here of leadership malpractice. I know that right conduct matters a lot to you, for its own sake, but this is not a church service, and I am going to concentrate on the *functional* consequences of commanders' ethical failure. It can lead to catastrophic operational failure.

That's actually the story of Homer's *Iliad*. Here's the one breath summary: The CG, Agamemnon, betrays what's right, first with the priest of Apollo, and then with his most effective and respected subordinate commander, the commander of his maneuver force, Achilles, by publicly dishonoring him in front of the whole army. This leads to the latter's combat-refusal, in effect, desertion, and then the near-desertion of the whole army the next day (the stampede to the ships in Book 2). What follows is a near fatal collapse of the Greek amphibious operation, with enormous losses, first from the plague sent by Apollo, and then from the weakening of the force, absent Achilles and his regiment.

So I emphasize the importance of moral leadership, because in its absence *very* bad things happen, and a lot of them:

- Loyalty goes out the window, to the point of physical desertion, even to the point of treason;
- Demotivation (this extends to the people who witness the betrayal of what's right or get knowledge of it)—motivation goes whooshing out of a unit like air out of a balloon, a kind of psychological desertion;
- Selfishness on steroids;
- Fulminating cynicism;
- Embitterment;
- Destruction of trust;
- Vengeful rage: "I hope all them motherfuckers die," as the 101AB Sergeant in *Achilles in Vietnam* said, which is also reminiscent of Achilles' berserker fury in the *Iliad*.[3]
- Running riot and other crimes against protected persons;
- Small units turning into criminal gangs.

3. Shay, *Achilles in Vietnam*, 24.

These all reflect the shrunken moral and social horizon that psychologically injured soldiers come to inhabit.

Moral injury damages the unit, can damage the nation, and chronically damages the soldier when he or she returns to home station or to civilian life.

So I have worked so hard on this because I see it as this important, yes, but even more because— we can do something about it! I have been an implacable critic of the US military personnel system, especially the officer personnel management system, because I believe it *mandates* careerism, the single most important ethical problem in the US forces. Not financial greed or sexual lust, but *careerism*. But making the case for renovating the US military personnel system is a huge subject for another day.

I'm almost finished, and I have to fulfill some promises:

First, I promised to mention the recent use of the phrase "Moral Injury" by others with a different meaning. This is the meaning advanced by three people I know well and respect: Retired Navy Captain psychiatrist, Bill Nash (the Marine Corps Combat and Operational Stress Control Coordinator in his last assignment before retirement), and Shira Maguen and Brett Litz of the National Center for PTSD in Boston.

They use the term "Moral Injury" this way: the consequences of having to do something that violates one's deepest ethical commitments. I'm here to tell you this *is* devastating, it is profoundly destructive of the well-being of the service member or veteran who carries that on his soul, and may, by pushing toward suicide, cost a life. To illustrate, so that this is not completely abstract: A Marine marksman in Fallujah finally locates an enemy sniper who has already shot a number of Marines in the unit. In his scope the marksman can see that the sniper has a baby strapped to his chest in what we would call a "snuggly," apparently, in the Marine's judgment, as a human shield. In full accordance with his understanding of the ROE, the Law of Land Warfare, and his duty, the Marine pulls the trigger, sees the round do its work, and lives with that for the rest of his life.

I fully concur with the importance and gravity of these horrific incidents that war will *always*, in ever-changing forms, produce. Ethical philosophers have addressed such situations under the heading "moral luck," by which they are speaking of moral *bad* luck. It's not that I am indifferent to this. It's just that, short of ending the human practice of war, there's not a lot we can do to eliminate the sort of Moral Injury that Nash, Maguen, and Litz have written about. It will always arise here and there in war even in the best circumstances, unquestionably more in counterinsurgencies and less in conventional operations in open terrain.

There is no contradiction between the two meanings of this phrase "Moral Injury," just that it's important to keep them straight. Unfortunately, Moral Injury as I define it often leads to Moral Injury as they define it. Command-driven atrocities ("crimes of obedience"), such as the My Lai massacre is a painful example.

So now I'll wrap with a riff on the practical physiology of ethics: *sleep* is fuel for the frontal lobes of the brain. The physiology here is clear and quite well established. Every hour of sleep loss drains the tank a bit. Emotional self-restraint, ethical self-restraint, and social judgment all depend critically on intact frontal lobe functioning. When you are out of gas in your frontal lobes, you become a moral moron. You lose the capacity to distinguish between friendlies, armed enemies, and protected persons—you fire them *all* up, accurately! but without discrimination. Emotional and ethical restraint go completely out the window, and social judgment goes to zero. Instead of *persevering* you *perseverate*—neurologist's symptom jargon for doing the same thing again and again despite a failing result.

In the military context sleep is a logistical entity like water, ammo, and fuel. It gets used up and has to be resupplied. It needs to be planned, disciplined, subject to intelligent policy, and respected for what it is: a fact of nature like gravity or distance. If you plan a 50k road march with your vehicles and only plan on 25k of fuel, people would think you an idiot, but we do this all the time with sleep. Twenty-five years ago you could have heard people boast that they ran 10k in the heat at Fort Hood and came back with full canteens. Today, when everyone has a Camelback, if anyone boasted that way you would ask, "What kinda nut is he?" Where we were then on water discipline twenty-five years ago is where we are now on sleep discipline.

The obstacles to having a sensible attitude toward sleep are primarily cultural and institutional: think back to when you were a company commander in theater: How comfortable were you being asleep when the battalion commander was awake? Afraid you would be seen as self-indulgent and weak, weren't you? I wrote about all this twelve years ago in a little paper in *Parameters: US Army War College Quarterly*, called "Ethical Standing for Commander Self-Care: The Need for Sleep."[4] I am delighted that the full text is now available for download online. If you read nothing else in this paper, read the two examples of catastrophic operational failure: one naval during WWII, when a lot of people died; the other in a division-size

---

4. Shay, "Ethical Standing."

force-on-force certification exercise, where nobody died, but the divisional artillery was entirely eliminated by the OPFOR.[5]

So when you become battalion commanders, find your own voice to say to your subordinate leaders that in order to do your job, you have to know that they are taking care of themselves. You will have to set the example by granting yourself enough sleep, and by being seen to value rather than punish self-care in your subordinate leaders.

Every recognition of our finite physical capacities, contrasted to our boundless spiritual capacities, makes us squirm. But I want to point out that it is an unfathomable mystery why God created us as partly physical beings, rather than as entirely and purely spiritual beings like the angels. I have no answer to that, but I do know that we're stuck with it. We are physical body and brain, mind, social participant, and culture inhabitant at every instant. If you neglect your self-care, particularly sleep, as a commander, aiming at more-than-human self-denial, you may catastrophically miss the mark of virtue that you so sincerely aim at. And in a fight, people may die because of it.

5. Editors' note: OPFOR stand for "opposing force." At US military training centers like the National Training Center at Fort Irwin in California, the resident OPFOR plays the role of the enemy force.

40

EDWARD TICK

Military Service, Moral Injury, and Spiritual Wounding

Ben's Story

Ben was an army tanker in the Iron Triangle in Vietnam, serving during the height of the war. "I don't know where I was in Vietnam," he says. "All we ever saw was deep, thick jungle." Ben was in fierce firefights during which he saw both friends and enemy combatants injured or killed. His unit also fought in Cambodia, "the place we never were."

During one incident Ben was sitting atop his track on the lookout for enemy combatants. As his mechanical beast rumbled through the jungle, Ben looked down at the ground next to his treads. A spider hole suddenly popped open off the jungle floor. He watched as a Viet Cong soldier tossed a hand grenade up toward him. Ben heard the clunk of metal hitting metal, then saw the grenade bounce off the side of his track. He watched the grenade fall backwards. His eyes met the Vietnamese soldier's eyes. Ben saw his look of unspeakable disbelief and terror. Then the grenade exploded.

Shortly thereafter hostilities ceased. Ben came to a bunker and looked in. He found three unarmed and confused Viet Cong fighters. Ben's sergeant told him to frag them. Ben declared that they were unarmed and had

307

surrendered. Fragging them would be murder, he said, and was against the laws of humane warfare.

But other squad members clambered for the opportunity. Some expressed willingness and glee to waste them. Ben walked off and listened in dismay as his comrades taunted the prisoners and one tossed a grenade for the execution.

"Even though one of their comrades had tried to kill me just twenty minutes earlier, I still knew that killing those unarmed prisoners was wrong and I wouldn't do it," Ben said. "When enemies were armed and trying to kill me, I had to defend myself. But nobody has the right to kill unarmed prisoners. They were just sad and helpless human beings, a lot like us."

We might think that, even though ordered to, Ben resisted doing wrong and therefore did not sustain Moral Injury. Is that the case?

Contemporary Interest in Moral Injury

In the last half decade there has been a flood of articles, books, radio programs, psychological tests for, and other explorations of Moral Injury. It is as if the concept of Moral Injury has been hiding in the bottom of humanity's Pandora's Box, waiting to be rediscovered. Why has it been so long ignored?

Directly put, we have not asked the right questions, studied the experiences of other cultures and times, used the right spiritual, ethical, and cross-cultural frameworks, listened deeply to our warriors' pain and to the ambiguities of their service, been honest about our country's moral inconsistencies, or facilitated a complete practice of warrior spirituality and tending of invisible wounds that includes attention to the soul and its deepest concerns.

We make war in ways that harm our own warriors. As a nation we want to continue these ways but without such harm. We maintain the belief that this is possible and that resiliency can be so strong as to resist moral breakdown and injury.

We rely on fear, mental illness, and biologically based models of care. Issues like shame and guilt are not commonly addressed. We believe we can treat the brain and neurological functioning while ignoring the full human being before us. Medical and pathological models of war wounding dominate. As pioneering psychiatrist Karl Menninger once observed, challenged people today may be considered either mentally ill or criminal, but "whatever became of sin?"[1]

---

1. Menninger, *Whatever Became of Sin?*

Clinicians can feel helpless, unprepared, frightened, or uncomfortable with their own responses, unprepared to deal with moral and spiritual issues, judgmental or repulsed by what they must witness. Chaplains may fear punishment or harm to their careers if they challenge the rules of engagement that produce Moral Injury.

Some practitioners contend that Moral Injury and post-traumatic stress disorder, though manifesting similar symptoms, are actually different animals. Others say that Moral Injury is at the root of PTSD. And some say that they are different aspects of the wounding of the whole person—Moral Injury wounds the character and soul while trauma can also wound us biologically, physiologically, cognitively, or psychologically. It seems to finally be accepted that doing what one judges to be wrong, even in life-threatening combat, harms the inner life, the psyche, the soul of the actor.

Jonathan Shay is credited with introducing Moral Injury into modern thinking by defining it as "a betrayal of what's right in a high-stakes situation by someone who holds power."[2] Such betrayal leads to "indignant wrath," in which "the primary trauma [is] converted . . . into lifelong disability." This rage is not the same as the berserker rage that can awaken on the battlefield when life is at stake, but arises from feeling mislead and betrayed by leadership such that it "impairs a person's dignity."[3] As veteran Joe Michaud wrote in a poem called "Shame,"

> now we're the Four Horsemen
>
> of the Apocalypse. Each freedom
> that is taken away from another,
> enslaves me. Each indignity
> suffered at our hands, belittles
> me. Each death from above
>
> by drone, each home invasion,
> each kidnapping, each rendition
> by our armed representatives, causes
> me to die a little, causes me to feel
> ashamed for the crimes of others.[4]

---

2. Shay, *Odysseus in America*, 240. Shay introduced the concept of Moral Injury in his *Achilles in Vietnam*, in which the entire first chapter is entitled "Betrayal of What's Right."

3. Ibid., 21.

4. Michaud, Joe. "Shame," 20.

Our warriors, acting with little choice on other's orders, may find these actions shameful or wrong. In the absence of leaders or society taking responsibility, the warriors take on that responsibility themselves and may carry it for life with crippling consequences. Veteran Glen Miller said, "As a LRRP team leader, I indeed prevented some cruel and immoral actions. On the other hand, I was nearby while witnessing two murders—no weapon, no honor, all fear. Moral Injury is inversely related to Just War." When the cause is unjust, whether it is the immediate individual action or the pursuit of an entire war, Moral Injury is inevitable.

During the Vietnam War, morality and legality were in constant question. Both veterans and anti-war activists protested all they judged as wrong—wrong war, cause, politics, enemies, actions, and interpretation of history. They felt betrayed by our country for committing these wrongs and sending them to enact them. Recall the 1971 testimony of John Kerry before the Senate Foreign Affairs Committee, who stated that the war and what we were asking veterans to die for was "a mistake."[5] Robert Jay Lifton's seminal work on veteran wounding *Home from the War: Vietnam Veterans, Neither Victims Nor Executioners* came out toward the end of the war. That early he observed the "moral inversion" that occurred in some soldiers: their ethical standards reversed and they "killed without inner justification."[6]

Shortly after the war Peter Marin wrote in *Psychology Today* that veterans live in "moral pain."[7] He declared that veterans and their helpers had to embark on a moral journey together that would be long and painful but could not be overlooked or therapy could prove "morally insufficient."[8] Or as my veteran client Dick cried from his depths, "Medications don't heal this kind of pain!"

William Mahedy, who served as a chaplain in Vietnam, also wrote shortly after the war. He observed that the reality of war is sin and we were participants in it; that veterans knew that they had witnessed, participated in, and perpetrated evil; and that this caused their suffering and was not reducible to stress. He also declared chaplains morally culpable for not naming that war what it truly was.[9] Or as Robert Emmet Meagher has recently written,

> Moral injury . . . is what used to be called sin. . . . The deepest and most intractable PTSD has its roots in what veterans

5. Kerry, "Vietnam Veterans against the War Statement."
6. Lifton, *Home from the War*, 37.
7. Editors' note: Peter Marin's essay is also collected here, in selection 27.
8. Marin, "Living in Moral Pain," 119–36.
9. Mahedy, *Out of the Night*, i, 149, 155, and elsewhere.

perceive as the evil they have done and been part of. . . . They have become convinced by their own experience of the essential criminality of war.[10]

Inevitability of Moral Injury in Warfare

"The Golden Rule" is so common in world religious, spiritual, and ethical traditions that it might be considered universal. "Do unto others as you would have them do unto you" has emerged through many traditions as a revelation meant to guide humanity's behavior. Commandments to not cause others pain, to treat others as we want to be treated, to protect and improve our own souls by doing right, to never return harm for harm, have been voiced by the great religions and spiritual teachers for millennia. We find them in the teachings of Hinduism, Zoraster, Confucius, Socrates, and the Old Testament. Two thousand years ago Jesus called us not only to love our neighbors as ourselves, but also to love our enemies and "do good to them that hate you" (Luke 6:27 NIV). When directly hurt we are to "turn the other cheek" (Matthew 5:39 NIV). The world's root moral traditions indicate that we are wounded whenever we harm others.

It is a fundamental truth that killing another human being under any circumstances may be the most traumatic act a person can perform. My Afghanistan veteran client declared, "The business of war is killing, and it makes everyone crazy." As Lt. Col. Dave Grossman writes, "Killing is what war is all about, and killing in combat, by its very nature, causes deep wounds of pain and guilt."[11] Or as declared by Iraq veteran and poet Brian Turner: "No matter / what god shines down on you . . . / it should break your heart to kill."[12] To kill is to entail Moral Injury.

The question should be not whether but how severely impacted the troop is by the act of killing. Moses dictated in Numbers 31:21–24 that purification after battle is necessary and required for all returnees. Indigenous cultures the world over have had extensive practices for cleansing and purifying the returned warrior after combat, including honoring and making amends for lives taken. But in our modern era, we ignore most necessities of warrior return, leaving it up to the warrior to find his or her way home and diagnosing them as disordered if they cannot. The result—our warriors

---

10. Meagher, *Killing from the Inside Out*, xvii–xviii.

11. Grossman, *On Killing*, 93.

12. Turner, *Here, Bullet*, 56. Editors' note: this poem is also collected here, in selection 1.

bring home invisible battle poisons still entrenched in their systems, even from moral behavior during warfare.

In the modern era the Geneva and Hague Conventions were early international and secular attempts to define the laws of war, codify its moral behavior, and attempt to preserve a humane code of conduct. The 1997 Mine Ban Treaty, signed by 162 countries but not the powerful big three of China, Russia, and the United States, represents one such effort. In fact, humanity has searched for millennia for principles and practices by which war can be rendered more humane, and through which we might limit the emergence of the bestial.

We only need to contemplate the Ten Commandments and examine whether during our practice of warfare we keep those second five commandments that dictate humanity's proper conduct toward others. Troops ask, and are tortured by, questions of whether our nation, our leaders, and they themselves as our frontline representatives, killed or murdered, stole, rendered false witness, coveted others' possessions, or committed adultery. They judge the leadership who sent them by these standards: Were there WMDs? Am I fighting for someone else's oil and profits? And what happens to our sexuality and intimacy under these conditions? Though we have all been trained in these core religious beliefs, we see that to enflame a people to war leaders violate these principles. Then during warfare it is inevitable that warriors may betray them, especially during politically and economically motivated conflicts in which the troops may not believe, or urban warfare where we cannot separate the innocent from the foe.

About 2,700 years ago Deuteronomy attempted to present a code for humane behavior during times of war. Chapter 20 insists on faith and sacrifice and details what actions are or are not allowed before and during combat and who is fit for service under what conditions. King David begged God not to allow him to kill wrongfully, and in Psalm 7 begged for death if he had without cause done violence to his enemy. Saint Augustine offered the first theological defense of war in the Christian tradition and attempted to expel its pain, guilt, and shame with divine approbations. Proponents of war have leaned on Augustine's Just War theory throughout the ages but have ignored his warning in *Literal Commentary on Genesis* that our sword blade thrust with envy and hatred cannot reach our neighbor unless it first passes through our own bodies.

We see that attempts to limit war's brutality and define moral behavior under its dire conditions date to the beginnings of civilization. The concept of Moral Injury may be universal, since instruction in moral behavior toward each other is at the foundation of the world's major religions. In which case, to participate in war and to take life at all constitutes moral wrongdoing and causes suffering to the actor as well as to the victim. In his foundational and prophetic book, *Out of the Night*, Chaplain Mahedy was correct: No matter how we justify our wars, our warriors are at once witnesses, perpetrators, and victims of the inherent sinfulness of war-making. And we must admit the truth of this together.

Whenever killing occurs Moral Injury is to some degree inevitable. And it is especially so under our modern conditions of war-making that include impersonal and long-distance killing; killing without being in danger ourselves; fighting in civilian sectors, the majority of casualties among civilians; destruction of infrastructures and environments; inadequate training in the impact of killing; sexual and other dangers from comrades; conditioned dehumanization of the foe; controversial wars without conclusions; lack of civilian support or involvement; neglect upon homecoming; and a host of other factors.

Moral Injury and Spiritual Wounding

When we honor the soul as that droplet of divinity planted in each of us, and observe the demands of military service and combat upon the soul, we are forced to conclude not only that Moral Injury is inevitable and especially so under contemporary conditions, but also that it is the tip of the iceberg of spiritual wounding. Not only may we be invisibly wounded in our moral frame and collapse in despair or dysfunction, but we may also suffer other dimensions of wounding that are registered in our deepest and most influential places, in the core of the self that shapes how it will function, or refuse to function, in our world.

Thus we must consider all dimensions of spiritual wounding. Troops endlessly express these in their confessions, counseling, and therapy, discussions with each other, public protests, and in their breakdowns and symptoms that are actually disguised and indirect communications. We must not just try to squash the symptom but always ask, "What is the symptom trying to say?"

We can declare these additional dimensions of spiritual wounding to warriors. All are possible. All can result from participation in warfare and acts of destruction. All are rendered far worse by neglect, ignorance, and bombardment by medications that cannot heal such pain. All can have disastrous consequences when veterans try to take their place in society. Warriors may feel soiled, polluted, unworthy of participation among the rest of us. They may feel that society and leadership has so misled, abandoned, and betrayed them that they choose not to be part of it—even unto choosing suicide. As Army veteran Nate Bethea recently wrote, "The common thread [among veterans] was not a tendency toward violence but rather toward self-hate . . . a fear of being permanently broken."[13]

Here are aspects of spiritual wounding to which I have heard our warriors testify and we have labored to heal. Each of these should be considered in the arena of invisible spiritual wounding:

* Broken faith

* Shattered trust

* Fall from grace

* Denied honor

* Unjust sacrifice

* Lost hope

* Lost innocence

* Shattered belief system

* Broken unity—with self, family, others, civilians, nation, life

* Nostalgia—the painful loss of the soul's true home

* Anesthesia—inability to appreciate beauty

* Amythos—the loss of a cosmological, universalistic, mythological, and historical vision and context into which to fit one's personal story.

All of these traits are ideally strong, well, and part of the healthy warrior identity. All these aspects of spiritual wounding constitute abandonment, harm to, and betrayal of the individual soul and its spiritual warrior archetype. All, and not just Moral Injury, must be treated with a transcendent spiritual vision and profound resolve. Or else.

Conclusions

If we are honest, listen to the testimonies of our warriors without diagnosis, spin, or obfuscation, practice empathy so that we feel with them what is torturing them inside, then we see that Moral Injury even occurs to those who do right. Ben, whose story opened this discussion, was severely wounded in heart and spirit. He functioned and held a job, but he retreated into isolation and alcohol abuse and did not believe he could ever again be a member of a caring community. And he kept his story to himself for over forty years

13. Bethea, "Sarah Palin."

because he did not want to cause pain or shame to his old military comrades. Finally he said, "I wanted to stop the execution but I couldn't. The most moral act I could perform was to refuse and walk away." Similarly Tommy, who stopped three atrocities in Vietnam; Michael, who saved children his squad was ready to kill in Afghanistan; Joe, who killed unarmed prisoners in Iraq when he discovered that they had committed atrocities—all testified to dimensions of suffering that was of the heart and soul and for which medication and conventional counseling were useless. Only by fully tending to the spiritual dimensions of their invisible wounding were they able to purify, reconcile, heal, and rejoin society.

These good warriors' stories demonstrate that it is possible for a soldier to do right and resist Moral Injury even in the combat zone. Very many do. Yet that does not necessarily protect troops from Moral Injury. He or she may feel sad, bad, wrong about the entire war, comrades' actions, leaderships' spin, or society's abdication of responsibility. Resist Moral Injury in the modern combat zone and it may still hurt and haunt. Moral courage may be the right choice but it may get you killed. It hurts when comrades betray what's right, and it is a deep invisible wound when one's courage goes unrecognized. Though Ben, Tommy, and Michael all did right and preserved innocent lives, each felt banished from society, because they judged society to be immoral in what it had asked of them and what some of its warriors did. Each felt they had to keep their stories secret in order to protect their comrades and also themselves from being judged for "unsoldierly" behavior.

We can take radical steps to alleviate the suffering caused by Moral Injury.

Troops could be recognized for moral courage, for doing the right thing under difficult and life-threatening conditions. We could award a Medal for Moral Courage just as we do for combat valor. We could give our warriors more incentive to make moral choices, to struggle with themselves as Ben did at the decision point, to take moral stands that may be contrary to contemporary rules of engagement but consistent with the highest spiritual, religious, and moral tenets of humanity. But as Ben said, "All I could do was turn my back and walk away." He has been walking away and grieving it for over forty years.

Finally, chaplains can and should play a special role in the recognition, evaluation, treatment, and response to Moral Injury. Just as we have medical and psychological evaluations for wounded warriors performed by specialists in those fields, we could have spiritual evaluations. Chaplains may be best, and can certainly be trained and prepared, for recognizing and addressing issues such as those listed above that are in essence moral and spiritual wounds, wounds and disorders to our souls, our cores, our deepest selves. Only in this way can we hope to offer our warriors holistic healing and a vision and practice that can indeed bring them home in body and soul.

41

ROBERT EMMET MEAGHER

Hope Dies Last

In thinking and writing about Moral Injury, our minds turn more or less automatically to veterans as the focus of our concern. Even the term "veteran" signals that concern. The word comes from the Latin *vetus* (aged, old, literally old or just old before one's time, experienced beyond one's years, worn, worn out). Sobering words to describe men and women, many of whom today have not yet reached their thirties. What, we might wonder, so ages, exhausts, darkens, bends, and sometimes breaks, many of our finest and most fit young citizens that they no longer feel able or entitled to pursue a full and fruitful life?

The ready, one-word answer in this context is "war." The often-assumed identification of "veterans" with "war veterans" is not surprising. After all, war is the work of the military, a fact of which we sons and daughters of the twentieth and twenty-first centuries need no convincing, especially in our present age, the age of what has been called "the forever war." Summing up his experience in a Marine Force Recon unit dropped into a jungle north of the DMZ, teeming with the enemy, Vietnam veteran Gregory Gomes explains that "Everyone who has lived through something like that has lived through trauma, and you can never go back. . . . You are seventeen or eighteen or nineteen and you just hit that wall. You become very old men."[1]

No war is without casualties—men and women who, even if they escape with their lives, all too often do so without their limbs, or eyes, or

1. In Junger, *Tribe*, 118.

317

former "good looks." Others survive their wars visibly unscathed but with broken hearts and broken souls. After the exhilaration, the rage, and the terror, it is the sorrow of war that endures. Strange to say, this sorrow—in all its many forms and faces—actually comes as a surprise to some, who imagine that wars ever end.

One such "innocent" was Sigmund Freud who six months into the "Great War" offered this blind reassurance to Germany's troops and to all those who hoped and prayed for their return, safe and sound, intact in mind and soul:

> When the fierce struggle of this war will have reached a decision every victorious warrior will joyfully and without delay return home to his wife and children, undisturbed by thoughts of the enemy he has killed either at close quarters or with weapons operating at a distance.[2]

Whatever threats to life and limb the war might pose to those who wage it, Freud was boldly confident, it seems, that no one need fear for their souls or, as he would prefer, their psyches. Superego be damned. Conscience would not be, could not conceivably be, a casualty of war. Or so he dreamed.

Freud was far from the first "thinker," however, to float the theory that war can be waged without moral violation and the destruction of character. In the West, the Roman Catholic Church, once it found itself vested with imperial authority and clout, made precisely that case: that it is possible to kill without sin, without stain, without guilt, without shame, without pollution, without being haunted by the souls of the dead, without (in today's currency) "Moral Injury."[3] Winning over rulers and regimes to this convenient doctrine has rarely required a hard sell, while warriors and war's victims have been more difficult to convince. To many, especially those who have known war up close, gotten their hands stained, had their hearts broken and their souls darkened, "Just War Theory" has made no sense of what they have seen and done. "A walk across any battlefield shortly after the guns have fallen silent is convincing enough," wrote WWII veteran J. Glenn Gray: "A sensitive person is sure to be oppressed by a spirit of evil there, a radical evil which suddenly makes the medieval images of hell and the thousand devils of that imagination believable."[4] Gray explains that "there is a line that a man dare not cross, deeds he dare not commit, regardless of orders and the hopelessness of the situation, for such deeds would destroy

2. Freud, *Reflections on War and Death*, II.20.

3. I have traced the origins and history of Just War Theory, as well as it lethal legacy into the present day, in *Killing from the Inside Out: Moral Injury and Just War*.

4. Gray, *The Warriors*, 51.

something in him that he values more than life itself."[5] That said, war calls on those who wage it to cross that line, more or less routinely.

The dark reality that Freud denied and Augustine occluded is one from which veterans are occupationally unable to escape. It is the awful work of war itself: the cleavage of humanity into enemy camps, the ensuing slaughter, the devastation of the earth and destruction of what men and women have made of the earth and of their lives. This work diminishes, distorts, and darkens us. It weighs on us, dismantling conscience.

So what in the world do we mean by "conscience"? I suggest that we begin with the assertion of the first-century Jewish philosopher Philo Judaeus to the effect that "Native and indwelling in every soul is a cross-examiner /. . . which is our accuser and our judge."[6] We may know this voice by different names, and it may say one thing to you and another to me; but I suspect that none or very few of us have never heard it. The experience of "conscience"—regardless of whose voice we believe it to be and regardless of what it says to us—is a common one and is aptly described in the generic word we use to designate it. "Con-science," from the Latin words for "with" and "knowledge," suggests communal, rather than private, idiosyncratic understanding, what in Greek is known as *syneidesis*, "mutual awareness, communication, being, as it were, on the same page."

Conscience is Janus-faced, looking both inward and outward, a mirror of the soul that at the same time reflects a community, with which the soul is either in harmony or at odds. Conscience exposes us to the approval or disapproval of eyes and ears from which there is ultimately nowhere to hide, because to hide from conscience is to hide from ourselves. The Roman statesman and philosopher Cicero once called conscience the *theatrum virtuti*, the "theater for virtue," where our deeds are manifest to others, a stage without dark corners, with no opportunity for concealment.[7] Even in what Cicero referred to as the *animi conscientia*, the "conscience of the soul," the court of innermost appeal, we find ourselves standing before a judge, a jury of our peers, or a mirror.[8] In the Christian tradition there is finally but one judge before whom we have no choice but to stand, *dominus deus*, the Lord God, whom Augustine in his *Confessions* addressed as *arbiter conscientiae meae*, "arbiter of my conscience" (V.6).

Welcome or unwelcome, approving or reproachful, the voice of conscience makes itself heard, warning us we are about to cross a line we

---

5. Ibid., 186.

6. Philo Judaeus, *Decalogue*, 87, cited in Konstan, *Before Forgiveness.*

7. Cicero, *Tusculanae Disputationes*, ii.64.

8. Cicero, *De Finibus Bonorum et Malorum*, ii.53.

oughtn't, rebuking us for already having done so, rewarding us with peace of mind for having watched our step. It is the voice of caution, guilt, shame, and well-being. But in saying this we are forgetting something. We are assuming that conscience has but one voice, that the spectators in the "theater for virtue" remain there in their seats forever, day and night, year after year, century after century, that today's silent arbiter(s) will be holding court tomorrow. All too often we find in life that the voice of conscience is plural, a crowd of voices sounding more like a rabble than a choir, condemning today what they recently applauded. Nowhere is this more apparent and inevitable than in the movement from peace to war and then, eventually, back again from war to peace.

War "alters the dimensions of morality within a man's consciousness," explains former Marine infantry Captain and Iraq War veteran Tyler Boudreau,

> and what is clearly wrong on the home front becomes natural on the battlefield. Killing, for instance, is a sin, unless you're in war, unless your life is threatened. Shooting an unarmed man is generally considered wrong, even in war, unless you think he's maneuvering against you. Then it's okay. Firing on the wounded or surrendered is not allowed, unless you believe they're faking. Then, by all means, fire away. So there are exceptions to the rules. That's what you pick up in the combat zone, the exceptions. The lines of morality shift and fade away, and so the soldier often doesn't even realize it's happening.[9]

Practicing the "arts of war" and preparing to deploy them, military recruits must be re-made, re-programmed, sworn into an elite band of brothers (and now sisters) willing to kill and die with and for each other, subordinating their bodies and souls to the success of the mission and the survival of the unit. Lesson one in their core curriculum is learning to kill. Boudreau makes precisely this point when he writes:

> I think it's fair to say that the taking of human life is something we, as a species, are inherently reluctant to do. I've read that in books, but I've felt it in my gut too. But the soldier kills for a living—it is his reason for being. Killing is not a by-product or some shitty collateral duty like peeling potatoes or scrubbing the latrine. It is the institutional point. It's not a trade secret. It just is. . . . And when a Marine shoots better than his peers, he's admired and he's handed medals and badges and promotions— all to encourage him to pull the trigger with another man in his

9. Boudreau, *Packing Inferno*, 165.

sights and kill him. Like it or not, that's desensitization. But desensitization doesn't eliminate morality from the consciousness. It merely postpones cogitation. Sooner or later, when a man's had a chance to think things over, he will find himself standing in judgment before his own conscience.[10]

Michael Yandell, a former Army explosive ordinance specialist, tells a similar story, a story that he says allowed him very little sleep when he came home from war. He writes of his "disillusionment," of the "erosion" of his "sense of place in the world":

> The spiritual and emotional foundations of the world disappeared and made it impossible for me to sleep the sleep of the just.. . . What began to erode for me in Iraq in 2004 was my perception of good and evil. What I lost was a world that makes moral sense. . . I was nineteen when I left for war. I did not know I was leaving a world that made sense—a world where people respected one another's lives and dignity, a world where violence and murder were understood to be wrong and punished by laws—and entering a world where all bets were off.[11]

Yandell has come to understand and accept that, while he can try to restore his moral compass to its civilian, peacetime settings, there is no turning back the clock and reversing time. The war, he concedes, is part of him now, a chronic illness, as it were, to be lived with. "Lived with" is the operative phrase here. In this he is one of the lucky ones, unlike his less fortunate, more gravely wounded comrades-in-arms, who at an alarming rate find their pain insufferable and life itself a burden they no longer can bear.

The simple truth is that the rules of war are not the rules of peace. War has always required a radical recalibration of conscience, of our shared understanding of good and evil, of right and wrong, the crossing of a line that something deep, profoundly deep in us, warns us not to cross. "War," after all, is a euphemism. As such it is an evasion. War is about killing. Lt. Col. Pete Kilner, makes this very point in his West Point class on the morality of killing: "there is one absolutely unique and defining characteristic of our profession—we are organized, equipped, and trained to kill people."[12] Even as part of a larger mission, says Kilner, killing is still "the biggest moral decision" one can make and "the biggest moral taboo" one can break.[13] World War II veteran and philosopher J. Glenn Gray, author of *The War-*

10. Boudreau, *Packing Inferno*, 78, 81–82.

11. Yandell, "The War Within," 12–13.

12. Kilner, "A Moral Justification," 55.

13. In Zabriskie, *The Kill Switch*, Kindle locations 101–3.

riors: Reflections on Men in Battle, argues further that the guilt and violation involved in killing, rather than rooted in the moral order, are metaphysical.

The combat soldier, before his first kill, knows well what was going through Hekabe's head when, realizing it was up to her to "see a bit of justice done," uttered these words: "I have outlived the world I knew. I think strange thoughts. My blood learns another law."[14] Killing has to be learned, and it is for many a lesson not easily learned. Issuing a weapon and training someone to use it are the easy part. The license and the eventual order to kill are another matter. Many combat veterans have described their acceptance of the moral and legal waiver to kill in war as a recalibration of their moral compass, a redefinition of right and wrong, others as a "kill-switch," whose default position is "off" but which the government knows how to turn "on" when the need arises. Turning it off again is another matter, less well understood and all too often overlooked.

"What happens when our boys kill?" writes Tyler Boudreau: "No matter how well we desensitize them, no matter how just the cause, the violence they inflict in battle will seep into their souls and cause pain. Even in self-defense, killing hurts the killer, too."[15] The odd fact here, however, is that it is not only "killers" who bear the wounds of Moral Injury, with all the often disabling anguish, shame, and despair that those wounds, arguably the deepest that war inflicts, bring. Studies reveal that even those who only train for war, witness its chaos and death, even second-hand, can also bear the inner stigmata of war's slaughter, savagery, and destruction.

Moral Injury is the legacy, the "karma" if you will, of killing and destroying. In war nothing is sacred in the original sense of that word: set apart, safe from violation. War is about dominance, dominance over other humans (men, women, children), and the accompanying widespread destruction of nature. No matter how "just" or necessary the cause, high-minded the intention, or hate-free the hearts of those who wage war, there is a moral price to be paid by all involved, however close to or removed from the battlefront they may be. We will learn this from our veterans, if we listen long and hard to what they have to tell and teach us. Moral Injury is a miasma that we all are at risk to contract. It is not easily contained. The all-volunteer, professional military, signed into law in 1973, promised a firewall between the war zone and the home front, between soldiers and civilians, between the haunted and the oblivious. Sheer illusion, like the civil defense shelters of the Cold War era, suggesting that we might survive a nuclear holocaust and move on to live another day. The entire nation goes to war

14. Euripides, *Hekabe*, 28.
15. Boudreau, *Packing Inferno*, 78, 81–82.

when it deploys its sons and daughters. That makes us a nation of warriors, a warlike people. Moral Injury is the signature wound not only of our military but of our militarized society as well. Our sky and our hearts cannot but be darkened by war's long shadow, and in that long night veterans are not the only ones who can lose hope.

However dark the truths we confront in an age of endless war, we must not lose hope. "You can't lose hope," cited the legendary Studs Terkel at age ninety-one from an interview with Jesse de la Cruz, a retired farm worker. "If you lose hope, you lose everything."[16] Without hope, nothing matters. To be hopeless, it is not necessary to despise life. It is enough to be indifferent. The condition of the hopeless is more like leprosy than cancer. Its instincts are self-destructive. Its logic leads to suicide, a road too many Americans, veterans or not, go down. Traditionally, within the Catholic tradition, suicide was regarded as the irredeemable sin, the sin against the Holy Spirit. Suicides were souls lost forever. "If you lose hope, you lose everything."

In the Christian tradition, hope is one of the three theological virtues: faith, hope and love. Of the three, according to Saint Paul, love is the greatest; but Studs was right, hope is the one you can't afford to lose. Paul also said that these three last, but he appears to have overlooked what happens to them in war. Love is the first casualty of war, because war is all about killing, and killing doesn't come easily or at all to those who have not yet learned to hate. For many if not most combat veterans religious faith is the next casualty, all the more so when a war and its warriors have been blessed in advance. Holy wars are an oxymoron, and so are the gods that sanction them. With love and faith fallen, all that remains is hope, the sole surviving source of a spiritual pulse, the last unsevered lifeline to creative affirmation. When that line is cut, the soul dies, whether or not the body dies with it.

I understand that any discussion of the soul and of the soul's death may seem forced or simply false, a ghost of the past, but not to veterans today nor to those committed to helping them. I have listened to the stories of many veterans from the wars in Vietnam, El Salvador, Bosnia, Afghanistan, and Iraq, as well as former combatants in South Africa and Northern Ireland, and the most spiritually wounded among them describe their state in words that might well have been ripped from Augustine's *City of God*, where in Book 13 he discusses "second death" or soul death, the death not of the *spiritus vivificans* (the breath of life in us) but rather the death of the *anima vivea* (the breath of love in us). Soul death has nothing to do with mortality. The truth is that people can, and many do, go dark in life long before they go dark in death. This soul death, this "going dark in life," may be understood

---

16. Terkel, *Hope Dies Last*, 9.

as a living death, a death in life. When I have conveyed words and ideas like these to profoundly haunted veterans, many find them remarkably descriptive of their own inner state. To veterans, Augustine's account of the death of the soul—its symptoms and its source—has the inescapable ring of truth.

What then, according to Augustine, is the source or root of this death? His answer to this is awkward but clear: sin, willful evil, is what kills the soul. Sin is another word we may rather be rid of, but it is a word we cannot afford to lose, especially when we are at war. "I believe the essential failure of the chaplaincy in Vietnam," explained the late Vietnam veteran chaplain William Mahedy,

> was its inability to name the reality for what it was. We should first have called it sin, admitted we were in a morally ambiguous and religiously tenuous situation, and then gone on to deal with the harsh reality of the soldier's life. . . . In theological terms, war is sin. This has nothing to do with whether a particular war is justified or whether isolated incidents in a soldier's war were right or wrong. The point is that war as a human enterprise is a matter of sin. It is a form of hatred for one's fellow human beings. It produces alienation from others and nihilism, and it ultimately represents a turning away from God.[17]

Sin and death are inseparable for Augustine; the one is the consequence of the other. Two different sins for two different deaths. Adam's sin is against the Creator and curses Adam to return to the dust from which he came. Cain's sin, on the other hand, is against the creation, against his own brother, and curses him to a living death, a life in darkness—life breath without life spark—until he too returns to dust. Cain's sin, the murder of his brother, is for Augustine the paradigmatic "mortal sin," the sin that kills the soul, the sin that hurls the soul towards hopelessness.

Towards hopeless, yes, but precisely here we must remind ourselves that hope dies last. So long as there is life there is a road back to hope. Nowhere that I know of in ancient literature, or since, is there a more moving account of the ascent from despair to life than in Euripides' *Herakles Furens* or *Herakles Gone Mad*, an ancient tragedy written by a veteran for fellow veterans in the throes of Athens' own "forever war."[18] In it, transparent to his own experience as a combat veteran, Euripides explores the trauma of

17. Mahedy, *Out of the Night*, 133.

18. Substantial portions of the following discussion are taken from my book *Herakles Gone Mad*. The Greek hero Herakles was absorbed into later Roman mythology and known as Hercules.

war and, even more, of the return to peace. *Herakles,* in short, is the story of a hero's homecoming.

In all of Greek myth there was no hero more beloved than Herakles. He combined phenomenal strength and courage with generosity and good-will. He was the stuff of which legends are made, a statue waiting to be cast. In Euripides' hands, however, Herakles is fragile and weary. He is haunted by what he has done and endured, and now must face still more violence. His homecoming is wrecked, and his own survival becomes a curse. With any imagination at all, Herakles is universal. Herakles' dramatic timing is at first impeccable. Fresh home from hell, he appears at the last possible auspicious moment, learns of his family's peril, and handily dispatches the vile usurper Lykos to the depths of hell, whose geography Herakles knows well by this time. Then something goes wrong. In fact everything goes wrong. Herakles suddenly turns on his own family and savagely slaughters them; and the only explanation given is that Lyssa, insanity personified, has descended on the house and loosened Herakles from his wits, driven him clear out of his mind. What are we to make of this madness *ex machina?* I believe this question is best answered by noting: first, that *lyssa* is the word Homer uses to name the battle madness of Achilles and Hector; and second, that Herakles' mad scene reads as a nearly clinical account of "misrecognition" or "misidentification" suffered by some combat veterans, while at the same time resembling the description of berserkers in numerous epic traditions as well as modern battlefield memoirs. In other words, Lyssa is merely a prop, an empty mask, as it were. Herakles' madness neither required then nor requires now any elaborate explanation for those who have taken part in the insane rampage of war. Theseus, for example, seems to understand not only what has happened to his friend but also how to go about helping him. For Athenians in 421 BCE, as now, a returning veteran who suddenly murders his wife and children is a tragic but hardly unfamiliar event.

As it happens, none of Herakles' labors were nearly as harrowing as what he now endures. None of them called for the courage that he must now summon and somehow find within himself. Being able and ready to die or to kill is, as it happens, far less of a challenge than to embrace life after one has hovered close to death and sent others into its dark mouth. War is undoubtedly hell, but the peace that follows can be an even greater hell for the warrior. In the front ranks, when a warrior goes down on one knee or plunges prostrate to the dust, he knows himself to be as good as dead. He is already a ghost. The same is true in peace. Herakles is down. He is over. Until, that is, a friend extends his hand, steadies him, and lifts him back to his feet. No one makes the ascent from hell alone, without a guide, without a friend.

The unbidden arrival of Theseus is every bit as timely as the earlier homecoming of Herakles. Knowing well the darkness of hell and what it means to be saved from it by a friend, Theseus knows just what to say now. The final dialogue between Herakles and Theseus represents a loving and confrontational exchange of comrades trying to live up to the challenge of friends, to have all things in common. Herakles warns his friend to flee, to run with all his might from Herakles' pollution *(miasma)*, and Theseus assures him that there is no such thing as pollution between friends. Theseus makes it clear that he is going nowhere, nowhere without his friend. And Herakles makes it equally clear that there is only one place he wants to go—to death, back to the netherworld, where he just came from. Theseus responds that this is the kind of talk he would expect from an ordinary man, but not from a hero. Theseus listens one more time to Herakles recount his nightmare and lacerate himself with bitter words, and then he extends his hand to him. It is time to get up and to go back to the great labor of living: "Enough tears, poor man," counsels Theseus. "Now, up on your feet" (1394). And, when he can't find the needed strength, Theseus lifts him to his feet, puts his arm around his neck in the yoke of friendship, and takes each slow step with him. Herakles' final words say it all, all that the play is meant to teach. They sum up what anyone who has come back from hell knows already: "Any man who would prefer great wealth or power to love, the love of friends, is sick to the core of his soul" (1425–26).

The lesson here is that in life, so long as we draw breath, we heal each other. Veterans heal other veterans. Once willing to die for each other, they must be willing to live for each other, to draw strength and hope from each other. We do well to recall here the first lines of the Chorus' entry in *Herakles*, a chorus of veterans, who having served out their lives in the service of their country stand by each other to the end (see selection 11):

> Leaning on our staves,
> A procession of propped-up old men,
> We make our way slowly to a great house
> . . .
> We are no more than ghosts, only half here,
> Things of the night or of dreams,
> Trembling, wanting to help, useless
> . . .
> When you lose your footing, reach out.
> Grab hold of a hand or robe.
> We are all old now. We stand or fall together.
> The same as in our spear-bearing youth,
> When we stood as one in the toil of battle

And brought home only glory
To our fatherland. (107–29)

Neither they nor Herakles stand any longer in the front ranks of battle. Instead, they hold their ground in the front ranks of a different, more grueling struggle to affirm themselves and each other in the face not of death but of life. Their enemies, their Furies, lie within. As friends, and this is what they call each other, they are ready to steady, to lift, or even to carry each other if need be from one day to the next, which is how life must be lived.

Bibliography

Abercrombie, Joe. *The Blade Itself (The First Law)*. New York: Prometheus, 2007.

Alexander, David W. "Combat-Activated Thymic Disorientation." PhD thesis, University of Essex, 2016. http://repository.essex.ac.uk/18020.

Allard, Carolyn B., et al. "Military Sexual Trauma Research: A Proposed Agenda." *Journal of Trauma & Dissociation* 12 (April 29, 2011) 324–45.

Alpert, Jon, and Ellen Goosenberg Kent. *Wartorn 1861–2010*. New York: HBO Documentary Films, 2011.

American Psychiatric Association. *Diagnostic and Statistical Manual of Mental Disorders*. 5th ed. Arlington, VA: American Psychiatric Association, 2013.

Anderson, Doug. "Bamboo Bridge." *Poems from Group 18: Open Field*. Northampton, MA: Open Field, 2011.

———. "Something Like a Soul." *The Massachusetts Review* 52 (Fall and Winter 2011) 1–6.

Anderson, Rosemarie. "Nine Psycho-Spiritual Characteristics of Spontaneous and Involuntary Weeping." *Journal of Transpersonal Psychology* (1996) 167–73.

Andreasen, Nancy. *The Broken Brain*. San Francisco: Harper Paperbacks, 1985.

Bailey, Beth. *America's Army: Making the All-Volunteer Force*. Cambridge, MA: Belknap of Harvard University Press, 2009.

Bastian, Brock, and Nick Haslam. "Experiencing Dehumanization: Cognitive and Emotional Effects of Everyday Dehumanization." *Basic and Applied Social Psychology* (November 7, 2011) 295–303.

Beauvoir, Simone de. *The Ethics of Ambiguity*. Translated by Bernard Frechtman. Secaucus, NJ: Citadel, 1958.

Beckham, Jean Crowell, et al. "Atrocities Exposure in Vietnam Combat Veterans with Chronic Posttraumatic Stress Disorder: Relationship to Combat Exposure, Symptom Severity, Guilt, and Interpersonal Violence." *Journal of Traumatic Stress* (October 1998) 777–85.

Beckner, Victoria L., and John B. Arden. *Conquering Post-Traumatic Stress Disorder: The Newest Techniques for Overcoming Symptoms, Regaining Hope, and Getting Your Life Back*. Beverly, MA: Quayside, 2008.

Beschloss, Michael R. *Reaching for Glory: Lyndon Johnson's Secret White House Tapes, 1964–1965*. New York: Simon & Schuster, 2002.

Bethea, Nate. "Sarah Palin, This Is What PTSD Is Really Like." *New York Times* (January 26, 2016). https://www.nytimes.com/2016/01/23/opinion/sarah-palin-this-is-what-ptsd-is-really-like.html?_r=0.

Biggar, Nigel. *In Defence of War.* Oxford: Oxford University Press, 2013.

Blake, Scott. *A Journey with P.T.S.D.* Essex, UK: Chipmunka, 2008.

Boal, Michael. "Death and Dishonor." *Playboy* (May 2004) 108–12, 134–41.

Bobrow, Joseph. "Waking Up from War, Part 2." Excerpt from "Waking Up from War: A Better Way Home for Veterans and Nations." *Huffington Post* (November 11, 2015). http://www.huffingtonpost.com/joseph-bobrow/waking-up-from-war-by-jos_1_b_8515302.html.

Boudreau, Tyler. "The Morally Injured." *The Massachusetts Review* 52 (Fall and Winter 2011) 746–54.

———. *Packing Inferno: The Unmaking of a Marine.* Port Townsend, WA: Feral House, 2008.

Bowlby, John. *Separation: Anxiety and Anger.* New York: Basic, 1973.

Brock, Rita Nakashima, and Gabriella Lettini. *Soul Repair: Recovering from Moral Injury after War.* Boston: Beacon, 2012.

Brooker, John W., et al. "Beyond 'T.B.D.': Understanding VA's Evaluation of a Former Servicemember's Benefit Eligibility Following Involuntary or Punitive Discharge from the Armed Forces." *Military Law Review* (Winter 2012) 1–328.

Browning, Christopher R. *Ordinary Men: Reserve Police Battalion 101 and the Final Solution in Poland.* New York: Asher/HarperCollins, 1992.

Broyd, Samantha J., et al. "Default-Mode Brain Dysfunction in Mental Disorders: A Systematic Review." *Neuroscience and Biobehavioral Reviews* (2009) 279–96.

Bryan, Craig J., et al. "Measuring Moral Injury: Psychometric Properties of the Moral Injury Events Scale in Two Military Samples." *Assessment* (October 2016) 557–70.

Buckner, Randy L., et al. "Anatomy, Function, and Relevance to Disease." *Annals of the New York Academy of Sciences* (March 2008) 1–38.

Butler, Joseph. *Fifteen Sermons.* London: Bell and Sons, 1964.

Calabresi, Steven G. "'A Shining City on a Hill': American Exceptionalism and the Supreme Court's Practice of Relying on Foreign Law." *Boston University Law Review* (2006) 1335–416.

Calhoun, L. G., and R. G. Tedeschi, eds. *The Handbook of Posttraumatic Growth.* Mahwah, NJ: Lawrence Erlbaum Associates, 2006.

Card, Orson Scott. *Ender's Game.* New York: Tom Doherty Associates, 1986.

Castano, Emanuele, and Roger Giner-Sorolla. "Not Quite Human: Infrahumanization in Response to Collective Responsibility for Intergroup Killing." *Journal of Personality and Social Psychology* (May 2006) 804–18.

Central Committee of the Communist Party of China's General office. "Communique on the Current State of the Ideological Sphere." *Chinafile.com* (April 22, 2013). https://www.chinafile.com/document-9-chinafile-translation.

Chartier, Tim. "Understanding Big Data: The Three V's." The Great Courses Daily. http://www.thegreatcoursesdaily.com/understanding-big-data-three-v.

Cicero, Marcus Tullius. *De Finibus Bonorum et Malorum.* Edited by Theodor Schiche. Perseus Digital Library. http://www.perseus.tufts.edu/hopper/text?doc=Perseus%3atext%3a2007.01.0036.

———. *Tusculanae* Disputationes. Edited by Max Pohlenz. Perseus Digital Library. http://www.perseus.tufts.edu/hopper/text?doc=Perseus%3Atext%3A2007.01.0044%3Abook%3D2%3Asection%3D64.

Cikara, Mina, et al. "From Agents to Objects: Sexist Attitudes and Neural Responses to Sexualized Targets." *Journal of Cognitive Neuroscience* (March 2011) 540–51.

Clark, Mokneque, et al. "Students, Scholars Debate Military Draft Reinstatement as Iraqi Conflict Heats Up." *The Columbia Chronicle* (January 13, 2003).

Clover, Charles. *Black Wind, White Snow: The Rise of Russia's New Nationalism.* New Haven: Yale University Press, 2016.

Collins, Gail. "3 Days of the Sotomayor." The Opinion Pages. *New York Times* (July 15, 2009). http://www.nytimes.com/2009/07/16/opinion/16collins.html.

Company Commanders. "Leading our Soldiers to Fight with Honor." *Army* (November 2006) 58–62.

Conrad, Joseph. *Heart of Darkness.* New York: Dover Publications, 1990.

Copland, Laura. "Staff Perspective: On Moral Injury." *Center for Deployment Psychology* (December 21, 2015). http://deploymentpsych.org/blog/staff-perspective-moral-injury.

Dao, James. "Drone Pilots are Found to Get Stress Disorders Much as Those in Combat Do." *New York Times* (February 22, 2013). http://www.nytimes.com/2013/02/23/us/drone-pilots-found-to-get-stress-disorders-much-as-those-in-combat-do.html.

Darehshon, Sara. "Booted: Lack of Recourse for Wrongfully Discharged US Military Rape Survivors." *Human Rights Watch* (May 19, 2016). https://www.hrw.org/report/2016/05/19/booted/lack-recourse-wrongfully-discharged-us-military-rape-survivors.

Department of Defense. "Fiscal Year 2014 Annual Report on Sexual Assault in the Military." *Department of Defense Sexual Assault Prevention and Response* (April 29, 2015). http://sapr.mil/public/docs/reports/FY14_Annual/FY14_DoD_SAPRO_Annual_Report_on_Sexual_Assault.pdf

———. "Instruction Number 2310.08E, Medical Program Support for Detainee Operations." *University of Minnesota Human Rights Library* (June 6, 2006). http://hrlibrary.umn.edu/OathBetrayed/Winkenwerder%206-6-2006.pdf.

Des Moines University. "Moral Injury from Sexual Abuse and War: Soul Wounds and Soul Repair (A Community Responsibility)" (September 27, 2013). https://www.dmu.edu/event/moral-injury.

Doehring, Carrie. "Resilience as the Relational Ability to Spiritually Integrate Moral Stress." *Pastoral Psychology* 64 (October 2015) 635–49.

Drath, Wilfred H., and Charles J. Palus. *Making Common Sense: Leadership as Meaning-Making in a Community of Practice.* Greensboro, NC: Center for Creative Leadership, 1994.

Drescher, Kent. "Moral Injury and Clergy." *VA National Center for PTSD* (August 28, 2015). https://www.patientcare.va.gov/chaplain/clergytraining/docs/CCTP_Webinar_Moral_Injury_Slides_08262015.pdf.

Duckworth, Tammy. "Introduction." In *Band of Sisters: American Women at War in Iraq,* by Kirsten Holmstedt, vii–x. Mechanicsburg, PA: Stackpole, 2007.

Edmonds, Bill. *God Is Not Here: A Soldier's Struggle with Torture, Trauma, and the Moral Injuries of War.* New York: Pegasus, 2015.

Egendorf, Arthur. *Healing from the War: Trauma and Transformation after Vietnam.* Boston: Houghton Mifflin, 1985.

Ephron, Dan. "He Should Never Have Gone to Iraq." *Newsweek* (June 30, 2008) 33–34.

Euripides, *Hekabe.* Translated by Robert Emmet Meagher. Wauconda, IL: Bolchazy-Carducci, 1995.

————. *Herakles Gone Mad: Rethinking Heroism in an Age of Endless War.* Translated by Robert Emmet Meagher. Northampton, MA: Olive Branch, 2006.

Farnsworth, Jacob K. "Dialogical Tensions in Heroic Military and Military-Related Moral Injury." *International Journal for Dialogical Science* (Spring 2014) 13–38.

Fontana, Alan, and Robert Rosenheck. "Trauma, Change in Strength of Religious Faith, and Mental Health Service Use Among Veterans Treated for PTSD." *Journal of Nervous and Mental Disease* (September 2004) 579–84.

Forest, Jim. "War and Peace in Orthodox Tradition." *IN COMMUNION Website of the Orthodox Peace Fellowship* (April 26, 2014). http://incommunion.org/2014/04/26/war-and-peace-in-orthodox-tradition.

Forward, Roy, and Bob Reece, eds. *Conscription in Australia.* Brisbane: University of Queensland, 1968.

Fox, Michael D., et al. "The Human Brain Is Intrinsically Organized into Dynamic, Anticorrelated Functional Networks." *Proceedings of the National Academy of Sciences* (May 19, 2005) 9673–78.

Frame, Tom. "The Influence of Religious Conviction" in *Moral Injury: Unseen Wounds in an Age of Barbarism,* edited by Tom Frame, 235-250. Sydney: University of New South Wales Press, 2015.

French, Shannon E. "Why Warriors Need a Code." In *The Code of the Warrior: Exploring Warrior Values, Past and Present,* 1–22. New York: Rowman and Littlefield, 1999.

French, Shannon, and Anthony Jack. "Dehumanizing the Enemy: The Intersection of Neuroethics and Military Ethics." In *Responsibilities to Protect in Theory and Practice,* edited by David Whetham, 169–95. The Netherlands: Brill/Martinus Nijhoff, 2015.

Freud, Sigmund. *Reflections on War and Death.* Translated by A. A. Brill and Alfred B. Kuttner. New York: Moffat, Yard, 1918.

Frey, William H., and Denise Desota-Johnson. "Effect of Stimulus on the Chemical Composition of Human Tears." *American Journal of Opthalmology* (October 1981) 559–67.

Friedman, Matthew J. "Post-Vietnam syndrome: Recognition and management." *Psychosomatics* 22 (1981) 931–42.

Fromm, Peter. "Hazing vs. Leadership: Some Thoughts on Getting My Arm Broken at West Point." In "Best Defense," blog by Thomas Ricks. *Foreign Policy Magazine* (December 2, 2011). http://foreignpolicy.com/2011/12/02/hazing-vs-leadership-some-thoughts-on-getting-my-arm-broken-at-west-point-2.

Fromm, Peter, Douglas Pryer, and Kevin Cutright. "The Myths We Soldiers Tell Ourselves." *Military Review* (September-October 2013) 57–68.

Galloway, Joseph L. "Commentary: 100,000 Reasons to Shed No Tears for McNamara." *McClatchy DC Bureau* (July 7, 2009). http://www.mcclatchydc.com/opinion/article24544984.html.

George, Seth. "Moral Injury and the Problem of Facing Religious Authority." *CGSC Ethics Symposium* (April 20, 2015). http://www.cgscfoundation.org/wp-content/uploads/2015/05/George-MoralInjuryandFacingReligiousAuthority-final.pdf.

Gerasimov, Valery. "The Value of Science in Prediction." *Voenno-Promyshlennyi Kur'er (The Military-Industrial Courier)* (February 27, 2013). Translated by Rob Coalson. https://inmoscowsshadows.wordpress.com/2014/07/06/the-gerasimov-doctrine-and-russian-non-linear-war.

Gilbertson, Ashley. "The Life and Lonely Death of Noah Pierce." *Virginia Quarterly Review* 84 (Fall 2008). http://www.vqronline.org/vqr-portfolio/life-and-lonely-death-noah-pierce.

Gino, Francesca, et al. "Contagion and Differentiation in Unethical Behavior: The Effect of One Bad Apple on the Barrel." *Psychological Science* (March 2009) 393–38.

Gladwin, Michael. *Captains of the Soul: A History of Australian Army Chaplains.* Newport NSW: Big Sky, 2013.

Glenn, Brandon. "Why It's So Difficult for Physicians to Be Empathetic and Analytic at the Same Time." *Modern Medicine Network* (July 31, 2013). http://medicaleconomics.modernmedicine.com/medical-economics/news/why-its-so-difficult-physicians-be-empathetic-and-analytic-same-time.

Gray, J. Glenn. *The Warriors: Reflections on Men in Battle.* Lincoln: University of Nebraska Press, 1998.

Gregory, Hamilton. *McNamara's Folly: The Use of Low-IQ Troops in the Vietnam War.* West Conshohocken, PA: Infinity, 2015.

Grossman, Dave. *On Killing: The Psychological Cost of Learning to Kill in War and Society.* Boston: Little, Brown, 1996.

Grossman, Zoltan. "From Wounded Knee to Syria: A Century of US Military Interventions." *academicevergreen.edu* (October 2001). https://academic.evergreen.edu/g/grossmaz/interventions.html

Guntzel, Jeff Severns. "Beyond PTSD to 'Moral Injury.'" *On Being* (March 14, 2013). http://www.onbeing.org/blog/beyond-ptsd-to-moral-injury.

Haidt, Jonathan. *The Righteous Mind: Why Good People Are Divided by Politics and Religion.* New York: Vintage , 2012.

Haidt, Jonathan, and Fredik Bjorklund. "Social Intuitionists Answer Six Questions about Moral Psychology." In *Moral Psychology: The Cognitive Science of Morality: Intuition and Diversity*, vol. 2, edited by W. Sinnott-Armstrong, 181–217. Cambridge, MA: MIT Press, 2007.

Haque, Omar Sultan, and Adam Waytz. "Dehumanization in Medicine: Causes, Solutions, and Functions." *Perspectives on Psychological Science* (March 9, 2012) 176–86.

Harakas, Stanley. "No Just War in the Fathers." *IN COMMUNION Website of the Orthodox Fellowship* (August 2, 2005). http://incommunion.org/2005/08/02/no-just-war-in-the-fathers.

Harris, C. S. *What Darkness Brings: A Sebastian St. Cyr Mystery.* New York: Penguin, 2013.

Haslam, Nick. "Dehumanization: An Integrative Review." *Personality and Social Psychology Review* (August 1, 2006) 252–64.

Hawkley, Louise C., and John T. Cacioppo. "Loneliness Matters: A Theoretical and Empirical Review of Consequences and Mechanisms." *Annals of Behavioral Medicine* (October 2010) 218–27.

Hendin, Herbert, and Edward Haas. "Suicide and Guilt As Manifestations of PTSD in Vietnam Combat Veterans." *American Journal of Psychology* (May 1991) 586–91.

Herman, Judith. *Trauma and Recovery.* Revised edition. New York: Basic, 2015.

Higgins, Hardie M. *To Make the Wounded Whole: Healing the Spiritual Wounds of PTSD.* Conshohocken, PA: Infinity, 2012.

Holmes, Richard. *Acts of War: Behavior of Men in Battle.* New York: Free Press, 1985.

Holmstedt, Kirsten. *Band of Sisters: American Women at War in Iraq,* New York: Stackpole, 2008.

Homer. *Odyssey.* Translated by Ian Johnston. http://records.viu.ca/~johnstoi/homer/odyssey19.htm.

Hoop, D.C. *PTSD: The Strugle within, from Saigon to Baghdad.* Raleigh, NC: Lulu, 2010.

Hoyt, Tim, et al. "Military Sexual Trauma in Men: A Review of Reported Rates." *Journal of Trauma Dissociation* 12 (April 29, 2011) 244–60.

Hunt, Andrew. *The Turning: A History of Vietnam Veterans Against the War.* New York: New York University Press, 1999.

Imiola, Brian, and Danny Cazier. "On the Road to Articulating Our Professional Ethic." *Military Review Ethics Reader: Special Edition* (2010) 11–18.

The Invisible War. Directed by Kirby Dick. Docuramafilms. DVD, 2012.

Jack, Anthony I., et al. "fMRI Reveals Reciprocal Inhibition between Social and Physical Cognitive Domains." *Neuroimage* (February 1, 2013) 385–401.

Jack, Anthony I., et al. "Seeing Human: Distinct and Overlapping Neural Signatures Associated with Two Forms of Dehumanization." *NeuroImage* (October 1, 2013) 313–28.

Jack, Anthony I., et al. "More Than a Feeling: Counterintuitive Effects of Compassion on Moral Judgment." In *Advances in Experimental Philosophy of Mind,* edited by Justin Sytsma, 125–80. London: Bloomsbury Academic, 2014.

Johnson, Susan M. *Emotionally Focused Couple Therapy with Trauma Survivors: Strengthening Attachment Bonds.* New York: Guilford, 2005.

Jordan, Kelly C. "Right for the Wrong Reasons: S. L. A. Marshall and the Ratio of Fire in Korea." *Journal of Military History* (January 2002) 135–62.

Junger, Sebastian. *Tribe: On Homecoming and Belonging.* New York: 12 Books, 2016.

Kerry, John. "Vietnam Veterans against the War Statement to the Senate Committee of Foreign Relations." April 23, 1971. The Sixties Project. http://www2.iath.virginia.edu/sixties/HTML_docs/Resources/Primary/Manifestos/VVAW_Kerry_Senate.html.

Kheirbek, Mazen A., and Rene Hen. "Add Neurons, Subtract Anxiety." *Scientific American* (July 2014) 62–67.

Kilner, Pete. "A Moral Justification for Killing in War." *Army* (February 2010) 55–60.

Kluckhohn, Clyde, and Dorothea Leighton. *The Navajo.* Cambridge, MA: Harvard University Press, 1946.

Knodell, Kevin. "A Network of Special Ops Veterans Wants to Change how America Reintegrates Troops." *War Is Boring* (June 19, 2016). http://warisboring.com/a-network-of-special-ops-veterans-wants-to-change-how-america-reintegrates-troops-6d128e0749fe.

Konstan, David. *Before Forgiveness: The Origins of a Moral Idea.* Cambridge: Cambridge University Press, 1962.

Kubany, Edward, et al. "Development and Validation of the Sources of Trauma Guilt Survey—War-Zone Version." *Journal of Traumatic Stress* (April 1997) 235–58.

Kube, Courtney, and Jim Miklaszewski. "Military Suicide Rate Hits Record High in 2012." *NBC News* (January 14, 2013). http://usnews.nbcnews.com/_news/2013/01/14/16510852-military-suicide-rate-hit-record-high-in-2012?lite.

Kudo, Timothy. "On War and Redemption." *The New York Times* (November 8, 2011).

Kulka, Richard A., et al. *Trauma and the Vietnam War Generation: Report of Findings From the National Vietnam Veterans Readjustment Study*. New York: Routledge, 2013.

Lau, G. J. *SitRep Negative: A Year in Vietnam*. Frederick, MD: Windroot, 2011.

LeardMann, Cynthia A., et al. "Combat Deployment Is Associated with Sexual Harassment or Sexual Assault in a Large, Female Military Cohort." *Women's Health Issues* 23(4) (July-August 2013) 215–23.

Legate, Nicole, et al. "Hurting You Hurts Me Too: The Psychological Costs of Complying with Ostracism." *Psychological Science* (February 27, 2013) 583–88.

Leslie, Kristen J. "'Ma'am, Can I Talk to You?' Pastoral Care to Survivors of Sexualized Violence at the United States Air Force Academy." *Journal of Pastoral Theology* 15(1) (August 7, 2005) 78–92.

———. *When Violence Is No Stranger: Pastoral Counseling with Survivors of Acquaintance Rape*. Minneapolis: Fortress, 2003.

Liang, Qiao, and Wang Xiangsui. "Unrestricted Warfare." *C4I.org* (February 1999). http://www.c4i.org/unrestricted.pdf.

Lifton, Robert Jay. *Home from the War: Vietnam Veterans, Neither Victims Nor Executioners*. New York: Simon and Schuster, 1973.

Litz, Brett, et al. *Adaptive Disclosure: A New Treatment for Military Trauma, Loss, and Moral Injury*. New York: Guilford, 2015.

Litz, Brett, et al. "Moral Injury and Moral Repair in War Veterans: A Preliminary Model and Intervention Strategy." *Clinical Psychology Review* (2009) 695–706.

MacNair, Rachel M. *Perpetration-Induced Traumatic Stress: The Psychological Consequences of Killing*. Westport, CT: Praeger, 2002.

Maguen, Shira, et al. "The Impact of Killing in War On Mental Health Symptoms and Related Functioning." *Journal of Traumatic Stress* (October 2009) 435–43.

Maguen, Shira, et al. "The Impact of Killing on Mental Health Symptoms in Gulf War Veterans." *Psychological Trauma: Theory, Research, Practice, and Policy* (March 2011) 21–26.

Maguen, Shira, and Brett Litz. "Moral Injury in Veterans of War." *PTSD Research Quarterly* (2012) 1–6.

———. "Moral Injury in the Context of War." *The National Center for PTSD* (February 23 2016). https://www.ptsd.va.gov/professional/co-occurring/moral_injury_at_war.asp.

Maguire, Mairead. "Appeal to His Holiness Pope Francis to Replace Just War Theory with a Theology of Peace, Nonkilling, and Nonviolence." *peacePEOPLE* (December 17, 2014). http://www.peacepeople.com/?p=706.

Mahedy, William P. *Out of the Night: The Spiritual Journey of Vietnam Vets*. New York: Ballantine/Epiphany, 1986.

Main, J. M., ed. *Conscription: The Australian Debate, 1901–1970*. Melbourne: Cassell, 1970.

Marin, Peter. "Living in Moral Pain." *Psychology Today* (November 1981) 68–80.

Marlantes, Karl. *What It Is Like to Go to War*. New York: Atlantic Monthly, 2011.

Marshall, S. L. A. *Men against Fire: The Problem of Battle Command*. Norman, OK: University of Oklahoma Press, 2000.

Marx, Brian, et al. "Combat-Related Guilt Mediates the Relations between Exposure to Combat-Related Abusive Violence and Psychiatric Diagnoses." *Depression and Anxiety* (March 2010) 287–93.

Masick, Erik. "Moral Injury and Preventive Law: A Framework for the Future." *Military Law Review* (2016) 223–89.

Mason, Steve. "A History Lesson." In *Johnny's Song: Poetry of a Vietnam Veteran*, 47. New York: Bantam, 1986.

———. "In Victory or Defeat." In *Warrior for Peace*, 101. New York: Simon and Schuster, 1988.

———. "(One) with It All." In *The Human Being: A Warrior's Journey Toward Peace and Mutual Healing*, 17. New York: Simon and Schuster, 1988.

Mattocks, Kristin M., et al. "Women at War: Understanding How Women Veterans Cope With Combat and Military Sexual Trauma." *Social Science & Medicine* 74 (February 2012) 537–45.

McCarthy, Marjorie M. "An Exploration of Moral Injury as Experienced by Combat Veterans." PhD diss., Antioch University, 2016.

McFate, Sean. *The Modern Mercenary*. Oxford: Oxford University Press, 2014.

McLay, Robert N. *At War with PTSD: Battling Post-Traumatic Stress Disorder with Virtual Reality*. Baltimore: John Hopkins University Press, 2012.

McMaster, H. R. "Lecture to the US Army 58th Judge Advocate Officer Graduate Course: The Role of the Judge Advocate in Contemporary Operations: Ensuring Moral and Ethical Conduct during War." *Army Law* (May 2011) 35–41.

Meagher, Robert Emmet. *Herakles Gone Mad: Rethinking Heroism in an Age of Endless War*. Northampton, MA: Olive Branch, 2006.

———. *Killing from the Inside Out: Moral Injury and Just War*. Eugene, OR: Cascade, 2014.

Menninger, Karl. *Whatever Became of Sin?* New York: Hawthorne, 1974.

Michaud, Joe. "Shame." *The War Crimes Times* (Spring 2014) 20.

Milgram, Stanley. *Obedience to Authority: An Experimental View*. New York: Harper Perennial Modern Thought, 2009.

Miller, Alice. *The Untouched Key: Tracing Childhood Trauma in Creativity*. New York, Anchor, 1991.

Miller, William Allen. "All the Voices Are in the Water." *Poems from Group 18: Open Field*. Northampton, MA: Open Field, 2011.

Mitchell, Greg. "Remembering the US Soldier Who Committed Suicide after She Refused to Take Part in Torture." *The Nation* (September 13, 2010). http://www.thenation.com/blog/154649/remembering-us-soldier-who-committed-suicide-after-she-refused-take-part-torture.

Morral, Andrew R., et al, eds. *Sexual Assault and Sexual Harassment in the US Military*. Vol. 2. Estimates for Department of Defense Service Members from the 2014 RAND Military Workplace Study. *RAND Corporation* (2016). http://www.rand.org/pubs/research_reports/RR870z2-1.html.

Morris, E. Ellen, et al. "Unseen Battles: The Recognition, Assessment, and Treatment Issues of Men with Military Sexual Trauma (MST)." *Trauma, Violence, & Abuse* 15(2) (November 2013) 94–101.

Muruzábal, Amaya. "The Monster as a Victim of War: The Returning Veteran in *The Best Years of Our Lives*." In *Hosting the Monster*, edited by Holly Lynn Baumgartner and Roger Davis, 23–42. New York: Editions, 1996.

Nash, William P., et al. "Psychometric Evaluation of the Moral Injury Events Scale." *Military Medicine* (June 2013) 646–52.

National Center for PTSD. "PTSD and DSM-V." *United States Department of Veterans Affairs* (June 10, 2013). https://www.ptsd.va.gov/professional/PTSD-overview/dsm5_criteria_ptsd.asp.

Newhouse, Eric. "Recovering from Moral Injury." In *Faces of Recovery* (forthcoming). Enumclaw, WA: Idyll Arbor.

Nez, Chester, with Judith Schiess Avila. *Code Talker: The First and Only Memoir by One of the Original Navajo Code Talkers of WWII.* New York: Berkeley Caliber, 2011.

Nisbett, Richard, and Timothy Wilson. "Telling More Than We Can Know: Verbal Reports on Mental Processes." *Psychological Review* (May 1977) 231–59.

Nolan, Keith William. *House to House: Playing the Enemy's Game in Saigon, May 1968.* Saint Paul, MN: Zenith, 2006.

Nye, Jr., Joseph S. *Soft Power: The Means to Success in World Politics.* New York: Public Affairs, 2004.

Office of the Commandant of the Marine Corps. *Commandant's Planning Guidance.* Washington, DC: US Marine Corps, 1995.

Office of the Special Advisor on the Prevention of Genocide. "Responsibility to Protect." *United Nations* (September 2005). http://www.un.org/en/preventgenocide/rwanda/about/bgresponsibility.shtml.

Office of the Surgeon Multi-National Force-Iraq and the Office of the Surgeon General United States Army Medical Command. "Mental Health Advisory Team (MHAT) IV Operation Iraqi Freedom 05–07 Final Report." *combatreform* (November 17, 2006). http://www.combatreform.org/MHAT_IV_Report_17NOV06.pdf.

———. "Mental Health Advisory Team (MHAT) V: Operation Iraqi Freedom 06–08: Iraq Operation Enduring Freedom 8: Afghanistan." *Army Medicine* (February 4, 2008). http://armymedicine.mil/Documents/Redacted1-MHATV-4-FEB-2008-Overview.pdf

O'Malley, Mary E. Barrs. "Military Sexual Trauma in Male Survivors: Violence, Emasculation, and Shame." DMin diss., Erskine Theological Seminary, 2016.

Orban, Michael. *Souled Out: A Memoir of War and Inner Peace.* West Bend, WI: Minuteman, 2007.

Osiel, Mark. *Obeying Orders: Atrocity, Military Discipline, and the Law of War.* New Brunswick: Transaction, 1999.

Owen, Wilfred. "Strange Meeting" and "The Parable of the Old Man and the Young." In *Poems.* London: Chatto & Windus, 1920.

———. "Soldier's Dream." In *The Complete Poems and Fragments of Wilfred Owen*, 182. Edited by Jon Stallworthy. London: Chatto & Windus, 1983.

Palmer, HC. "If I Die in a Combat Zone." *Narrative Magazine*, Winter 2015. www.narrativemagazine.com.

Papadopoulos, Renos K. "Failure and Success in Forms of Involuntary Dislocation: Trauma, Resilience, and Adversity-Activated Development." In *The Crucible of Failure*, vol. VII, 25–49. New Orleans: Spring Journal, 2015.

———. *Therapeutic Care for Refugees: No Place like Home.* London: Karnac, 2002.

Parker, Michael. *John Winthrop: Founding the City Upon a Hill.* New York: Routledge, 2013.

Patitsas, Timothy. "The Opposite of War Is Not Peace: Healing Trauma in *The Iliad* and in Orthodox Tradition." *Road to Emmaus* XIV 1 (2013) 27–50.

Pressfield, Steven. *The Warrior Ethos.* New York: Black Irish Entertainment, 2011.

Pressman, Sarah D., et al. "Is the Emotion-Health Connection a 'First-World Problem'?" *Psychological Science* (February 26, 2013) 544–49.

Pryer, Douglas A. *The Fight for the High Ground.* Fort Leavenworth, KS: CGSC Foundation, 2009.

———."Moral Injury and the American Service Member: What Leaders Don't Talk about When They Talk about War." *CGSC Foundation* (May 1, 2014). http://www. cgscfoundation.org/wp-content/uploads/2014/05/Pryer-MoralInjuryandtheAme ricanServiceMember-1May14.pdf.

———. "Moral Injury and the American Soldier." *Cicero Magazine* (June 2, 2014). http://www.ciceromagazine.com.php56–15.dfw3–1.websitetestlink.com/features/ moral-injury-and-the-american-soldier.

Putzel, Michael. *The Price They Paid: Enduring Wounds of War.* Washington, DC: Trysail, 2015.

Pyka, Martin, et al. "Impact of Working Memory Load on FMRI Resting State Pattern in Subsequent Resting Phases." *PLoS One* (September 25, 2009). https://www.ncbi. nlm.nih.gov/pmc/articles/PMC2745698/pdf/pone.0007198.pdf.

Raichle, Marcus E., et al. "A Default Mode of Brain Function: A Brief History of an Evolving Idea." *Proceedings of the National Academy of Sciences* (2005) 676–82.

Ritchie, Elspeth Cameron. "Army's Former Top Psych Doc Says Military Believed to Routinely Underreport Suicide Data in Reserve Forces." *The Military Suicide Report* (April 22, 2012). http://themilitarysuicidereport.wordpress.com/2012/ page/79.

Rockel, Stephen J., and Rick Halpern. *Inventing Collateral Damage: Civilian Casualties, War, and Empire.* Toronto: Between the Lines, 2009.

Romo, Barry. "The Never Ending War." *The Veteran: Vietnam Veterans Against the War* (Fall 2010), 8.

———. "Veteran's History Project." Interviewed by Cesar Ruvalcaba. American Folklife Center, Library of Congress. http://memory.loc.gov/diglib/vhp/bib/loc. natlib.afc2001001.106.

Sakharov, Archimandrite Sophrony. *Saint Silouan, the Athonite.* Crestwood, NY: Saint Vladimir's Seminary, 1991.

Sassoon, Siegfried. "Suicide in Trenches" and "Survivors." In *The War Poems of Siegfried Sassoon*, 39 and 60. London: William Heinemann, 1919.

Schmidt, Eric. "Keynote Speech at Guardian Activate 2010." https://www.youtube.com/ watch?v=kBeWzg5_ShU.

Scranton, Roy. "*Star Wars* and the Fantasy of American Violence." *The New York Times* (July 2, 2016). https://www.nytimes.com/2016/07/03/opinion/sunday/star-wars- and-the-fantasy-of-american-violence.html.

Seamone, Evan R. "Dismantling America's Largest Sleeper Cell: The Imperative to Treat, Rather Than Merely Punish, Active-Duty Offenders with PTSD Prior to Discharge from the Armed Forces." *Nova Law Review* (2013) 478–522.

Segrest, Timothy. *Reflections of PTSD: With My Perfect Flaws.* Bloomington, IN: Indiana University Press, 2008.

Shakespeare, William. *The Life of King Henry V.* Folger Shakespeare Library. http:// www.folgerdigitaltexts.org/download/pdf/H5.pdf.

———. *The Tragedy of Richard III.* Folger Shakespeare Library. http://www. folgerdigitaltexts.org/download/pdf/R3.pdf.

Shay, Jonathan. *Achilles in Vietnam: Combat Trauma and the Undoing of Character.* New York: Simon and Schuster, 1994.

———. "Ethical Standing." *Parameters: US Army War College Quarterly* 28 (Summer 1998) 93–105. http://ssi.armywarcollege.edu/pubs/parameters/Articles/98summer/shay.htm.

———. "Jonathan Shay Extended Interview." WGBH/PBS *Religion & Ethics Newsweekly* (May 28, 2010). http://www.pbs.org/wnet/religionandethics/?p=6384.

———. *Odysseus in America: Combat Trauma and the Trials of Homecoming.* New York: Scribner, 2002.

———. "Moral Injury." *Psychoanalytic Psychology* 31 (April 2014) 182–91.

———. "Moral Leadership Prevents Moral Injury." *Fort Leavenworth Ethics Symposium: Exploring the Professional Military Ethic, Symposium Report* (November 15–17, 2010) 313–16. http://www.cgscfoundation.org/wp-content/uploads/2014/03/FtLvnEthicsSymposiumReport-2010.pdf. Used by permission of Jonathan Shay.

———. "No More Sugar Coating: Combat Trauma and Criminal Behavior." In *The Attorney's Guide to Defending Veterans in Criminal Court*, edited by Brockton D. Hunter and Ryan C. Else, 57–72. Minneapolis: Veterans Defense Project, 2014.

Sherman, Nancy. *Stoic Warriors: The Ancient Philosophy behind the Military Mind.* Oxford: Oxford University Press, 2005.

Silk, Jonathan. "Making Sense of Killing." *Army* (November 2005) 89–98.

Simmons, Marvin. "Veterans Voice Radio Show," hosted by Marvin Simmons (December 18, 2015). KBOO 90.7 FM, Portland, Oregon.

Sites, Kevin. *The Things They Cannot Say: Stories Soldiers Won't Tell You about What They've Seen, Done, or Failed to Do in War.* New York: HarperCollins, 2013.

Skedros, James. "War, Byzantium, and Military Saints." *Road to Emmaus* XIV (2013) 3–24.

Sledge, E. B. *With the Old Breed: At Peleliu and Okinawa.* New York: Presidio, 2007.

Smith, David Livingstone. *Less than Human: Why We Demean, Enslave, and Exterminate Others.* New York: Saint Martin's Griffin, 2012.

Sophocles. *Philoctetes.* Translated by David Grene. In *Sophocles II*, edited by David Grene and Richmond Lattimore, 194–254. Chicago: University of Chicago Press, 1957.

Stander, Valerie A., and Cynthia J. Thomsen. "Sexual Harassment and Assault in the US Military: A Review of Policy and Research Trends." *Military Medicine* 181 (January 2016) 20–27.

Suris, Alina, and Lisa Lind. "Military Sexual Trauma: A Review of Prevalence and Associated Health Consequences in Veterans." *Trauma, Violence, & Abuse* 9 (October 1, 2008) 250–69.

Taubert, Eberhard. *The Eternal Jew.* Directed by Fritz Hippler. Deutsche Film Gesellschaft, 1940.

Terkel, Studs. *Hope Dies Last: Keeping the Faith in Troubled Times.* New York: New Press, 2003.

Tick, Edward. "Military Service, Moral Injury, and Spiritual Wounding." *The Military Chaplain* 89 (Spring 2016) 4–8.

———. "The Wounded Warrior." In *Warrior's Return: Restoring the Soul after War*, 20. Boulder, CO: Sounds True, 2014.

Toner, James H. *Morals Under the Gun.* Lexington, KY: University Press of Kentucky, 2000.

Trading Economics. "United States Gross National Product, 1950–2017." tradingeconomics.com (2017). http://www.tradingeconomics.com/united-states/gross-national-product.

Trudeau, Garry. *The War Within: One More Step at a Time.* Kansas City: Andrew McMeel, 2006.

Turner, Brian. "Eulogy" and "Sadiq." In *Here, Bullet,* 20 and 56. Farmington, ME: Alice James, 2005.

———. *My Life as a Foreign Country: A Memoir.* New York: W.W. Norton, 2014.

Tuttle, Bill. "BillT." *Castle Argghhh!* Blog (July 7, 2009). http://www.thedonovan.com/archives/2009/07/mcnamara_day_tw.html.

US Department of Army. *Army Doctrinal Publication 6–0, Mission Command.* Changed no. 2, 2014. Washington, DC: US Government Printing Office, 2012.

———. *Army Regulation 27–26, Legal Services: Rules of Professional Conduct for Lawyers.* Washington, DC: US Government Printing Office, 1992.

———. *Army Regulation 635–200, Active Duty Enlisted Administrative Separations.* Washington, DC: US Government Printing Office, 2005.

———. *Army Regulation 635–40, Physical Evaluation for Retention, Retirement, or Separation.* Washington, DC: US Government Printing Office, 2006.

———. "'NEW' Discharge Upgrades and PTSD to Apply." *Review Boards Agency* (2014). http://arba.army.pentagon.mil/adrb-ptsd.html.

US House of Representatives. "House Report 112–110: Department of Defense Appropriations Bill, 2012." *House Report* (June 16, 2011). https://www.congress.gov/congressional-report/112th-congress/house-report/110.

Walsh, Froma. "Traumatic Loss and Major Disasters: Strengthening Family and Community Resilience." *Family Process* 46 (June 2007) 207–27.

Wang, Yuan-Kang. "The Myth of Chinese Exceptionalism." *Foreign Policy* (March 6, 2012). http://foreignpolicy.com/2012/03/06/the-myth-of-chinese-exceptionalism/.

Webster, Alexander, and Darrell Cole. *The Virtue of War: Reclaiming the Classic Christian Traditions East and West.* Salisbury: Regina, 2004.

Willis, John D. "Moral Injury: Insights into Executive Morality and Toxic Organizations." *Leadership Ethics Online* (November 27, 2012). http://www.leadershipethicsonline.com/2012/11/27/moral-injury-executive-morality-toxic-organizations.

Wilson, John P., Matthew J. Friedman, and Jacob D. Lindy, eds. *Treating Psychological Trauma and PTSD.* New York: Guilford, 2001.

Wizelman, Leah. *When the War Never Ends: The voices of Military Members with PTSD and Their Families.* Lanham, MD: Rowman and Littlefield, 2011.

Wood, David. "The Grunts: Damned If They Kill, Damned If They Don't." *Huffington Post* (March 18, 2014). http://projects.huffingtonpost.com/projects/moral-injury/the-grunts.

———. "The Recruits: When Right and Wrong are Hard to Tell Apart." *Huffington Post.* (March 19, 2014). http://projects.huffingtonpost.com/projects/moral-injury/the-recruits.

———. *What Have We Done: The Moral Injury of Our Longest Wars.* New York: Little, Brown, 2016.

Wood, Graeme. "What ISIS Really Wants." *The Atlantic* (March 2015). https://www.theatlantic.com/magazine/archive/2015/03/what-isis-really-wants/384980.

World Health Organization. *International Statistical Classification of Diseases and Related Health Problems.* 10th ed. Geneva: World Health Organization, 1993.

Yandell, Michael. "The War Within." *The Christian Century* 132 (January 2, 2015) 12–13.

Zabriskie, Phil. *The Kill Switch*. Amazon Kindle Single, 2014.

SOLDIER'S heart

Soldier's Heart is a 501(c)3 that was founded in 2006 by psychotherapists Dr. Edward Tick and Kate Dahlstedt. Our mission is to transform the emotional, moral, and spiritual wounds that inevitably result from war and military service and that are at the core of Post-traumatic Stress Disorder. We help active-duty troops and veterans to not merely seek readjustment and "normalcy," but develop new and honorable identities as lifelong spiritual warriors who still have missions to serve and wisdom to give. We offer genuine homecoming, reintegration, and a path for post-traumatic growth. We also empower and equip families, clinicians, clergy and other care providers, and caring civilians and communities to support our troops and veterans not just through charities but also in meaningful, involved and transformative ways to support establishing new identities and inclusiveness.

Soldier's Heart philosophy and methodology are modeled on co-founder Dr. Edward Tick's pioneering books *War and the Soul* and *Warrior's Return.* We have developed a proven holistic, community-based, spiritual method of healing that goes beyond conventional treatment methods and relies on time-honored worldwide warrior rituals adapted to current needs and society and deep community involvement. Our methods incorporate what we have learned from intensive lifelong involvement with and study of worldwide spiritual traditions, indigenous cultures, mythology, and warrior traditions.

Countless veterans and members of the military have experienced significant and lasting healing after working with us. Thousands of chaplains and behavioral health professionals from the U.S. Army, Air Force, National Guard, Special Operations forces and Veterans Administration chaplains and clinicians have received training from Soldier's Heart.

At Soldier's Heart, we do not consider PTSD to be a mental disorder. Instead, we believe it is a normal reaction to a traumatic experience. It is the expression of anguish, dislocation, and rage of the self as it attempts to cope with its loss of innocence and reformulate a new personal identity.

In an effort to identify what could be the major cause of suicide among American veterans, professionals across multiple disciplines–including clinical psychologists, social workers, ethicists and clergy–are with greater frequency now using the phrase "moral injury." Military leaders warn of the real danger of spiritual and moral trauma and advocate education about moral injury and its relationship to spirituality and stress.

At Soldier's Heart, we have recognized that moral injury is as old as war and war causes moral trauma as well as "injury" because it results not from happenstance but from the violence that human beings do. We recognize that warriors have survived violent exchanges with others, suffer for it, and are forever different. For decades we have embraced this moral truth in the center of military service and directly address the moral wounds our veterans carry and practice rituals for cleansing and sharing these wounds as well as forms of service for atoning from them.

We offer retreats that create a safe place for veterans and active-duty servicemen and women to share their military experiences. We also offer family retreats, workshops, trainings, educational programs, and lectures on a wide variety of topics. Our retreats are not only "getaways" for r &r and do not rely on conventional programming. Rather, we lead attendees through a time-honored six-step process of return that includes tending by the community, affirmation of warrior destiny, purification and cleansing, storytelling, restitution and initiation as an elder warrior. This process lays down a blueprint for the return journey that the survivor can continue to utilize through the life cycle.

Through our retreats, trainings, overseas warrior healing journeys and many forms of community and public service and education, Soldier's Heart has been uniquely successful in transforming the lives of wounded warriors and supporting them to develop and practice the lifelong identity of returned honorable elder warriors necessary to society's well-being.

For more information on Soldier's Heart, Inc. please visit our website www.soldiersheart.net

Edward Tick, Ph.D., Co-founder and Director

Kate Dahlstedt, MA, Co-founder and Director of Military Women's and Family Programming

INDEX

Made in the USA
Lexington, KY
07 July 2018